A BLACKFOOT HISTORY
THE WINTER COUNTS

A BLACKFOOT HISTORY
THE WINTER COUNTS

SIKAITAPI ITSINNIIKI
TELLING THE OLD STORIES

Paul M. Raczka

Blackfoot Books
P.O. Box 1481
Old Blackfoot Agency
Choteau, Montana 59422

Blackfoot Books

ISBN 978-0-692-77264-5

Library of Congress # 2016916337
Printed in Canada by Friesens Press, Altona, Manitoba

Front cover illustration: Bull Head and grandson Percy Smith, North Peigans, “Sign Talkers”, pastel and watercolor, 39” x 26”, Artist Winold Reiss, courtesy Tjark Reiss. Current collection, Buffalo Bill Center of the West, Cody, WY.

To my father, the first storyteller in my life.
And to ALL storytellers, whoever they may be, past, present and future.
May their stories live on forever, for they carry the essence of life itself.

ACKNOWLEDGMENTS

It has been over 45 years since my life among the Blackfoot People started. And 36 years since the publication of the small book on Bull Plume's winter count by the Old Man River Culture Center on the North Peigan Reserve. During those 45 years the stories never stopped coming, Some first hand, others on tape, and yet others from the dusty archives of museums and libraries. They are still just as alive as when first spoken, and are the stories of a people through the history of time.

The bedrock of these acknowledgments are still those who were a part of the first winter count book [included here as Bull Plume #1, improved and corrected]. They are the two grand old ladies of the North Peigan Reserve, Ekistanopataki [Mrs. Buffalo] and her sister Sisinaki [Mrs. Many Guns] who have long passed away at 109 and 111 years old. Their help, encouragement and sharing of knowledge in those early days cannot be measured. Others of the North Peigan were Joe and Josephine Crowshoe Sr., John Yellowhorn, Billy Strikes With a Gun, and Albert Little Mustache Sr. From the South Peigan Mike Swims Under, and the North Blackfeet [Siksika], Ben Calf Robe. From the Blood-Blackfoot one of my earliest teachers Bob Black Plume, and long time friends and relatives Ed and Ruth Little Bear. All have long since passed on and are greatly missed. Through the many years there have been others who have added to my knowledge and understanding of Niitsitapiiysin [the Blackfoot way of life] and encouraged making this book a reality.

Leonard Bastien and Allan Pard, were also instrumental in that first book, and patient in my early struggles with the language. My partners in the All Brave Dog Society, they persevered while we tried to bring order out of chaos. Now they are the elders who carry many of these stories into the future. Shirley Crowshoe, granddaughter of Ekistanopataki, who was always at hand for translations and comments over these many years, continues her own work with bringing the stories, and language back. Sadly, one of my strongest proponents in doing this book, Narcisse Blood of the Blood-Blackfoot, tragically passed away before it went to press. He was one of the many who insisted this book needed to be done, and constantly asked when it would be finished, spurring my efforts forward.

Two non-Blackfoot added their comments and conversations to this work that were invaluable; Dr. Hugh Dempsey, now retired from the Glenbow Alberta Institute, and Dr. Jane Richardson Hanks, both preeminent scholars of the Blackfoot people and their history. Their own bodies of work have become classics in the field.

Many others from the distant past, and not so distant past, have contributed to this work, and I apologize for omitting their names. Many are cited within the work and my thanks go out to all of them.

And last, but certainly not least, are the many archivists and librarians at the Glenbow Museum Archives, Royal Alberta Archives and Montana Historical Society Archives who helped find requests of obscure documents, photos, and books over the years. They are the unsung heroes of any researcher. My thanks to all.

FORWARD

Blackfoot winter counts are not only records of important annual events but they also provide a rare look at the culture and lifestyle of a prairie nation at various times in its history. The winter counts themselves have been the subject of much examination and study. We know that the keepers of the winter counts (there were several of them) selected the most important event for the year. Sometimes they recorded an epidemic or battle that affected the whole nation, and at other times they selected personal events within their own families. Either way, each entry reflected an episode in tribal history.

In this book, Paul Raczka looks beyond the simple listing of occurrences to tell the story behind the winter counts. He uses them as entries into the rich and varied history of a prairie people from the "dog days" to the twentieth century. These winter counts are doorways and when opened they reveal stories of warfare, leadership, victories, and disasters over a 214-year period.

Raczka begins with the Bull Plume's winter count of 1764, recorded simply as "Big Smallpox scare." This was one of the earliest records of an epidemic that swept through the Blackfoot time after time, decimating the three tribes of Blackfoot, Blood, and Peigan that made up the Blackfoot nation. Raczka uses this and other entries to tell the stories of these Blackfoot people. Drawing on his vast knowledge of the tribes, the tales told to him by elders, and documents of the period, he provides a fascinating glimpse past the winter counts and into the camps and lodges of a prairie people.

Hugh A. Dempsey
Chief Curator Emeritus, Glenbow Museum, editor of Alberta History quarterly

Our words are very important.

My name is Eagle Speak.

This time that my life came from, I really feel cautious when we are speaking about things and about the way we live.

Spotted Eagle *[the author, ed.]* told me that I can talk about his stories. They just wrote them down, the Piikani, and the way that we lived. He didn't come from a collage or big school. He lived around the Piikani and he was around all the ceremonies that I was at. Here he was, he really paid attention and had a very good understanding about everything that was going on.

And with me, my Piikani language is what made my life good. Right away I understood what he wrote. I have made very good use of my knowledge of Piikani ways, all the things that were given to me, and all the good things. Now the way that we live is very different. There we live now, being humble and helpful is not there any more. We are making the western way of life important. This makes the way we live now very hard. This makes our life very hard now. We just get sick from it. We have to put up with all the things that we are hit with – the dangerous things, alcohol and the things that they smoke. It makes the way we live very hard. The children, the elders, we are all hit with it.

Our leaders, fathers, their thoughts and rules here, Spotted Eagle, I saw what he wrote, the Piikani, he has become a part of all the elders of many hundred years old; the way it was. I really feel good about it. It is just like I took back my previous life and thinking. Then I understand all these writings. They will be very helpful for our grand children, all of the children that are not born yet. We are given what we can tell stories about. We just put it behind us. This, our Whiteman speaking , *[English, ed.]* is how we lost it.

All the things that my parents and elders invited me to know. I heard them,"Try very hard to be strong, be strong about what you hear people say, help people, be kind and gentle, these are things that will be helpful to you." Well, stories, these are the laws. They are not written down. The way the stories go, the one who told the story helps us to know ahead of time.

That is the way with our bundles. Why we don't make mistakes. They all have stories. The same for the songs. We are all relatives to the things that fly around, the water people, the ground people, we are all related to these things. The songs came from them and they are transferable. *[Etsik pumaksin, passed on through ceremony, ed.]* This is how we understand life now, the written material. I saw them as stories that Spotted Eagle put together. Our fathers made available to us so we can know the stories. So we can know about our fathers stories, how the life was back in the olden days. The schools don't have them written among their stories. We can just take back all the stories and knowledge that they took away. Now we can start telling the real stories about how it was. Our children can hear them and they can understand how our fathers lived. It is far different than the way we live now.

I really believe that their *[the elders, ed.]* work is put ahead of everything. This type of work *[now, ed.]* is put way low in importance. We don't get benefits for it. They *[the elders, ed.]* interview and tell about our Holy things, they are all a part of it. This is how these writings are all about ourselves, the way that we were taught and how I understand you. It is totally different than the way I live. I am humiliated and I am scared about it, the English speaking. We still talk in two ways, they are not real, these are things that I know, after I start re thinking. This is the way we live, and now when our children complete school, they will understand real life, real thoughts and then we can live like the writings and stories. Because they are our laws and rules, so that they can continue to be told with them that still speak our language. It is most important that our mistakes are the blame of our English speaking. Our Native language has made us very pitiful and humble. It was made so that we can understand what is not good and that we should not use all these things that are bad for us. Loneliness, scary thoughts, fright, are what had made us all sick.

Our language is most important in our life. With this we can understand life and about our Creator. This is why I am really guiding them straight. Spotted Eagle will get many good things and good luck in life because of these really good things that he has told stories about.
Well, that is all,

Peter Strikes With a Gun, Former Beaver Bundle owner, Former Head Chief of the Piikani Nation, North Peigan-Blackfoot, Brocket, Alberta

Peter Strikes With a Gun, as well as Earl Old Person, grew up speaking Blackfoot as their primary language, and continue to do so in their every day life. To give the reader a feel for the rhythm and thought process of the language we've translated Peter's Blackfoot statements as closely as possible. Our thanks to Marvin Weatherwax Sr. for his help in doing this.

Oki, my name is Earl Old Person. I'm a member of the Blackfeet tribe of the Blackfeet Reservation. My Indian name is Cold Wind, Istosopot, and my other Indian name is Charging Home, Akayapakyapi. Cold Wind is a name I gave to myself when I was a very small boy, and I heard the Indian name Istosopot and I was concerned and wanted to know what it meant. And my mother told me it was "Cold Wind". And I told my mother from here on my name is going to be Istosopot. So I'm known by this name, by all people. But the name that was given to me by my grandfather, old Bear Medicine, he gave me the name Akayapakyapi, Charging Home, it was a warrior's name. This was my mother's father, old Bear Medicine. Not too many know me by this name, but that was my name given me when I was just a baby.

I've lived a long time, around many things, and by many people that I observed. People that I admired many times over by the things that they stood for. Not because I knew them personally that well, but the stories I had heard of them. And it brings pride to people when you hear these kinds of stories. We have people today that have become very concerned, and were very interested, in knowing about our ways and how our people lived , and the things that we are trying to follow, just by knowing and hearing of some of their ways. And the people I'm talking about, these people who are non-Indian, white people. But they have taken a lot of time to gather information, to find out about things of the Native people, what they stood for.

I read books. I like to read books, especially when things that I read pertain to my people and to the Natives of Indian country. When I hear of the many things that they had done to cause we the people today to exist and to continue, looking back and try to relive some of those things that we are able to do and show our young people that they may be able to use I thank and admire those people that take that time, a non-Indian, and be able to put it into a way that we could read and to help the ways of our people. We have a lot of our young people today thats trying to find things to understand where we come from, how our people lived, the things our people done to help our ways to continue. We cannot go back to the old ways of how our people were known as warriors, how they lived the harsh times. But we can learn to become strong and to be a person that's determined to continue the things that we are able to do to help our young people understand our way of life; this through reading books, this through hearing stories. Our elders are gone that can go back and tell stories that they would want us to hear and understand. But we still have those people that took enough time to bring out some of those things that they were able to gather, put together, and to show we the people of the present days, to understand and be able to relay those things to our young people, to the people that are wanting to understand the ways of our Native people. So today, I really commend people like Paul Raczka who are one of those individuals that have done things to put together something that our people can follow.

It may have been a time that perhaps it was difficult for them to gather these informations. But through their determination they continued finding those ways, because they had concerns about the ways of our Indian people. And just by hearing some of the stories, reading some of the stories, of our people, of their braveness, of them being very strong, it brings to us that had it not been for them; had it not been for them being strong, and being individuals that did not give up, we continue to exist, we continue to observe those things that they stood for. So many thanks to all that help bring together our history, whether its by the Blackfeet, of the Blackfeet, or other Nations. We're all together in this and we're going to be together as we go forth. Thank you.

Earl Old Person, Lifetime Traditional Head Chief of the Blackfeet Tribe, South Peigan-Blackfoot, Browning, Montana

CONTENTS

ILLUSTRATIONS

CHAPTER 1

INTRODUCTION

"Sikaitapi itsinniiki" *is just that – "telling the old stories". Each story stands alone and carries its own lesson. Each was told at the appropriate time and place to pass on a teaching related to the situation. That is what Blackfoot history really is – a lesson to learn, from things that happened in the past. The Siksikaitsitapix, the Blackfoot People*[1]*, take that definition literally. Within the Blackfoot world view an exact date for an event is not necessarily the most important lesson. Memorizing specific dates of events is not as important as learning the "teachings" the event provided.*

To benefit from this collection of teachings it is necessary to suspend the Euro concept of history, the Euro reckoning of time, and the standardization of the importance of events. It will become clear to the reader that in the winter counts presented here an event may be recorded a year or two in either direction from the date recorded in Euro-Canadian/American history. It will also become clear that a reverse process was used by some of those non-Blackfoot, who first recorded these winter counts, to fit them into their time line of history. Rather than starting with a date and recording an event, the existing event was placed in a date established, or presumed, within the Euro-history calendar. In some cases this was done by the Blackfoot keepers of the individual winter count during the reservation period to make it acceptable, and legitimate, in non-Blackfoot concepts of "written history".

The early reservation period brought an over powering movement by the dominant society to "civilize" the Blackfoot people into Euro lifestyle and beliefs. One of the ways they attempted this was to trivialize Blackfoot culture and world view. In their view it was of "no worth", "primitive" and needed to be eliminated for the people to "advance" into civilized society. Many Blackfoot people fought these attempts and maintained the traditional culture. A few attempted to show the dominant society the value of Blackfoot worldview, history and culture. This was accomplished to a limited extent with an influx of scholars to the reservations seeking to record that very culture. They sought out the intellectuals of Blackfoot culture and found those individuals who saw this as an opportunity to present, and preserve, the legitimacy of their culture and history to Euro society.

These scholars, or their field workers, wrote down the stories as they were told. However, when the information was published it was in many cases modified to fit the scholars' preconceptions or theories. For years these stories, written in the words of the Blackfoot people, sat unread. Other stories are still told by elders and Medicine Bundle

[1] The terms for the Blackfoot People [Siksikaitsitapix] as spoken in Blackfoot are Piikani for the English terms Peigan-Blackfoot in Canada, and Piegan-Blackfeet in the U.S.; Kainai, Blood-Blackfoot of Alberta and Siksika-Blackfoot or North Blackfeet, in Canada. The spelling used will be determined by the original source. North Peigan of Canada, South Piegan/Blackfeet of the U.S., Bloods of Canada and North Blackfeet of Canada. The Blackfoot as a group called themselves by several names; Siksikaitsitapix, Niitsitapix [Real People] and Saokitapix [Prairie People].

owners. By bringing both together we hope to tell those stories as the Blackfoot people know and tell them: Blackfoot world view and history, presented by those Blackfoot intellectuals, standing within the world's history, and every bit as valid as that of the dominant society.

History is a matter of perspective. Usually it is told from that of the victor, but in all cases it is from the viewpoint of the writer. Each writer brings his own experiences and interests to his writing, and that affects the perspective of the events being written about. It also affects just which events are considered noteworthy of recording or remembering. Therefore, knowing something about the writer and his personal history is almost as important as the events recorded. In that way we can judge his recordings and insights on the basis of his personal perspectives.

And that is the basis for this book, a history of the Blackfoot Nation told by the Blackfoot people. It is a history that starts at the very beginning, and is passed down through oral tradition, until the time of writing. What little is known of the writers will be included so the reader can form his own judgments. Their biographies and qualifications are just as important as the stories themselves, for they form the perspective of the story as it is presented.

The stories selected here are part of a large pool of oral history that still exists among the Blackfoot people. The same story may vary with details among different tellers, but the overall teaching always remains the same. Those selected were given by persons of tribally acknowledged ritual knowledge and were often Medicine Bundle holders or tribal leaders.

What is missing from these written accounts is the visual beauty and emotion of the storyteller. Watching the story being told was involving the listener totally into the experience, with both the teller and listener forgetting the present surroundings. Hand gestures, including sign language at times, and body movements, were accompanied by songs in the correct places. A dying skill these days.

For those who argue oral history does not accurately portray history we would like to point out a couple of things. When a group of people depend only upon an oral passing of knowledge the accuracy of that knowledge becomes much greater than in a society dependent upon written knowledge. For example, songs for many Blackfoot ceremonies were recorded in 1903 and 1904. When comparing them to those in use today [by individuals who had no access to the recordings], not only were the words the same but also the vocables in the main part of the song. This is over a one hundred year period. Also, despite the claim by Euro-historians that the Blackfoot originated in the Slave Lake area of northern Alberta, newer archaeological research tends to support the early Blackfoot oral history. The evidence is beginning to show that proto-Blackfoot lived where their history states – along the eastern front of the Rocky Mountains at least as long ago as 300-400BC. It seems oral history is proving more accurate than we give it credit.

The majority of these stories were told to, and recorded, by non-Native people who had an overwhelming interest in the Blackfoot worldview and history. They had the opportunity to write the stories of the last of the buffalo people, in the words and viewpoints of those people. Those Blackfoot of past years felt the need to have their history and viewpoint recorded for future generations of their own people, but for many years these stories sat in ledgers and notes in private libraries and dusty archives. A few were inserted in books and articles to lend authenticity to non-Native writers' viewpoints, but they were usually just considered anecdotal and "quaint". Others used them as fillers in histories written about the Euro North Americans and their accomplishments. A very few authors published them with all the authenticity and respect they deserved. But these authors were few and far between. Their works are also included as part of this history.

Each person in the long chain, from the early Blackfoot to the present, had their strengths and weaknesses. These also are important to note and recognize. For the early Blackfoot it was their qualifications as ceremonialists, for it was in the ceremonial teachings the complete stories were passed. For later generations it was their ability to remember, or interpret events recorded in the winter count pictographs or syllabic writings. Then there was the final telling to the non-Blackfoot, the skill of the translators and their knowledge of "old" Blackfoot language and Blackfoot culture. Some of these interpreters were converted Christians who tried to put a more "civilized" spin on the stories being told. Others had never been involved in the traditional religion and ceremonies and didn't really understand what was being told. And yet others were "just doing a job" and had no interest in the material, or perfecting the translations.

The non-Blackfoot recorders of these stories fall into two categories; one group recorded the stories exactly as they were told, the others recorded them and then interpreted them to fit their own preconceived theories. In these cases we went back to the recorder's original field notes for the true story.

BLACKFOOT LANGUAGE, INTERPRETERS AND TRANSLATIONS

The Blackfoot language is a beautiful, complex language which carries philosophical and world view information that defies simple, direct, translation. Much like the pictographs in the winter counts, individual words contain more information than meets the eye [or ear]. This world view is built upon the interpretation of specific events or emotions, and assigned a word or phrase agreed upon by the people. Thus even though an individual has a conversational ability in the language unless he/she has been exposed to the context and circumstances in which it is used, a direct translation would lack information. In many of these stories the speaker, who spoke English as a second language, insisted on telling the stories in Blackfoot to insure the correct information was given. Discussions followed concerning specific words or phrases to arrive at the closest English equivalent to the Blackfoot world view concept being expressed. This was also helpful concerning intended meanings in previously translated stories.

The term "World View" is often tossed about in literature without a clear understanding of the term. One way to explain it is to take a simple word like owl. When you say the word "owl" to a person whose first language is English they would mentally interpret it as " bird of prey, hunts at night, eats mice and other rodents, wise, associated with the supernatural at times". A Blackfoot word for owl, "Sipistto", creates a very different mental image. He is literally, "night announcer" and can come to warn people of a potential death or bad luck. He is also the spirit of a past Medicine Pipe Owner. His prepared skin is in the Medicine Pipe bundle itself, adding the owl's spiritual power to help the people. By wearing his feathers a man would gain his spiritual power in going to war. ["Putting on the owl feathers", preparing for war] [Ben Calf Robe, Siksika-Blackfoot,1976 to the author]. Two very different cultural visual images and interpretations for the same bird. Thus, a "Blackfoot World View" is created within, and by, the language, giving us a very different way of looking at, and interacting with, the world in general. It is for this reason Blackfoot elders [as well as those of other tribes and cultures] consider the loss of the language the beginning of the lose of identity as a separate and distinct people.

Words also change meaning, as well as implied meaning, depending on the context in which they are used. In other cases, once the subject is established, a different or shorter version of the subject word is used during the same conversation.

For example when discussing "Antelope" Saokiawakassi [lit. Prairie Deer], the complete word is first used to establish the subject. Thereafter, in the conversation it may be referred to just as awakasi, deer, [antelope being considered a part of the deer family]. However, participants in the conversation understand that it is still referring to antelope.

A "Sacred" language of sorts also exists. Words that mean one thing in common everyday conversations change meaning when used in the sacred or "Holy" context. For example the word "matapi" means person in everyday conversation. However, when discussing holy subjects, or the Blackfoot World View, it could also mean spirit. Thus when a person says he was visited by a person it could mean just that in everyday conversation. But if they were discussing holy matters he would mean he was visited by a spirit. Context of the conversation is all important.

The understanding of these changes is important in the reading of the story translations done by various researchers. Several other things need to be considered when using the translations. First, is the World View and ceremonial knowledge of the original Blackfoot speaker. Secondly the same knowledge of the interpreter comes into play. They have to know the true meaning of the word within the context of the conversation. Third we have the knowledge and fluency of English by the interpreter. Here, in most cases, we have a person with a "high" understanding of their native language and a rudimentary knowledge of a second language. And last, we have the recorder who may, or may not, have preconceived ideas regarding the topic of discussion. A recorder who is a true ethnographer will write exactly what was translated without embellishing or modifying it to fit their own preconceived ideas, or the current theories regarding the topic. [See Curtis and Grinnell's interpretations in the section "In to Blackfoot Country".]

As A.C. Haddon, an anthropologist who worked with Edward Curtis for a time, explained, "It is therefore not to be wondered at that the published accounts of American Indians, and indeed of all native peoples who are investigated in a similar manner, are liable to vary and to be of varying reliability. The chances of misunderstandings creeping in are considerable even when informant [speaker, ed.], interpreter, and investigator are watchful and honest. How much more so when one of the three links in the chain is careless or prejudiced." [Gidley, 1982]

IN THE BEGINNING...

"At a certain time, it happened that all the earth was covered with water. The Old Man [Napiw] was in a canoe, and he thought of causing the earth to come up from the abyss. To put this project into execution he used the aid of four animals, - the duck, the otter, the badger and the muskrat. The muskrat proved to be the best diver. He remained so long under water that when he came to the surface he was fainting, but he had succeeded in getting a little particle of earth, which he brought between the toes of his paw. This particle of earth the Old Man took, and blowing on it he swelled it to such an extant as to make the whole earth of it. Then it took four days to complete his work, and make the mountains, rivers, plants and beasts." *[Unknown Blackfoot in Hale, Report of the British Association for the Advancement of Science, 1886, p. 224]*

This is one version of the story of the flood. Others tell of Napi on a log with a duck, otter, beaver, and muskrat. The important points of the story are that the muskrat brought up the earth, thus insuring his importance in the Blackfoot religion. The other is that there were four animals, and Napi blew on the particle of earth four times to recreate the earth.

It is also important to realize that these stories were all translated from Blackfoot and that the translations depended on how well the interpreter spoke, and understood, Blackfoot <u>and</u> English. And then we have the writer's word changes into what he felt the public at large would understand. This would account for some differences in the stories and how they were explained in English by the various writers.

Another important point to remember is that this story is in response to the question as to how the earth was created. The Blackfoot story teller is giving the account as to how <u>this earth we are standing on</u> was created. Again, this is a teaching for a specific event. The careful listener would have questions about how Napi, and the animals, could be floating on a log if the earth hadn't been created yet. Where did the animals and the log/canoe come from? If we remember Blackfoot history is not a linear reciting of events, but rather individual <u>teachings</u> we would be aware there is another story here somewhere.

Here then is the story of the flooding of the <u>first</u> earth while Napi [Old Man] was traveling with his friend the wolf.

"...One morning they awoke, and Old Man said: 'Oh my young brother, I have had a bad dream. Hereafter, when you chase anything, if it jumps a stream, you must not follow it. Even a little spring you must not jump.' And the wolf promised not to jump over water.

Now one day the wolf was chasing a moose, and it ran on an island. The stream about it was very small; so the wolf thought: 'This is such a little stream that I must jump it. That moose is very tired, and I don't think it will leave the island.' So he jumped on to the island, and as soon as he entered the brush, a bear caught him, for the island was the home of the Chief Bear [*a Water Bear, one of the Underwater People, ed.]* and his two brothers.

Old Man waited a long time for the wolf to come back, and then went to look for him. He asked all the birds he met if they had seen him, but they all said they had not.

At last he saw a kingfisher, who was sitting on a limb overhanging the water. 'Why do you sit there, my young brother?' said Old Man. 'Because,' replied the kingfisher, 'the Chief Bear and his brothers have killed your wolf; they have eaten the meat and thrown the fat into the river, and whenever I see a piece come floating along, I fly down and get it.' Then said Old Man, 'Do the Bear Chief and his brothers often come out? And where do they live?' 'They come out every morning to play,' said the kingfisher; 'and they live upon that island.'

Old Man went up there and saw their track on the sand, where they had been playing, and he turned himself into a rotten tree. By and by the bears came out, and when they saw the tree, the Chief Bear said: 'Look at that rotten tree. It is Old Man. Go, brothers, and see if it is not.' So the two brothers went over and clawed and bit the tree, and although it hurt Old Man, he never moved. Then the Bear Chief was sure it was only a tree, and he began to play with his brothers. Now while they were playing, and all were on their backs, Old Man leaned over and shot an arrow into each one of them; and they cried out loudly and ran back on the island. The Old Man changed into himself, and walked down along the river. Pretty soon he saw a frog jumping along, and every time it jumped it would say, 'Ni-nah Okai-yu!' And sometimes it would stop and sing: 'Ni-nah Okayi-yu! [Chief Bear!] Ni-nah Okai-yu! [Chief Bear!] Napi I-nit-si-wah Ni-nah Okai-yu! [Old Man kill him, Chief Bear!]

'What do you say?' cried Old Man. The frog repeated what he had said.

'Ah!' exclaimed Old Man, 'tell me all about it.'

'The Chief Bear and his brothers,' replied the frog, 'were playing on the sand, when Old Man shot arrows into them. They are not dead, but the arrows are very near their hearts; if you should shove ever so little on them, the points would cut their hearts. I am going after medicine now to cure them.'

Then Old Man killed the frog and skinned her, and put the hide on himself and swam back to the island, and hopped up toward the bears, crying at every step, 'Ni-nah Okai-yu!' just as the frog had done.

'Hurry,' cried the Chief Bear.

'Yes,' replied Old Man, and he went up and shoved the arrow into his heart.

'I cured him; he is asleep now,' he cried, and he went up and shoved the arrow into the biggest brother's heart. 'I cured them; they are asleep now'; and he went up and shoved the arrow into the other bear's heart.... [*White Calf, South Piegan-Blackfoot, to George Bird Grinnell, ca. 1891, BLACKFOOT LODGE TALES, 1962, pp 150-152*]

These bears were Underwater People, and when the others found out what happened, they covered the earth with water in revenge for the killing of one of their own. And that is how we find Napi floating on a log in our first story, and the creation of the earth we are standing on today.

Some scholars say these stories are tribal answers to finding fish and water plant fossils on the hill tops. Others say it is an example of Christian theology creeping into Blackfoot thought via the Noah's Ark story. But perhaps there is a third option from a time before the Blackfoot became Blackfoot and were "the ones who used stones".

Modern geology is providing us with some interesting information. We know the last glacier age was 20,000 years ago, but we are finding that there were many mega floods that hit Blackfoot country over the years. Some caused Glacial Lake Missoula, with ice dams that broke and changed the landscape drastically. Others where not so large, but continued over the years with damming, flooding, and changes to the environment. There were "little ice ages" continuing into the 1850's to various extents. Couldn't our stories be the result of proto-Blackfoot being affected by one of these, and explaining what they witnessed? What we are finding out is that "hard" science is constantly changing its "facts", and that they are coming closer to what the old stories have said all along.

THE NORTH COUNTRY....

"Our tribes came southward out of the wooded country to the north of Bow River. We began to make short excursions to the south, and finding it a better game country and with much less snow, we kept coming farther and farther, and finally gave up altogether our old home. This happened before my grandfather's *[Sistsawana, Bird Rattle, ed.]* time. We call that former home 'Ishtssohatsi' ['in the brush']. The Peigan led in this movement and were followed by the Bloods and later the Blackfeet *[Siksikai, ed.]*. We *[meaning the Peigan, ed.]* all hunted in the plains between Milk River and the Yellowstone, the Peigan finally wintering on the Musselshell or the Upper Missouri, the Bloods on Belly River, south of the site of Fort Macleod, the Blackfeet on Bow River, or its tributary, High River. Of course, individual families and small bands of the Blackfeet would sometimes spend the winter among the Peigans."

"Tearing Lodge further states that Bird Rattle used to say that through the forest country ran a big river, which informant thinks was larger than the Missouri. After the Peigan had begun to make short trips into the prairies, they one winter returned to the big river, to find white men on the other side. These men traded with them, and as the people began to go further south the white men followed them with their goods. Later, when they returned to the big river, they found a fort built on the other side, which Tearing Lodge believes was Edmonton House."
[Tearing Lodge, South Peigan-Blackfoot, 1898, at the age of ca. 68, to Edward Curtis, Curtis mss; Seaver Center for Western History, L.A.]

From this information, and the opinion of George Bird Grinnell who was with him interviewing Tearing Lodge in Blackfoot country in 1898, Curtis formed his conclusion that the Blackfoot people originated and migrated from the north near Lesser Slave Lake Alberta, and the big river referred to was the Peace River.

Both published that conclusion, and thereafter other researchers quoted their findings as fact. Grinnell tried to add to the strength of his conclusion that the Cree name for the Blackfoot was "Slave Indians". Slave Lake bears the same name therefore it must be the home of the Blackfoot. He adds that Henry's Cree guides stated that the "Knisteneaux" [Slave Indians] and Beaver Indians made their peace at Peace Point from which the river gets its name. [Henry-Thompson Journals, Vol. II, page 510, N.Y. 1897] However, he would not be the first researcher to face confusion with Cree names for various other groups. David Smyth covers this name confusion thoroughly in his thesis, "The Niitsitapi Trade" [Smyth, 2001] and shows other tribes were also called "Slave Indians" and misidentified as Blackfoot.

Both Curtis and Grinnell were stretching parts of the information to fit their theories. The "forest", or "bush" as they say in Canada, starts south of Red Deer, Alberta, approximately 400 miles south of the Peace River, and well south of the Blackfoot northern boundary of the North Saskatchewan River. Going back to both Curtis' and Grinnell's original notes we find that the big river that Tearing Lodge refers to is literally "Big River" [Omakati, in Blackfoot], the Saskatchewan River. All other historical accounts of meetings with the Blackfoot place them along the Saskatchewan at various times. None show them near Lesser Slave Lake or the Peace River. Another clue given by Tearing Lodge is that when they went back north they found "a fort built on the other side". This would probably be Buckingham House or Fort George, built on the North Saskatchewan River in 1791 [See winter count for 1791.] .

Tearing Lodge and his wife, South Peigan. Told Grinnell and Curtis stories from his father's time. Edward Curtis Photo, ca. 1909

Some of this confusion can be due to the interpreter as we mentioned elsewhere, and some can be interpretation of the story by researchers with preconceived theories. For example quoting from the Curtis mss. again; "Their genetic legend is so modernized that the creation is placed on the Teton River in Montana. The aged wiseman [Tearing Lodge, ed.] who gave the story of the creation on the Teton River, the following day told how his paternal grandfather had discussed the life of the people when living at the lesser Slave Lake [Curtis and Grinnell's opinion as to the location, ed.] hundreds of miles north and generations before they moved south to Montana. When asked to reconcile his historical statement with the legend he merely smiled, shrugged his shoulders and said, 'That is the way the people tell it'." *[Curtis mss.; Seaver Center for Western History, L.A.]*

To this we can add the story that after Napi created the Blackfoot people he rested on a butte where he made a stone image of himself. This stone outline is still in existence on the Teton River just west of Choteau, Montana.

If we are to accept this story of the Blackfoot being in the south what would be the reason they were found along the North Saskatchewan River? One possible answer may come from the far southwest United States. We know as a fact that one of the smallpox epidemics that hit the Blackfoot people came through the Shoshone people to the south. [See 1764 winter count.] If an earlier [and possibly "first"] epidemic had hit the Blackfoot from the same source, they would have fled as far away from the source as possible. And that would be to the far northern border of their land. An unknown, and untreatable [by their methods] killer of the people would cause panic and fear they had offended their spiritual helpers and guardians of their land.

Is it possible such an event occurred? From the journals of fray Juan de Prada of 1638 we may find a possible answer, and source. As the Franciscan Commissary General of New Spain {New Mexico, etc.] he reported Pueblo Indian numbers declined due, "to that extent on account of the very active prevalence during these last years of smallpox and the sickness which the Mexicans called cocolitzli [typhus, ed.]" From 60,000 they were reduced to 40,000 people during the years 1636-1641. [Hackett, 109-110] This, along with forced slavery, and abuse by the Spanish, caused a great flight of Pueblo Indians from the Spanish country to the Plains Indians. Some fled to the Plains Apache country to the east, while others escaped to the Utes in the north. Since the Utes, as well as the Comanche and Apache to the east, were old trading partners among the pueblos, there would be a favorable welcome for them. Both the Comanche and Utes were related to the Shoshone and were frequent trading partners – especially for horses.

"Saturday, March 25th. The Snakes continued to move. I had no idea the Snakes were so numerous. The Plains Snakes, said to be 1000 men, annually go to the Spanish settlements to trade and steal horses. The Lower Snakes are not less than 1500 men, independent of women and children." [Williams, 1971]

It would take only one infected individual to spread the diseases among them and on to the Blackfoot southern border.

The time-line would be about right for the Blackfoot to have fled north, stayed until they were comfortable the disease to the south had run its course [one or two generations?], recovered their numbers and strength, and discovered enemy tribes were beginning to move into their original country. This would be about the time first contact with European traders placed them on the north boundary of their country and moving back to the south.

Strengthening their southern origin we find Wissler had collected other stories from the Peigan; "The Piegan, especially, claim that they came up from the south from a region beyond, or to the west, of the mountains and that they formerly lived north of their present reservation, sometimes wintering in the foothills, among the trees. The incidents in some of their myths, especially those of the Old Man [Napi, ed.], are often definitely located in the north, but this north is in all cases placed between Macleod and Edmonton [Alberta, ed.], within the territory assigned to the Blackfoot..." [Wissler, 1910; 17]

As we've mentioned earlier, each story is a teaching and a response to a question or situation, and they are not given in a linear manner. For the Blackfoot, both stories are true. In the time before the people became Blackfoot, the stories [including many of the Napi stories] are situated in the south country from the Yellowstone [Ponoka Omakati, Elk River] north. They could indeed have become "Blackfoot" along the Teton during "the time when we used stones". *The stories are neither "modernized" nor confusing for the Blackfoot people. Archeological evidence is finding that the use of the Blackfoot Buffalo Calling Ceremony, and painted Iniskim [Buffalo Stone], was happening in southern Alberta and northern Montana at least 1,500 years ago.[AD 600-1725 AD]*

A story collected by J.W. Schultz.
"Very long ago there was a tribe of people living far to the south, on the other side of the mountains. Somehow game became very scarce there, and the people began to starve. In this tribe there was an old man who had three sons, all grown and married, and he felt very sad to see them and their little children starving and growing thinner every day. One morning he called his sons to his lodge and said, 'My children, listen. I have mourned a great deal for you lately. I have felt very badly to see you and the little ones starve. For myself, I do not care. I am now very old, and the time is near for me to die. I have been praying a great deal for you lately, trying to find some way for you to survive. Last night my Dream talked to me. Hear what he said and then do as you think best. My opinion is that he spoke well. He said, 'Kyi, old man, take courage. This is not the only country. Beyond these mountains is a very big land. There you will find plenty of food. Stay here no longer. Before you get any weaker, cross these mountains with your children. Thus shall you survive.''

"For some time no one spoke. All were thinking of the Dream's words. At last one of the sons said, 'Maybe this is the truth. I am willing to go. If we stay here we will surely die. If we cross the mountains we may find the game. If we do not find it, we can die there as well as here.'

" 'True! True!' said the other sons, 'we can try. Let us hurry and get ready.'

"It did not take them long to start, for they left all their property behind, except for a few robes. There was no trail, and the mountains were steep, so they traveled very slowly. They could not go fast, for the women had to carry the smallest children, and all were weak from hunger. Sometimes the men killed a bird or a rabbit, and some days they found some roots or berries to eat. Other days they had nothing, and at night they went to bed hungry and the children cried themselves to sleep. When they first started they thought that when they had climbed the mountains in sight and reached the top they would be able to see the new country on the other side; but beyond these were many others, and they kept climbing up and down, up and down, until they thought there were nothing but mountains beyond. So one day they talked of giving up, they were so weak, when they suddenly saw that they had passed the last peak. Beyond was the great prairie, reaching to the end of the world. By sunset they reached it, and camped beside a little stream. Already they had seen plenty of game, great bands of buffalo, elk, and antelope. Early in the morning the sons started out to hunt, but they had bad luck. They could not get near enough game to kill it. But their father was a powerful person. He made a black medicine *[sikokasim. Black Root, ed.]*, a very wonderful medicine, and rubbed it on his oldest son's feet, and it enabled him to run so fast that he got right up beside a fat cow and killed her with one arrow.

"Then they feasted, first giving the tongue to the Sun, and once more they felt well and easy, and the children again ran about and played as they had in other days before starvation came. The old man gave his eldest son a new name. 'Hereafter,' he said, 'your namc is Siks-i-kaho [Blackfoot] *[Blackfeet, ed.]*. It shall be the name of your children, too,'

"Now the other sons were jealous. They said, 'Is our elder brother better than we? Why may we not have some of this black medicine, too?'

"'Wait,' said their father. 'You shall each have a new name. First go to war, and when you return I will give you new names for yourself and your children. Here we will found three tribes, and this shall be their country.' The young men soon got ready and started, one going south, the other east.

"It was winter when the one who went east returned. He brought scalps with him, and also some weapons which he had taken from the enemy. His father named him Kai-nah [Bloods]. From him and his children this tribe started.

"The other son did not return until the middle of the winter. He also brought scalps and weapons, and some wearing apparel of curious make; so the old man named him Pi-kun-i [Piegan]. He was the first of this tribe." *[Crazy Dog, Blackfoot, told to J.W. Schultz, to Grinnell; Grinnell, 1892; 154-156] [A similar story was told to Clark Wissler in the early 1900's.]*

The transition from their land across the mountains to this "great prairie, reaching to the end of the world" *also meant learning new hunting methods. Stalking and ambush no longer were as effective as in the wooded country. While they could see game all around them,* "they could not get near enough game to kill it". *Again, the father provided the solution. His spiritual power instructed him to make a Medicine with the Black Root and rub it on his oldest son's feet.* "...it enabled him to run so fast that he got right up beside a fat cow and killed it with one arrow".

What this story tells us is that the proto-Blackfoot learned to become "persistence hunters", an effective hunting method used by early man in plains environments around the world. It consists of simply running after a specific animal until it drops from exhaustion. It is the same method used by wolves, in relays, in bringing down their much faster prey. And indeed, Blackfoot elders consistently say that "the people learned to hunt from the wolves." *By keeping a steady pace, and keeping the animal in sight, the prey eventually collapses from oxygen debt, and/or heat exhaustion. Buffalo, elk and deer are built to escape with short bursts of speed which creates oxygen debt and overheating, but humans can run at a steady pace without hitting that debt. Sweat glands and the lack of fur also allow humans to run for long periods without over heating. As long as the hunters could, isolate and, keep the animal in sight, regularly pushing it to its break away short sprints of speed, he will eventually catch up to the animal who will be suffering from exhaustion. Man can run at a steady pace for hours without incurring total oxygen debt, prey animals cannot.*

In other words, for the early Blackfoot to become the Saokitapix *[Prairie People, their other name, ed.] and survive on the* "great prairie" *they became what we today consider ultra-marathon runners. Like the wolf, they no doubt hunted as a group, and with their brain as well. That meant examining the herd for the weakest animal, memorizing its tracks and droppings; the younger hunters pushing the herd until it became separated from it, and then keeping it from rejoining the herd [the group effort], while the average hunters pursued the animal; and eventually, the experienced hunters finishing the last leg of the race by running it to exhaustion, and the final conclusion. This allowed the hunters to walk up to the animal and kill it without personal danger. It was also much more effective a hunting method for the open prairie than stalking or ambush.*

Historic records show that tribes on the Prairie and Plains as well as Northern Mexico regularly ran down deer and wild horses. And in modern days humans beat horses at the 50 mile Man Against Horse Race in Arizona for several years. For the Blackfoot, one race was recorded in 1886 between Scabby Dried Meat, a Siksika, and several other runners, including non-Natives. It was a four day race on an indoor track lasting four hours each night. The winner would be the one completing the most laps for the four days in the fastest time. The fourth night Scabby Dried Meat ran 84 miles and was the eventual winner. [Calgary Herald October 30, 1886]

Earlier documented evidence from among the Pawnee was recorded by Luther North, head of the Pawnee scouts during the Sioux wars. While carrying dispatches to Fremont, Nebraska he met a young Pawnee boy traveling from Genoa, Nebraska to Fremont to visit his father. The boy was running and North was horseback going at a jog/trot. The boy ran the 73 miles on one drink of water and with nothing to eat. He averaged 7 miles per hour, at about 9 minute miles. He was not considered one of the noted runners. In another case a noted runner ran from Pawnee Agency to the Wichita Agency, a distance of 120 miles, in 24 hours and came back in 24 hours or less, all over rough, hilly, stony country. [Grinnell, 1973, 84]

These last citations, while not specifically concerning the Blackfoot, show that early North American prairie hunters were capable of distance running for long periods of time. These were the skills needed to survive on the prairie. In short, anyone capable of running the 26.2 miles of a modern marathon in 3 to 5 hours could survive as a prairie hunter.

Yellow Kidney, South Peigan-Blackfoot, gives us a bit more strength to the Black Root story. In describing the ceremony of the Buffalo Calling [using the Piskan or Buffalo Jump, ed.], he mentions how the woman [who found the first Buffalo Stone] uses the Black Root in the ceremony. "She rubs a piece of Licorice Root *[Black Root, ed.]* over the feet, head and back of the auaki. *[Runner who leads the buffalo into the wings of the Piskan, ed.]* This is believed to cause the bison to stumble and fall, and the herd will be more easily secured." *[Yellow Kidney, Schaeffer notes, ca. 1950]*

THE LAND AND ANIMALS:

Two other very important events are also mentioned in these stories. The first is the second dream given the old man. In it he has reached accord with the animals of this new land. They have given him the means to hunt the animals of the Plains, which were new, and foreign to the people. It was the black root, and the ceremony that accompanied it, that allowed the people to be successful in hunting the large animals. It was the animals themselves that had given permission to be hunted, and had shown the method to do it in a spiritual and respectful way.

Other spiritual gifts, like the Beaver Bundle, Sun Dance and Thunder Medicine Pipe, would be given with methods of contacting and using the animals and land, and the spiritual power that went with them. In each of these the covenant and integration of the people with all the animals and spirits was established, and the possession of the land reinforced. And in the ceremony of each bundle it is repeated and renewed during every opening.

Beaver Bundle belonging to Mad Wolf, South Peigan, ca. 1906. McClintock photo, Beinecke Archives, Yale University

In the transfer of the Beaver Bundle to the original receiver Misumiksistuk [Ancient, or Long-Time-Beaver] was making a formal apology [kittoh pikim mott] to the man for his son stealing the man's wife. He brought his Water-Pipe as a gift and called on his friend the Sun [who had already made a covenant with the people] to help make peace between them. Beaver then called all the water birds and animals to help him. "Then the Old Beaver sang: 'Let a man come in.' Then appeared a bunch of people came in and filled the tipi, Old Beaver at the head *[the men sitting on the north side of the tipi, ed.]*. Old Beaver: 'Let the women come in.' Then came in a lot of women who sat as far as the beaver woman *[on the south side of the tipi, ed.]*. Beaver Old Man: 'Let all the young men come in.' Beaver Old Man: 'Let all the children come in.' Outside the tipi they heard noises from thc young men and children. There were all different kinds of birds and animals. The Beaver Old Man said to the old man: 'Each is going to give you something for the bundle.'...Each gave his own hide or feathers. Each person sang four songs as he gave the hide. Each said, 'I give my hide to the man.'" *[White Headed Chief, Siksika-Blackfoot, to Hanks, 12 June 1938]*

While these were primarily those birds and animals associated with the water, the second half of the Beaver Bundle was given in another ceremony and contained all the rest of the birds and animals in Blackfoot territory. The amopistaan [ceremonial bundle] established the covenant between them and the Blackfoot people. Thus legitimizing Blackfoot spiritual claim to, and use of, the land and animals.

Secondly, the sons traveling to the south and east, in addition to defeating any peoples they met, also marked the territory of the Blackfoot people. As they traveled the edges of their new home they would create an "earth drawing" at certain spots. In some cases these were rock formations, in others they were painted on the rock faces, and at a few they became the "Holy" places where spiritual contact was made, and help was given to the Blackfoot people. These powerful, spiritual markers outlined the boundaries of their land, reduced, and even prevented the spiritual power of enemy tribes that entered Blackfoot territory from being effective.

Rock outline of Napi figure where he laid down to rest after creating the Blackfoot People. Choteau, Montana. Photo courtesy John Murray Blackfeet Tribal Historic Preservation Office

Sun River marker, author's photo

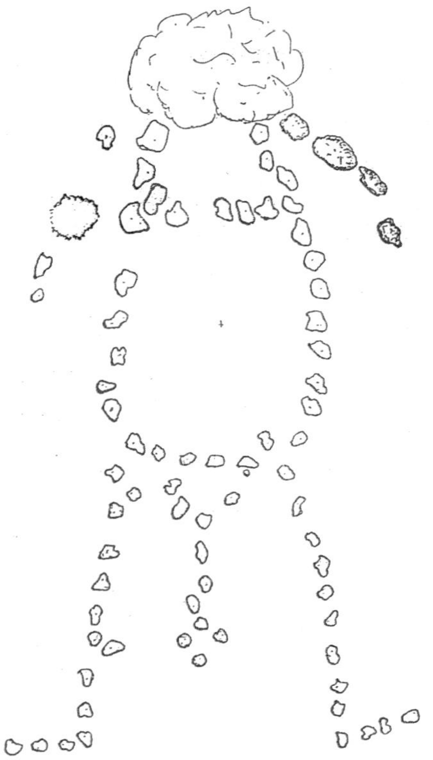

Napi Figure, Madison River. Drawing by Professor Carling Malouf, 1958, of a rock effigy with a bush for the head located along the Madison River near Three Forks, Montana. Malouf papers, Archives and Special Collections, University of Montana.

Recorded war stories often give the geographic location of enemy camps and if they were within Blackfoot territory. The protocol for telling of these stories required detail description of the journey, participants, events, and length of time. When recounted as part of certain ceremonies they became religious and any fabrications would lead to dire consequences to the teller.

Based on Blackfoot oral history [also neighboring tribes oral histories and Euro-historical documents] concerning wintering, and hunting camp sites, the area considered by the Blackfoot Confederacy to be theirs runs from where the North Saskatchewan River comes out of the mountains at Rocky Mountain House, south along the foot hills to the Helena/Three Forks area; east to Livingston, then following the Yellowstone River to the Forsyth/Miles City area; north to Glasgow near the mouth of the Milk River and from there north into Saskatchewan, east of Swift Current, to North Battleford [passing east of the Eagle Hills, site of first contact], to the North Saskatchewan River and following that to Rocky Mountain House. Markers such as the stone Napi figures at Choteau and the Madison River, as well as paintings at Sun River Canyon, marked these boundaries. These borders were, of course, contested by enemy tribes and, as the Blackfoot became more horse orientated they shifted closer to the foothills where the environment was more conducive to wintering their horses. In later years the location of trading posts would also be a factor in the shifting moves. Those enemy tribes would often place their own markers next to the Blackfoot ones in hopes of making them ineffective so that they might move onto the land themselves.

Physical locations where spiritual events occurred were the symbols of contracts between the spiritual realm and the people. This gave the people spiritual permission to live on the land in the area and became a boundary marker, or spiritual gate controlling access of outsiders. Through the years others would be given, and the ties reinforced, until the entire land would be covered with sites. Each added to the power of the people and their claim to the land. The Blackfoot people completed their covenant with the Above People, Earth People and Underwater People, and this land was theirs. The knowledge of the covenants was strengthened with the elders passing on the stories of these events within the transfer of the bundles or ceremonies. As they often said, "Those stories, that is why we know this is our land from the beginning." *[Mike Swims Under, Joe Crowshoe, Bob Black Plume, personal communication]*

Map of traditional Blackfoot territory based on oral history of Blackfoot and neighboring tribes. Author's drawing.

Old Swan's Map:

In 1801 Peter Fidler, trader and surveyor for the Hudson's Bay Company, asked Old Swan, a prominent Siksika [North Blackfeet] chief to draw a map of the country south and west of Chesterfield House at the junction of the Red Deer and South Saskatchewan Rivers. This map, along with several others done by Siksika and Gros Ventre men, has been examined, interpreted and modified through history. First by Fidler himself, who tried to incorporate the information into Euro map making, and then by Aaron Arrowsmith, London cartographer at the time, where it became the basis of exploration for that part of North America. Eventually it was used by the Lewis and Clark Expedition who, using Euro latitude and longitude map technology, began to doubt the truthfulness of the map. In subsequent years scholars would dissect and analyze Old Swan's map and speculate on its accuracy or inaccuracy.

It was, once again, a conflict of cultures. The map was not drawn with Euro values [specific distances, curves of rivers, hills, mountains, etc.] in mind, but rather those of the Blackfoot themselves. It was a pictographic map, similar to all pictographs used by the people. Not meant to convey the entire story, but to remind the teachings of the markers [drawings]. In actuality it is a map of the Old North Trail, the fabled north-south road along the east side of the Rocky Mountains used since the arrival of man in the area. Stripping away the writing on the original map shows the beauty and simplicity of the map, and traditional teachings.

As the markings were being made the "teachings" would also be given. Thus the "student" would know what landmarks to look for at certain points in the journey. These would be significant markers easily seen at a distance and usually already known from stories and origin myths. A horseback rider would not be out of sight of at least one of the markers for more than a day or two's ride. Being a "regionally nomadic" people exact time and distance where not crucial factors in their travels. Thus a statement that it would take three days to get to another point would really vary on if it was a war party on foot or horseback, a group consisting of old people and children, or how large the total group.

Many of the markers are still known and recognizable to many Blackfoot people, as well as others, living along the Old North Trail [Rocky Mountain Front]. Most are intended to be "read" traveling along the foothills to the east of the mountains. Those out on the plains are references to both the probable location of Blackfoot camps that would be important to a trader seeking them out [such as the Cypress Hills, a favorite hunting area]. Or, to give an indication of your location should you wander too far east from the mountains.

Others would be culturally significant such as "Cut to yis", Pine Butte west of Choteau, Montana, and west of the Napi stone effigy where the Blackfoot People were created. "Ki oo peski", Bear's Tooth, while suggested to be both north of Helena, Montana or in the Absaroka Mountains in Wyoming, is in all probability Haystack Butte southwest of

Augusta, Montana. This prominent, and important, feature is easily seen even when the mountains are covered in clouds. It was also known as "Hunters Lookout" and used as such to locate the buffalo herds. It is in position with the Rattle Hills to the east, which would be Square, Shaw and Crown Buttes. Both these markers are located in prime winter buffalo hunting territory of the Blackfoot Nation. The area is filled with numerous Piskan, or buffalo jump [actually, buffalo corral], sites.

In addition various other tribes were marked on the map where they might be encountered. A list of tribal names and identification is provided in the Tribal Names Appendix under "Old Swan".

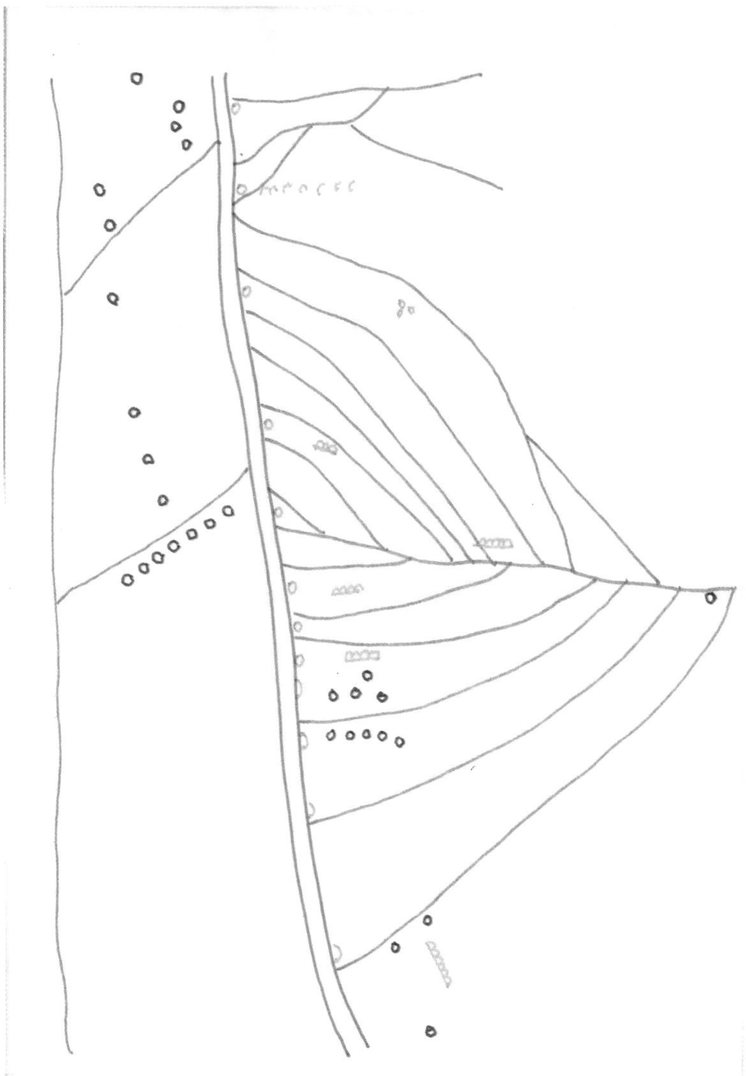

Old Swan's map minus added writings showing its pictographic form. Blue indicating waterways, green, geographic markers and black, tribal locations. Red double line indicating the Rocky Mountains. Author's drawing.

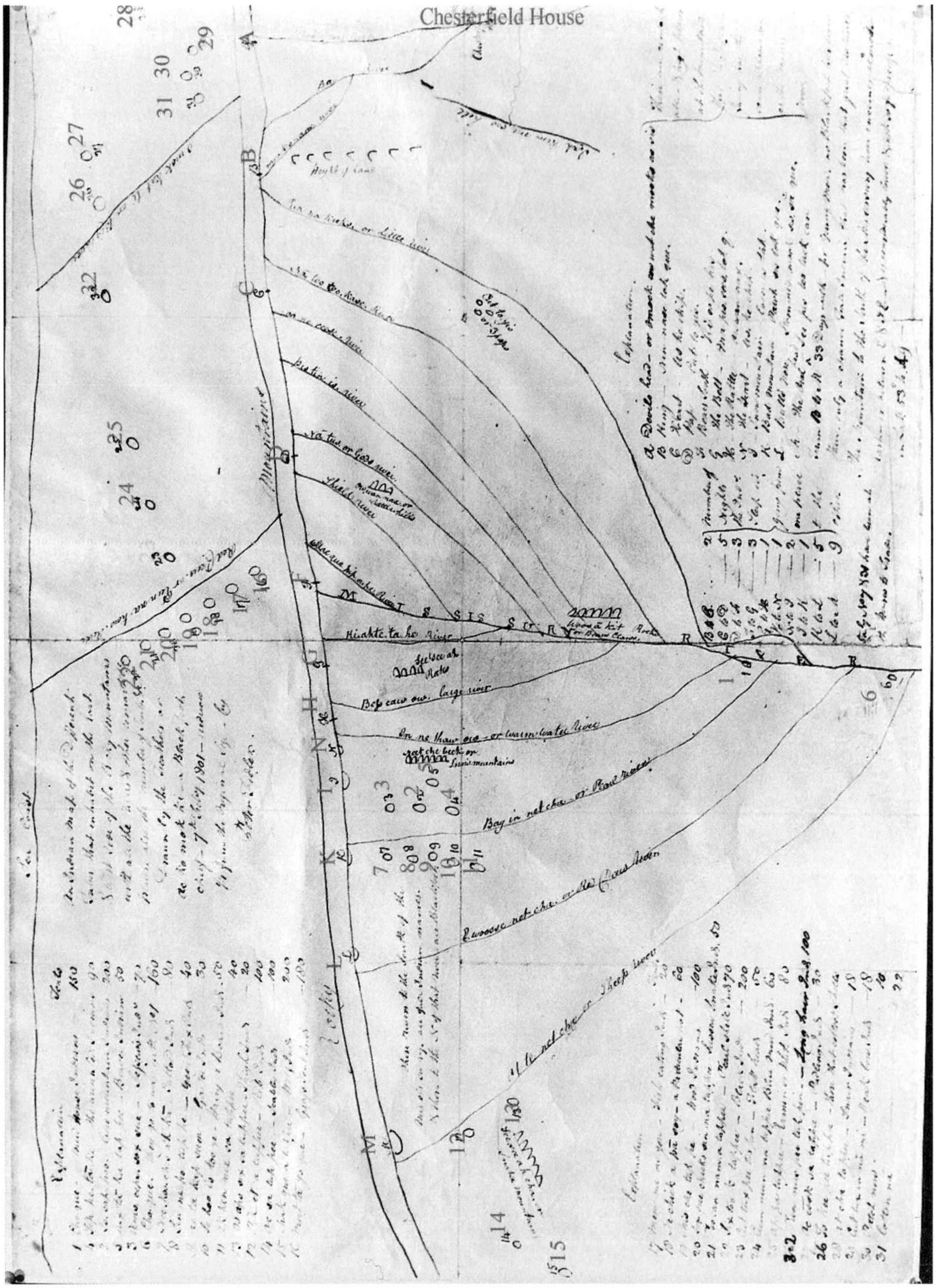

Old Swan 1801 map from the Hudson's Bay Company archive including Fidler's notations. Numbers in red showing tribal identifications and letters showing geographic markers added by author.

Lettered geographic markers:

A. Omok kow wat che mooks as sis, Devil's Head; Devil's Head Mountain, Alberta. [Swan's Bill, ed.]

B. Nin nase tok que, King: Chief Mountain, Montana

C. Oos ke chip, Heart; Heart Butte, Montana

D. Cut to yis, Pap: [Pine Butte, Montana, west of Napi figure where Napi created the Blackfoot near Choteau, Montana, ed.]

F. Ki oo pe kis, Bear's Tooth [Haystack Butte, Montana, ed.]

G. Ma pis sees tok q, The Belt

H. Ow wan nax, The Rattle

N. Us ke chip, The Heart

I. Coon is tak, Snow Mountain

K. Pawk sis tok que, Bad Mountain

L. Stommix mook sis sa que, Bull's Nose [More than likely this is the rock formations just south of Dillon, Montana on a well known route from Blackfoot country (the Three Forks wintering area of the Peigan Small Robes Band), to Snake Indian country, passing Dillon, Montana, Kutois - Blood Clot Hill, at Dell, Montana and on through Monida Pass, all the way to the Great Salt Lake. ed.]

M. See pis too tuck can, The Owl's Head

As we have mentioned before there have been numerous speculations concerning locations on Old Swan's map. But if we read it as a pictograph, it becomes much more accurate. Travel along the Old North Trail was made at a distance from the mountains, following the path of least resistance along the foothills. For much of it shown, it runs through Blackfoot territory, land very familiar to the Blackfoot People. If this map was given to a Blackfoot many of the landmarks would be familiar [as we've mentioned earlier] and further explanation not necessary. They would know to travel further out from the mountains while keeping them in view. And indeed, this information might have been conveyed to Fidler orally at the time, or taken for granted by Old Swan.

Regardless, this is a significant map, leading to the further exploration of the country, and made by the Blackfoot People.

The First Dogs...

"I will tell you how the early Blood Indians lived. As I heard it, I will tell the story without adding any lies. These were the people who first lived and are called the-people-who-used-stones; who lived a hard life and traveled by foot. Their homes were made of hides as well as their clothing, shoes and bedding. These hides came from the buffalo. Theirs was a hard life in that they had to hunt by foot. They were the people who used stones to fasten their homes to the earth. They did not use sticks to tie their teepees down, instead, they dug up rocks and used these.

When he was on the hunt, he would take down his teepee and bring it to where the buffalos were. All the people would tie their teepees together, forming a corral and gradually advancing on the animals. Inside this corral, he found it easy to kill the buffalo. They would shoot them on the area around the kidneys. They found that the buffalo died faster by shooting them there. The buffalo would fall in a sitting position and their hides were cut off starting from the shoulders. Cattle are different for when they are skinned they are turned over with their legs in the air. The buffalo would have rolled over had they been skinned this way.

That is how my grandmother, Twice-Killer, told me the story. She lived to be 105 years old. When she died, the skin on her face was like elastic hanging loose when she died. She had no hair left and she was blind. She lived a long life.

My father, his mother, and his mother's mother, all were alive at one time. My father's name was Bottle. These were the people who told me this story.

One day, the people noticed animals crawling out of a large body of water. They were all kinds of colors. The water was their home. The Indian started trapping by using trees and hide and baiting the traps with meat. When the animal approached the meat, it was trapped. They took the animals home, and it was not long before they became tame. As time went on, the animals no longer ran away and the dogs started breeding. Soon everyone had dogs. They used it for carrying their belongings when they were moving and at the hunt, the dog was used to carry the meat by the fastening of two poles to his back where the hide was draped between these poles and served as a hold for the meat.

Time passed, and the dog had become the animal of burden. How many years had passed since it was captured is not known since there was no recorded time then and the white man had not yet arrived." *[Jim Bottle, Blood-Blackfoot, to Kenneth Peacock, July, 1968; translated by Leo Fox]*

The earliest archaeological evidence of the dog in Canada is at a 6,400 year old site in Crowsnest Pass, Alberta. [Reeves, 1974]

SCARFACE…

…"Early in the morning, the wolverine showed him the trail, and Scarface followed it until he came to the water's edge. He looked out over it, and his heart almost stopped. Never before had any one seen such a big water. The other side could not be seen, and there was no end to it. Scarface sat down on the shore. His food was all gone, his moccasins worn out. His heart was sick. 'I cannot cross this big water,' he said. 'I cannot return to the people. Here, by this water, I shall die.'

Not so. His helpers were there. Two swans came swimming up to the shore. 'Why have you come here?' they asked him. 'What are you doing? It is very far to the place where your people live.'

'I am here,' replied Scarface, 'to die. Far away, in my country, is a beautiful girl. I want to marry her, but she belongs to the Sun. So I started to find him and ask for her. I have traveled many days. My food is gone. I cannot go back. I cannot cross this big water, so I am going to die.'

'No,' said the swans; 'it shall not be so. Across this water is the home of that Above Person. Get on our backs, and we will take you there.'

Scarface quickly arose. He felt strong again. He waded out into the water and lay down on the swans' backs, and they started off. Very deep and black is that fearful water. Strange people live there, mighty animals which often seize and drown a person. The swans carried him safely, and took him to the other side. Here was a broad hard trail leading back from the water's edge.

'Kyi,' said the swans. You are now close to the Sun's lodge. Follow that trail, and you will soon see it.'

Scarface started up the trail, and pretty soon he came to some beautiful things, lying in it. There was a war shirt, a shield, and a bow and arrows. He had never seen such pretty weapons; but he did not touch them. He walked carefully around then, and traveled on. A little way further on, he met a young man, the handsomest person he had ever seen. His moccasins were sewn with bright colored feathers. The young man said to him, 'Did you see some weapons lying on the trail?'

'Yes,' replied Scarface; 'I saw them.'
'But did you not touch them?' asked the young man.
'No; I thought some one had left them there, so I did not take them.'

'You are not a thief,' said the young man. 'What is your name?'
'Scarface.'
'Where are you going?'
'To the Sun.'

'My name,' said the young man, 'is Apisuahts [The Morning Star]. The Sun is my father; come, I will take you to our lodge. My father is not now at home, but he will come in at night.'

Soon they came to the lodge. It was very large and handsome; strange medicine animals were painted on it. Behind, on a tripod, were strange weapons and beautiful clothes – the Sun's. Scarface was ashamed to go in, but Morning Star said, 'Do not be afraid, my friend; we are glad you have come.'

They entered. One person was sitting there, Kokomikeis [the Moon], the Sun's wife, Morning Star's mother. She spoke to Scarface kindly, and gave him something to eat. 'Why have you come so far from your people?' she asked.

Then Scarface told her about the beautiful girl he wanted to marry. 'She belongs to the Sun,' he said. 'I have come to ask him for her.'

When it was time for the Sun to come home, the Moon hid Scarface under a pile of robes. As soon as the Sun got to the doorway, he stopped, and said, 'I smell a person.'

'Yes, father,' said Morning Star; 'a good young man has come to see you. I know he is good, for he found some of my things on the trail and did not touch them.'

Then Scarface came out from under the robes, and the Sun entered and sat down. 'I am glad you have come to our lodge,' he said. 'Stay with us as long as you think best. My son is lonesome sometimes; be his friend.'

The next day the Moon called Scarface out of the lodge, and said to him; 'Go with Morning Star where you please, but never hunt near that big water; do not let him go there. It is the home of great birds which have long sharp bills; they kill people. I have had many sons, but these birds have killed them all. Morning Star is the only one left.'

So Scarface stayed there a long time and hunted with Morning Star. One day they came near the water, and saw the big birds.

'Come,' said Morning Star; 'let us go and kill those birds.'

'No, no!' replied Scarface; 'we must not go there. Those are very terrible birds; they will kill us.'

Morning Star would not listen. He ran towards the water, and Scarface followed. He knew that he must kill the birds and save the boy. If not, the Sun would be angry and might kill him. He ran ahead and met the birds, which were coming towards him to fight, and killed every one of them with his spear: not one was left. Then the young men cut off their heads, and carried them home. Morning Star's mother was glad when they told her what they had done, and showed her the bird's heads. She cried, and called Scarface 'my son.' When the Sun came home at night, she told him about it, and he too was glad. 'My son,' he said to Scarface, 'I will not forget what you have this day done for me. Tell me now, what can I do for you?'...

[Scarface asked for the girl he loved, and for Sun to remove the scar from his face. Sun gave the girl to him, and in a sweat lodge removed his scar. Scarface was now called Mistaken Morning Star, because without his scar he looked so much like Morning Star even Moon couldn't tell them apart. He also gave Scarface the Okan, or Sun Dance.]

"Then said the Sun: 'When any man is sick or in danger, his wife may promise to build me a lodge, if he recovers. If the woman is pure and true, then I will be pleased and help the man. But if she is bad, if she lies, then I will be angry. You shall build the lodge like the world, round, with walls, but first you must build a sweat house of a hundred sticks. It shall be like the sky [a hemisphere], and half of it shall be painted red. That is me. The other half you will paint black. That is the night.'...

"The young man was now ready to return home. Morning Star and the Sun gave him many beautiful presents. The Moon cried and kissed him, and called him 'my son.' Then the Sun showed him the short trail. It was the Wolf Road [Milky Way]. He followed it, and soon reached the ground." *[Curly Bear, South Peigan-Blackfoot, to Grinnell, 1898, Field Notes, Seaver Inst.]*

Among the gifts Mistaken Morning Star brought back were a shield, the bow and arrows, and other weapons, and a beautiful buckskin Hairlock Suit with scalps hanging from the sleeves and leggings representing the cranes he killed. It was the first time the people saw bows and arrows, which would make their lives easier from now on. From this time on the people also called the Sun Apistotooki, Creator or Arrow Maker [apssi – arrow, apistotaki – make something].

If we take some elders interpretation of Apistotaki as Arrow Maker, as well as "Creator", we can then come closer to the date when the Okan or Sun Dance, came to the Blackfoot. Archeologists believe the earliest date for the use of arrows in Blackfoot country is around 200 AD. They base this on the small points [arrowheads] found at various sites. However, as with all science, there are different opinions on the date for the introduction of arrows. Owen Evans at the University of Oklahoma did some field trials with arrows. [Brennan, 1959] He believed that the early, first arrows were developed without fletching on them [the feathers on the arrow]. He tested arrows without fletching and found that arrows with heavier points and a heavier shaft traveled farther and more accurately then the small point arrows without fletching. This would mean that possibly those early, heavier points identified as from spears or atlatls were actually used as arrows with the bow. And that would mean that bows and arrows are considerably older than first believed. Which would mean the early Okan, or Sun Dance, among the Blackfoot is considerably older than 200 AD.

THE FIRST HORSE…

"A long time ago there was a poor boy who tried to obtain secret power so that he might be able to get some of the things he wanted but did not have. He went out from his camp and slept alone on mountains, near great rocks, beside rivers. He wandered until he came to a large lake northeast of the Sweetgrass Hills [Lake Pakowki]. By the side of that lake he broke down and cried. The powerful man who lived in that lake heard him and told his son to go to the boy and find out why he was crying. The son went to the sorrowing boy and told him that his father wished to see him. 'But how can I go to him?' the lad asked. The son replied, 'Hold onto my shoulders and close your eyes. Don't look until I tell you to do so.'

They started into the water. As they moved along the son told the boy, 'My father will offer you your choice of the animals in this lake. Be sure to choose the old mallard and its little ones.'

When they reached his father's lodge, the son told the boy to open his eyes. He did so and was takcn into the father's lodge. The old man said to him, 'Son, come sit over here.' Then he asked, 'My boy, why did you come here?' The boy explained, 'I have been a very poor boy. I left my camp to look for secret power so that I may be able to start out for myself.' The old man then said, 'Now, son you are going to become the leader of your tribe. You will have plenty of everything. Do you see all the animals in this lake? They are all mine.' The boy, remembering the son's advice, said, 'I should thank you for giving me as many of them as you can.' Then the old man offered him his choice. The boy asked for the mallard and it's young. The old man replied, 'Don't take that one. It is old and of no value.' But the boy insisted. Four times he asked for the mallard. Then the old man said, 'You are a wise boy. When you leave my lodge my son will take you to the edge of the lake. When you leave the lake don't look back.'

The boy did as he was told. At the margin of the lake the water spirit's son collected some marsh grass and braided it into a rope. With the rope he caught the old mallard and led it ashore. He placed the rope in the boy's hand and told him to walk on, but not to look back until daybreak. As the boy walked along he heard the duck's feathers flapping on the ground. Later he could no longer hear that sound. As he proceeded he heard the sound of heavy feet behind him, and a strange noise, the cry of an animal. The braided marsh grass turned into a rawhide rope in his hand. But he did not look back until dawn.

At daybreak he turned around and saw a strange animal at the end of the line, a horse. He mounted it and, using the rawhide rope as a bridle, rode back to camp. Then he found that many horses had followed him.

The people of the camp were afraid of the strange animals. But the boy signed to them not to fear. He dismounted and tied a knot in the tail of his horse. Then he gave everybody horses from those that had followed him. There were plenty for everyone and he had quite a herd left over for himself. Five of the older men in camp gave their daughters to him in return for the horses he had given them. They gave him a fine lodge also.

Until that time the people had only dogs. But the boy told them how to handle the strange horses. He showed them how to use them for packing, how to break them for riding and for the travois, and he gave the horse its name, elk dog. One day the men asked him, 'These elk dogs, would they be of any use in hunting buffalo?' The boy replied. 'They are fine for that. Let me show you.' Whereupon he showed his people how to chase buffalo on horseback. He also showed them how to make whips and other gear for their horses. Once when they came to a river the boy's friends asked him, 'These elk dogs, are they of any use to us in water?' He replied, 'That is where they are best. I got them from the water.' So he showed them how to use horses in crossing streams.

The boy grew older and became a great chief, a leader of his people. Since that time every chief has owned a lot of horses." *[Head Carrier to Chewing-Black-Bones, South Peigan-Blackfoot, to Ewers, 1955; 294-295]*

Blackfoot oral history stories relate obtaining horses from the Shoshone [Piksiiksiinaitapix], Flathead [Kotokspitapix], and Kutenai [Kutenaitapix]. These were obtained by trade, gifts and as war trophies. [Joe Crowshoe, North Peigan-Blackfoot, Bob Black Plume, Blood-Blackfoot, and Willie Eagle Plume, Blood-Blackfoot, interviews with the author, 1970's field notes]

Some scholars claim these peoples were enemies, at war with the Blackfoot, and not about to trade horses, or teach the Blackfoot how to use them. While it is true they were often at war with each other, like all people they saw occasional advantages to peace and trade. If the situation warranted, they would be friends and trading partners; if not, then enemies. This not only changed from day to day, or group to group, but depended on the circumstances of the moment.[Fiddler 1792. p.16]

Oral history recorded by scholars through the years gives ample evidence of changing alliances. The Shoshone had horses, but lacked direct access to European trade goods, even until the time of Lewis and Clark in 1805. The Blackfoot had trade goods, including and especially, guns. So whenever the two enemies couldn't get enough of the things they need by raiding, a peace and trading were the next logical method.

BLACKFOOT POTTERY

"She said that to make a cooking pot they first dug a hole in the ground, making the sides as round and smooth as possible. Then they took a flat stone and placed it in the bottom of the hole. Then they lined the hole with a thick layer of clay. Next they took a mixture of a certain red rock which had been broken into small pieces with a stone hammer, heated and again pounded until the rock was as fine as flour, and river sand or sand rock pounded fine, mixed with water into a dough. After the clay lining was smoothed and shaped with an elk horn, this dough was put in the cavity and roughly plastered over the clay layer. When it began to dry out, two holes were punched in this inner layer opposite each other and near the top edges of the sides. Then a large stone, just the right size and shape to fill and form the inside wall of the pot, was placed in the cavity. Next a fire was built over the hole. It heated the stone very hot. After this firing had dried out the pot, it was removed from the hole by [1] digging away the top portion of the outer clay lining, [2] lifting the pot by the handle holes with the rock inside it, and [3] turning the pot over carefully and extracting the rock." *[Victory-All-Over-Woman, Blood-Blackfoot, over 100 years old, told to Weasel-Tail, Blood-Blackfoot, when he was a young man, told to Ewers when he was in his middle eighties; 1945;292-293]*

"The vessel was built up by hand. No mold was used. Then it was greased inside and out and placed over a fire to dry. This fire must not be too hot or the pot would crack. The vessels were quite thick and fragile. They were easily broken, so people had to be very careful with them. Two shapes of vessels were made. One was a cooking pot with a constriction near the top around which the handle was wrapped. The other was a flat dish." *[Mrs. Frank Racine, Blood-Blackfoot as her grandmother described Blood pottery making by her great-grandmother in the early 1800's. Ewers, 1945; 294]*

In 1935 Dr. Kenneth Kidd interviewed six North Blackfeet-Blackfoot and five declared that they had heard or knew of Blackfoot making pottery.

"According to some informants the pots were made of a white sticky clay, found in rocky places, which was moulded [sic] into shape and stood beside the fire to dry...Such pots were used for boiling.

"The other tradition relates that a bag of the required size was made from buffalo skin. Sand [evidently clay and sand] mixed with water was plastered on the inner surface of the bag and allowed to dry in the sun. The skin cover was then removed. Sometimes a handle made from the neck-gristle of a bison was attached through holes made in the rim."
[Pretty-Young-Man, North Blackfeet-Blackfoot, 1935, to Kidd; Ewers, 1945; 293]
In 1810 Alexander Henry found trade kettles scarce among the Blackfoot, but by 1833 Culbertson estimated that there was one in every lodge. So it's very probable that by about 1825 the fragile clay pots were replaced by the traders' brass kettles as an everyday utensil.

WHEN THE BLOODS FIRST GOT GUNS

"Once while a few Bloods had camps somewhere near the timber country on the north of High River in Canada, all the able bodied men had all went out to run buffalo. While the women and children, and a few old men were left at camps. And a war party of Cree came along and attacked the few lodges of the Bloods, and took nearly all the women and children as prisoners.

Then the Crees started on their way with the women and children. One of the men who was one of the Cree followed up the tracks of some women who had escaped from the Blood camp. There were four of these Blood women and they made for some timber which was not far from the camps. And as there was snow on the ground, the Cree man had no difficulty in following them up, and soon overtook them, and ordered them to all turn back and go with him. The four women went along with the man. And as the main war party of Crees had women and children with them they could not go a great distance with out camping. Now after the four women and the Cree had gone some distance, the women noticed that the man was getting very tired and weak. For when he would sit down he would have some trouble in getting up again. So one of the women said to the others, 'The next time this man sits down let the four of us tackle him and I will kill him, for you can see that he is weak and won't be able to do much fighting.' So as they were all going along they came to a small stream of water. And the Cree man laid down on his belly to drink some water. And as soon as he did the four women jumped on him. Two of them held him by his legs, while the other two got a hold of his arms and head, and they pushed his head in the water and held his head under the water until he was drowned. Then the four Blood women pulled him out and scalped him, and started back to their own camps.

Now by this time the Blood who were out hunting came back, and learning what had happened, they all followed up the Cree war party and met the four women coming back. And when the women told them how they had killed the Cree who had captured them, the other Bloods said they would all turn back and not tackle the Crees. But one of the Bloods said, 'The Crees have taken my wife and children, and I am going to follow them and try and get my family back, although they may kill me.' Now the woman whom had scalped the Cree had some of her kin folks taken prisoner and said to the man, 'I will go with you.'

So the man and woman went together to overtake the Crees. And as the Crees didn't travel very fast, the man and woman soon overtook them. And when the Crees saw the man and woman they thought it was one of their party, as they missed the man whom the women had killed. Now when the Crees seen that they were Bloods, they were anxious to find out about their own man, and said they better ask this Blood if he knew anything about the Cree who was left behind. So the Crees seated the man and woman down on a blanket. And one of the Crees filled a pipe and said a prayer over the pipe first and went to the Blood and said, 'Now we want you to speak the truth only and if you are going to tell the truth, you can smoke this pipe. And if you are going to tell a lie, don't smoke this pipe. We want to find out what became of the Cree man whom we left to follow up. And if you tell us the truth about him, even if your people has killed him or not, we will grant whatever you have come here for.'

Now the Blood did not care to tell about how the Cree was killed, as he was afraid of the Crees. Now the woman said to the man, 'Go ahead and smoke the pipe. You don't know anything about killing the Cree. I was the one who killed him and I will tell them how we killed him.' So the Blood took the pipe and smoked it. And said to the Crees, 'This woman knows how the Cree was killed and she will tell you all about him.' So the woman told the Crees that she and the other women had killed him. And when the Crees heard of this they were pleased to get the truth about their man. So they did as they agree to do and let the man have his wife and children back whom they had kidnapped. And also the Blood woman relatives and then the Crees said to the Blood man, 'Next summer we will meet and make peace with each other. And then you shall all get your women and children back.'

So the man and his wife and children, and the other woman and her kin folks, all went back to their people. And the next summer the Crees and the Bloods met and made peace. And the Bloods got their women and children back. And four of the Blood Chiefs were given rifles by the Crees. And the Bloods did not know how to shoot with the guns. And the Crees set up a mark, and showed the Bloods how to shoot with the guns. And when the Bloods would shoot with the guns they were afraid of them and would drop the guns when they would go off. And finally they got used to shooting. Now the Bloods gave the Crees horses for presents. And as the Crees could not ride much they would fall off the horses when the horses would go on a trot or lope. So the Bloods gave the Crees the laugh because they could not ride horse back. And later on the Piegans got firearms. And while a few Piegans were on thc war party a great many Snake Indians attacked the few Piegans. And the Piegans opened fire on them with their guns and as the Snakes never heard or seen guns, they all took to their heels and run away and were afraid of the guns of the Piegans. And also the Crows run from the Piegans when the Piegans first took some shots at them from their rifles, as the Crows did not know anything about guns at the time." *[Three Bears, South Piegan-Blackfoot to Duvall, 1911;621-626; same story from Heavy Runner, South Piegan-Blackfoot to Duvall, 1911]*

CHAPTER 2
KEEPERS OF THE WINTER COUNTS

Keepers of the winter counts are those individuals who are known to have recorded events within these winter counts. The winter counts are identified by the name of the last keeper. Earlier recorders are given as far back as known. All are Blackfoot First Nations people with the exception of Missionary Reverend Canon W. R. Haynes who entered several events after the death of Bull Plume. David Duvall recorded the Elk Horn, Big Brave [Mountain Chief] and Mrs. Big Nose Winter Counts.

The importance of the winter counts was recognized and preserved by a number of non-Blackfoot and it was due to their efforts we still have these important documents. They are Anthropologists Jane and Lucien Hanks for the Many Guns Winter Count, Harry Biele for the Percy Creighton Winter Count. Historian Hugh Dempsey, Trader and Indian Agent R.N. Wilson and Catholic priest Father Emile Legal all had versions of the Bad Head Winter Count. Father Legal also collected the Crane Bear Winter Count. Reverend Haynes recorded both versions of the Bull Plume Winter Count from which this author published the first Bull Plume Winter Count. Indian Agent Capt. L.W. Cooke recorded Big Nose [aka Three Suns] events.

APATOHSIPIIKANI [NORTH PEIGAN-BLACKFOOT]

Bull Plume, North Peigan-Blackfoot; Winter Count 1764-1924

There are two versions as to where the original winter count originated. But there are indications we might also be speaking of two different winter counts. The first is from Bull Plume directly and from whom the journals were obtained. He states he received them from his grandfather Wolf Child. Bull Plume left two copies of his winter count, both in old journals [#1 is dated 1912]. One is in the author's possession [#1] and the other is in the Glenbow Museum Archives donated by Chester Arthur, former Indian Agent at the North Peigan Reserve [#2]. Both have event entries that are written in the same hand, that of W.R. Haynes, missionary at the North Peigan Reserve. The Arthur journal also contains Bull Plume's last will and testament, as well as listings of the tribes and chiefs signing the Lame Bull Treaty of 1855 with the United States government, and the 1877 Treaty #7 with the Canadian government. This journal also contains an additional pictograph to the right of several years listed and these are interpreted as "Pictograph" below Bull Plume #2. The additional pictographs and will may indicate this as being the secondarily produced winter count.

In both Bull Plume #1 and #2 the entries were begun in the journal at the lower left hand page and continued from bottom to top on the next and continued to be read bottom to top. This would indicate the original hide drawings were done in a counter clockwise direction similar to other tribal winter counts. At one point Haynes became confused and wrote the entries top to bottom, but this mistake was soon corrected.

Reverend Canon Haynes spent fifty-six years as an Anglican missionary among the Blackfoot people. In that time he learned the language, and expressed an unusual interest in Blackfoot culture. Haynes came to the North Peigan Reserve in 1897, to run the new school which became Victoria Home. In 1903 he was ordained minister in the Anglican church and remained among the North Peigans until his death in 1937 at the age of seventy-two. His work with Bull Plume on the winter count left us with a historic treasure.

Bull Plume #1 was printed in 1979 by this author with the Old Man River Culture Center on the North Peigan Reserve. Corrections interpretations and additional information have been added to this volume. The original hide has never been located.

Bull Plume, North Peigan-Blackfoot. Glenbow Archives, Calgary.

Missionaries Rev. Cannon W.R. Haynes [left] and Rev. J.W. Tims at the Blackfoot Sun Dance camp ca. 1880's. An interesting group shot of the missionaries sitting in front of the Holy Lodge at the Sun Dance ceremony with the main ceremonialists sitting behind them. The Canadian flag has been changed in the photo to that of the Canadian Missionary Society. More than likely this was intended to be a fund raising photo for the church back east showing their loyal converts behind them. Unknown photographer, Glenbow Archives .

The second origin version is recorded by Walter McClintock in "The Old North Trail". In an interview Brings-Down-the-Sun claims Bull Plume got the information from him and that he got them from his father Iron-Shirt. He mentions a few events as proof of his claim. He also states the original was on a buffalo hide. [McClintock; 1968, 417] Several of the events he relates to McClintock are not in Bull Plume's version, which leads to speculation there may have been two different winter counts in existence. "He [Bull Plume, ed.] has a record originally on an antelope skin and a buckskin nicely tanned, but now transferred to a paper book, which is said to go back 157 years." [Grinnell; Notes July 6, 1911]

Brings Down The Sun and Bird Woman, North Peigan-Blackfoot. ca. 1909, McClintock photo, Beinecke Archives, Yale University

Iron Shirt, father of Brings Down the Sun. Carl Bodmer painting 1883, courtesy Northern Natural Gas Co. Omaha, Nebraska

There was a rivalry between Bull Plume and Brings-Down-the-Sun at the time McClintock interviewed Bring-Down-the-Sun which should be taken into consideration. While in one statement he claims Bull Plume was an orphan, and his family unknown, in the next he tells of his father receiving a Medicine Pipe from Wolf Child, Bull Plume's grandfather. Readers familiar with intra-tribal rivalries are aware that not all statements should be taken as fact but rather "of the moment". And so we leave it to the reader to draw their own conclusion.

Bull Plume/Old Agency Winter Count 1868-1909

Written in a small notebook, this winter count contains pictographs without interpretations. The author of this count was unknown for many years until, while comparing pictographs with the other winter counts, Bull Plume's name glyph was recognized on the last page. The original is in the Glenbow Museum Archives. An unusual feature of this journal is that it contains several pages of a calendar of sorts. The days of the week are marked as a single line and each Sunday is marked with a cross. In addition, pictographs of the waning and waxing of the moon are marked for each month as well as Sun Dances and historical events for each year.

It was an attempt by Bull Plume to reconcile the traditional Blackfoot "New Moon" calendar with the Julian calendar. Blackfoot reckoning calls for a new month each new moon. As a Beaver Bundle owner [whose duties included keeping track of the monthly cycle], Bull Plume kept track of the moons with this system. A strong intellectual, and proponent of Blackfoot culture, he was no doubt trying to establish the validity of the culture in comparison to Euro culture. Unfortunately, he found that the two calendars were not compatible long term. When he got to a month containing two new moons in the Julian calendar, he abandoned his attempt, and day markings in the journal ended.

However, the pictographic entries continued. By comparing them with known events, dates were established. And by "reading" the non-conforming pictographs, as well as comparing them to known events in other winter counts, we were able to add additional information.

AMSKAPIPIIKUNI [SOUTH PEIGAN-BLACKFOOT]

The South Peigan [or Blackfeet, as they prefer to be called in the States] winter counts were all collected by David C. Duvall [1878-1911] in the early 1900's. Duvall was an extraordinary individual, son of a Blackfeet [South Peigan] mother and a French-Canadian fur trade employee at Fort Benton, he was well educated and had a strong interest in the culture of his people. Not only was he fluent in conversational Blackfoot, he also strove to learn the "High Blackfoot" spoken by the old time traditionalists in order to get a better understanding of the information they were giving him. When Clark Wissler, from the American Museum of Natural History discovered him during his fieldwork among the Blackfoot, he hired him immediately. And over the next several years Duvall provided the information that Wissler eventually turned into several books published by the museum. Fortunately, Duvall's hand written notes still exist in several archives. Where Wissler was an anthropologist who produced theories and interpretations of the culture and ceremonies, Duvall meticulously recorded the exact words of the speakers. These intellectuals of the Blackfoot Nation were his relatives, and were scrupulous in giving him the total facts. And he was equally conscientious in putting them down word for word. They made sure he knew the overall understanding of the events and stories, and the context in which they fit. As a result we have information untarnished by anthropological theories, given directly from the mouths of those who "lived" what they spoke of. His contributions can never be undervalued.

Elk Horn, South Peigan-Blackfoot. ca. 1909 McClintock photo, Beinecke Archives, Yale University

ELK HORN, South Peigan-Blackfoot; Winter Count 1850-1904

An accomplished warrior of the old days, Elk Horn appears to have kept his winter count in the form of "memory sticks", each recalling specific events. This gives strength to the use of winter counts as "teachings" rather than calendar events with specific dates. In recording the events, Duvall mentions that Elk Horn became confused at one point and couldn't remember the exact order of a few events.

Big Brave, also known as Mountain Chief, 1913, Joseph Dixon photo, author's collection

BIG BRAVE, South Peigan-Blackfoot; Winter Count 1850-1886

Big Brave, also called Mountain Chief after his father, was a well known warrior of the old days. A strong traditionalist, he was also a main source of information gathered by

Duvall for Wissler in his publication "Ceremonial Bundles of the Blackfoot Indians", by the American Museum of Natural History in 1912. Painted by artists and photographed many times, he was the epitome of a Blackfoot warrior. Duvall provides two versions of his winter count which are basically the same. Any additional information, not given in the first, is listed as Big Brave #2.

Three Suns, also known as Big Nose, South Peigan-Blackfoot. 1881, Arthur Canning photo, Montana Historical Society

BIG NOSE, South Peigan-Blackfoot; Dated war record 1845-1881

From a pictographic hide painted by Big Nose of his war adventures, and given to acting Indian Agent Captain L.W. Cooke, with Big Nose relating the events and dates. Big Nose, also known as Three Suns, was head chief of the southern branch of the Montana Blackfeet.

MRS. BIG NOSE, South Peigan-Blackfoot; 1850-1854(?)

The widow of Big Nose related several events to David Duvall in January 1911 when questioned about winter counts. Comparing those events with known dated winter counts gave us approximate dates for the events she related.

KAINAI [BLOOD-BLACKFOOT]

Bad Head, [Blood, ed.[, 1855, Gustav Sohon drawing, Washington State Historical Society, Tacoma, WA.

BAD HEAD, Blood-Blackfoot; Winter Count, 1810-1883

A band chief among the Bloods, he was also known as Father-of-Many-Children. R.N. Wilson states the original winter count was done "in symbolic pictographs on a tanned skin". [Wilson, 1958, 367] But once again the original hide has not been found to this date. Both Wilson and Father Emile Legal [who also received the winter count directly from Bad Head] wrote the original details in Blackfoot although there are differences in the spelling by both. They also added comments to certain events that they felt were true, but later proved to be incorrect. While both of these men obtained the winter count independently, it is not certain who obtained it first. Both men were in Blackfoot country from 1881, and could have gotten it prior to Bad Head's death in 1885, but he was very old by this time. Wilson came to Blackfoot country in 1863 with the Northwest Mounted Police, but it is more likely he collected the count in the 1880's while operating a trading post on the Blood Reserve near Standoff, Alberta. Legal's copy ends in 1885 with Bad Head's death, but Wilson's continues until 1889, which indicates another writer added the subsequent years.

Jim White Bull, Blood-Blackfoot, 1959, Gordon Crighton photo, Glenbow Archives

White Bull/Bad Head, Blood-Blackfoot; Winter Count 1809 [1811]-1906

The brother of Jim White Bull, Blood-Blackfoot, in 1906 was asked by Head Chief Ermine Horse, and Chief Owl to record the stories of the Blood people. Jim White Bull took this over at the age of 19 in 1911. Much of the information was passed on from Bad Head to Ermine Horse, but also continues to 1906. Some of the dates vary from Bad Head's account, as well as some of the translations. While White Bull starts his in 1809 with the death of Crying Bear, the actual event was recorded by Bad Head in 1811. We have shifted his dates to match those of the Bad Head account. His original dating can be read in the Blood tribal newspaper, Kainai News, for February 15, March 15, and May 20, 1969 issues.

Bad Head/ Dempsey; Winter Count 1810-1883

This version was published by well known Blackfoot historian Hugh Dempsey and the Glenbow Museum.[Dempsey,1965] Dempsey and his father-in-law James Gladstone, a Blood-Blackfoot and fluent speaker, translated the original script of both Legal and Wilson into English. As well, Dempsey added historical references to place the events in context, and included the entries of White Bull.

Percy Creighton, Blood-Blackfoot, ca. 1930, Winold Reiss photo, author's collection.

Percy Creighton, Blood-Blackfoot; Winter Count 1831-1938

The original source for this winter count is unknown. It was collected by Harry Biele from Creighton on the Blood Reserve in 1939 and is with the Ester Goldfrank papers in the National Anthropological Archives. The Yellow Fly and Creighton winter counts are the same until 1858, which may provide us with the source of some of this winter count. Both were well educated men and no doubt knew each other.

SIKSIKA [NORTH BLACKFEET-BLACKFOOT]

The Siksika winter counts are interesting in that they seem to derive from the same source. Legal collected the Crane Bear winter count in 1909 while a missionary among the Blackfoot tribes. Hanks states that the Many Guns winter count was started 31 years after the Siksika settled on the Reserve which would be around 1912. Yet he also states Many Guns took over the winter count in 1911. This would indicate the Many Guns winter count, started by Wolf Sun and Tomorrow Coming Over the Hill was probably in existence well before the date of 1912. The other Siksika winter counts give no clue as to the date of their creation.

Many Guns, North Blackfeet-Blackfoot, 1949, F. Gully photo, Glenbow Archives

Many Guns, Siksika-Blackfoot; Winter Count: 1831-1963

"Many Guns has a calendar, with a square or "O" for each year, and a word in syllabics[2] which recalls the story for that year. Not a picture symbol. Two old men about 1900 devised this calendar, after discussion and compilation of existent stories. Many

[2] Syllabics was invented in 1840 by James Evans, a missionary, to enable writing Indigenous languages of Canada. His work started with Ojibwa and soon expanded to Cree and Blackfoot.

Guns bought it from them, and now owns it. It is a single sheet of brown paper, with entries sometimes multiple, in two columns. Years in Arabic figures have been added.

"The two old men 1) Apinako'tamiso [Tomorrow Coming Over the Hill], 2) Makuyatos [Wolf Sun], were paid $5 apiece and a quilt and tobacco for the calendar by Many Guns, who said he wanted 'to buy your minds and intelligence. In the future when you're gone I'll keep on going.' *The calendar goes back long before treaty. 31 years after they settled on reserve permanently the two old men wrote it down in syllabics, a key word for each year." [Hanks Mss. Paul Fox interpreting Sept 4,1938] Lucian Hanks recorded the events and years as told by Many Guns and this forms the base of the Many Guns Winter Count included here. Other translations of the syllabic notes written by him were done after his death.*

Many Guns took over the Winter Count in 1911, the same year Apinako'tamiso died. Kept it until 1942 and then was taken over by his son Thomas Many Guns.

In 1912 James Eagle Child was sent by Clark Wissler to find cultural resource people among the North Blackfeet at Gleichen, Alberta Canada. On September 16, 1912 he writes to Wissler, "I know of one old man that know [sic.] every thing he write the dates and names of certain person and all the medicine things. He can tell us every thing we want to know. But he's gone out with his son-in-law to the farmers *[to work for the white farmers, ed.]*...P.S. The old man I spoke of writing and keeping track of the former times he write in Indian way." *[syllabics, ed.] Again on the 24th of September he writes,* "... They have another Indian here called Wolf Top Knot. *[Many Guns' other name, ed.]* The Indians spoke of as a fine member and of olden times has written all the names and certain stories that happen two hundred years ago back and has kind of history of the former times. When I first get here I spoke to him about it and he said he was busy that he would when he had time." *[Glenbow Museum Archives, Duvall Papers, Wissler correspondence, pp 630-632 and pp 634-35] Wissler, it seems, never sent Eagle Child to get the information, nor did he pursue it himself.*

"There lived on the Blackfoot Reserve an old man who kept the records of the race fresh in his mind, Running Wolf [the male wolf] [Wolf Sun?, ed.]. He was always pointed out as the man who knew these things." [Morris,1909, p.124]

In 1968 and 1969 several other translations of Many Gun's syllabic notes were done by Dave Melting Tallow, a Siksika-Blackfoot, which give a few variations of the readings. These are entered under Many Guns with the numbers 68 or 69 following. As well the original written syllabic document still exists and all are in the Royal Alberta Museum Archives.

Crane Bear, Siksika-Blackfoot; Winter Count 1828-1877

The Crane Bear winter count was documented by Father Emile Legal in 1909 while stationed at the North Blackfeet reserve in Alberta. The document is written in French and has small pictographic type images with each entry. Unfortunately, Legal was no artist, and they amount to no more than scribbles. The original is in the Oblate Missionary files kept at the Royal Alberta Museum Archives. The entries are very similar to both Many Guns', Running Rabbit's and Yellow Fly's winter counts. The initial date being three years ahead of Many Guns with the events listed following the date difference. Additional events are also recorded that differ from the other Siksika winter counts.

Teddy Yellow Fly, ca. 1938, Arnold Lupson photo, Glenbow Archives

Yellow Fly, Siksika-Blackfoot; Winter Count 1831-1877

Teddy Yellow Fly was married to Many Guns' daughter, and Many Guns winter count may be the source for his winter count. It is also similar to Running Rabbit's winter count. The initial date is similar to Many Guns, but a few events listed are different. The original is in the Glenbow Museum Archives.

*Yellow Fly served on the early chiefs council on the Siksika Reserve and was well thought of in this role."*Teddy Yellow Fly is highest chief, has more power than Duck Chief *[Head Chief ca. early 1900's, ed.]*. He is generous and keeps his promises – has a good head. Everybody likes him and says good things for him. He talks good for the tribe and helps fellows in trouble out. He is for the Blackfeet." *[Ben Calf Robe, Hanks,1941]*

"Teddy Yellow Fly was the most intelligent and brilliant Indian the writer ever met. He came to a premature and mysterious death by drowning in the Bow River off Centre Street in Calgary in 1950. His formal education at an Indian Residential school ended when he passed the fifth grade, but as a young man he attended a Provincial Agricultural College, the School of Technology and by reading and collaboration with anthropologists and others increased his knowledge far beyond that of the average white man. He wrote many leading articles on various phases of Indian life and culture and broadcasted all over Canada and also over United States stations. He was the real leader of the Blackfeet people though he ranked only as a minor chief. He was a large farmer and rancher and also a splendid office accountant; which work he did in his spare time. In fact he was brilliant, but was his own worst enemy." [Gooderham, 169]

A strong proponent of Treaty and Blackfeet rights, he was often at odds with Agent George Gooderham while he worked for the rights of the Siksika-Blackfoot people.

Houghton Running Rabbit, center, writing interpretations of his father's pictographic war record painted on a buffalo hide for Edmund Morris, 1909. Edmund Morris photo Provincial Archives of Manitoba, Winnipeg.

Running Rabbit, Siksika-Blackfoot; Winter Count 1830-1937

Houghton Running Rabbit's winter count starts with the date of 1830 with the event listed being the same as Many Guns' of 1831. Subsequent events continue with the one year difference. There were two separate journals with entries by Running Rabbit, one starting in 1830 going to 1937, and the other in 1866 going to 1901. The events are basically the same with a few entries expanded upon. Both are entered here under Running Rabbit's name. The original journals are in the Glenbow Museum Archives.

Joe Little Chief; Siksika-Blackfoot; Winter Count 1830-1956

While basically the same events are recorded by Little Chief, he presents them in an anecdotal style and expands on events with his own interpretations. This may cause some confusion and should be taken into consideration. The original is in the Glenbow Museum Archives.

CHAPTER 3

THE WINTER COUNTS

Events recorded in the winter counts were in linear order and not necessarily subject to the actual year in our calendars. Each individual keeper decided what event was significant enough to be recorded. In some cases these were tribal and others, personal events. Euro-calendar dates were marked according to estimates, or further information, given by the Blackfoot Keeper at the time of recording. Others were based on historical records concerning those events. Since the Blackfoot calendar year started in the Euro-calendar month of October the actual event could be recorded in the previous,current or future year of the Euro-calendar. The importance of the event was the "teaching" and not necessarily the exact date it occurred.

A winter count is basically a yearly record of significant events. In Blackfoot world view the year began in October of our calendar year. Keepers of the Beaver Bundles kept a monthly count with sticks within their bundles and each new moon they would have a small ceremony where specific songs were sung for each month. Sometimes called a "Moon Ceremony" they were important indicators of the coming seasons and events within Blackfoot cosmology.

It was when "the time of plenty" begins to end and earth begins her cleansing. Cold Maker comes and claims the weak, washing the earth in a blanket of white. It became the time when only the strong and healthy of the animals and man survived. And when it ended, life began anew, strong, clean, and fresh.

This became a dividing point of sorts. Significant events were decided upon to include in the winter count, that would remind the people of what was important enough not to forget. This dividing point was not a hard and fast rule. Events could slide over to the year before, or after, the actual date of occurrence, but they were always recorded in sequence. The most important function of the winter count was to record the events and accomplishments of the people in a system of chronology. While Euro-history demands an exact date, history for the Blackfoot world view is more often an individual event in relation to a teaching. Time was not a critical factor.

We have mentioned this "Blackfoot World View" before and perhaps another explanation would be that the difference between Blackfoot and Euro world views is the relationship viewing nature. For the Blackfoot this relationship is between nature and man. This means an equality between "real" people [humans], spirits, and animal spirits, as well as the physical world itself. The Euro world view is that man has dominion over nature. This causes the two worlds to view and interpret an event differently. An example of this would be the 1855 Treaty. For the Blackfoot it was a treaty of peace, for the Euro-Americans it was a land surrender. In the Blackfoot view they had already made a sacred covenant with the land [and animals] to use it, which gave them permission to be there. They then allowed the Americans to also use the land, not to own it, a concept that was beyond their reality. For the Americans they believed they now owned the land. In the winter counts we will encounter several of these events with cultural differences providing different interpretations.

Another factor to consider with the winter counts and the information they contain is that a series of epidemics hit the Blackfoot through their history. In these cases it would be the intellectuals of the tribe that were among the first to go. They were the Medicine Bundle owners that the sick went to for help. As a result, they were among the first exposed to these diseases, more so than the average person. While these losses caused a fragmentation of stories and teachings there was still a consistency in the teachings and their relationship to the world view.

In the later years the recording of Sun Dances are common. At this time they were against the law, so putting one on was an act of defiance against this government control. It showed that the people were still holding on to their traditional religion despite the orders of government and pressures of missionaries. They were still Blackfoot and the recorded event showed that.

The specific event recorded was decided upon by the keeper of that particular winter count. These events ranged from those involving the entire Blackfoot Nation to those of the immediate band or even just the family. This can be seen when we compare the several different winter counts in the following text.

The Bull Plume winter counts are the only ones containing pictographs. Crane Bear's winter count had them at one time, but when Father Legal tried to copy them with the text his artistic skill left much to be desired, and they are totally illegible. He did include additional information on each event as Crane Bear gave the story. All the others are short, written descriptions. Those from the Siksika were primarily written in syllabics and then translated into English. Many Guns' winter count is perhaps the most reliable of these as he provided the teaching and complete story as he translated the syllabics to Hanks. In later years others translated the syllabics from Many Guns' original calendar and these are included as sub-sets.

PICTOGRAPHS

Pictographs are individual drawings that serve as reminders of specific events, and like the Blackfoot language, are very descriptive. The earliest type were the petroglyphs carved, or scratched, on rock and aren't really very different from pictographs. In later years those same rock faces also contained painted images [pictographs] as well as the carved ones. Some would say this was a form of early writing, but it was not meant to convey a specific word. Rather they were reminders of total events. Blackfoot knowledge was based on memory and transfer through oral tradition and pictographs were meant to jog the memory rather than to tell the total story. A person who "knew" the story could fill in the details. A person who could "read" pictographs could get the general idea, in most cases, but not the full details.

Another type of pictograph was drawn or painted on shirts, robes, tipis, tipi liners and in later days on panels of canvas. These depicted the war adventures and important events of specific individuals and generally contained more details of the event while the winter counts contained only one image.

In the following text the pictograph and story of the event will be given from the Blackfoot viewpoint whenever possible. The Euro interpretation, and/or comments, of the same event will be shown in italics, if known. This will give us two world views of the same event.

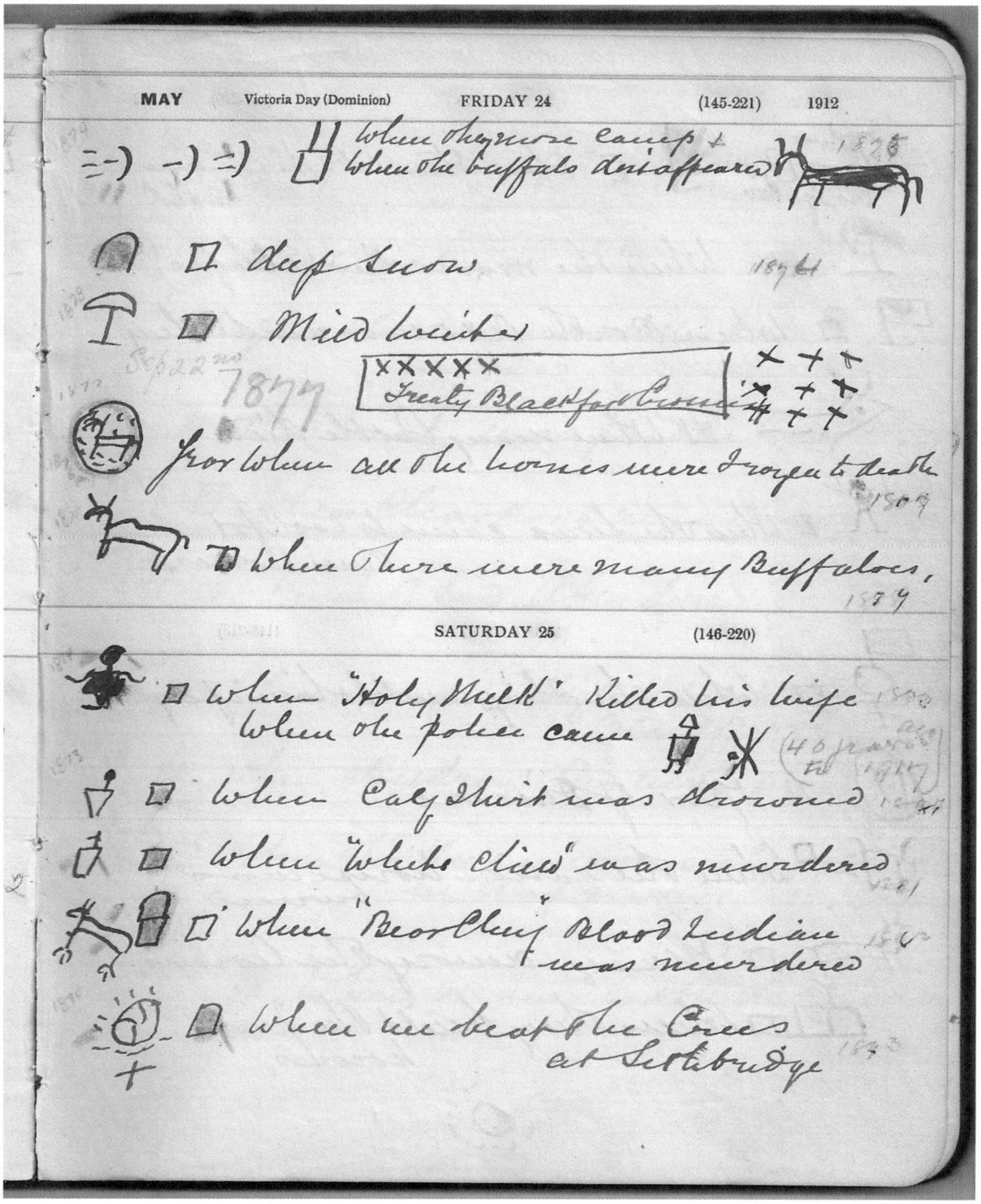

Bull Plume #1 ledger 1874, author's collection

When Wolf chief Died Suddenly
When the River flooded in winter
When the Blood stole many horses
When the Piegans Killed 50 Crees.
Dwarf Black Plume
When the Sioux stole many of our horses.
The year of stealing horses. while they were busy buying at the store
The Horse slipped out of tent & ran away,
When the Piegans line of guards was broken by the Sioux

Bull Plume #2 ledger 1845, Glenbow Museum Archives

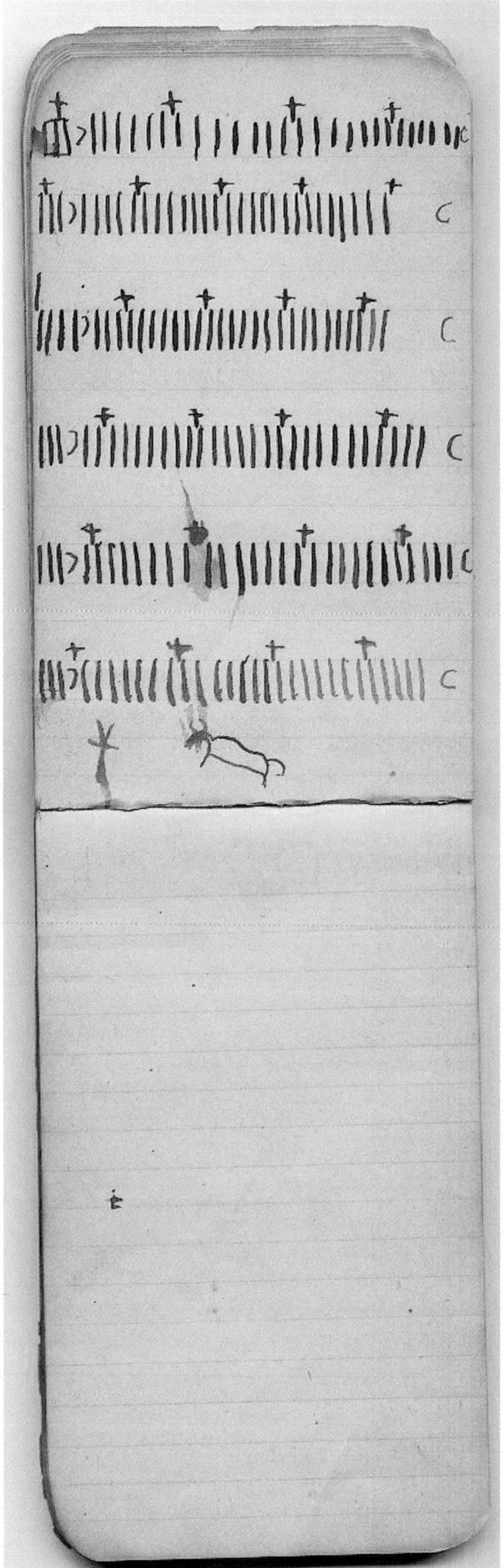

Bull Plume Old Agency Notebook,
Glenbow Museum Archives

WINTER COUNTS LINEAGE:

BULL PLUME WINTER COUNT:

Two conflicting lineages for Bull Plume #1 and possibly two separate winter counts.

From Bull Plume:
 # 1: From his grandfather Wolf Child to Bull Plume to Reverend Canon William Haynes.

Bull Plume #2, Wolf Child to Bull Plume to Agent Chester Arthur [written in the same hand as Bull Plume #1, most likely Haynes].

Bull Plume #3, Bull Plume to old Agency building basement.

As claimed by Brings-Down-the-Sun for Bull Plume #1:
Little Mountain to his son Iron Shirt, to his son Brings-Down-the-Sun, to Bull Plume. No surviving example.

ELK HORN WINTER COUNT:
Elk Horn to David Duvall to Clark Wissler.

BIG BRAVE [MOUNTAIN CHIEF] WINTER COUNT:
Mountain Chief to David Duvall to Clark Wissler.

BIG NOSE [THREE SUNS] WAR RECORD:
From a pictographic hide painted by, and given to acting Indian Agent Captain L.W. Cooke, with Big Nose relating the events and dates.

MRS. BIG NOSE WINTER COUNT:
Mrs. Big Nose to David Duvall to Clark Wissler.

BAD HEAD WINTER COUNT:
#1 Bad Head to R.N. Wilson

#2 Bad Head to Father Emile Legal

#3 Hugh Dempsey used the above two winter counts, plus that of White Bull, translating the original Blackfoot words with the help of his father-in-law James Gladstone, and added historical context.

WHITE BULL WINTER COUNT:
From Bad Head to Weasel Horse and Chief Owl to White Bull's brother, to White Bull.

PERCY CREIGHTON WINTER COUNT:

Percy Creighton to Harry Biele to Ester Goldfrank.

MANY GUNS WINTER COUNT:

From two old men, Makuyatoai [Wolf Sun] and Apinako'tamiso [Tomorrow Coming Over the Hill].

RUNNING RABBIT WINTER COUNT:

Unknown who he received it from but it is duplicate to events in the Many Guns account with his first event of 1830 being the same as Many Guns 1831.

LITTLE CHIEF WINTER COUNT:

Duplicate of Many Guns with years and some events liberally interpreted.

YELLOW FLY WINTER COUNT:

Duplicate of Many Guns. He was the son-in-law of Many Guns for a time, so this may be his source.

CRANE BEAR WINTER COUNT:

Crane Bear to Father Emile Legal.

CHAPTER 4

THE EARLY DAYS

The earliest entry we have is in the Bull Plume winter counts, and it is one of tragedy. The feelings of loss and helplessness contained in this small symbol, are tremendous. The glory and power of the Blackfoot Nation was crushed as no real enemy could possibly have done. The country was empty and the people spread to the far corners of the land. Perhaps the recorder felt he was recording the last words of his people. Or, perhaps, he wanted to insure that the people never forgot this great tragedy.

Instead of an ending, it became the start for two hundred and fourteen years of Blackfoot history, written by the Blackfoot people. In time, other winter counts came into existence and added to this history.

The Early Days consists of recovery and the blossoming of the Blackfoot people.

1764

NORTH PEIGAN

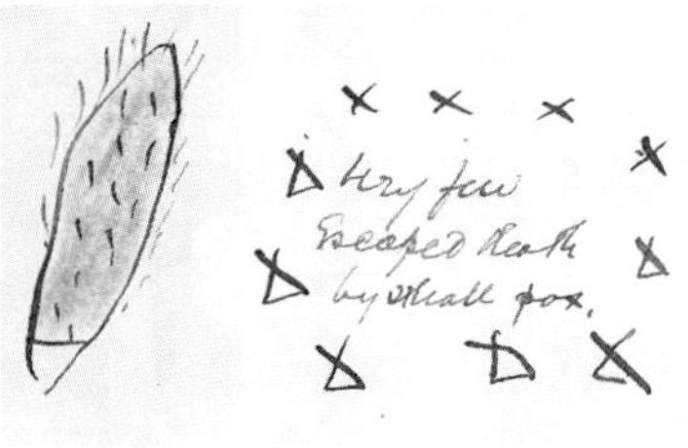

BULL PLUME #1: Big Small Pox Scare *Very few escaped death by smallpox*

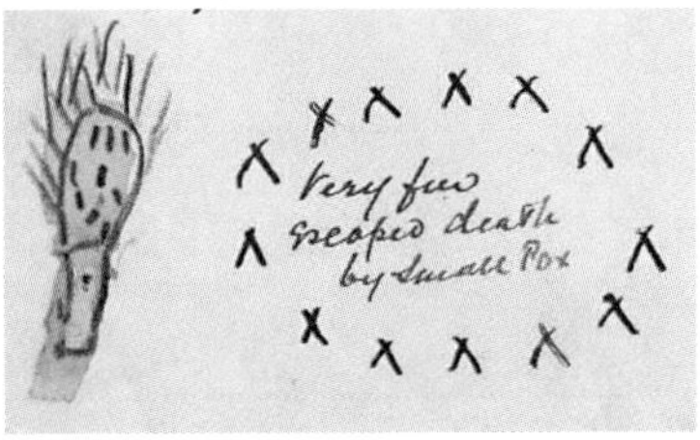

BULL PLUME #2: Big Small Pox Scare V*ery few escaped death by smallpox*

"...about one third of us died, but in some of the other camps there were tents in which every one died. When at length it left us, and we moved about to find our people, it was

no longer with the song and the dance; but with tears, shrieks, and howlings [sic]of despair for those who would never return to us. War was no longer thought of, and we had enough to do to hunt and make provision for our families, for in our sickness we had consumed all our dried provisions; but the Bisons [sic] and Red Deer were also gone, we did not see one half of what was before, whither they had gone, we could not tell…Our hearts were low and dejected, and we shall never be again the same people."
[Saukamappee to Thompson in 1781, p337]

1765

NORTH PEIGAN

BULL PLUME #1: Elk Bull Died

BULL PLUME #2: Elk Bull Died

1766

NORTH PEIGAN

BULL PLUME #1: Beaver Woman got away – *Escaped from the Crees after being captured in battle and got back to Blackfoot, her own people.*

BULL PLUME #2: Beaver Woman got away

Young Cree warriors, E. Brown photo, author's collection

1767

NORTH PEIGAN

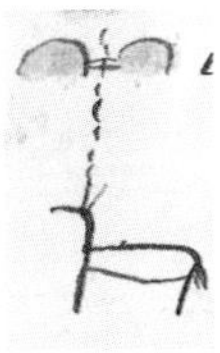

BULL PLUME #1: When we got the mules (stole them)
When the people went over the mountains *and stole the mules*

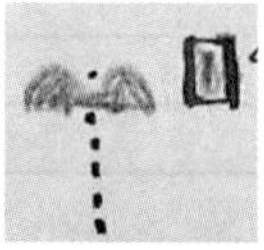

BULL PLUME #2: When we got the Mules
When the people went over the mountains

This is not the first appearance of mules among the Blackfoot as Anthony Henday saw four in 1754.

1768

NORTH PEIGAN

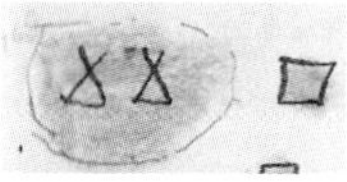
BULL PLUME #1: Big fire when all the camp was burned

BULL PLUME #2: Big fire when the camp was burned

1769

NORTH PEIGAN

BULL PLUME #1: When we took the Snake Indians wives and children

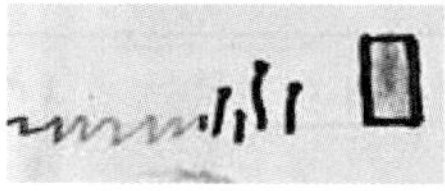
BULL PLUME #2: When we took the Snake Indians wives and children

"Now we must revenge the death of our people and make the Snake Indians feel the effects of our guns, and other weapons; but the young women must all be saved, and if any has a babe at the breast it must not be taken from her, nor hurt; all the Boys and Lads that have no weapons must not be killed, but brought to our camps, and be adopted amongst us, to be our people, and make us more numerous and stronger than we are."
[Speech of an old chief related by Saukamapee to Thompson, Tyerrell; 339.]
This indicates the Blackfoot felt the Shoshone were responsible for the epidemic.

Shoshone [Snake] warriors and women, Muybridge photo, Central Pacific Railroad, Corrine, Utah. Author's photo.

1770

NORTH PEIGAN

BULL PLUME #1: When the berries stayed on the trees all winter

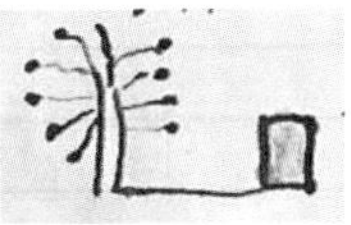

BULL PLUME #2: When the berries stayed on the trees all winter

1771

NORTH PEIGAN

BULL PLUME #1: When the old women went astray.

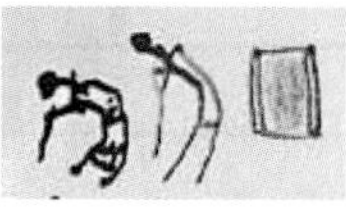

BULL PLUME #2: When the old women went astray.

1772

NORTH PEIGAN

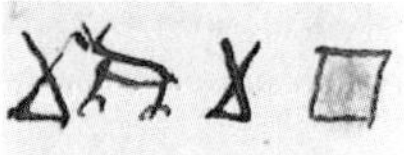

BULL PLUME #1: When the bears came into camp

BULL PLUME #2: When the bears came into the camp.

1773

NORTH PEIGAN

BULL PLUME #1: When many horses were drowned.

BULL PLUME #2: When many horses got drowned.

1774

NORTH PEIGAN

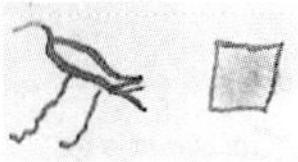

BULL PLUME #1: Thundered in winter.

BULL PLUME #2: Thundered in winter.

This is a significant event in Blackfoot religion. The arrival of Thunder in the spring is the signal for the Medicine Pipe owners to open their bundles and renew the tobacco in them. The usual time for this to occur is in the spring when Thunder ordinarily appears. However, strong traditionalists will open their bundles *<u>whenever</u>* *they hear the first thunder of the year.*

Wild Gun, his wife Matsoaki and daughter with Thunder Medicine Pipe. ca. 1909, Edward Curtis photo

Old Chief dancing with Thunder Pipe at first Thunder spring opening. ca.1906, McClintock photo Beinecke Archives. [This looks more like Crow Chief, South Piegan - Blackfoot}

"A long time ago the people were camped out on the plains. One day it really started to rain, and the thunder and lightning got really bad. A man and his wife were sitting in their tipi waiting for the storm to let up. For some reason the man fell asleep. When he finally woke up it was dark, his wife was gone and there was no fire in the lodge. The storm had ended, so he thought his wife probably went out to visit her relatives. He built up the fire and waited for her to come home. It started getting later and later and he began to worry about her. Then he began to get mad that she'd stayed out so late, and went out to look for her. He went to her relative's camps, and then to her friends, but no one had seen her that day. Now he started getting worried thinking that she may have gone for wood and some enemy had captured or killed her.

The next morning she still hadn't returned, so he began looking for her again. All around the camp he looked. He went down by the water, and down in the brush, and looked for tracks. But he didn't find anything. Back in his tipi he sat for a long time thinking how she could have just disappeared, and he began feeling very sad because he loved her a great deal. That man just sat there crying and praying, asking Natosi to pity him and help him. Then it just came to him, like someone had put the words in his head. He knew what happened; that Thunder had knocked him out and stolen his wife. Well, he was no coward; he'd go get her back. And so he started out, wandering on the plains and asking everyone he met where Thunder lived, because nobody knew where his lodge was.

First he asked Badger, because Badger had a lot of power and might just know where Thunder stayed. But Badger told him he didn't know and didn't want to know. Thunder was too powerful and kills anyone who makes him angry. He told the man to just forget about the woman and go home before he too gets killed. The man went on, starting to feel discouraged. When he met some of those water birds he thought, 'they traveled all over; they might know where Thunder lived'. But they didn't know and told him the same thing, 'forget about her and go home. Thunder will kill you.' Finally he met up with Wolf. Now Wolf was a great traveler, and seemed to know all the country. But when he asked, Wolf told him the same thing the others had, that he didn't know and besides, Thunder would kill the man. Now that man started crying and feeling really sad. He was afraid he'd never find his wife, and if he did, Thunder would probably kill him. Wolf looked at the man crying there and he began to pity him. Well, Wolf told him, 'there is one who is not afraid of Thunder. If you have courage you can ask him to help you. He lives in a stone lodge right inside that mountain pass. *[This is Crow's Nest Mountain in Crow's Nest Pass, Alberta, ed.]* His namc is Misum Omahkaistoa *[Ancient Raven, ed.]* and he has great power. He might pity you, but don't say I didn't warn you.'

The man traveled for a long time and finally entered the mountain pass. There he found a mountain shaped like a tipi made of solid stone. He looked, but couldn't find any entrance. He began crying, 'Ahai-ai, ahai-ai', in a pitiful way, and walking around the lodge. Finally a voce called out from inside, 'Peet *[come in, ed.]*'. When he walked around to the east side, there was a door. Going inside he looked around and saw it was like a regular lodge with beautiful linings and backrests, and robes to sit on. Straight at the back sat Raven. Raven pointed to a seat next to him and handed the man a bowl of food. The man took the food but just sat there with his head hanging down, not eating. 'Napii, *[friend, ed.]* what troubles you so that you can't eat?' So the man told him the whole story how Thunder stole his wife, and how everyone was afraid to help him, or even tell him where Thunder lived. Then he told how he met Wolf and Wolf told him Raven was the only one powerful enough to help him, and that's why he came here. He hoped Raven would pity him and help him get his wife back.

Raven thought about this for a long time. Finally he told the man not to worry, that they'd go see what they could do to get his wife back. Now the man felt a lot better, and began to eat. In the morning they would start.

Next morning they started south to Thunder's home. It too was a mountain, not far south from Raven's lodge *[Chief Mountain, Alberta, ed.]* As they traveled the man started to remember all the things the birds and animals had told him about Thunder, and he began to get scared. Raven was powerful, and could read the man's thoughts. He just looked at the man and said, 'Don't worry, we'll be successful'.

Thunder had great power, so he knew when they got close to his lodge. There was a loud boom of thunder and he called out, 'Who are you and what do you want here? You'd better leave before I get angry.' Raven answered back, 'We've come for this man's wife you stole.' 'Well, you can't have her. I'm not giving her back.' Thunder answered. 'We're not leaving without her', Raven answered. Thunder got mad and made a big storm. He began throwing lightning at Raven. Raven just dodged the lightning and began singing his power song, 'Wind is my Medicine, Cold is my Medicine'.
When he started to sing the wind came up strong, and it began to blizzard. Thunder kept throwing his lightning but the snow and ice began to slow him down. Pretty soon he was

almost covered. 'Wait, wait', he called, 'you win. You can have the woman back.' Raven said, 'Well it's not over yet. You owe this man something for his suffering.' 'Well', Thunder said, 'I'll give him my Holy Pipe. But he has to bring it outside and show it to me when he hears me come back in the spring. If he calls on me then, I'll know it is him and won't hurt him or his people, and I'll help them.' The man agreed to do this, and took the pipe. And then Raven said, 'What about me? You put me to all this trouble; I should get something.' Then Thunder agreed to share the year with Raven. For half the year Raven can have the cold so people will remember his power. The other half will be warm and Thunder will be in charge. So that's how come we have winter and summer. But sometimes Thunder and Raven fight over the seasons again, and we see them throwing lightning and thunder in the middle of a snow storm. *[Dick Pard, North Peigan. Author's field notes 1973]*

1775

NORTH PEIGAN

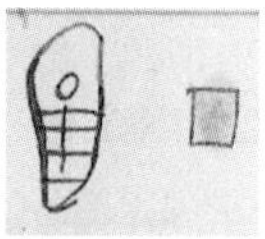

BULL PLUME #1: When the baby was lost.

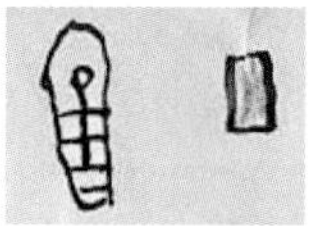

BULL PLUME #2: When the baby was lost.

A camp on the move was a sight to see. The people would spread out for a quarter mile in width with the men riding to the front and sides. The young men would bring up the rear and all would be visiting and talking with the excitement of a new camp for the night, and prospects for future hunts. The young babies would be in their cradleboards or moss bags tied to the cross of the travois of a gentle pack horse or on the pack of a dog. It is not hard to imagine the tragedy of a broken string on a runaway horse or dog. Even a baby could not be found in the waist high grass when the day's journey covered several miles.

Another story tells how one of these lost babies was cared for and returned to the people with a powerful gift.

"A camp was traveling away back in early days before horses were known. Dogs were loaded and all walking on foot, a woman had her child on a little dog travois. A rabbit ran across their trail and the dogs all took after it. The dogs all disappeared over a ridge and when they returned the baby was missing from the dog's travois. All searched for it but found it not. A bear found it, took it to its hole, fed it berries. Bear also gathered plenty of buffalo chips which he turned into pemmican by magic; the bear reared him and when he was a large boy the bear called all the other bears together and told them to put the boy son of his in possession of bears' charms, etc.. They gave him a belt of bear fur, also other ornaments - 4 arrows and a bow, and sent him home to the Indian camp. He entered his mother's and father's lodge and they enquired [sic] who he was. He said, 'I am the child lost when the dogs ran after the rabbit, a bear took me and reared me and here I am!'

He put one of his arrows in the bow, aimed at his brother, shot him and he fell. The parents cried, 'Oh why have you killed your brother?' Said he, 'No, I am only initiating him, no harm will come to him. The boy then doctored the other and brought him to life again, and taught him the bear dance and songs and they took in other members, and so the society of Braves came down to us." *[Scalp Roller to Wilson, 1893, Wilson 1958, 337-8] Rather than the origin for the Brave Society [Mutsix] as a whole, Scalp Roller gives the origin for the Bear Brave, one of the leaders of the society.]*

1776

NORTH PEIGAN

BULL PLUME #1: When the elks went through the ice.

BULL PLUME #2: When the elks went through the ice.

1777

NORTH PEIGAN

BULL PLUME #1: When "Pretty Weasel Woman" committed murder.

BULL PLUME #2: When "Pretty Weasel Woman" committed murder.

When the word "murder" is used it refers to the killing of a tribal member by another tribal member.

1778

NORTH PEIGAN

BULL PLUME #1: The great wind.

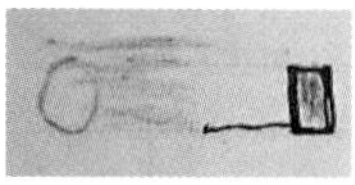

BULL PLUME #2: The great wind.

Winds of 50 to 60 miles per hour are a common event in Blackfoot country. For one to be recorded in the winter count as "the great wind" it must have been well above those numbers.

1779

NORTH PEIGAN

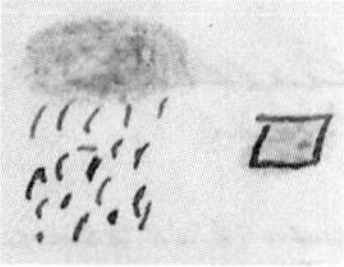

BULL PLUME #1: When it hailed in winter.

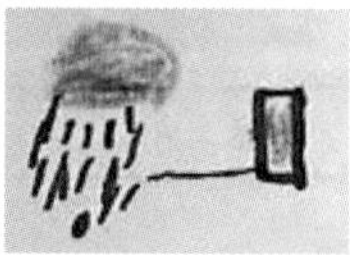

BULL PLUME #2: When it hailed in winter.

1780

NORTH PEIGAN

BULL PLUME #1: Cough disease or first appearance of Consumption.

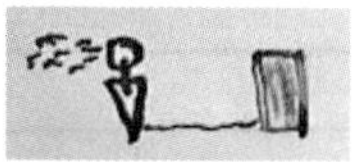

BULL PLUME #2: Cough disease

This is the 1781 small pox epidemic which is referred to in most publications on the northern plains. Cough disease, or "little small pox" was another name for measles. Mathew Cocking observed, "Before the fatal attack of small pox, all these nations of Indians were much more numerous than they are at present…It is computed that at least one-half of the inhabitants were carried off by it." (Cocking; 1908; 203)

1781

NORTH PEIGAN

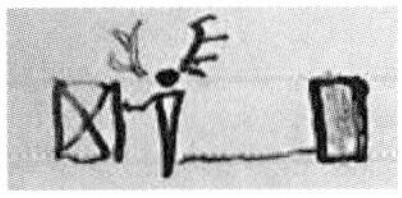

BULL PLUME #1: When "Holy Elk" won the battle.

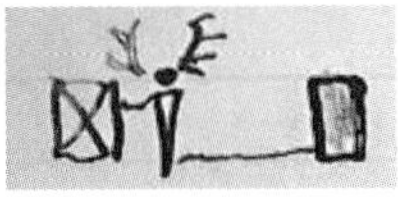

BULL PLUME #2: When "Holy Elk" won the battle.

For the Blackfoot war was a way to wealth and prestige. A man's accomplishments were recognized, and well known among the people.

War Parties:

War party leader – itamó i
War party – có o
Revenge party – ksiamsiso

Three classes of warrior:

1. ometa pakistsyu – "he's getting ahead"
   A young man who has been on 5 or 6 war parties but who hasn't got very many horses, killed an enemy or otherwise particularly distinguished himself.
2. sai sotapsyu – "he's getting famous"
   About ten war parties, many horses, possibly killed an enemy.
3. niatapse e sotapseyu – "famous warrior"
   Brave warrior, reputation for generosity, helps old and poor, leader of successful war parties. A man must be a warrior of the highest rank to become a chief.

Bravest Deeds:
Being surrounded by the enemy and escaping, rescuing wounded comrade from midst of enemy, protecting the retreat of a war party, turning back to help a man whose horse has given out. Capturing guns is an especial honor. There is no formal recognition of rank. It is a question of gradually building a reputation and becoming generally recognized."
[Lazy Boy, South Peigan to John Collier, 1938]

1782

NORTH PEIGAN

BULL PLUME #1: When they took the shield.

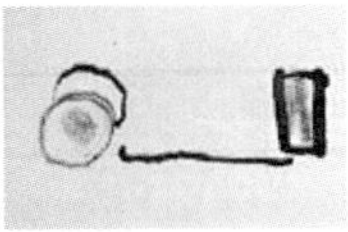

BULL PLUME #2: When they took the shield.

The capture of a shield was an important coup. Being both an article of war and a religious item it was a much sought after trophy, especially those of the Crow tribe which were highly decorated similar to the Blackfoot shields.

Maka, South Peigan-Blackfoot with shield, McClintock photo, Beinecke Archives, Yale University

Shield and Single-Horn Headdress on tripod in South Peigan-Blackfoot Sun Dance camp, 1906, McClintock photo, Beinecke Archives, Yale University

1783

NORTH PEIGAN

 BULL PLUME #1: Eclipse of the sun in winter.

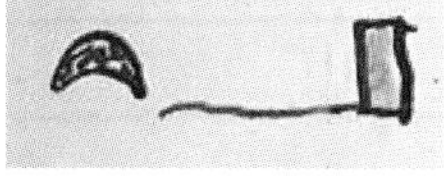 BULL PLUME #2: Eclipse of the sun in winter.

April 12, 1782; visible in SE Saskatchewan & central Manitoba; annular eclipse where the moon does not cover totally cover the sun, leaving a thin ring of light.
August 16, 1784 Solar eclipse [partial eclipse] [Peter Broughton, Chairman, Royal Astronomical Society of Canada]

1784

NORTH PEIGAN

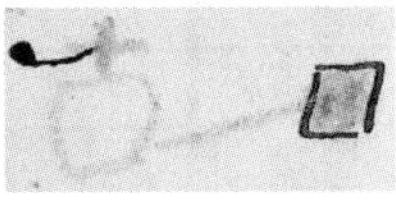

BULL PLUME #1: When the whitemen with short hair first came.

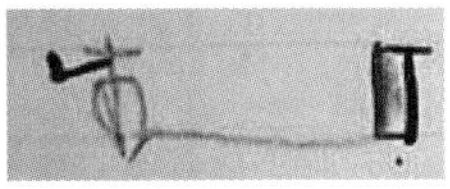

BULL PLUME #2: When shorthaired whitemen first came.

Prior to this the Cree and Assiniboine were the main traders to the Blackfoot. Occasionally the Hudson Bay Company would send out agents to the Blackfoot to encourage them to come east to trade. These men usually had long hair since it was a definite asset in dealing with the Indian people.

Our account could well mean the arrival of free traders from Montreal, newly formed into the Northwest Company. They established Umfreville's House on the North Saskatchewan River at the present Alberta-Saskatchewan border.

1785

NORTH PEIGAN

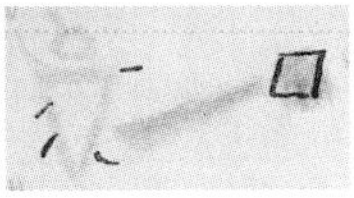

BULL PLUME #1: When "Young Man" was killed.

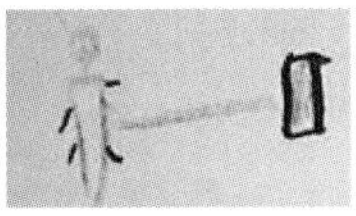

BULL PLUME #2: When "Young Man" was killed.

1786

NORTH PEIGAN

 BULL PLUME #1: When the woman was killed outside.

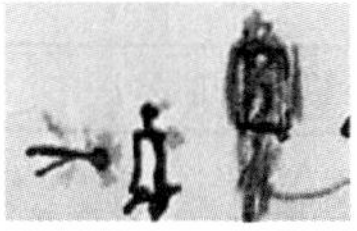 BULL PLUME #2: When the woman was killed outside.

1787

NORTH PEIGAN

 BULL PLUME #1: Disease among the antelope.

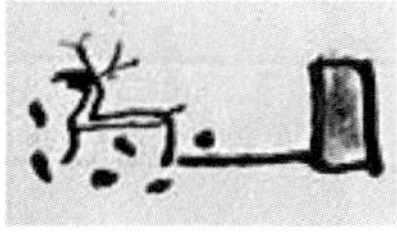 BULL PLUME #2: Disease among the antelope.

Antelope were also an important food source for the Blackfoot. They were the desired hides, along with Mountain Sheep, to be used for clothing; being light weight, and the strongest of the food animals hunted by the Blackfoot. .

Antelope Hunt
There were seven families. The oldest man invited others to his lodge to talk about how they would get food. The old man told them,' Last winter we drove the antelope in the snow bank. Do any of you have the untanned hides from this kill?' 'Yes,' they said, 'We have some.'

The old man said, 'Soak the green antelope hides. Then carve out a piece of wood in shape of antelope. We'll then put hides over this frame, and allow them to dry. Then we'll remove the hides from the drying frame.' Then had one man get into dried hide, stored bow and arrow in front of breast ready for use. Then had him walk around to see if he resembled an antelope. Tied hoofs to his arms and legs. Two men were dressed in this manner. Told them to go west side of camp to avoid camp smoke and leave decoy hides out on prairie. Then told them to scout for a band of antelope.

The oldest man told them, 'Go into hills early in the morning. Find some antelope manure and urine, put it on yourselves, then don your suits and seek out antelope.

Approach as close as you can without frightening them and then retreat so as to get them to follow you. Have your bow and arrows ready at your breast. [Had sticks running down into front legs of hide.] 'Then brace yourselves on two sticks while you shoot with bow and arrow.'

After they had killed several antelopes, they returned to camp with two heads. The old man then sang and held a ceremony and left decoys outside camp so as to avoid contaminating with smoke smell. They took the heads home. The old man said, 'The female up there has a song. She warns the others of danger. We'll stop her.' He took tinder and stuffed it into the ears of the antelope. After this the smart female couldn't hear them any more. The old man sang the song.

The second time they went up, they killed the leader. Thereafter the antelope would approach the hunters closely and the latter killed them easily. After this hunt, the old man said, 'We'll move down the river now and devise some other way of hunting antelope. Then they made their antelope fall. Made a decoy of coyote hide and stood far off from antelope. The coyote feigned chasing the two decoy men towards the fall, and the antelope followed them. The two decoys then threw themselves prostrate and allowed antelope to run themselves over cliff. *[Yellow Kidney, South Peigan-Blackfoot; Schaeffer, 1950, 126, 1-3]*

1788

NORTH PEIGAN

BULL PLUME #1: The winter when the stars fell.

BULL PLUME #2: The winter when the stars fell.

1789

NORTH PEIGAN

BULL PLUME #1: When "Ringing-Smoking-Pipe" stole many horses.

BULL PLUME #2: When "Ringing-Smoking-Pipe" stole many horses.

Bringing home the horses, 1906, McClintock photo Beinecke Archives, Yale University

1790

NORTH PEIGAN

BULL PLUME #1: Took 8 Cree tipis in battle.

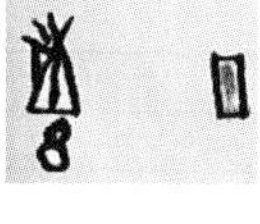

BULL PLUME #2: Took 8 Cree tipis in battle.

Painted Cree tipis, Fort Qu'Appelle, Saskatchewan, Phillip Godsell photo, Glenbow Museum Archives

1791

NORTH PEIGAN

BULL PLUME #1: When log houses were first built.

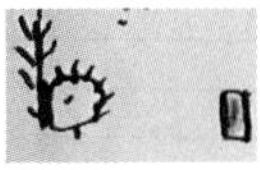

BULL PLUME #2: When the wooden house was built.

"After the Piegans had begun to make short trips into the prairies, they one winter returned to the big river [this is the Saskatchewan River, (Omakatay – Big River), ed.], to find white men on the other side. These men traded with them, and as the people began to go further south the white men followed them with their goods." *[Tearing Lodge, South Peigan, to Edward Curtis and George Bird Grinnell in 1898; 3]*

Chesterfield House, of the Northwest Company, was built in 1800 on the South Saskatchewan River below it's junction with the Red Deer River . It was the furthest south of any post, and well within Blackfoot territory. Buckingham House (Hudson's Bay

Company, 1791) and Fort George (Northwest Company, 1791) were built on the North Saskatchewan River.

In 1791 Peter Fiddler, a geographic surveyor for the Hudson's Bay Company, traveled with a Peigan Band through southern Alberta. Living in the chief's lodge while they traveled the open, wood-less prairie, he gives us an insight to another importance of the buffalo to life on the plains. "Burnt Cow dung [buffalo, ed.] as usual. The fire is first made of small dry wood then afterwards the dry Dung. A small stick or 2 is kept constantly in the middle of the fire, perpendicular & bits of Inside fatt are placed upon it that melts & falls down gradually into the fire & makes the Buffalo dung burn much better than without this. This kind of fuel makes a great quantity of ashes. When the Dung is dry it does tolerably well; at present it is rather wet, on account of the fresh snow thawing & wetting it, it takes a long time for the air to dry it well again, particularly at this season of the year." [Fiddler, 1991, 26-27]

1792

NORTH PEIGAN

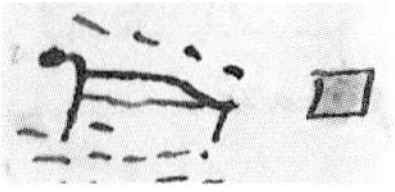

BULL PLUME #1: When there were many wolves.

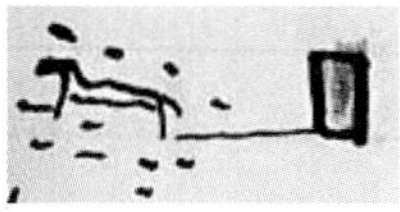

BULL PLUME #2: When there were many wolves.

1793

NORTH PEIGAN

BULL PLUME #1: When "Many Killed" were taken in battle.

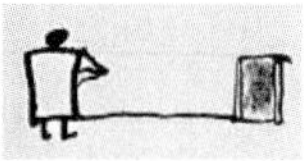

BULL PLUME #2: When "Many Killed" was taken in battle.

Many Killed was most likely the name of a woman captured.

1794

NORTH PEIGAN

BULL PLUME #1: Before the battle when all was quiet.

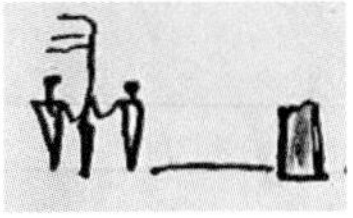

BULL PLUME #2: “ “ “

The Gros Ventre, allies of the Blackfoot, plundered Manchester House in the fall of 1793 and South Branch House in 1794. Thompson, p. ixvii)

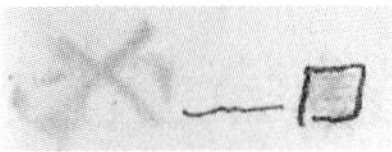

BULL PLUME #1: When the Thunder Pipes were taken.

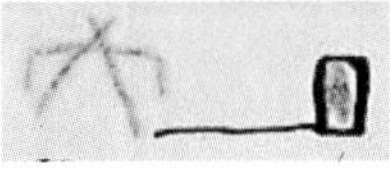

BULL PLUME #2: “ “ “

Thunder Medicine Pipes were important Medicine Bundles among the Blackfoot. Evidently more than one was captured during a battle.

Medicine Pipe on tripod behind lodge, 1920, H.F. Robinson photo, author's collection

1795

NORTH PEIGAN

BULL PLUME #1: When "The Dog" was killed. *The Dog, is the name of a chief.*

BULL PLUME #2: When "The Dog" was killed. *The Dog, is the name of a chief.*

The Gros Ventre, allies of the Blackfoot, divided this year. "April 9, 1795, Gros Ventre split into two groups, one [90 lodges] to snakes. The Snake Indians have suffered a severe loss in war this year if rumour [sic] be true, a party of the first two mentioned tribes [Blood and Siksika] having killed no less than 20 men and two women in an expedition against them." [Mc Gillivray, 69]

1796

NORTH PEIGAN

BULL PLUME #1: When "Bull Chief" was murdered.

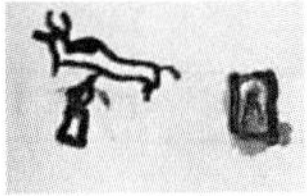

BULL PLUME #2: When "Bull Chief" was murdered.

Murder, in these cases, refers to the killing by a member of the tribe or their allies.

1797

NORTH PEIGAN

BULL PLUME #1: When "Old Man Crane" was murdered.

BULL PLUME #2: "Old Man Crane" was murdered.

1798

NORTH PEIGAN

BULL PLUME #1: When we fought 6 days in the foothills.

BULL PLUME #2: When they fought 6 days in the foothills.

1799

NORTH PEIGAN

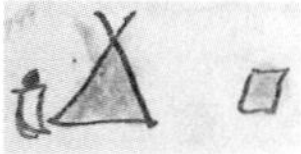

BULL PLUME #1: When "Woman Sitting" lost the battle.

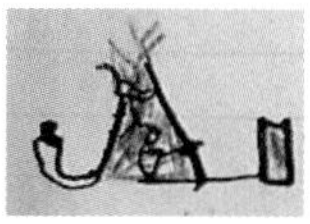

BULL PLUME #2: When "Woman Sitting" lost the battle.

1800

NORTH PEIGAN

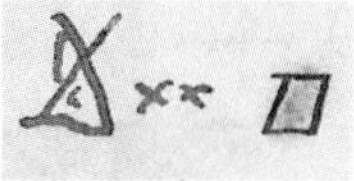

BULL PLUME #1: The Crow tent. This tent is still in existence (1913). *When they stole it.*

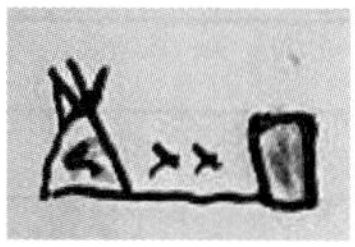

BULL PLUME #2: The Crow tent. This tent is still in existence.

The Crow tent refers to the Crow Lodge tipi design. It was received in a dream by Fox Head of the Buffalo Chip Band of the Peigans. The reference to having "stole it" is in pencil and obviously added incorrectly at a later date. More than likely it refers to "when they sold it" to another family. The Crow Lodge is very famous among the North Peigan since the dream was given at the confluence of the Old Man River and Crow Lodge Creek on the North Peigan Reserve. The design is still in existence among the North Peigan people.

"Fox Head's wife had a dream about the crows. In her dream she was told by the crows to paint this design on their tipi and they would always have good luck. When her husband started painting the design lots of crows came and were sitting in the trees near him calling and making noise. When they set up the tipi and had the ceremony a few of those crows flew over and sat on the tipi's poles. Then they knew it was a powerful design." [*Joe Crowshoe, North Peigan-Blackfoot; 1976, to the author; field notes]*

Maistoikokoup, Crow Bird Lodge

Yellow Kidney has owned this lodge three times and each time he learned tale of its origin. Hence he is familiar with details. His father before him owned the lodge, when Yellow Kidney was a child. It was turned over to his relatives later and then took back to Buffalo Chip band. [He prayed to Thunder Chief before relating story for long life for interpreter and recorder. Implicit was idea that he was relating the truth].

The Crow Painted Lodge originated among Buffalo Chip band, while latter were camped in Porcupine Hills, along Old Man River. *[At Crow Lodge Creek, ed.]* This is when Peigan roamed in early days. This took place before Blackfoot had horses.

At this camp the people were short of food and some were already hungry. The band chiefs assembled in council and agreed to hold a bison drive.

The drive was successfully held. The hunters started to butcher the dead buffalo. One person who couldn't remove his share of the kill, left it inside the corral until next day. However he took home a few pieces of meat to his lodge. The crows started to flock around the corral in great numbers. The people of the camp retired.

Before daylight the hunter was awakened by his wife, who told him to bring in the balance of the meat back to camp on the travois. He harnessed the dog and started for the corral. By this time day had started to break. Upon nearing the corral he saw a lodge pitched nearby. It was painted, with figures of seven crows on the south, and seven on the north side. The hunter was curious as to how it got there. Upon approaching closer, he saw many crows sitting there. A female crow at the end of the row was singing;
'My Man! You'd better get up. There's a man coming towards us. We should have a smoke.'

The male crow became angry and jealous. He sang in reply;
'The people on the outside of us are enemies. I hear their weapons.'
The female replied;
We'll have a smoke. We'll pray for good luck for the people.'

She reassured her husband about the hunter and continued. 'I want to give this human our lodge. He will feed us.' Now the male crow had regained his good humor. He joined his wife in presenting the lodge to the hunter. He told the latter 'We give you this lodge, with all the power that's in it.' Then the hunter immediately returned home, leaving his kill for the crows to eat. Before they had told him, 'The reason we give you this lodge is this. These are all our children here. You have fed them.'

Upon arriving home, the hunter was greeted by his wife, 'Where is the meat?' He replied, 'I have given it to the crows to eat,' without mentioning their gift of the lodge. That night upon retiring, the hunter dreamed that the crow people appeared to him and said, 'You saw the lodge. You must make one like it. Paint it like the one on the hill.'

The next morning he awakened his wife and told her to boil a quantity of meat. He planned to invite the old people to his lodge and relate his dream. After they had arrived, he said, 'Now I want to talk to you. We have been given wonderful aide. I saw a painted lodge yesterday up at the corral. There were two rows of crows painted upon the cover, each row standing upon a red line representing the blood of the bison. In the rear where the lines join, a buffalo skull is drawn. That represents the fat on the side of a buffalo's head, which is the favorite food of the crow.'

The old people remarked, 'This is a very wonderful gift from the crows. We'll use it as a protection for our people and also to insure good fortune in securing bison. The lodge will be used to draw the bison to us. Today you must take down your lodge and paint it like the dream lodge. You must do this at once.'
So the hunter started. He took several travois and placed them against his lodge for ladders. He then marked out the outlines of the crows, the base line and the skull. The horns of the latter curved downward rather than up. Soon he had all the designs filled in. He cut a red robe into small triangular pieces and attached one to each of the bird's beaks to represent bison meat. In the corner of each smoke wing, a bison tail was attached. In the rear between the top and the skull, seven more bison tails were attached. A blue cross was painted on the top rear to represent the butterfly.

After the lodge was painted, the owner told the people, 'Tonight we will go through the ceremony taught me by the Crow people. We will borrow some rattles from the Beaver Bundle men, and then we'll use the drum. We'll make a blood soup with berries to eat afterwards. That is what the Crow woman did. She sang first, accompanied by the rattles. The women will sing first, and then the men will drum and sing. Then everyone will rise and dance. Everyone will make all the noise possible, so much as to nearly tear the lodge down.'

The women sang their song first and the men followed, accompanied by the drum. [These are incitement dances used in war.] When the time came for the buffalo skull song, white clay was applied to it's top and sides. Four different Medicine objects are used in the lodge ritual [which is why it has a great deal of power and is still used today.] At the conclusion of the ritual, the buffalo drive woman said, 'I will give these two buffalo stones to the lodge for use in the ceremony. I will give my rattles at the same time.' Thus she helped out the lodge owner. *[Yellow Kidney, South Peigan-Blackfoot; Schaeffer, 1950, 125-7-11]*

The Crow Lodge made of buffalo hide, ca.1909, McClintock photo, Beinecke Archives, Yale University

1801

NORTH PEIGAN

BULL PLUME #1: When we took the stars and stripes from the River Indians.

BULL PLUME #2: When we took the stars and stripes from the River Indians.

The people referred to are Pend d'Oreille, called Niituhta-tapix (River People) in Blackfoot.

Capturing a flag from the enemy was considered an important coup. Flags were regarded as having power as war medicines and captured flags often were used to wrap major Medicine Bundles. This represented power over their enemies. The fur trade companies all had their own flags which were given to the chiefs. When arriving at the fort to trade, the proper flag would be carried at the front of the column. The American Fur Company created a number of different homemade flags that were given out, or sold, and came in a variety of styles. Many were cheaply made and often hand painted with eagles in place of the blue stared section. The design of the American flag was not yet standardized at this point in time. Rudolph Kurz relates in his journal of having painted a number of flags for Edwin Denig during his stay at Fort Union. It is more than likely the flag mentioned came from traders along the west coast rather than from any eastern trading post. See the fort drawings of Thunder Chief in the year 1831 for a Native interpretation of the American Fur Company flags

"September 20. Mr. Denig has again contrived some employment for me, i.e., to paint the picture of an eagle, life size, on cotton cloth; then to sew thereon stripes of red and white cloth in alternating stripes about 15 feet long, thus providing flags for Indians. They are to pay the handsome price of 20 robes apiece for these standards; so only the wealthiest among them can afford to enjoy the distinction of presenting on." [Kurz; Hewitt, 1970,133]

A fur trade flag hangs on the wall behind the visiting Assiniboine at Fort Union; Rudolf Kurz painted a number of these for company trader Edwin Denig while working for his keep at the fort. ca.1851, Rudolf Kurz drawing.

"I think it is significant that an American Flag should be captured by the Peigans four years before the Lewis and Clark expedition came west... the area was still considered part of the Spanish possession but there were rumors and indications from David Thompson that Americans had penetrated the area even prior to Lewis and Clark." (Dempsey; personal communication, 1978)

1802

NORTH PEIGAN

BULL PLUME #1: "Still Smoking" stole many horses. *From the Crees*

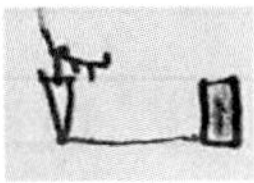

BULL PLUME #2: "Still Smoking" stole many horses. *From the Crees*

"One summer (I think 1802) a large camp of Stone Indians, had sent some young men to a Blackfoot camp, who brought away about thirty horses, they were quickly followed to the Stone Indian camp, and about three nights afterwards, the Blackfeet Young men took not only the greater part of the horses stolen from them, but collected as many more and drove them all off to their own camp." (Thompson; 1916; p368)

The notation about Cree Indians had been added in pencil later. It is more likely Thompson's identification of Stone Indians (Stoney/Assiniboine) is the correct one. The Blackfoot word for Crees is Asinawa and for the Assiniboine it is Nitsissinawa ["real" or "original" Cree]. The Blackfoot name for Stoney Indians is Sa ahsi sakitaki.

BULL PLUME #1: When "Big Rattlesnake" was killed. *Fighting the Crees.*

BULL PLUME #2: When "Big Rattlesnake" was killed. *Fighting the Crees.*

"My father once told me of an expedition from the Blackfeet, that went south by the Old Trail, to visit the people with dark skins. Elk Tongue and his wife, Natoya, were of this expedition, also Arrow Top and Pemmican, who was a boy of twelve at that time. He died only a few years ago at the age of ninety-five. They were absent four years. It took them twelve moons of steady traveling to reach the country of the dark skinned people, and eighteen moons to come north again. They returned by a longer route through the 'High Trees' or Bitter Root country, where they could travel without danger of being seen. They feared going along the North Trail because it was frequented by their enemies, the Crows, Sioux, and Cheyenne. Elk Tongue brought back the Dancing Pipe. He bought it nearly one hundred years ago and it was very old then. The South Man, who gave it to him, warned him to use it only upon important occasions, for the fulfillment of a vow, or the recovery of the sick." [*Brings-Down-the-Sun, North Peigan, ca. 1910 to Walter McClintock, p435-6.*]

This trip was one to visit the Arapaho tribe, or Southern Gros Ventres as the Blackfoot called them. At one time the Arapaho and Gros Ventre were one tribe, and both allied with the Blackfoot. When the Arapaho split off and moved to the Wyoming, Colorado area, they still maintained close ties with their relatives in the north. Visits between the groups were frequent. On this trip Elk Tongue received the Circle Dance Medicine Pipe, which Brings-Down-the-Sun calls the Dancing Pipe, as a gift. He was not the first Band Chief to lead his people south for an extended visit, nor the last.

We can determine the approximate year for this visit by Brings-Down-the-Sun's estimate of Pemmican's age at 12. Pemmican, also known as Wolf Calf later in life, was one of the group of Peigans that met Lewis and Clark in 1806, when he was 16 years old. This would put the date for Elk Tongue's trip at either 1801 or 1802.

Elk Tongue Chief, 1855, Gustav Sohon drawing, Washington State Historical Society, Tacoma, WA

Circle Dance Medicine Pipe obtained from the Arapaho dancing through the South Peigan camp led by Shorty White Grass, 1909, McClintock photo, Beinecke Archives, Yale University.

1803

NORTH PEIGAN

BULL PLUME #1: Disease among the buffalo.

BULL PLUME #2: Disease among the buffaloes.

This would have been an event of tragic proportions. Buffalo were the mainstay of Blackfoot existence. Their entire lives centered around the buffalo, and many ceremonies concerned obtaining the buffalo for survival. One such was the Piskan, or Buffalo Jump/corral, which reached back to the B.C. periods.

CALLING THE BUFFALO:

One of the most ancient forms of hunting, the Piskan or Buffalo Jump/Corral, was preceded with a ceremony. The ceremony itself changed with the addition of other spiritual instruction given through the course of time. The description below is mainly from Yellow Kidney of the South Peigan. Other information was supplied by members of the South and North Peigan and is included to clarify the ceremony and procedure. While the use of the actual ceremony has not been done for many years, the elements and songs are still in use within other bundles, and are well known.

"At the camp people were short of food. Some were already hungry. The chiefs assembled in council and agreed to hold a bison drive.

The band chief advised all to go to work erecting the corral and making it strong. All available elk antlers were first gathered to be made into chisels. They were driven by stone pounders in cutting trees. As each tree fell the bison bellow, 'Hu! Hu!' was given.

The drive site was a cliff facing south. Trees were set in holes dug about the circumference of the proposed corral. Strips of bark peeled from white berry bushes were braided into strong line and used as weaving elements run in and out along the corral posts. The latter were so strong that a bison could scarcely break through. In this way the corral was erected.

One or two fast runners were selected from the youths. A pit was dug at the side of the cliff, into which these runners could quickly conceal themselves as the bison pushed past them over the drop.

Next rocks were piled up to form "V" shaped wings leading to the drop. These rock piles were called 'women'. *[also,* "ochtokikat"*, same name as for the ears on a tipi. Mrs. Buffalo, North Peigan, 1978, Field Notes.]* Next to the cliff were two larger piles, each occupied by a courageous hunter. The balance were manned by as many persons [men, women and children] as were available. Each one prayed that herd might be driven over without injury to himself. [The piles were just used as markers for the hiders to use. They crouched down by them covered with their robes and if the herd came close to them they would shake just a leg of the robe to scare them back to the center line. Children weren't used because they might get scared and run away. Mike Swims Under, South Peigan, 1997]

The bison is 'smart, mean and fierce'. As a protection against enemies, they keep to the open grasslands as much as possible.

The medicine woman *[or man, ed.]* sings buffalo songs and accompanies herself with rattles. The old and brave people assist her in singing. She directs the fastest runner to be brought to her. Then she lights the pipe and goes trough the ritual. One or two 'licorice roots' are employed next. The root is rubbed on the feet, head and back of the runner, in order to induce the buffalo to stumble and fall. Thus, it is hoped, the animals can be secured more easily. She then directs the runner to do his best. *[See the origin myth for the beginning use of this root.]*

She takes a buffalo chip and molds it into the figure of a buffalo. *[This is prior to the gift of the buffalo stone. After the stone arrives it replaces the buffalo chip figure.]* She then covers it with grease and red paint, and places it besides the altar. The later is located beside the smudge. The runner is now instructed to imitate the bison. Next she warns the people to watch the buffalo chip figure. If it fails to move in the ritual to follow, it indicates that the drive will be unsuccessful and the people will continue to be hungry.

Now the medicine woman starts to sing. All the men accompany her. [At this point the Iniskim song is included to the ceremony after its arrival among the Blackfoot. *Swims Under, South Peigan, 1997.]*

Omaiaki	matokit	nitatos
You, woman	pick me up	I'm holy

2nd song:

omaninnai	otaki	naxksoyiu
You, man	I want a kidney to eat	

All the people watch the buffalo chip.

3rd song:

omaninnai	otoki	nakssowi	okiti	nakssowi
You, man	I want	rump meat to eat		brisket to eat

After this the runner starts out of the lodge. The runner starts out in the darkness and walks twice entirely around the buffalo herd picked out to be driven. By the time he has completed his walk, it has started to get light. [This is done around the time the Morning Star rises. *Swims Under, 1997*] Previously he had been told that a big old bull, the leader, would be lying before the herd. He had been instructed to get as close as possible to this animal. Further, that would see him and arise to its feet. At this the runner was to yell twice, "iii! iii! At this signal the bull would take after him. In the meantime, while circling the herd and approaching the midpoint, the runner must pray to the coyote for supernatural power to run swiftly, so that the bull might not overtake him.

The runner, after circling the herd, stands in the opening of the wings near the bull. He shouts, the bull arises sees the runner and takes off in pursuit. The remainder of the herd follow. Now the runner is between the opening of the wings, with the herd in full gallop behind. As the animals pass each pile of rocks, the person behind it throws up one leg of his robe to direct the herd. After they pass, all the guards arise and fall in behind, yelling their loudest.

During all this the ceremony continues in the tipi.

This song is to charm the buffalo.

4th song:
This song is the Iniskim talking to the runner.

Omaauaki	motoau	inniua
Runner!	I take	the buffalo

The lead buffalo will unhesitatingly jump with the herd into the corral.

5th song:
This is the woman talking about the piling of meat upon the corral post during butchering.

Nipiskani	iksisakosstok	aiitsimitsu	natoyui
My corral	has so much meat	it begins to smell	it [the corral] is holy

6th song:
This refers to a specific buffalo runner, Red Antelope, and is just before the Morning Star arises.

Mikauakasi	nipuaut	matoxpiu	kaksinok	koxkauaki
Red Antelope!	Arise!	We want everyone to see you. Start and drive [the buffalo]		

7th song:
This is the leader of the buffalo speaking.

Oxsokui	natoyiu	taiyakssauxpaipiu
My trail	is holy	I jump unhesitatingly [into the corral]

After the arrival of the Iniskim an actual dance was added between the 6th and 7th songs. This was done by young girls wearing buffalo robes with the hair out. It was the same as the buffalo dance for the Beaver Bundle. They danced so that young cows would fall in the trap since they made the best meat.

Yellow Kidney talks about Red Antelope, a famous Buffalo Runner of the South Peigans:

The fastest runner in the tribe was named Mikoaukasi, "Red [Painted] Antelope [Clothing]". *[It's not clear if this name was passed on with the position, or the name of just one individual, as many names were passed on with a Medicine Bundle when it was transferred. ed.] [The words "Painted" and "Clothing" in his name are implied in the Blackfoot language. ed.]* His clothing was made of antelope skins, the fastest animal known to the Blackfeet, and painted with red earth. Further, he wore two tail feathers of the Sparrow Hawk, the fastest bird, in his hair as a power token from this bird. His clothing represented power from Antelope.

Hard Wind Old Man [Iyikssopapi] is a spirit, as is Wears Red Feather In Hair [Ikotsi-kimani]. The former has control of the wind; the latter a cloud spirit. These two spirits, plus Red Antelope are responsible for luring the bison into the corral, hence food is offered them on buffalo chip plates. If people failed to feed Hard Wind Old Man, the wind would blow with great force. Likewise the cloud spirit, if not propiated, would cause a hard rain and wind. He was regarded as the most powerful of the two. Red Antelope had power from both.

Before the runner starts out, the medicine woman talks to him, 'I'm going to get a corner of the liver and some fat to feed you'. She arranges portions of these two foods upon three buffalo chips, used as plates. She also calls upon Hard Wind Old Man and Wears Red Feather in Hair for aid. The three buffalo chips are then placed upon a clean grassy spot on a hilltop for the two spirits. Red Antelope eats his share on a hill upon returning from the drive.

Red Antelope has two supernaturals for his guardians.

Red Antelope was very particular about his ceremonial clothing. After wearing it to drive in the bison, he removed it, roll it up with sweetgrass, and stored it some distance from camp. The last was to avoid contamination by human scent or odor of smoke from camp fire. Either would frighten buffalo during drive.

The leader of the ceremony is called the 'autapatan'. The runner that brings in the buffalo to the jump is called 'auakiu'. *[Yellow Kidney to Collier, 1938]*

Yellow Kidney, South Peigan-Blackfoot, ca. 1930's, Winold Reiss photo, author's collection

1804

NORTH PEIGAN

 BULL PLUME #1: When the Sioux were killed.

 BULL PLUME #2: When 4 Sioux were killed.

1805

NORTH PEIGAN

BULL PLUME #1: When the Crows died.

BULL PLUME #2: When the Crows died.

CHAPTER 5

ARRIVAL FROM THE SOUTH

1806 contained an event that would ultimately affect the land of the Blackfoot. For the Blackfoot it was so insignificant that it was not mentioned in any of the winter counts. Yet it was to open the door to Blackfoot country from the south and bring a trickle that turned into a flood. Pressure from these people in the south would increase and brought changes to deal with them.

1806

NORTH PEIGAN

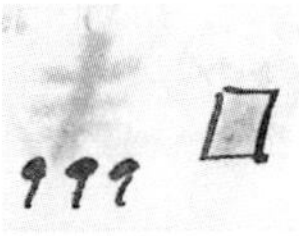

BULL PLUME #1: Many foolish children were killed.

BULL PLUME #2: Many foolish children were killed.

There is a story about a group of children who disobeyed their parents and went off to pick pine gum while they were camped in the foothills. They were all killed by Assiniboines. The story tellers are not sure if this is the same reference as the winter count. (Mrs. Buffalo & John Yellowhorn, North Peigan; author's field notes 1976)

"That afternoon they met eight Indians who proved to be Piegan, Blackfeet a tribe Lewis and his small party had wanted to avoid. They talked and all agreed to camp together that night on Two Medicine River. Lewis was awakened the next morning by sounds of a struggle as the Indians tried to make off with the expedition's guns and horses. Reubin Field stabbed one of the Indians to the heart, then the party pursued the others who were fleeing with the horses. Lewis was forced to shoot one of the Blackfeet in self-defense. It was the first and only instance of actual armed violence between the explorers and Indians in the whole expedition." [Lewis & Clark Journals, July 26, 1806]

Wolf Calf, South Peigan-Blackfoot aged 108 years, 1896 Thomas Magee photo, H. Scriver collection, author's collection.

"When I first heard of whites I was a young man *[approx. 16, ed.]*. Four Bears and Almost-a-Dog were not yet born. We started a war party from the north. We came to Birch Creek and there we met some white men camped in the bend where there is now a saloon. We camped on the knoll where the saloons now are. Chief of the war party was Sidehill-Calf. He said to his son, 'Look out for the best horse these white men have, and steal him.' Three young men went out from the camp and stole three horses. When a white man went out to look at the horses he missed these three and went back and spoke to the other whites and made a great fuss. The Indians had gone forward to meet the whites and make peace with them. When the whites discovered their horses gone all the Piegan men left except four chief men who stopped, thinking they could make the whites stop shooting. Then three of these chiefs ran and Sidehill-Calf alone remained. He was just going to start to run when two white men came up to him and killed him with their knives. Then the Piegans and white men had a battle." He can't tell how many got killed; he just knows of the one with the knife. *[Wolf-Calf (Pemmican) to Grinnell, 1890]*

1807

NORTH PEIGAN

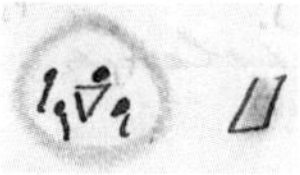

BULL PLUME #1: When all were frozen out.

BULL PLUME #2: When all were frozen out.

1808

NORTH PEIGAN

BULL PLUME #1: Getting paint and taken captive. *Near Turtle Mountain, by Crow Indians.*

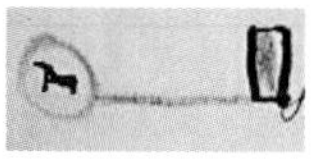

BULL PLUME #2: Getting paint and taken captive.

The location and tribe are again in pencil. There is a location for getting earth paint on the Castle River, Alberta, near Turtle Mountain, called Crow Eagle Reserve, another near Cutbank, Montana and also on Two Medicine River.

1809

NORTH PEIGAN

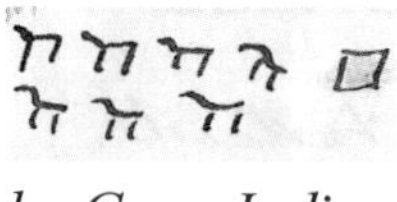

BULL PLUME #1: When many horses were taken in the night. *Stolen by Crow Indians.*

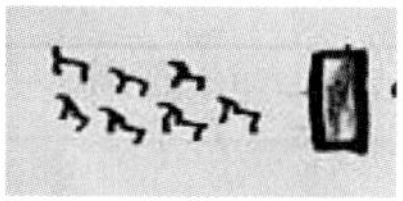

BULL PLUME #2: When many horses were taken in the night.

1810

NORTH PEIGAN

BULL PLUME #1: When "Spotted Calf" was killed.

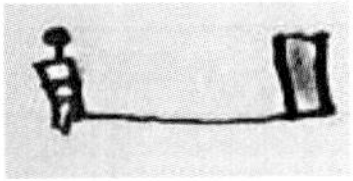

BULL PLUME #2: When "Spotted Calf" was killed.

BLOOD

At this point in our journal we add Bad Head's winter count from the Blood-Blackfoot tribe. Three copies of his winter count were made; one by Robert Wilson, second by Father Legal, and the third by Jim White Bull. Wilson's account will be used as the primary account listed as Bad Head. The Wilson and Legal copies may have come from Bad Head directly and the White Bull count came through traditional Native transference of knowledge; from Bad Head to Weasel Horse to White Bull's brother, to White Bull. In 1965 the Wilson version of the winter count was published by Hugh Dempsey, through the Glenbow-Alberta Institute. Some of his interpretations are included with the counts.

BAD HEAD
[WILSON]: (*That is the winter of 1810-1811*) Ka-orsoyixitsitotoyrpiyan
The Indians see for the first time, the horses with cropped tails of the American soldiers.

[DEMPSEY]: Cropped tails/when they came. *This was probably the Astoria expedition under Wilson P. Hunt which passed just south of Blackfeet country in the summer of 1811. Irving (1897:187) observed that the party cropped the tails of horses purchased from the Arikara so as to distinguish them from Indian ponies.*

It could also be when Fort Henry or Three Forks, was built between the Jefferson and Madison Rivers. Pierre Menard of the St. Louis Missouri Fur Company built the fort in hopes of trapping the area and establishing peaceful relations with the Blackfoot. In April two groups of trappers set out from the post. Within ten miles of the fort one group was attacked and killed or captured five of the 18 men. Later that month a second group lost three men to the Gros Ventre and Bloods. Members of these groups arrived at Rocky Mountain House with considerable materials from their encounters with the American "trespassers". [Smyth, 2001; 368-369]

1811

NORTH PEIGAN

BULL PLUME #1: When we were driven in battle. *By the Crees.*

BULL PLUME #2: When they were driven in battle.

"By the Crees." is again added in pencil at a later date.

In 1807 David Thompson established trade relations with the Flathead and Kutenai tribes west of the mountains, despite attempts by the Peigan to stop them. This meant that for the first time the Westside people had access to the guns of the white traders in large quantities. " The Salish Indians during the winter (of 1809-1810) had traded upwards of twenty guns from me, with which they thought themselves a fair match for the Peeagan Indians in battle on the Plains. In the month of July when the Bison Bulls are getting fat, they formed a camp of about one hundred and fifty men to hunt and make dried Provisions as I had requested them;... they crossed the Mountains by a wide defile of easy passage, eastward of the Saleesh Lake (Flathead Lake) here they are watched by the Peeagans to prevent them hunting the Bison, and driven back, and could only hunt as it were by stealth; the case was now different, and they were determined to hunt boldly and try a battle with them: they were entering on the grounds, when the scouts, as usual, early each morning sent to view the country came riding at full speed, calling out, 'the Enemy is on us;' instantly down went the Tents, and tent poles, which, with the Baggage formed a rude rampart; this was barely done, when a steady charge of cavalry came on them, but the Horses did not break through the rampart, part of pointed poles, each party discharged their arrows, which only wounded a few, none fell; a second and third charge, was made; but in a weak manner; the battle was now to be of infantry. The Saleesh, about one hundred and fifty men, took possession of a slightly rising ground about half a mile in front of their Tents, the Peeagans, about one hundred seventy men drew up and formed a rude line about four hundred yards from them; the Saleesh and the white Men lay quiet on the defensive; the Peeagans, from time to time throughout the day, sent parties of about forty men forward, to dare them to battle; these would often approach to within sixty to eighty yards, insulting them as old women,.. the evening ended the battle; on the part of the Peeagans, seven killed and thirteen wounded; on the part of the Saleesh, five killed and nine wounded; each party took care of their dead and wounded; no scalps were taken, which the Peeagans accounted a disgrace to them;... This was the first time the Peeagans were in a manner defeated, and they determined to wreck their vengeance on the white men who crossed the mountains to the west side; and furnished arms and ammunition to their Enemies." (Thompson; 1916; 423-424)

Flathead warrior, unknown photographer, author's collection

BLOOD

BAD HEAD: Orkesay aseniwitomotsarpi "Crying Bear" has been destroyed.

WHITE BULL: The year Crying Bear was been destroyed by the Cree Indians up north.

1812

NORTH PEIGAN

BULL PLUME #1: When we fought with the Crees.

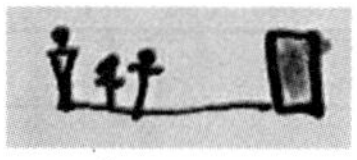

BULL PLUME #2: When they fought with the Crees.

[The drawing symbol for the Assiniboine, is shown in both Bull Plume Winter Counts (i.e. Cutthroats), ed.]

BLOOD

BAD HEAD: Ekartsiw otsenik Kotorxispettapi The Gambler has been killed by a Flathead Indian.

WHITE BULL: Gambler was been killed by a Flathead Indian in west.

DEMPSEY: *In April, 1813, the traders at Edmonton House reported that "...the Bloods and Blackfeet are determined to steal every Horse belonging to White Men in revenge for the death of their Relations, fifty of whom have been killed by the Flat Heads since last summer (1812). White Men, they say, by supplying the Flat Heads with Arms, are the principal cause of their great loss." (Edmonton House entry for April 28, 1813)*

1813

NORTH PEIGAN

BULL PLUME #1: When "Crazy Dog" was killed.

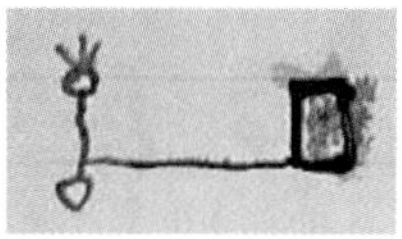

BULL PLUME #2: When "Crazy Dog" was killed.

BLOOD

BAD HEAD: Itakesaopi Many went on the War Path

WHITE BULL: Many Blood Indians went on war path to Crow Indians on near Sheep River or Big Horn River in Montana.

1814

NORTH PEIGAN

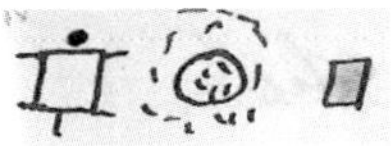

BULL PLUME #1: Great battle with the Peigans.

BULL PLUME #2: Great battle with the Peigans.

The symbols drawn here show a buffalo hide and a circle indicating a camp or battle position, surrounded by lines indicating people.

BLOOD

BAD HEAD: Ikinay itsenitarpi Top Knot has been killed.

WHITE BULL: Air Top was been killed by Crow Indians in Little Big Horn River in Montana.

1815

NORTH PEIGAN

BULL PLUME #1: Fight in the thin bush.

BULL PLUME #2: Fight in the thin bush.

The drawings, with the forked center pole, show this was during a Sun Dance

BLOOD

BAD HEAD: Matsi pokanitomotsarpi Mad children destroyed by the Crees on Belly River.

WHITE BULL: Mad Child has been destroyed by Cree Indians on lower Belly River

LEGAL: *Mad Child was a Blood Indian who was killed by Crees on the banks of the Belly River, not far from the site of the first Blood Agency.*

DEMPSEY: *This may be the incident reported by traders in the summer of 1815 when a Cree and Assiniboine war party attacked a camp of twenty Blood and Sarsi lodges, killing four men and a woman. The Bloods retaliated and by winter several had been killed on each side. (Edmonton Houses entry for Oct. 11, 1815)*

1816

NORTH PEIGAN

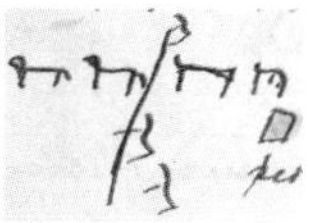

BULL PLUME #1: When the Peigans broke the River Peoples' line of march.

BULL PLUME #2: When the Peigans broke the River Peoples' line of march.

The Peigans came upon a camp of Pend d'Oreilles on the move, and attacked

BLOOD

BAD HEAD: Asekarsin tsenitarpi A Blood Indian named "Extending His Paw" had been killed by another Blood.

WHITE BULL: Blood Indians named "Extending His Teeth" has been killed by another Blood Indian.

1817

NORTH PEIGAN

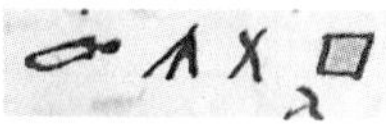

BULL PLUME #1: When "Red Crow" half frozen went into camp and was killed.

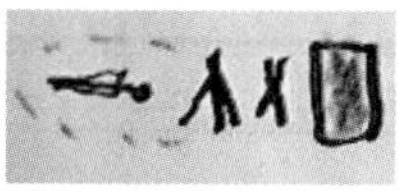

BULL PLUME #2: When "Red Crow" half frozen went into camp and was killed.

Red Crow [not the Blood chief] set up camp instead of pushing on to the main camp. The enemy found him and killed him.

BLOOD

BAD HEAD: Ominis itsenitarpu "Buffalo Paunch" killed by his brother.

WHITE BULL: Buffalo Paunch killed by his own brother.

1818

NORTH PEIGAN

 BULL PLUME #1: When "Wolf Child" was set upon.

 BULL PLUME #2: When "Wolf Child" was set upon.

BLOOD

BAD HEAD: Stokan The Blood Indians had their Sun-dance in the winter time.

WHITE BULL: Blood Indians had their Sun Lodge in winter time.

DEMPSEY: *The Sun Dance was usually held in early summer when the Saskatoon berries were ripe. On this occasion, a winter camp of Bloods on Sheep River was in danger of being attacked by war parties of Crees. A holy woman vowed that if they were spared from harm she would sponsor a Sun Dance immediately. When no attack came, the ritual was held.*

Another version, still told on the Blood Reserve, identifies the attackers as Crow Indians.

1819

NORTH PEIGAN

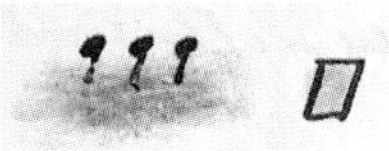 BULL PLUME #1: When 3 persons were frozen to death.

BULL PLUME #2: When three persons were frozen to death.

BLOOD

BAD HEAD: Saskinapastsimesin Coughing epidemic

WHITE BULL: Blood Indians had been sick with the Coughing epidemic.

DEMPSEY: *In the winter of 1819-20, traders at Edmonton House reported that a measles epidemic had wiped out one third of the Blackfoot and Gros Ventre tribes. (Edmonton House entries for Feb. 6 and March 15, 1820)*

1820

NORTH PEIGAN

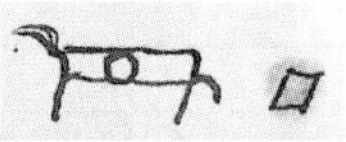

BULL PLUME #1: When the Big White Bellied horse was taken.

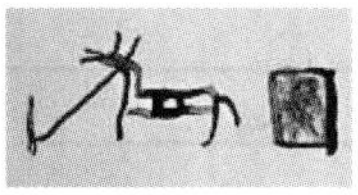

BULL PLUME #2: When the Big White Bellied horse was taken.

This would be a very famous race horse or buffalo running horse.

BLOOD

BAD HEAD: Nis-otokinay itsenitarpi "Four Horns" killed by a Pend d'Oreille

WHITE BULL: Four Horns was killed by South Peigans

DEMPSEY: *He was a North Peigan who was killed by a Pend d'Oreille Indian.*

1821

NORTH PEIGAN

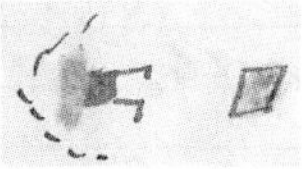

BULL PLUME #1: When "The Dwarf" fell through the ice.

BULL PLUME #2: When "The Dwarf" fell through the ice.

BLOOD

BAD HEAD: Katookinaw itsenew A great chief "No Top Knot" dies.

WHITE BULL: A great chief

1822

NORTH PEIGAN

BULL PLUME #1: When "One Cutting" hung himself.

BULL PLUME #2: When "One Cutting" hung himself.

BLOOD

BAD HEAD: Ekkakiw otsipsitapipi etotoartay A White man named by the Indian the small or short man takes a place at the confluence of Musselshell and the Missouri river.

WHITE BULL: White man named by the Blood Indians "Short Man" in Missouri River.

DEMPSEY: Limping/when he first came here/where the rivers meet.

Wilson was told that the winter count referred to a fort built at the mouth of the Yellowstone by Andrew Henry and W.H. Ashley. Legal, on the other hand, was informed the post was at the confluence of the Red Deer and Belly Rivers. [This was Chesterfield House, established for the Hudson's Bay Co. by Donald McKenzie (1800).]

1823

NORTH PEIGAN

BULL PLUME #1: When "Bull Horse" shot himself.

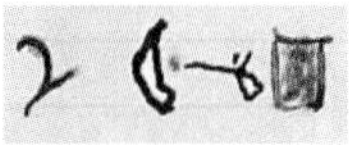

BULL PLUME #2: When "Bull Horse" shot himself.

BLOOD

BAD HEAD: Innospiw otsitesenipi "When Long Hair died"

WHITE BULL: Blood Indian his name Long Hair died that year

1824

NORTH PEIGAN

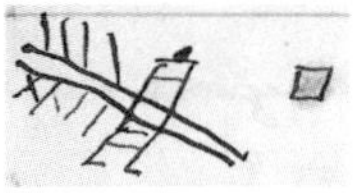

BULL PLUME #1: When "Spotted" was killed by the falling of a tree.

BULL PLUME #2: When "Spotted" was killed by the falling of a tree.

BLOOD

BAD HEAD: Sapo Nit-omatapiskotspi The Bloods drove away the Crows

1825

NORTH PEIGAN

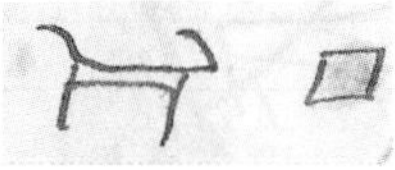

BULL PLUME #1: When they eat dogs. *Buffalo had gone south, so they had to eat their dogs.*

BULL PLUME #2: When they eat dogs.

To the Blackfoot there was nothing quite as disgusting as eating dog. They must have been on the edge of starvation to be forced into this position.

BLOOD

BAD HEAD: Itaka-ennastop Several Indian tribes make a treaty of peace: Bloods, Gros Ventres, Koutonais and Nez-perces.

WHITE BULL: Several Indian tribes make a treaty of peace with Short Man. Blood Indians, Gros Ventres Indians, Flat Head Indians and Nez Perces Indians, South Peigans Indians, near Yellowstone River.

DEMPSEY: *On Sept. 22, 1825 Peter Skene Ogden (Rich, 1950:85), of the Hudson's Bay Co. traveling with a large party of Flatheads, recorded making a treaty with a camp of two hundred lodges of Bloods and a few Gros Ventres and Peigans.*

"For two or three months my old father and the other chiefs had been making plans to get together a great party of braves to go to war across the mountains, to capture women and children and to kill enemies and get horses. As made up at last the party numbered 632 warriors. There were Gros Ventres 200, Piegans 200, and the rest were Bloods and Blackfeet.

Rising Head was a great warrior, a brave man. His name before had been Little-Foxes-Medicine. The old father and the other Indians tried to keep me back. They said it was going to be a big war party. There would be plenty of danger. 'It is foolish to go,' they said. 'Indians will kill you. Your relations will cry.' But I said, 'I want to go. I want to travel and see the country.' I did not want to kill Indians and take scalps, but I wanted excitement.

We started, I with my old father Rising Head, from the Beaverhead River. A war party goes pretty slowly and we traveled most of the time in the night, on account of the sun which during the day was hot as fire. We saw some trails of Indians – old ones on which it had rained, or into which the dust had blown. We passed through the country occupied by many tribes of Indians, but saw none, and at last we came to where I could see the Salt Lake. We were all on horseback. I had two horses. At length we turned about to go home, having made no war. Returning we came to a place between the Snake and Flathead country called Kut-o-yis [clot of blood]. *(Near Dell, Montana towards the Idaho Montana line, a butte sticks out onto the plains around it. In the setting sun it turns blood red and one can easily see why it was named "Clot-of-Blood.)* One night we sent out scouts to look over the country and see if they could see anything. One of these scouts came in and said that they had seen a white man riding a horse. The people were discouraged and wanted to go home. They said, 'We have no luck.' They killed about 300 beaver.

I said to my father, 'Well, let us go home, but first I will go out and try to find these people. I would like to have a new shirt, some ammunition, and some tobacco.' They tried to prevent me by saying, 'Come on, we will go home and go to the Fort and get what you need. Do not go to see them. They may rush on you and kill you.' But I started and a band of braves went with me, but by and by they all turned back, and I went on alone. I had a good horse and a good gun, a double barreled pistol and a good knife in my belt.

The whites must have seen me coming and been watching me through a spy glass. I went on, and presently saw a dust rising and thought some Indians must be running buffalo. Over a hill came a white man riding on a big brown horse and behind him a big Flathead Indian, naked as when he was born, but with bow and arrows. After him rode six more Indians. This white man was named Dixon. I had been with him at school in Montreal. I was nearly naked and looked like an Indian and he did not know me. He called out in English, 'Who are you? Is it war or peace?' and he rode on. I was vexed that he should ride on without stopping to speak with me, and I thought to myself, 'Ah, my friend, before night your head may be on the ground. I can make it war or I can make it peace, as I please.'

After him followed these Flathead Indians charging down on me. Their chief was in the lead. He was naked; a feather was tied about his waist, and he wore a bull's horn war bonnet, one horn of which was painted red, the other green. He had a bow and arrows, and carried in his hand a big hatchet which he held up in the air, and as he rode along he was making a prayer. I did not know whether his prayer was good or bad. I got off my horse and waited, having all my arms ready. I depended most upon my knife. If he made a charge on me I could rip him up. I did not know just what to do. I was doubtful. He had yellow hair and a good face. He rode up to me and sprung off his horse and coming up to me held out his hand to shake hands with me. I gave him my left hand, for I was holding my pistol and knife in my right. When he took my hand, he held it up to heaven and made a prayer. Then all my bad feelings went down. I felt that when my hand was held up to heaven, I was safe. There were six Indians with him, a Flathead, a Nez Perce, a Pend d'Oreille, a Snake and others representing seven different tribes in all. All these six came up and shook my hand, and each held it up to heaven and made a prayer. Then they wanted me to sit down and smoke and make peace. I was a little afraid to do so, but it was alright.

We sat down. Dixon had ridden a wide circle, and presently he came back. His horse was wild and two of the Indians got up and caught a long line that was dragging from the horse's neck and stopped him. Dixon dismounted and came towards me. I got up holding my knife in my hand, for I was afraid of him. He looked mean. When he came up to me, he knew me at once. He said, 'In the name of God, what brings you here?' I answered, 'In the name of God, what brings you?' Then we talked. He said, 'Are you alone?' I pointed off to the east and said, 'Do you see those four pines over there on that ridge? Behind that point is a creek, and on that creek are some Blackfeet, many, many. I am with them.' Then Dixon said, 'There was a poor white man of our party killed three days ago.' I said, 'I can't help that. I know nothing about that. The Blackfeet will soon be here. When I left camp I said to my father, 'Don't move till I come. If I do not come, if I am killed, do as you please.'

Dixon said, 'There are 112 persons in my camp trapping beaver for Sublette. The Blackfeet may attack us. What shall we do?' I said, 'Get on your horse and come with me.'

We started and rode mile after mile without stopping. At last when we rode over a hill we saw the Blackfeet, with the soldiers in the lead. Before I left camp I had said to Rising Head, 'If I am killed, you can go avenge me on white or red, but if you see me coming with a white man, try to be good and kind and keep the young men from doing anything bad.' The Blackfeet were coming with war bonnets on their heads. They looked fierce – like devils. Dixon was frightened. I said to him, 'Come on.'

We rode up to the soldiers and I jumped off my horse and made a speech. I said, 'Father, I have always heard that you were a great and powerful chief and could do anything you pleased. Now here is my brother, he was a little boy when I left home. I hope that you will not harm him. I have not seen his camp, but I hear that there are other white men there. Do not harm them. Take pity on them and pity me. If you hurt them you hurt me.'

The Indians with Dixon were coming on. I said to him, 'I am afraid those Indians will be cut to pieces. I should not like to have them killed. They have been good and kind to me. Tell them to go back, for God's sake.' They came on, and as they came the Flathead chief held up his hand to heaven and said, 'Glorious day. I am glad to die today by the hand of my enemies.' I called out to the Father of All in a loud voice, speaking in Blackfoot so that all might understand and prayed saying, 'Now Father, let me know today how great a chief you are and do not let these Indians be cut up. I hope that you will come down and put a new heart in all these people, so that there shall be no harm done to these seven Indians.' I called out to the chief, 'Now father, give life to these poor Indians who have been good and kind to me, that the Father of All may take pity on you and give you life in battle.' The Blackfeet listened to what I said and no one tried to harm these Indians. They all seemed friendly.

Then I said to my old father, 'I will go to their camp. You come and follow me and do not let any one be harmed.' I called out to a Gros Ventres named Crow Bull, to a Blood chief, and to a Blackfoot, 'Have pity on me and help me.'

I rode off and went to the white men's camp, and found the people half dead with fear. They were so frightened they could not talk, for they had learned that the Blackfoot war party was coming. When the Blackfeet came up, I called out to rising Head: 'Now my father do not stop here, but pass on to a good camping place beyond, where you can stop and dance all day and all night.' All the night I had about one hundred men of my party stationed about the camp, helping me to watch.

Next day I called Peter Ogden and said, 'Put down in a pile all the tobacco and Ammunition you have.' They did so, putting down a big keg of powder, two big rolls of tobacco, and two bags and a half of balls. This was put to one side and the Blackfeet called up. As each man came up he threw down what beaver skins he had, and I measured out the goods, weighing the powder and ball. All night I worked trading. The party of white men were well paid for their goods for in the morning there were 240 beaver skins. As the Indians traded they got on their horses and rode off, and at last it came near the end, and there were left only myself and a few head men. Then the Ogden party cooked a lot of food and asked us to help ourselves. They gave me a lot of old clothes.

After we had done smoking, my old father jumped up and danced a war dance about me as if I had really defeated this party. They wanted to change my name, but I said, 'No, Rising Wolf is my name and Rising Wolf let it remain so long as I walk the plains.' *[Hugh Monroe to Grinnell, ca. 1890; manuscript, Southwest Museum, Los Angeles.]*

"In 1825 the Cheyennes and Arapahos were all still living north of the Platte, near the Black Hills. In that year or the next the Gros Ventres came down from Canada to visit their kinsmen, the Arapahos, and with those Gros Ventres came eighteen or twenty young Blackfeet. These young Blackfeet were all men, they had no women with them. They said their tribe had been fighting with the whites up in Canada, their relatives were all dead, they did not care to stay in Canada any longer, and so had come down to live with the Cheyennes and Arapahos and to steal horses from the Kiowas and Comanches, as they had heard these tribes were very rich in horses…The Gros Ventres returned to Canada some years later, but the Blackfeet never went back. Most of them married into the Cheyenne and Arapaho tribes, and their children and grand-children are still living with us down here."*[Colony, Oklahoma, ca.1905, ed.] [George Bent, Hyde,1968,32,]*

1826

NORTH PEIGAN

BULL PLUME #1: Mange amongst cattle.

This obviously refers to buffalo and not cattle.

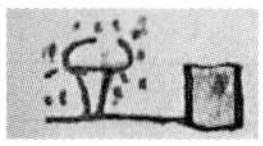

BULL PLUME #2: Mange amongst the Buffalo.

BLOOD

BAD HEAD: Nisa-orkokinisiw itomaraikamotspi Sapo The Bloods stole a great number of horses from the Crows near the butte called "Goose Neck".

WHITE BULL: Blood Indians captured a great number of horses from the Crow Indians, the butte called Strong Goose Neck Butte.

DEMPSEY: Strong Goose Neck, or more correctly Merganser Neck, is a butte located just west of Belt, Montana.

1827

NORTH PEIGAN

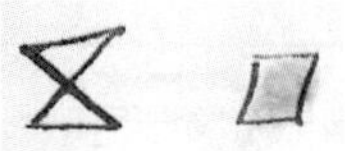

BULL PLUME #1: When the ground was covered with ice.

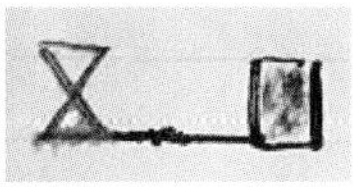 BULL PLUME #2: When the ground was covered with ice.

BLOOD

BAD HEAD: Ttaka-eniskoyew Many died

WHITE BULL: Many Bloods Indians died that year with sickness

1828

NORTH PEIGAN

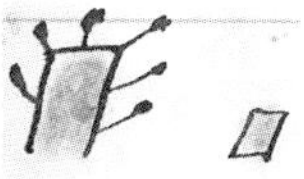 BULL PLUME #1: When the Peigans lost the battle.

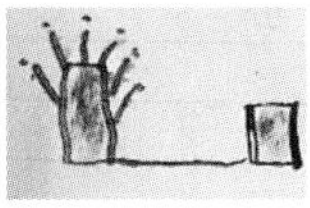 BULL PLUME #2: When the Peigans lost the battle.

Oct. 1828 Peigans battled Crow, Shoshone & American trappers "In October 1828, word arrived at Edmonton House of a battle pitting the Piikani against the Crow and Shoshone, and also of the killing of some 18 more American trappers by the Blackfoot alliance." [Smyth, 201; 413]

BLOOD

BAD HEAD: Sapo-Maxika itsonitarpi A chief named Crow-Foot was killed by a Crow Indian

WHITE BULL: A chief named Crow Foot was killed by a Crow Indians in war path

DEMPSEY: *Crowfoot (properly Crow Big Foot) was the leader of a party of fourteen Blackfoot ambushed and killed while en route to a peace parley with the Shoshone. The event occurred south of the Missouri River. In later years the name Crowfoot was taken by another man who eventually became chief of the North Blackfoot. (Dempsey, 1959)*

NORTH BLACKFEET

Here the Crane Bear winter count starts and gives us a North Blackfeet [Siksika] viewpoint.

CRANE BEAR: Blackfoot Crowfoot was born that year, at the time when the cherries were ripe.

[Running Rabbit and Little Chief give the date for Crowfoot's birth as 1830. The other events follow in order with Crane Bear's starting two years earlier than the others, including Many Guns'. ed.]

1829

NORTH PEIGAN

BULL PLUME #1: When the Peigans fought with the Elks. *In the states.*

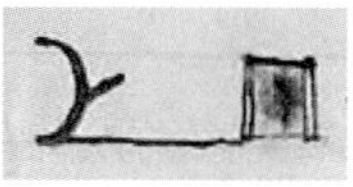

BULL PLUME #2: When they fought with Elk Horses.

More than likely this is the Arikara who are called "horns" or "elk" referring to their manner of wearing the hair with two pieces of bone standing up. (Swanton, BAE Bulletin 145; 1952; 273)

Little Brave, Arikara. photo courtesy "G.A.Custer, His Life and Times"

BLOOD

BAD HEAD: Ikitsiketapi otsitomotsarpi Seven Crow Indians have been destroyed on the American border.

WHITE BULL: Seven Crow Indians destroyed by Blood Indians on near American border. Two guards that night over them, one of them is Eagle Runner and other one is Gros-man. Calf Shirt's father captured medicine axe.

DEMPSEY: Seven Persons/have been destroyed.

This winter count is remembered by modern Bloods because of a coincidence associated with it. In 1829, seven Crow Indians were killed near Buffalo Horn Butte, a short distance west of Chinook, Montana. The Bloods were led by Spotted Bear, who captured a pipe-hatchet during the fight. About forty years later, Calf Shirt, a son of Spotted Bear, led a war party which killed seven Crees and he also took a pipe-hatchet (White Bull). The later event is recorded in the White Bull winter count for 1870 and Seven Persons Creek, in south-eastern Alberta, is named for the incident.

NORTH BLACKFEET

CRANE BEAR: Buffalo – Wolf Peace – Blackfeet and their enemies both dread making war on each other, and make peace that year, in time for the hunt.

[1831, Running Rabbit & Little Chief; 1832 Many Guns, ed.]

1830

NORTH PEIGAN

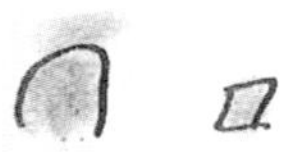

BULL PLUME #1: Deep snow.

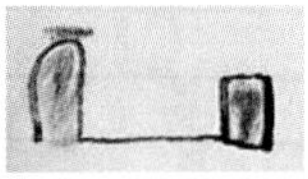

BULL PLUME #2: Deep snow.

BLOOD

BAD HEAD: Itenepitsop Very sever winter. Many go on the war path and are frozen to death

DEMPSEY: When we were freezing.

NORTH BLACKFEET

RUNNING RABBIT: White Flathead: Crowfoot born

LITTLE CHIEF: The year 1830 White Flat Head also Crowfoot were born. Flat Head was a Blood Indian his father and mother were both Bloods.

Crowfoot's mother was a Blood woman and his father was a Blackfoot. Crowfoot was born at the Bloods. He stayed at the Bloods till he was about four or five years then this Many Manes came to the Bloods and took Crowfoot back to Blackfoot Crossing and he was given the name Bear Ghost. He grow up a fine young man when he was old enough to ride that is about eight or nine years he learned how to ride a horse after he learned how to shoot with bow and arrow til he was a chief of the Blackfeet.

CRANE BEAR: Low on the Red Deer River, at a place Also known as Morkinistres, the Elbow, a Blackfeet, Ninnapeksew *(Chief Bird, ed.)* won a victory over Crees who attacked him. *(1833, MANY GUNS, ed.)*

CHAPTER 6

SHIFTING TIDES AND THE BEGINNING OF CHANGE

Pressure began to build on the eastern front of Blackfoot country. The merger of the Hudson's Bay Company with the Northwest Company released two-thirds of their work force, the majority being Metis. They soon formed groups of their own, or joined the Woods Cree and Bush Ojibwa in moving onto the plains permanently. As pressure on the eastern buffalo hunting grounds of the Blackfoot, and the opening of trade with the Americans, began it changed the lifestyle and locations of the Blackfoot in response.

1831

NORTH PEIGAN

BULL PLUME #1: When the whites from the South and North met.

BULL PLUME #2: When the whites from the South and North met.

This was the establishment of the first American post among the Blackfoot – Fort Peigan- at the mouth of the Marias River. In 1830, Jacob [Jacques] Berger, a former employee of the Hudson's Bay Company, and a fluent Blackfoot speaker, led a small party of four men and a trading outfit provided by the American Fur Company into the Blackfoot country. Considered a "suicide mission", he convinced Kenneth McKenzie, superintendent of the Upper Missouri Outfit of the American Fur Company, that he could establish trade with the hostile Blackfoot. Meeting with several Piikani who recognized him, he was invited to the main camp and spent the next twenty-two days distributing liberal gifts and reciting the prices the Company would pay for furs. He managed to convince ninety-two men and thirty-two women to return to Fort Union with him. There, after being treated royally by McKenzie, they invited him to establish a trading post in Blackfoot country. Traders, who would be invited guests and protected, were welcome but poaching trappers would never be allowed. In the spring of 1831 construction was started on the fort [Fort Peigan]. Under James Kipp the fort offered higher prices than the Canadian companies and in a very few days obtained 6,450 pounds of beaver skins. (Bradley; Book "F"; 244-247) This would be roughly 19,350 beaver skins.

There was also another encounter between the HBC and American traders. In the summer of 1832 Chief Trader and Factor John Rowland of Edmonton House, took a group down into American territory to meet with the Peigans. He hoped to convince them to return to trade with HBC and not the Americans. While camped in the south he was visited by James [Jimmy Jock] Bird a former employee of the HBC and recently working for the American Fur Trade Company.[Smyth, 2001;442-444]

While the Hudson's Bay Company considered Bird a traitor, the Blackfoot people considered him one of them, and looking out for their best interests. His actions in this instance, as well as others in the future, prove that he was indeed working for the interests of the Blackfoot People.

James Bird, Gustav Sohon drawing, 1855, Washington State Historical Society, Tacoma, WA.

This may also be the year Brings-Down-The-Sun was born. He told McClintock he was born the year "...when white men were seen for the first time in our country." (McClintock; 1968; 423)

BLOOD

BAD HEAD: Kipp otsitsitapipi etotartay A white man named Kipp established a post at the confluence of Bear River and the Missouri.

DEMPSEY: Kipp/when he lived there/where the rivers meet.

In October, 1831, James Kipp and seventy-five men established Fort Peigan at the confluence of the Missouri and Marias Rivers. (Chittenden, 1954, 333)

PERCY CREIGHTON: White Flat Head (Abs ok kinay) a well known headman who acted as leader. With a war party he pursued the Cree and made a big killing west of Red Deer.

NORTH BLACKFEET

YELLOW FLY: The year when "White Direct Head", famous warrior. Trailed his enemy and killed him. Crowfoot a year old

RUNNING RABBIT: Their peace with the wolf

MANY GUNS: Isatsima = to follow late, people went to war. Itsuyoxkomi = a man, follow 4 days late to the war party.

MANY GUNS 65.68: Roaring In The Water

MANY GUNS 65.69: The Scrapper and Making Sound In The Water

LITTLE CHIEF: In the year 1831 the Blackfeet had a lot of enemies of which they fought in that year the Blackfeet had a fight with the Iroquois which were bitter enemies of them they fought with the Hurons after they fought with Iroquois after that fight with the Iroquois the Hurons Indians their chief his name was Wolf made peace with the Blackfeet. *[This is obviously a very confused interpretation.]*

CRANE BEAR: Big House [*One of the American forts?, ed]* The Crows made their Sun Dance in winter, and defeated the Blackfeet, Blood and Cree.

In 1831 Josiah Gregg encountered "Arapahoes, Gros Ventres, and Blackfeet were assembled in great numbers on the Cimarron River". [estimated to number two to three thousand with five hundred tipis] This is in Oklahoma near the Colorado border. [Gregg, pp227-28, 231-32, 1954] They were still there in 1835 as recorded by Col. Dodge. [Dodge,140-144, 1835]

"In August, 1825, seven hundred families of Blackfoots visited the Arapahoes, and remained with or near them until the ensuing summer..." [W.H. Ashley, 1831] Authors and scholars have long debated on the identity of these people with many claiming them to be all Gros Ventre, with only a few Blackfeet. The following story told by Little Light of the North Blackfeet [Siksika] in 1938, sheds light on this important historic event.

Leaders of the All Brave Dogs Society dance in camp, 1920, H.F. Robinson photo, author's collection

All Brave Dogs,1920, H.F. Robinson photo, author's collection

Acustie, Leader of the North Peigan All Brave Dogs wearing the leader's dog skin necklace around his neck. c. 1895, Steele & Company, Winnipeg. Glenbow Archives

"The Dog society *[All Brave Dogs, ed]* came from tribes living in the east ["*down stream" in Blackfoot, ed.]*. It is not a very important society *[meaning within the religious structure of the Blackfeet, ed.]*. There was one band called the Omakxkiatsimani. *[Big Dried Food Case People, ed.]* There was a good looking bachelor in the Siyaks name Mixkoksi who was son of the chief of the band. He had something to do with the wife of the chief of the Omax. This woman was a frightful liar. She told her husband, the chief of the Omax, that Mixkoksi had stopped her while she was getting water and told her he wished to know her better. But that was not true. The woman had made it up. Mixkoksi did not know anything about it. This did not seem to bother her husband. But at another time the wife said she went for some water and Mixkoksi stopped her and made love and asked her to go with him. She said she was going to tell her husband about the affair. But Mixkoksi said, the husband is not ikstoyisanaps. *[a "respected person", iktoyisanaps, ed.]* When the husband heard this, that made him mad. He was going to kill the bachelor.

There was a hoop and dart game. This was just a game. There were no societies playing. The husband was lying on his stomach watching when he saw Mixkoksi. But Mixkoksi did not see him. He was lying on his stomach watching too. The husband got one of the long tent pegs, put on a robe, and hid the tent peg under the robe. The husband came and stood at the feet of Mixkoksi and said; 'I thought I was ikstoyisanaps, but you said I wasn't.' Mixkoksi knew nothing about it and asked what he meant. The husband said; 'You know what I mean.' He hit Mixkoksi on the head and knocked him out. Just as he was going to give him a 2nd blow, the crowd stopped and held him. After this the husband went home. The bachelor was taken home, and the dent in his skull was pulled out. Then he came back to consciousness. Then Mixkoksi asked a man from another band who was chief of the band, 'you go and tell the man I don't know why he hit me.' The husband told the messenger that it was funny Mixkoksi did not know why he was hit. Mixkoksi had tried to make love to his wife twice and had said that the husband was not iksoyisanaps. The messenger went back to Mixkoksi's lodge and told the chief of the Siyaks that Mixkoksi, his son, was in wrong, that he had tried to make love two times to the wife of the chief of the Omaks and had called him no iksoyisanaps. Mixkoksi said the woman was lying, that he had only seen her from a distance and that he had been injured for nothing. The messenger went home. Mixkoksi told his father that if the story were true he would not have cared. But since it was not, he would go and kill the man who had hit him for nothing.

When Mixkoksi's wound was all healed, he told his father to have the Siyaks go up north to the wood lands and that he would stay and kill the man that hit him. The chief told the herald to announce to the band that in the morning they would break camp and go. When morning came, Mixkoksi went a little way and stopped and said he was going with his little brother. The rest should hurry and go way up north. Then Mixkoksi told his little brother to wait until he should return, even if it were a long time. Mixkoksi went toward evening back to the camp of the Omax and hid near it. From his hiding spot at night Mixkoksi went to the chief's lodge. Mixkoksi had some dry grass in his pocket and a rifle. When he got in the chief was snoring. Mixkoksi put some grass on the fire to give him a light , took a good aim at the chief and shot him. Mixkoksi fled out of the lodge and went back to his little brother. Mixkoksi told him that he had shot the chief and that they should beat it. They kept going but did not catch up with the band until they were at the wood landing the north. Then he told that he had killed the chief of the Omax. The band of the dead chief did not follow but stayed where they were. The Siyaks came to the Sun Dance of the Crees. The leaders said to their enemies that they were going to go around with the Crees because they had killed a chief. The Siyaks stayed so long among the Crees that men and women spoke Cree just as good as Blackfoot.

There were four young bachelors of the Omax who resolved to find Mixkoksi and kill him. They thought the Siyaks were with the Crees because they had not been seen for so long. One of the bachelors was the best friend on Mixkoksi; his name was Oxksksowatsimi [Many Feathers]. Oxksksowatsimi the oldest of the four, said that Mixkoksi was a kind of fellow who can do anything when he is mad. They went to the Crees and arrived on a night when there was going to be a big smoking ceremony among the Siyaks. Mixkoksi was not there but over visiting the Crees. The four bachelors from the Omax looked in the lodge where the smoking ceremony was being held. They looked into each lodge too but could not find Mixkoksi. The second oldest of the bachelors said that they should find Mixkoksi's father and kill him instead of Mixkoksi.

Oxksksowatsimi didn't agree to it. Oxksksowatsimi said, it would back on them if they killed the father because he was an old religious man. If you kill the father I will beat it. Oxksksowatsimi and one other went away. The remaining two went to the back of the lodge where the smoking ceremony was being held, cut a hole just behind Mixkoksi's father and shot him in the back of the neck. Oxksksowatsimi and the other had left. When the chief of the Siyaks was killed, all agreed to follow. But it was too dark.
They decided to wait for day light. That night all the good horses were tied up ready for the morning. Then they started in the morning. The fellows did not see the killer because they passed him. The one was slower than the other. The killer was left behind. When they stopped for a rest, they saw a fellow running toward them. They shot the fellow and did what they wanted with his body. *[Little Light commented that bad luck followed the killer by giving him a slower pace. Hanks]*. The three remaining refugees went back to the Omax camp and told the result of the trip. They had not killed Mixkoksi but the chief of the Siyaks. The three had tried to stop the killer, but he had not agreed and had killed the chief. Then he was killed [the killer]. The new chief of the Omax said the Siyaks were dangerous when they get angered. It was only right that the remaining three should leave the Blackfoot camp and go down south. The chief of the Omax said they would go down south too. They were afraid of the Siyaks. One girl from the Siyaks had married a man from the Omax. They had children. As they were about to go the woman said she would stay. The man agreed to say with his children, even if the Siyaks should kill him. The Omax did not travel in the day because they were afraid of the Snakes and the Crows. They came finally to a tribe of Blackfeet. *[The name of the tribe is unknown, but they are said to speak the same language and live in the south. Hanks]*

After two years the Siyaks had said that they would come back and fight the Omax. The Siyaks did not know the other band had left. 20 men were going to come over to the Blackfoot camp for the Omax. The rest would stay and camp. The Siyaks numbered about 200 in all. The 20 men of the Siyaks came over and looked for the Blackfoot camp. One would go out and scout. They found the camp near the Bow River. The scout went back and told the rest. They sneaked up and stayed near until morning. Then they saw a man and his wife riding out. The woman had his fast horse behind her and rode another. He was going out for buffalo. Some one said he would go and ask the man where the Omax was, and the rest should charge on them. Maybe the man was not an Omax, and they should not charge him. The man and the woman were the ones that stayed back and did not go with the Omax., but the 20 Siyaks did not know that. They saw the man get off his horse and get on the fast horse. The man gave the slow horse to his wife. He started out and shot some buffalo that ran toward the 20 Siyaks. They recognized the horse as one that had been given to the Brother in law of one of them. They made signs to him that they were not enemies from another tribe and then went up and greeted him with a kiss. The woman came along afterwards. The man told the 20 Siyaks to sit down, that they would have a meal. When the woman came, the woman stopped. The man made a sign for her to come, that here were her relatives. She was very glad to see them because she had not seen them for a long time. Mixkoksi was the oldest of the 20 Siyaks. Mixkoksi asked if the Omax was still at the camp. The man said the Omax had fled to the other Blackfoot tribe in the south. Mixkoksi said they would come and look for the Omax some other time. It would be better to bring the Siyaks to the rest of the tribe since the enemy were not there. The 20 Siyaks went to the camp of the brother in law and rested their horses. Then they wet north and told the people that the Omax had fled. When the Siyaks went back to their camp, it was found that the Siyaks were talking Cree rather than Blackfoot.

When the Siyaks had been with the tribe for a year, the Omax had been with the other Blackfoot for one year. Then they had seen the dance of the Crazy Dogs *[the All Brave Dogs, ed]*. They liked it and learned all the songs. The Omax said they would come back and make peace with the Siyaks. They wanted to go back to their own tribe. At the same time Mixkoksi thought they would go and look for the Omax. He did not know when the party started that the Omax had started back at the same time. The Siyaks were traveling and had gone near the Blood Reserve. The Omax was on the other side. Oxksksowatsimi was scout for the Omax to see if there were any enemies. Mixkoksi's group was resting. One of the Siyaks went up on a hill to guard. The scout saw four men coming. They thought they might be enemies. They got the guns all set and waited for the men to come up the hill when they would shoot the four men. The four men did not know of the ambush. When the four men got a certain distance away, one of the Siyaks said, 'One of the men is Mixkoksi's friend.' They said to wait and see if it was the friend of Mixkoksi. They recognized the friend and said they would find out why they were coming and maybe have the fight right there. When the four men were quite near, Oxksksowatsimi looked up and saw Mixkoksi. Then Oxksksowatsimi dropped his gun and ran to Mixkoksi and hugged and kissed him. Then the others did the same, and all were glad of it. All sat down, and Mixkoksi asked Oxksksowatsimi what was the cause of his trip. Oxksksowatsimi said his band was over the hills, and he was scouting. Mixkoksi said they were out looking for his band. Oxksksowatsimi said that he has missed Mixkoksi a great deal, and he decided to come back and try to make peace with the Siyaks. Mixkoksi said it was a good idea. They had met, and they wanted peace. The Siyaks had killed two Omax men, and the Omax had killed only one Siyaks man, said Oxksksowatsimi. Oxksksowatsimi said that all should go back to the tribe from there, since they had made peace. Oxksksowatsimi said that all should go back to the Omax camp. Mixkoksi did not agree and said they should all go back to the tribe from there, since they had made peace. Oxksksowatsimi said, 'When we come to the Blackfoot camp, we will give the Siyaks horses, and then I will give you Mixkoksi my fastest horse and a suit of buckskins.' Mixkoksi just started home, but the Omax went back to the Omax and said they had met Mixkoksi and there were lots of Siyaks with him. They had made peace, and the band should travel faster.

When the Omax heard that peace had been made, they were very happy. When Mixkoksi got back to the Blackfoot, he said the Siyaks had made peace. The other men said it was up to Mixkoksi, that he was a big man, and they were glad to make peace. The Omax would soon be there. When the Omax came, they took up their own side of the circle. Then the Omax got all their fast horses. These were taken to the Siyaks. The next day the Siyaks gave horses to the Omax, and peace was made for good.

Then the tipi belonging now to Duck Chief was given by the Blackfoot in the south. It came into the hands of the northern Blackfoot. Eight tipis came into the hands of the northern Blackfoot. When the Omax were settled in the Sundance, the fellows of the Omax showed the Blackfoot the dance of the Crazy Dogs *[the All Brave Dogs, ed.]* [The Omax did not really buy it from the southern Blackfoot but they saw it and imitated it. It was one of the biggest steals that is known; much laughter]."

When did the foregoing incident happen? The event may have happened 150 years ago. There was a woman who was a little girl who went south with the Omax. Her name was Sisoyaki. She was a very old lady when she told Little Light this story. When she got married, she was a wife of Crowfoot. Another old man told the story again to Little Light who went up north with the Siyaks. He was a little boy when this happened, and he was the father of Billy Mayfield. His name was Ponokaistamik. Ponokaistamik was one of the chiefs of the Siyaks. The two people agreed in their stories. *[Hanks, M8458 Box 1 File2]*

"...It was so far south they had always warm climate & saw negroes working in the fields. They stood this three or four years but wanted to see their own people. On the home journey they were attacked by the Snakes in Montana. Her parents & most of the others were killed. A cousin caught up Sisoyake then ___ up on his shoulders & rode on. Later the smallpox later broke out amongst them & carried off nearly all who were left. From a powerful band they were now reduced to a few families." *[Sisoyaki, Sikiksika-Blackfoot, to Father Doucet to Edmund Morris, 1907; 1985; 45]*

Sisoyaki, wife of Crowfoot, North Blackfeet-Blackfoot, 1905, Edmund Morris photo, Provincial Archives of Manitoba, Winnipeg.

“Natosistsi was in the Omaxkistsimani – Siyaks fight…and went down east with the Omaxkistsi. He got there the North Door tipi up east. *[A painted tipi design, ed.]* Old Weasel Calf, father in law of Mrs. Weasel Calf, was a 10-12 year old boy when they went down east. There were four tribes down east and the last *[first?, ed.]* one spoke ‘our’ language.

1. nitsi poyi – speakers of real words
2. aksi tapi – scarlet mark people
3. tsipistoitapi – owl people
4. aksi tapisaksi – scarlet mark on hip people.

#1 talked only a little differently from us, but all are friends, so warred together. *[Buck Running Rabbit, 1938, Hanks notes, personal correspondence, author’s possession.]*

Two possible identities for this Blackfoot speaking group are given below.

The Arapaho were divided into five divisions; 1. Gros Ventre,[Begging People] 2. Besawunena, [Big Lodge People] 3. Hinanaeina 4. Ha-anahawunena 5.Nawathinehena [South People], and each had its own dialect. The Ha-anahawunena dialect was said to resemble Blackfoot, but they were the first to lose their separate identity. The four divisions south of the Gros Ventre consolidated into the Arapaho and adopted the language of the Hinanaeina. [Fowler,2001; 840]

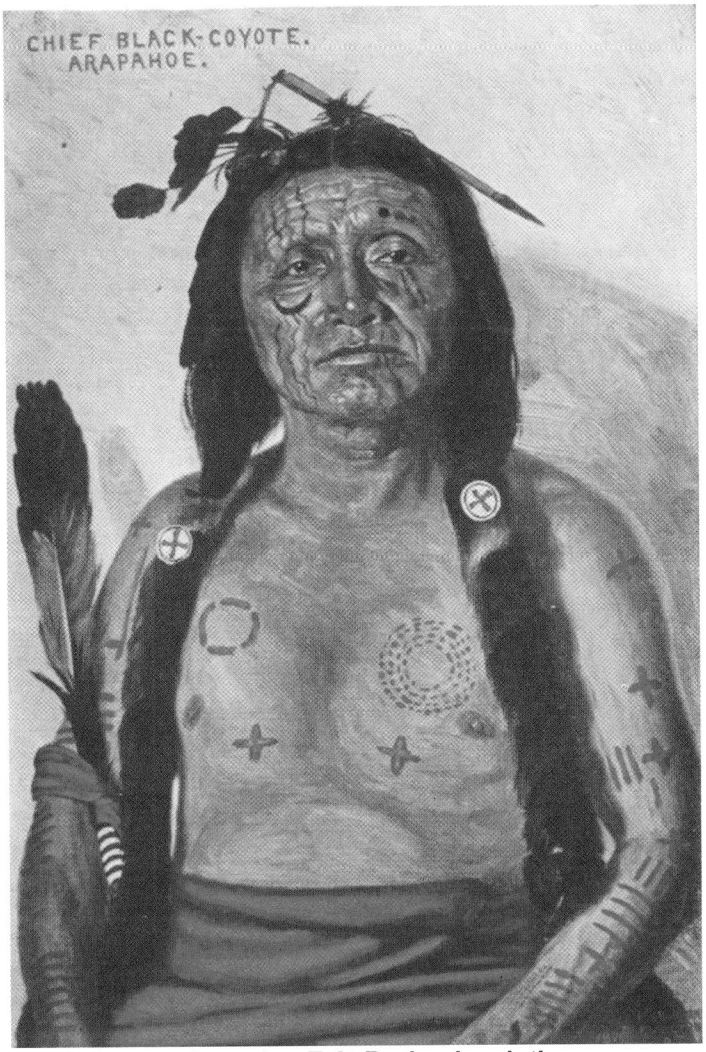

Black Coyote, Arapaho, E.A. Burbank painting

The Blackfeet that came and stayed with the Southern Cheyenne and Arapaho may also be this group who spoke "nitsi poyi" or "real words" of the Blackfoot. George Bent knew of them arriving in 1826 and marrying into the Arapaho and Cheyenne tribes. "I knew five or six of these old Blackfeet. The last of them, Small Eyes, died of old age about the year 1880. He lived with me for a time in my lodge in 1867. These Blackfeet never learned the Cheyenne language. They always talked to us in the sign language, which was used by all the Plains tribes. *[George Bent to George Hyde, 1968; 33-34] It stands to reason they would have camped together, and their wives would have learned Blackfoot, perhaps forming a small band among the southern Arapahos and Cheyenne.*

Fort Union, Carl Bodmer painting

Father Nicolas Point; b. 1799, d. 1868

In 1846 Father Nicolas Point traveled through Blackfoot country as "recorder" [a field artist] for the Jesuit Missionary expedition. He made hundreds of drawings and watercolors of the geography and peoples encountered. During his stay at Fort Lewis in Montana he also collected some of the earliest known Blackfoot drawing on paper. John Ewers wrote an essay on these drawings in Ethnohistory, Vol. 18, No.3 [Summer 1971] titled "A Unique Pictorial Interpretation of Blackfoot Indian Religion in 1846-1847". Ewers speculated the artist was "unknown" in his essay. However, after studying the drawings we've found the name glyph for the artist Thunder Chief, a well-known name among the Blood-Blackfoot. Thunder Chief's name is written at the top of one page in Blackfoot. Ewers assumed this was Father DeSmet or Father Point's Indian name due to the pictograph of a priest standing next to it. However, Father Point's Blackfoot name was "Tusks" [White Calf, Lancaster, 1966; 20] and Father DeSmet's was "Beaver Teeth" [Morris, 1985; 127]. Examining the other drawings we find a drawing [name glyph] above several of the other pages indicating a Thunderbird. Traditionally this would be Thunder Chief's signature.

The importance of these drawings lies in that they give us the Blackfoot viewpoint of the traders and the interaction of the trading post in Blackfoot culture. The people, workers, cooks, engagee's, traders, and their birds and animals foreign to the Blackfoot are depicted in Blackfoot pictographic style. Those of Blackfoot life, religion and the animals of the west were no doubt, to inform Point's superiors back east about the west and support his own drawings. It is also some of the earliest pictographs done in the media of paper and watercolors.

"Religion & Superstition", Thunder Chief drawing, 1846, collected by Father Nicolas Point, Archives of the Jesuits in Canada, Montreal

This page appears to be made up of four separate pages placed on one sheet. At the bottom left are two Antelope with only the forelegs of another at the lower right. Above them are drawings of the Moon and Sun. Both have wavy lines coming from them. In pictographic language this shows that they have spiritual power.

To the right of these drawing is one showing a very important story of Blackfoot religion. It concerns a Thunder Medicine Pipe man and his daughter. The man sits in front of his earth painted altar of red and black with eagle plumes at the corners. He is painted all in the sacred red paint and has his hair tied in an "Okinayossin", Medicine Pipe owner's top knot. Above him are the male and female Thunder Birds, with "wavy power lines" coming from their claws and bodies, symbolizing their spiritual power. To the far right we see a bear with a woman riding on its back. This is the daughter of the pipe owner who was stolen by the bear, being returned. The story accounts for the hide of the Black Bear being a part of the Thunder Medicine Pipe bundle, and prohibition of the pipe owner from mentioning bear's name, for he became the owner's son-in-law. As a "formal apology" [Kittoh pikim moot] for stealing the girl, the bear gave his hide to wrap the bundle and the ability to use roots for doctoring by the pipe owner.

At the top of the page we see an image of a priest, believed to be Father Point, a Buffalo Shield and a painted tipi. The shield is interesting in that either the same shield, or a descendant copy of the original shield, is currently in the collection of the American Museum of Natural History in New York. However, in this drawing a decorated buffalo tail is attached to the right of the shield in an upright position similar to that when a buffalo charges. For this drawing to be done by our artist he must own, or have owned this shield in the past. He would not have chanced Spiritual displeasure by drawing it. This also holds true for the Horned Snake tipi shown next to it. It also, must have been owned by our artist. In this drawing the artist shows both the male and female snakes on the same side of the tipi. The actual tipi would have the male on the south side and female on the north side of the cover.

At the very top of the page is written "Ksistekomina" twice. Speculation was that this was Father Point's Blackfoot name. It translates as "Thunder Chief" in English. However there are several images done by our artist that show Thunder Birds above the head of a Blackfoot man. It is more than likely these are name glyphs for Thunder Chief, and would give us the name of our artist.

"Employees of the fort", Thunder Chief drawing, 1846, collected by Father Nicolas Point, Archives of the Jesuits in Canada, Montreal

This is possibly Fort Lewis [1845 – 1847] on the Missouri and near the present town of Fort Benton. Done in the one dimensional style of early pictographs the drawing shows all four sides of the fort. Above the hand painted flags of the American Fur Company with their eagles and stripes, are portraits of two wood cutters and the mule drawn wagons used to haul the wood to build the fort.

"Exterior & interior of the kitchen", Thunder Chief drawing, 1846, collected by Father Nicolas Point, Archives of the Jesuits in Canada, Montreal

Rather than drawings of the kitchen these images more likely show the feast getting ready to be served to the important men of the visiting tribe. "Then the great men, about fifty in number, were brought into the festive hall, where they found not only the great calumet but also kettles of corn and jars of water mixed with molasses." [Point, 1967, 210] With the fort factors supervising, Native wives of the employees are carrying pots of cooked food into the main room for the feast. Part of a Thunder Bird is above the heads of the woman and factor. In pictographic language this could be a name glyph for Thunder Chief indicating that he was a part of the feast, or that the feast was for him.

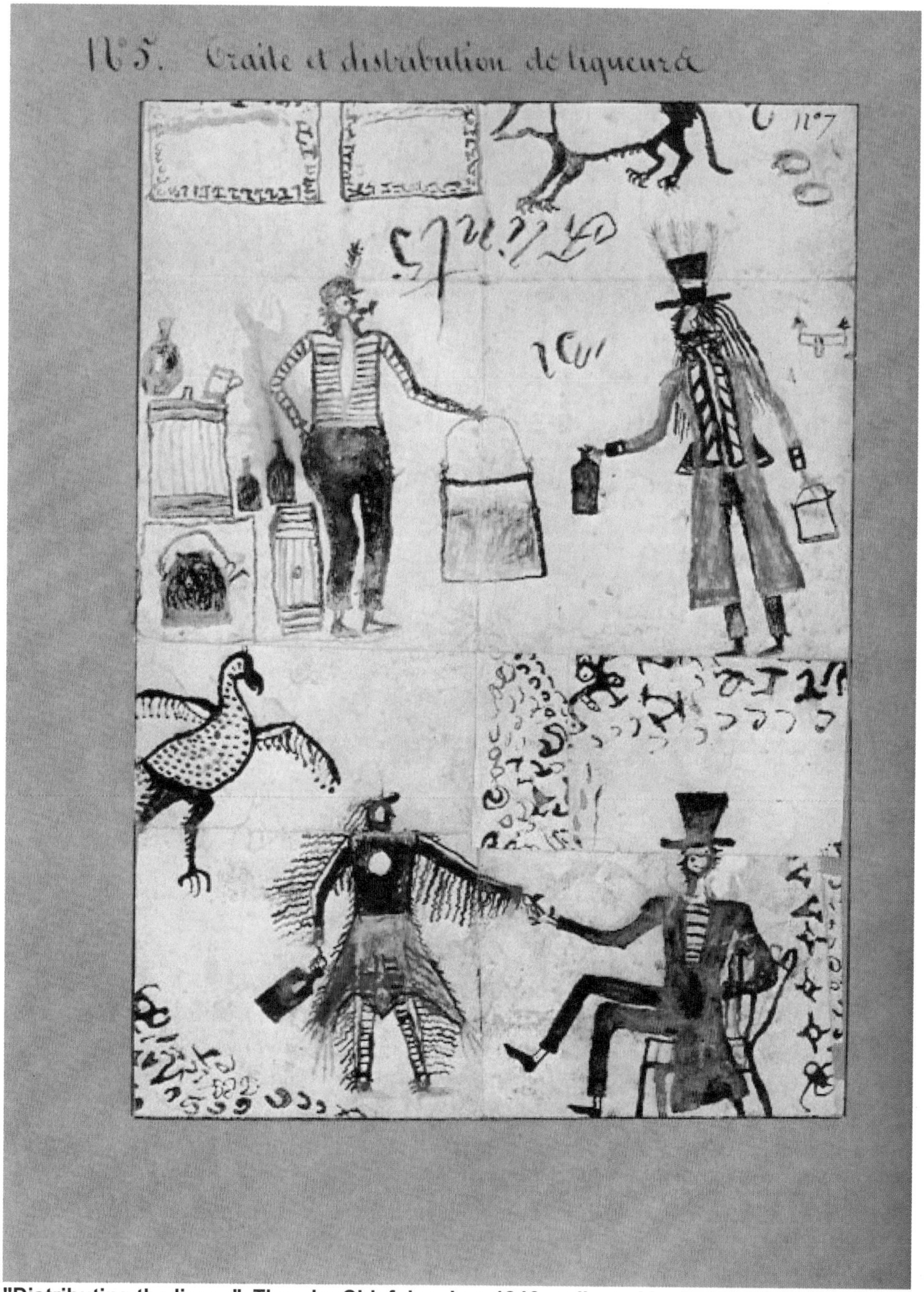

"Distributing the liquor", Thunder Chief drawing, 1846, collected by Father Nicolas Point, Archives of the Jesuits in Canada, Montreal

The bottom of the drawing shows an important man shaking hands with the factor of the fort and being given a bottle of whiskey. He is wearing a Hairlock Shirt painted in red and black, with scalp lock leggings as well. His hair is tied in an "Okinayossin", or Medicine Pipe owner's top knot. Behind him is a Thunderbird. This would be an image of the artist himself, with his name glyph. In another drawing the name "Thunder Chief" is written above the drawings. Since drawings of Thunderbirds appear in other of the drawings at random spots, it's possible the artist was "signing" them, or indicating he was involved, as well.

The top half of the drawing shows an employee of the fort handing out liquor to another important man. The man wears a "Chief's Coat" of red trade cloth, given to leaders by the traders, and carries containers to fill. He also wears a top hat decorated with four plumed sticks coming from his hat band. Upon arriving at the fort the chiefs were often given kegs of alcohol to be taken back to the main camp and shared out with his people prior to beginning trade. The cat like figure above his head may also be his name glyph, but we can only see a part of it.

"Then the men at the fort brought out a huge copper kettle of whiskey outside the gate and passed cups of it to the circle of chiefs. Afterwords, the chiefs were invited inside where the factors dressed them all in fine cloths and gave them each a gallon of whiskey." [Many Tail Feathers, South Peigan-Blackfoot, to Schultz, 1929]

"Employees of the fort", Thunder Chief drawing, 1846, collected by Father Nicolas Point, Archives of the Jesuits in Canada, Montreal

The top of the page shows three employees of the fort with one holding a paint horse. No doubt this was a well known buffalo running or race horse given as a gift to the trader. Below them is a black horse with the brand of "V" on its hip. In front of the horse is a trader riding another black horse that has a Spanish ring bit on. Both of these horses would have been famous horses for our artist to portray them.

"Interior of steamboat & calumet ceremony", Thunder Chief drawing, 1846, collected by Father Nicolas Point, Archives of the Jesuits in Canada, Montreal

Labeled "interior of steamboat and calumet ceremony" there is some question as to this interpretation. At the bottom of the page could well be the interior of a steamship with the crew smoking a Native made pipe, but there is nothing in the image to indicate a "calumet ceremony" as such. The man holding the pipe [or calumet, as Point states] has a written document above his head would indicate he is the man in charge. To the right are two employees of the fort, one holding a large sword.

Above this drawing is an image of a steamboat, three squares, and a strange creature of some sort. Since the drawings are cut from their original pages it's almost impossible to get a true reading of the images. However, the three squares [one is drawn over the boat] may be letters, or written documents of some sort. The one at the far right seems to be a folded paper with the two flaps at the top. Written documents were a source of amazement to Native people at the time, and important enough to document in their drawings.

However, the most important part of this page is the top half, which doesn't even get mentioned in the text. Here we have a Blackfoot moon calendar being matched up with a European calendar. The bottom lines with crosses indicate the weekdays plus the cross for Sunday. At the top we have a Blackfoot moon calendar measuring the weeks between new moons. What's exciting about this is that it is very similar to the one done by Bull Plume in the Old Agency Winter Count in the early 1900's.

Between the two calendars there is a man in a red chief's coat at the right and a factor of the fort on the left that has been cut in half. He holds a paper in his hand that shows him to be in charge. These letters of recommendation were written for Natives to show to the factors of other forts indicating the bearer was friendly and a good person.

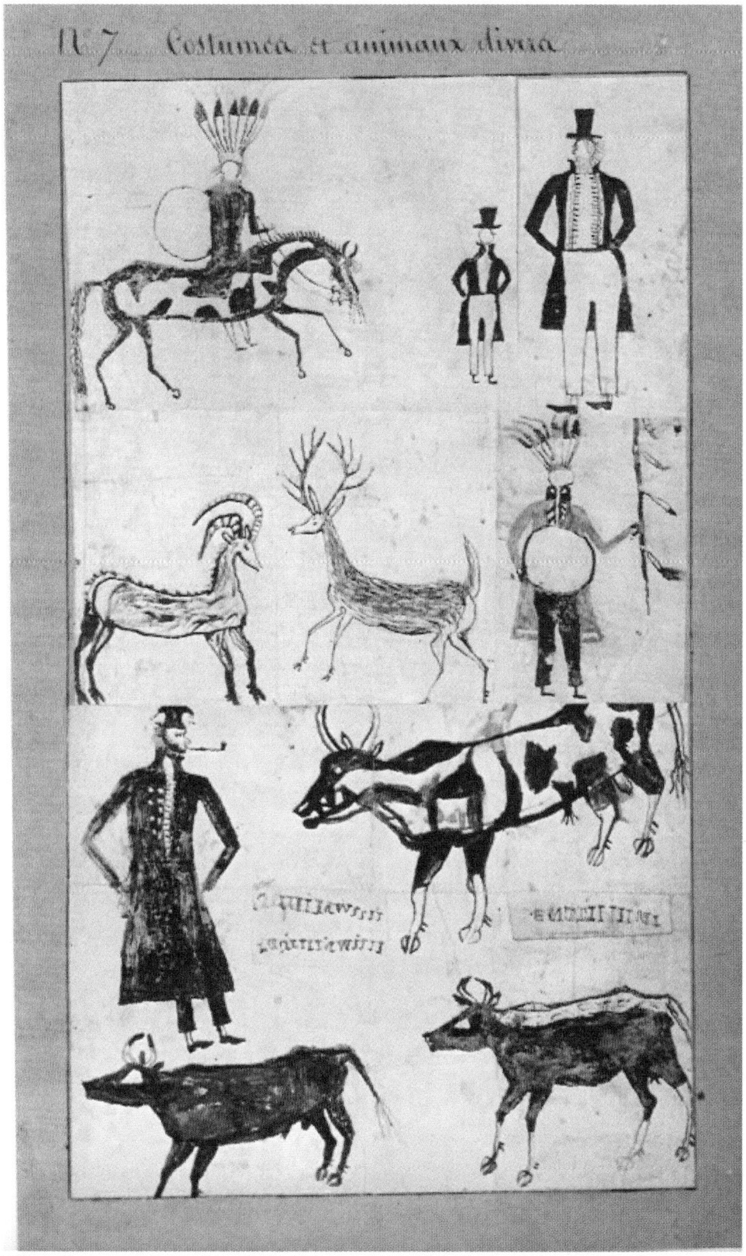

"Costumes & animals", Thunder Chief drawing, 1846, collected by Father Nicolas Point, Archives of the Jesuits in Canada, Montreal

Titled "animals and humans in costumes" this page shows several domestic cattle at the bottom of the page and one of the Engage employees of the Fort with his distinctive peaked hat. Above him is a drawing of a Mountain Sheep, a Whitetail deer and a Blackfoot leader wearing a Chief's Coat, carrying a spear and shield, and wearing a Straight-up headdress.

At the top there is an image of a Blackfoot leader riding a paint colored horse, wearing a Straight-up headdress and carrying a shield. His horse has on a Spanish ring bit with the chains of dangles hanging under his chin. In front of him are two traders.

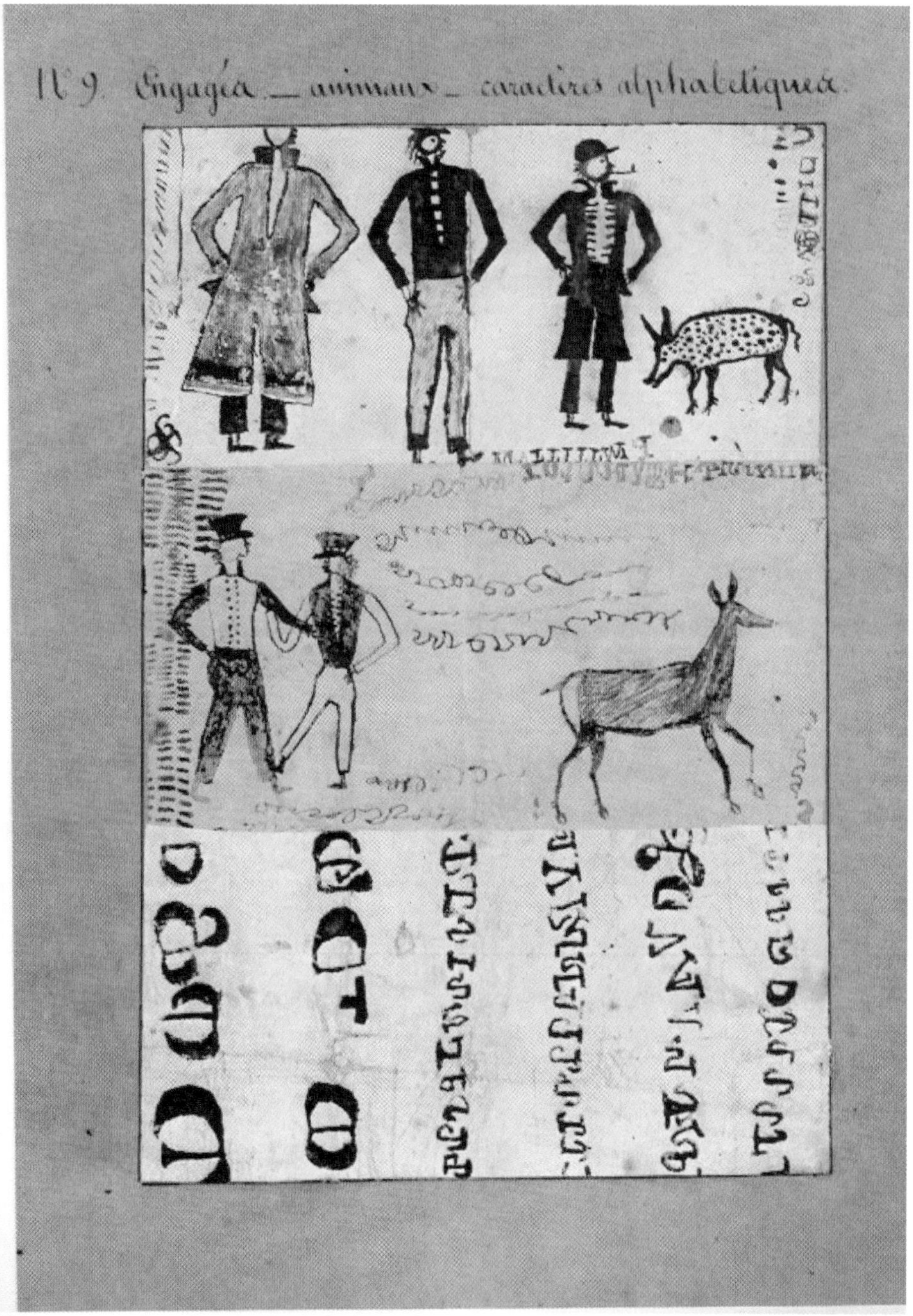

"Engagees & animals & alphabet characters", Thunder Chief drawing 1846, collected by Father Nicolas Point, Archives of the Jesuits in Canada, Montreal

Composed of three separate pages the bottom third shows our Native artist's attempt at alphabet characters. Above that are two traders and a female Blacktail Deer. Between the men and deer are squiggly lines with the artist's attempt at script writing. At the top are three employees of the fort. The man on the left wears a green capote. At the far right is a domestic pig from the fort.

"Boats & sleds", Thunder Chief drawing, 1846, collected by Father Nicolas Point, Archives of the Jesuits in Canada, Montreal

Another page consisting of five separate pages placed on one page. The bottom left shows two non-Native men rowing a boat. To their right are two more men poling a pirogue. Above them is a trader traveling with a dog sled. Above him, and to the right, are two domestic roosters. Many of the trading posts, as well as some individual Native people, kept roosters and chickens. Another boat and oarsmen with the bottom half of a Native in formal dress wearing Hair Lock leggings and a trailer headdress.

"Barge being towed", Thunder Chief drawing, 1846, collected by Father Nicolas Point, Archives of the Jesuits in Canada, Montreal

From August to winter freeze-up the upper Missouri trading posts had to be supplied by barges, rather than the steamboats, due to the low water level. They were often towed with long ropes by men walking on the shore line. This drawing shows how it was done, as well as details of the barge. Most of these barges had the elk skull with antlers attached at the top of the cabin, shown in the drawing. The drawing also shows the Lookout and the flag of the American Fur Company. In the section of the flag where the stars usually are the company had an eagle, which our artist depicted with some squiggles in red. These flags were hand painted and also given out to the chiefs.

Also in the drawing the artist has a cow moose running along the shore line in front of the barge. Right above the barge drawing a black horse is shown in a corral. Upper center of the drawing has a crescent moon with squiggly lines around it. This may be the artist's attempt to portray the script writing of the white culture and not the spiritual power of Moon.

"Indian Letter". unknown Native artist, 1842, collected by Father Nicolas Point, Archives of the Jesuits, Montreal

Written in 1842 by another Native artist, this page shows activity at one of the forts. At the bottom is an Indian camp with the artist shown in the middle of the camp. The river divides the drawing with a barge flying the trader's flag. Dashed lines show the path of the Indians coming to the fort from the left. At the gate of the fort the factor meets the Chief of the tribe who extends a hand of friendship. His horse is drawn behind him in the old style of drawing. The lines with circles attached to the front are his people behind him. Tipi poles above the fort indicate another camp.

1832

BLOOD

BAD HEAD: Otsitsitokkanipi omarxistowan itstoyemuv An American (or Big Knife) winters at the place called the Straight, or Narrow Place, on Milk River.

WHITE BULL: Americans or Big Knives winters at the Milk River

DEMPSEY: *In July, 1832, David D. Mitchell and sixty men established Fort McKenzie on a narrow ridge separating the Teton and Missouri. (Chittenden, 1954, 336).*

PERCY CREIGHTON: Wolf Peace Making. The Blood, (with some Peigan & Sarcee) pretended to make peace with the Cree and fought with them instead.

NORTH BLACKFEET

YELLOW FLY: The Wolf Peace Treaty Year. A treaty with an enemy tribe.

RUNNING RABBIT: Crooked Back Bone, Calgary

MANY GUNS: Ito kuyinestsu pi = literally, "wolf-peace" meaning they did not trust each other like wolves. Bad-peace, peace between Crees and Blackfeet. "Not too sure-still afraid."

MANY GUNS 65.68 & .69: The Truce

MANY GUNS File 7: The first peace with Crees were like wolves because Blackfeet and Crees were afraid to meet each other, lest guns be hidden under the blankets.

In 1828 the Cree and Assiniboine made peace with the Blackfoot. However, by 1830 the peace became fragile with some bands of the eastern Cree attacking the Blackfoot. At this point neither group was sure of the intentions of the other when they met. By 1832 the peace was definitely broken and the groups again at war.

LITTLE CHIEF: Crooked Back Bone was born there was not much moving because the Indians had hardly any horses they went on expedition and got lot of horses they were Blackfeets, Bloods & Peigans, Sarcees

Crooked Back Bone grew up to be a fine young man went on war party and was a war chief for a long time till he got killed in the year of 1881

CRANE BEAR: A Blackfeet, Ippawaw, is shot in the chest, but the ball slides to the ground without wounding him.

1833

NORTH PEIGAN

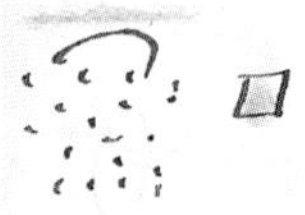

BULL PLUME #1: When lots of stars fell. *Shooting stars.*

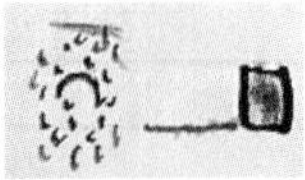

BULL PLUME #2: When lots of stars fell.

Possibly the Leonoid Shower which occurred in November.

BLOOD

BAD HEAD: Kakatosen otsitsoriapi Very remarkable shower of stars, the Bloods were camped near High River.

WHITE BULL: Blood Indians were camped near High River, stars are falling down.

DEMPSEY: *This meteoric shower was seen throughout much of North America on the night of Nov.12, 1833, and is recorded in the winter counts of other plains tribes (see Mallery, 1893:280 and Praus, 1962:14)*

Major Alexander Culbertson noted the following at Fort McKenzie, "Brilliant display of falling stars and total eclipse of the sun observed at Fort McKenzie in 1833. Both were regarded by the Indians as forerunners of some great catastrophe." (Bradley; vol. VIII; 134)

PERCY CREIGHTON: A man by the name of Hump Back killed an Cree enemy prisoner at a celebration at which there was dancing, etc. The enemy was scalped.

NORTH BLACKFEET

YELLOW FLY: The year "Hunch Back", a warrior, was killed.

RUNNING RABBIT: The Sundance; burn feets

MANY GUNS: Ksam skiniwa = "humpback". A Cree chief by that name was killed by Big Plume, i.e. Omaxsapope. Had three names ---"Big Plume" which he gave to Blood Indian when he gave the Blood his Medicine Pipe. 2nd name = Nineipiksi –Chief Bird. 3rd name = Epikskunaki (Take A Gun And Don't Shoot It). Big Plume was a bigger chief than Crowfoot (because Ikaki a white trader was his friend); All traders respected him, he could go into store and take anything. In war he took trophies too. That year Crowfoot was born.

MANY GUNS File 7: Blackfeet went on an "itaisi" (buffalo hunt with tipis) left some members a home. It was Big Plume's band. Crees attacked those left and destroyed the tipis and 8 Blackfeet women & 2 children were captured.

"When Omaxsapopai *[Big Plume, ed.]* got home from the hunt only one woman was left, who told him the story of the deaths and capture. His other wives and some of his children had all been killed. Everything taken by the Crees [cleaned out], including the tipi and Medicine Pipe of Omaxsapopai. This happened in the winter.

Next summer [early[Omaxsapopai got some followers to ksimuxksis o [pay back]. They went by Edmonton and Ekaki [white trader] who was a good friend of Omaxsapopai. Ekaki asked Omaxsapopai, "What are you doing?" Omaxsapopai, "I'm here to pay back, do the same trick to them because I'm so lonesome for my family." [they were dead]. Ekaki told Omaxsapopai, You better not, just go home, in spite of two children of yours captured and eight others. Some men of mine trading, are going to the Crees, and they'll buy the captives and your Medicine Pipe back." Omaxsapopai agreed. Omaxsapopai then turned back with his war party and went home because of the promise. Ekaki sent his men to tatsikya.kopi [a place]. Ksistatipuka [Beaver Child] was the head white man of this bunch of whites sent to the Cree at tatsikya.kopi. Ekaki told them to tell the Crees, 'Your friend Ekaki has heard from his friend Omaxsapopai that Crees have gotten ten women and a Medicine Pipe. Ekaki wants to buy them <u>all</u> back – not just one of them.'

Ksistatipuka therefore invited all the old Cree and chiefs. Chiefs brought into Ksistatipuka's house and door locked. Old men told to stay nearby outside. So Ksistatipuka told the chiefs the message from Ekaki, 'Bring the ten women and pipe <u>in here</u>, and I'll give you a big keg of whiskey.' Chiefs refused, saying, 'The Blackfoot do the same to us, and so we're not going to give them up.' Ksistatipuka then said, 'Then this summer we won't give you any bullets or powder and nothing sharp, like knife or axe. We'll wait until you're clean out. Then we'll send a message to Omaxsapopai to attack you and he'll kill you off like a stick killing ducks. We're going to lock you chiefs up here because it is your fault, not giving these women up.'

Chiefs got scared, so one said, 'Tell one of our children to come in, so I can send a message by him out.' A man Cree came in. Chiefs: 'We have sad news for you. We are to be locked up here *[unless the captives are released – J.R.]* . It would be bad for you to give our bodies up. Bring in the ten and the pipe therefore.' Man went out, announced out loud that they should be brought in. Women [nine] brought in and pipe one missing. The other woman was taken down east, captured by Willow People [another branch of Crees]. Ksistatipuka: 'Well, I'll buy her later.' The whiskey was given out then and all launched into a good time. 'Ksistatipuka was just trying to scare the Crees and it worked.'

Ksistatipuka and his men returned with goods and the pipe and women. Got to Edmonton. About ten young Blackfoot men happened to be there getting tobacco. Ekaki told them the news and sent a message by them for Omaxsapopai to come up and get his Medicine Pipe and the women.

Now Ekaki was a great friend of Omaxsapopai. Of course Omaxsapopai was head chief of whole Blackfoot nation. A lot of tipis went up to get the women [parents, etc. of women]. Ekaki then gave Omaxsapopai a drink. Omaxsapopai got drunk so Ekaki had to put him to bed upstairs. 'Ekaki treated Omaxsapopai just like a brother.' Ekaki kept going upstairs to see if he were sober. When sober, Ekaki gave Omaxsapopai his Medicine Pipe and said, 'You're also going to get a big union flag. When you want peace, put it up. Rest of time, keep your pipe covered with it.' Now Ekaki had Indian powers – had strong dreams. Ekaki had a song that went with the flag. Ekaki stood beside his friend and sang, 'White man above is hearing me'. *[Many Guns sings it then and there]* – and draped flag around Omaxsapopai like a blanket. Then Ekaki sang again. Took it off and covered pipe with it...Before this pipes never had coverings it was whites who told us to do this, so now we use red shawls. Ekaki was the last white to have Indian power in him.

Omaxsapopai then got a lot of presents from Ekaki and Omaxsapopai always divides these presents among the band members who had come up with him, for there were more than he could carry himself.

Omaxsapopai returned, and all began to gather for Sun Dance, half circle Blackfeet, half Blood.

THE STORY OF HUMPBACK, OR CROOKED-BACKBONE:

Omaxsapopai was still thinking of his Medicine Pipe and Crees and revenge, so he decided to give his pipe away, so he could get the best running horse available. He got four old men to untie his pipe bundle. He rode around quietly and ascertained which was the best horse. He wanted the 'catch' the owner of it. He got off his horse and examined the fine horse. 'This is the horse I want.' Some young boys were standing around, so Omaxsapopai asked, 'Napi!' [Omaxsapopai always kind spoken and called even young lads Napi.] *[Napii means 'friend', ed.]* Omaxsapopai pretending: 'I have lost a horse like this. Whose is it?' Boy: 'It belongs to Somebody, a Blood.' Omaxsapopai: 'Well, who?' Boy: 'Somebody. That's his real name.' Omaxsapopai was doing this secretly to find out the owner. Omaxsapopai: 'I think I'll take the horse. It must be mine.' Kids: 'No! It's his!' Omaxsapopai was just doing this to make sure whose horse it was. Kids: 'Somebody raised it from a colt.' Omaxsapopai: 'Where is his tipi?' Kids: 'There!' So Omaxsapopai examined the tipi carefully so he'd know whom to catch.

Then the four old men collected nine men for the ceremony of catching the Blood Indian Somebody. Omaxsapopai: 'Three will go this way to Somebody's tipi, two that way, so Somebody won't suspect us; three with owl, weasel and pipe will go with me. Sneak around and wait at his tipi for each other.' When they got there Omaxsapopai accosted a boy. Omaxsapopai: 'Boy, run and see if Somebody is in his tipi.' Boy peeped and he was, so Omaxsapopai walked in and caught Somebody. Omaxsapopai blew his whistle and at Omaxsapopai's home the drums began to beat. So Somebody was taken back to Omaxsapopai's tipi, was fixed up. Omaxsapopai: 'Don't be scared. Just give me one horse.' All the Blood relatives however, gathered horses because relatives always help, so a bunch of horses arrived with the beautiful runner in the midst.

Medicine Pipe people on the way to capture the new owner, McClintock photo, Beinecke Archives, Yale University

Omaxsapopai told Somebody: 'Young married man, I'm going to give you a good name, because you haven't got one. You're going to have my name Omaxsapopai – and when you invite me this evening call me Nineipiksi *[Chief Bird, ed,]*, which will be my new name henceforth.' So Somebody invited Omaxsapopai by that name that evening [a pipe recipient invites the owner for four nights].

After the four nights of dancing Omaxsapopai said: 'Young married man, in two days I'm going to war. You have to be taught to skin and hunt and shoot again. So you're to come with me.' [After receiving a pipe you have to be taught to eat, drink, wear clothes, everything all over again. Definite instructions have to be given.]

Two days later Omaxsapopai came round, gave smoke to some Blood chiefs who all refused. Somebody was the only Blood who agreed to come, and one from Peigan band, present also at the Sun Dance. All the others were Blackfeet and they set off to war.

As they approached the Cree they found them in circle camp too, so they decided to wait till night before attacking. Omaxsapopai sent four men out at night and said, 'Inspect the layout of the tipis for best plan of attack. Then make marks with manure how we should line up to attack them!'

Now there were two captured Blackfoot women: (1) Pokoki; Cree husband – matsiinam [nice looking]; (2) Konski; husband probably same as other's living among these Crees.

These women had been captured long before the 10 and were still unredeemed.

The party came close to the piles of manure, but not right on them, and waited. Towards dawn they threw up dung, because 'if you see it come down, you know it's getting dawn. If not, it's still too dark to attack.' So the men awaited there the hour of attack. Then Omaxsapopai said, 'We're going to try a good scheme! When you approach the dung piles, make a noise like buffalo. This will bring out more Cree to shoot at; otherwise we might not be able to kill as may or more than they have killed Blackfoot.'

So the men grunted as they approached. Now the two Blackfoot women [sisters] were in the same tipi. Their husband heard the sound, rose, came out and called to his wives. 'Come! Buffalo are near, come and chase them!' Women rose, and said to each other, 'Alas, we have to carry meat on our backs here. Meat is also brought in all mixed up – badly cut up, not cut right and orderly like the way the Blackfoot do it. It's no fun now going to chase the buffalo. The way the Blackfoot bring in meat on horseback makes a hunt lots of fun. Now it's no fun to hear the call to hunt.' But they got ready to come. At that moment the Blackfoot men called out the great war cry, 'Hear, my friend, I'm here!' The Crees ran out. All shooting then started up. Lots were killed and lots captured. Omaxsapopai had miracle power – could shoot without loading. So at daylight Omaxsapopai said: 'Now listen, don't anyone get in front of me.' Omaxsapopai then killed eight men in a row, but suddenly the Peigan disobeyed and ran in front of Omaxsapopai, and that stopped the miracle. Omaxsapopai was sorry he had to stop for he wanted to see how many Cree he could kill. The Peigan ran back to Blackfoot lines and sat down, but 'because he broke the old man's rules, he was killed by the Cree as he sat there.'

Then a message came to Omaxsapopai; 'There's one man we can't kill. Guns won't go off at him. He has a hump back.' So Omaxsapopai came round and he tried to shoot the hump back, but his gun also misfired. 'He must have more power than me!' So Omaxsapopai made four passes at the man with his gun and fired and the hump back was killed. Omaxsapopai: 'Send a message to my brother Somebody *[Pipe recipient]* to come.' Somebody came. 'Somebody, take your gun and shoot at this Cree, then say, 'I, Omaxs, killed this Cree.' Then scalp him.' So Somebody did so. Thus Omaxsapopai taught Somebody how to kill and scalp again. Somebody could recite this as a deed always from then on, even though he had not actually killed the Cree. Of course Omaxsapopai had named himself on the dead Cree as true killer.

So when they got home Omaxsapopai and Somebody renamed themselves out on the dead Cree. Somebody would say; 'I, Omaxsapopai, killed in an imitation fashion a Cree - through Ninepiksi and the Medicine Pipe.'

When they first started to shoot the Blackfoot women rushed out, having heard it was Blackfoot. They hid in a bush. A Blackfoot saw them and started to shoot at them, thinking them Cree. They called out and it turned out to be their own brother [a miracle!] 'wonderous'. Brother called, 'Is that you, Pokaki?' 'Yes, and Konski.' So their brother saved them, brought them behind the Blackfoot lines and told them where to sit in back to be safe. The two arrived there and said to the other Blackfoot, 'Our brother sent us here to be safe.'

The battle was won by the Blackfoot. Half the Cree escaped into the bush to hide. The half that stayed to fight was killed. The Blackfoot took half the tipis of the Cree. The Blackfoot cleaned out the tipis near them. Horses from all round were taken.

Also: when Omaxsapopai killed Humpback, Apstsapo [a Blackfoot] [younger than Omaxsapopai] was standing beside him. Omaxsapopai told Apstsapo to run and get the gun. 'A man won't do that!' Apstsapo was a humpback himself. Apstsapo and Omaxsapopai were both Saiyeks. Apstsapo was grand father to old Turning Rope; therefore a brother to Omaxsapopai. Omaxsapopai was therefore very generous and kind. No one would ever give a gun deed away like that usually, but Omaxsapopai did it for his brother.

Crowfoot would never have done anything so generous. Omaxsapopai did this to Apstsapo because Apstsapo was crippled and humpback and couldn't do anything really by himself. Apstsapo was trying hard but couldn't ever get very much. So Omaxsapopai just helped him to become a chief.

Joke: When the Blackfoot grunted like buffalo and deceived the Cree, the Cree had called to their camps, 'Come on and get out to catch the calves.' 'Cree were the calves themselves and were caught instead!'

After the Blackfoot fought they returned to 'sit-backers'. *[Those that remained at home, ed.]* Blackfoot sang a victory song, composed for the occasion; 'Humpback, get up and chase the buffalo.'

The Blood still have 'The Long Time Pipe that Omaxsapopai gave them by giving it to Somebody.' *[Told by Many Guns to Hanks, Box 8, File 7]*

LITTLE CHIEF: In the spring the Indians had just enough food till April the month of the frogs they moved to Berry Flat hunting the buffalo killed a lot of meat and in June they had their Sun Dance at Berry Flat they moved along the Bow River for the winter they were luck because the buffalo was plentyful there all winter they had meat

CRANE BEAR: Ippawaw is killed.

1834

NORTH PEIGAN

BULL PLUME #1: When they fought on the side of the river.

BULL PLUME #2: When they fought on the side of the river.

BULL PLUME #1 shows the symbol for Blood Indians, BULL PLUME #2 shows the symbol for white men, both in a canoe, indicating water.

There are several events this may refer to; one being the time the Bloods and Peigans fought each other at Fort McKenzie in August 1833 ,two days after the Assiniboine/Cree attack [Maximilian;109] Iron Shirt, one of the recorders of this winter count was present there, or, to the battle at Bow River between the Bloods and Peigans. When the Peigans killed two of the Blood's "greatest chiefs and wounded a third in one of their quarrels which so enraged the Blood Indians who immediately rushed upon the Peaguns and destroyed a whole camp by killing the men and taking women and children prisoners and proceeding to two other small camps, served then in the same manner." [Rowland to Governor, Chief Factors and Chief Traders, Edmonton House, 10 January 1834, fo. 62d., Simpson Correspondence, D.4/26, reel 3M54, HBCA] [ref: HBCA fo 6d; B.21/a1; Bow Fort (Peigan Post) PJ 1833-34, 7 Dec 1833] Or it may refer to the event given in Bad Head's winter count.

Assiniboine and Cree attack at Fort McKenzie, Carl Bodmer watercolor, courtesy Northern Natural Gas Co, Omaha, Nebraska

BLOOD

BAD HEAD: Sapo-itotayiskatarpi The Bloods help themselves with the horses of the Crows.

WHITE BULL: Blood Indians help themselves with Crow Indian horses at near Elk River.

PERCY CREIGHTON: The enemies (Cree) made a raid on the Sun Makers Lodge and tried to kill her. They did not succeed & were driven off by the Bloods.

NORTH BLACKFEET

YELLOW FLY: The year of the Sun Dance massacre.

RUNNING RABBIT: The stars fall down

MANY GUNS: Kietokiiks = Prairie Chickens. This year the Prairie Chickens were formed.

"A man, Napiokus, dreamed of the Prairie Chickens and gave it away. His great grand-son Red Eagle died 1937. Napiokus had dreamed of the Prairie Chickens when young, and again and again, but decided no to notice the dream till later. So he collected calf skins and things. Gathered all the young men and gave them the stuff, for they wanted to be in a society.

This Napiokus was Grandfather uncle *[Grandfather's brother, ed.]* of Many Guns therefore maaxs *[aaahs ? elder relation, ed.]* to Many Guns. Napiokus was glad the young were willing to have it. Two minipukas *[favored children, ed.]* got their tipis for the bunch to pitch in middle of camp-circle. Napiokus fixed up four things: Suit, bow and arrow, shield, rattle, as required regalia. Prairie Chickens lost the bow and arrow and shield now. *[1938, ed.]*

Napiokus fixed them all up [hard work!] and then called, 'Come and see what your children are going to do. They'll dance early in morning! Sleepy-heads will be awakened by Prairie Chickens!' Prairie Chickens dance four mornings then scatter two by two out to dance at front door, acting like Prairie Chickens.

Having waked up all people, people rushed out without even washing faces. Some might give out presents.

The first time they danced three mornings only. Then the bunch went to war secretly. 'Prairie Chickens flew away' and the fourth dance was danced when they got back. All got home safely." *[Many Guns to Hanks, M68458.8.7, box 1, file 7, pp 209-210]*

LITTLE CHIEF: The stars fell down this is how it happen that year a Medicine man the above spirits such as the moon the stars gives him is power he was very powerful every body knew him and about his power every-body went to him when thy got sick he cured them he helped the poor and the sick his name was Bull Got Lift (E st me pe kis na) in a battle with the Crees also some half breeds they were out hunting when the Crees sighted them and give chase they were three Blackfeets so they had fast horses as they were far away from the Crees Bull Got Lift's horse step in a hole and hurt his leg he told his friends never mind me save yourself and they left him the Crees got to Bull Got Lift they all got off their horses the Crees said we better not kill him he is a Medicine Man we will sure have bad luck but the half breeds said kill him so one half breed shot Bull Got Lift and killed him as soon as he was killed it turn dark the moon was not seen in the sky all the stars look like they were falling down or they were jumping to each other it stayed that way for nearly two days the Crees half breeds got very bad luck

CRANE BEAR: A Blackfeet, Apisaokikiniw, pursued by the Cree, is saved by the unexpected presence close to him of a bear, the sight of which made them afraid and made them take flight. *(Apsaokikin = White Flat Head, ed.)*

[1838, RUNNING RABBIT & MANY GUNS, 1836, LITTLE CHIEF, ed.]

1835

NORTH PEIGAN

BULL PLUME #1: When the Peigans beat the Sioux in battle.

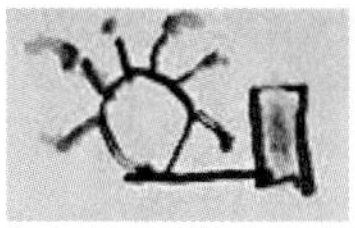

BULL PLUME #2: When the Peigans beat the Sioux in battle.

BLOOD

BAD HEAD: Otsitsoyeuitarpi Peikenekiva Natsitapin Two Peigans jump in the river (Bears River) and get killed.

LEGAL: Two Peigans being pursued by an enemy jumped into the Marias River and were killed.

PERCY CREIGHTON: The Indians were traveling all night. Many stars were falling. This year was known as the falling of the stars.

NORTH BLACKFEET

CRANE BEAR: The Crows were completely routed by the Blackfeet.

[1837, MANY GUNS; 1838, Running Rabbit & Little Chief, ed.]

YELLOW FLY: The year the stars fell

RUNNING RABBIT: Holy Coming Down killed (Morning Coming Over Hill) (he didn't go through his body, Upside Down Blanket) (Crow Indian stole Upside Down Blanket)

MANY GUNS: Kakatosiks = stars
Otsitsinisiipists = falling

LITTLE CHIEF: Holy Coming Down got killed in a battle with the Crees he was a great war chief

1836

BLOOD

BAD HEAD: Pokan otsitaoutsiskarpi Epidemic of constipation amongst children

DEMPSEY: Children/when they had strangulation of the throat. *Many children were said to have died of this ailment (Legal). which informants believe was diphtheria.*

PERCY CREIGHTON: An Indian by the name of Holy Coming Over The Hill – a well known headman was killed by the Crow.

NORTH BLACKFEET

CRANE BEAR: The Kootenay were coming to trade. The Blackfeet made war on them and defeated them. *[1839, MANY GUNS, ed.]*

YELLOW FLY: The year "Sacred Messenger". A warrior, was killed.

RUNNING RABBIT: White Flathead, with bear

MANY GUNS: Pix tsitapiks = 9 persons. The time 9 Crees were killed.

MANY GUNS 65.68: The nine men and the time we were burning our feet

LITTLE CHIEF: White Flat Head was out hunting he killed a young buffalo got off his horse started to butch the buffalo when a bear came out of the bush and attacked him he fought with the bear for a long time finely he killed the bear he was badly scratch and biting but he was a very powerful Medicine Man when he got to his tepee his saw how bad he was took him in the tepee he told his wife go out do not let anybody come in I will fix my I will be alright which she did after awhile she was told by her husband Come in when she went in the tepee her husband looked the same as before he fought with the bear when all the people saw him they said what a powerful man he is

1837

NORTH PEIGAN

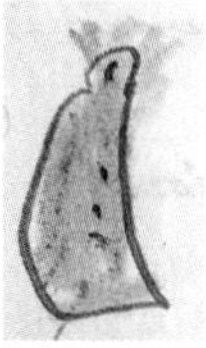 BULL PLUME #1: Year of smallpox, second time.

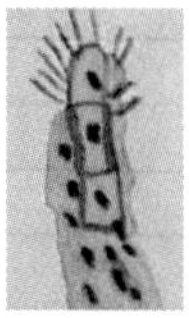 BULL PLUME #2: Year of smallpox.

BLOOD

BAD HEAD: Aponsin Small pox

WHITE BULL: Indians had Small pox many died with disease.

DEMPSEY: *The disease was brought to the Upper Missouri on the steamboat St. Peters of the American Fur Company. About two thirds of the Blackfoot nation, or six thousand people died during the epidemic. (Bradly, 1900)*

BAD HEAD: *Wilson adds this as a separate year,* "1838, Itsosin stoyew People recover from the disease."

DEMPSEY: When it ended in winter *The smallpox epidemic began in June 1837 and was the subject of the 1837-38 winter count. The cold weather helped to control the spread of the disease and by the spring of 1838 it had run its course (Chittenden, 1954: 620). Therefore, the outbreak, spread and termination of the epidemic all belong in the same winter count. However, so great was the impact of the disaster that the beginning and end were given as separate accounts.*[3]

In the spring of 1837 the American Fur Company steamboat started up river from St. Louis carrying infected clothing. The boat made it to Fort Union where the disease would have been kept under control had not a stolen blanket spread the disease to the surrounding tribes. A.M. Harvey, clerk for the American Fur Co. tried to out run the disease to Fort Benton. Before he had proceeded far, three cases broke out on his keel boat. He stopped at the mouth of the Judith River and sent word to Major Culbertson at Fort Benton.

---

[3] *(1837 spring) Calendar reckoning by Oct .*
In Dempsey he puts two years together for 1837. Wilson's account of BH does not, and adds "When it ended" as a separate year. With the other known dates following Dempsey's version appears to be correct.

Culbertson intended to keep the keel boat where it was until cold weather set in and the disease died down. But there were five-hundred lodges of Peigans and Bloods camped near the fort, waiting for the trade goods the keel boat was bringing. When they heard of Culbertson's plan they threatened to bring the boat up themselves. He tried to convince Them of the fatal effect of the disease, but they could not believe that it could do them any Injury.

In five days they completed their trade and spread to the west and north. For two months not an Indian was seen at the fort. Culbertson, concerned to know how the Indians had fared, went to the three forks of the Missouri where the Peigans generally camped. "A few days' travel brought him in sight of a village of about sixty lodges. Not a soul was to be seen, and a funeral stillness rested upon it. They approached with anxious hearts and awed by the unwonted quiet, for the vicinity of an Indian village is not apt to be the scene of oppressive silence. Soon a stench was observed in the air, that increased as they advanced; and presently the scene with all it's horror was before them. Hundreds of decaying forms of human beings, horses and dogs lay scattered everywhere among the lodges...Two old women, too feeble to travel, were the sole living occupants of the village.")Bradley; vol. III; 221-225)

Over six thousand Blackfoot died in this epidemic. About two-thirds of all the people. The Cree, meanwhile, had been vaccinated by the traders in their country at Fort Pelly and at the Saskatchewan. As a result there was scarcely a case among them. With the Blackfoot numbers decimated the Cree and Ojibwa were able to push further onto the Plains. (The Plains Cree; Milloy; 71 & The Ojibwa of Western Canada; Peers;142)

PERCY CREIGHTON: White Flat Head – died of old age.

NORTH BLACKFEET

CRANE BEAR: First Small Pox (1839 RR; 1841, MANY GUNS, ed.)

YELLOW FLY: "White Direct Head" year

RUNNING RABBIT: ________ made war (with Blackfoot)

MANY GUNS: Itesapa = Crow. Ninayopi = scalp dance, victory dance

MANY GUNS 65.68: The time we made a right new man

MANY GUNS 65.69: The time we rejoiced, The time we were burning our feet and Holy Coming Down.

LITTLE CHIEF: The Crees had a war with the Blackfeets Bloods Peigans Sarcees but as they were a few Crees the four tribes soon chased away killed a lot

1838

NORTH PEIGAN

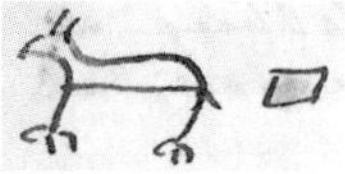

BULL PLUME #1: When "Bear Moving" was bitten by a bear.

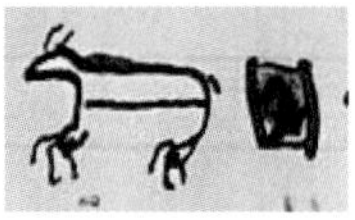

BULL PLUME #2: When "Bear Moving" was bitten by a bear.

BLOOD

BAD HEAD: Onistena otseintarpi White Calf Chief killed by a white man at (Fort) Benton

DEMPSEY: *Wilson was told the Blood Chief was killed by a white trader on the Missouri. Bradley (1900) stated that in the spring of 1838, A. Culbertson, factor in charge of Fort McKenzie, killed a Blood known to the traders as Big Road.*

PERCY CREIGHTON: The Blood had a big battle with the Crow and succeeded in killing many.

NORTH BLACKFEET

CRANE BEAR: A Crow has his nose cut off. (see 1840, RR & LC; 1841, MANY GUNS, ed.)

YELLOW FLY: The year of the Crow Victory Dances.

RUNNING RABBIT: Killed Crow Indian, made war dance (Running Rabbit born) (Crow Indians, killed them all by camp)

MANY GUNS: Two names:

(1) Apoksiyuwa = White Under The Front Fore Leg (a renowned Blackfoot horse's name). The horse was stolen by Crows.

(2) Apsaokikin = White Flathead and alias Kixsipipita = Spotted Eagle. Apsaokikin went to war vs. Mountain People e.g. Snake and Flatheads. Blackfoot scattered. Apsaokikin ran the other way. Apsaokikin was all alone, the enemy encircled him. Apsaokikin saw a bear which went after him. Apsaokikin prayed, "Father, I came for your help." So bear charged the Indians. "Saved by a bear".

MANY GUNS 65.68: Wore His Robe Inside Out and White Flathead

MANY GUNS 65.69: Had His Robe Inside Out was captured. White Flat Head. Bob Tail Robe.

LITTLE CHIEF: They moved south they meet the Crow Indians they camped with them it was in June so one Crow Indian made the Sun Dance Running Rabbit was born in treaty No. 7 he was made a head chief of the Blackfeets he died in the year 1911 Jan. 22nd.

1839

NORTH PEIGAN

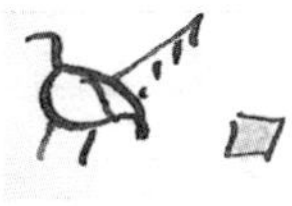

BULL PLUME #1: When "Eagle" was killed.

BULL PLUME #2: When "Eagle" was killed.

BLOOD

BAD HEAD: Potsiw otsenitarpi An old squaw called Potsiew (which can mean "Met") was killed, the killer remaining unknown.

DEMPSEY: *Dempsey translates this name as "Meeting Someone".*

WHITE BULL: An old woman called which can mean Met was drowned St. Mary's River

PERCY CREIGHTON: The Indian have a big battle with the Kootenay and killed many.

NORTH BLACKFEET

CRANE BEAR: A Blackfeet, Mississaw, (Sits ?, ed.) goes insane. (1841, RR, ed.)

YELLOW FLY: The year of the Kootenay War.

RUNNING RABBIT: Small Pox

MANY GUNS: Pikuni = Kutenaa. Peigans and Kootenay had a war.

LITTLE CHIEF: The four tribes moved to the south they moved back to Blackfoot Crossing in the fall they moved to the Red Deer River camp there for the winter

1840

NORTH PEIGAN

BULL PLUME #1: When "Calf Feeding" was killed.

BULL PLUME #2: When "Calf Feeding" was killed.

BLOOD

BAD HEAD: Another Squaw named Hind Face was killed by a Blood Indian

DEMPSEY: *This woman was killed by a drunken Blood.*

PERCY CREIGHTON: Big Small Pox Epidemic. Many deaths among the Indians.

NORTH BLACKFEET

CRANE BEAR: A Blackfeet has his leg cut off, after it was frozen crossing a river. [1841, Running Rabbit, ed.]

YELLOW FLY: The big epidemic year.

RUNNING RABBIT: Cut Nose, Crow Indian (Eagle Rib, born)

MANY GUNS: Umaxkapiksi = Big small pox

LITTLE CHIEF: They moved to the Blackfoot Crossing in the month of June Mr. Cut Nose a Crow Indian came to visit the Blackfeets he was welcome he was given a lot of horses also a lot of dry goods he than back south the late Eagle Rib was born at treaty No. 7 he was made head chief he died in 1909

1841

NORTH PEIGAN

BULL PLUME #1: When "Crow Moving" and his band were killed.

BULL PLUME #2: When "Crow Moving" and his band were killed.

BULL PLUME # 2: When "High Chief" was killed. *This is an extra event added to BULL PLUME #2, Both events are shown.*

BLOOD

BAD HEAD: Mahertawatow itomotsarpi "Going Crow" killed by a party of Crows

DEMPSEY: Walking Crow/when he was killed

PERCY CREIGHTON: A warrior by the name of Cut Nose, killed a Crow Indian in a battle.

NORTH BLACKFEET

CRANE BEAR: A Blackfeet (Natos onistaw) *[Sun Calf or Holy Calf, ed.]* is pursued by the Crow with no letup for four days, without being able to eat, but he drinks his own urine and is saved.

YELLOW FLY: The year a Crow Indian Chief without a nose was killed.

RUNNING RABBIT: Cut Hair Inside made Sundance. (Sit was craze [sic.]) (Sun Calf went long war)

MANY GUNS: Kaxkaniwa = Cut Nose. This was a Crow, and was killed by Blackfoot.

LITTLE CHIEF: A Blackfoot Mr. Cut Hair In Side made the Sun Dance just camping around by the Bow River in the fall after they all got this supply of meat they moved east of the Blackfoot Crossing for the winter

1842

NORTH PEIGAN

 BULL PLUME #1: When many horses died from starvation.

 BULL PLUME #2: When many horses died from starvation.

At this point, in BULL PLUME#2 a second pictograph is added for each year, on the right hand side of the page. We will give an interpretation of it whenever possible.

 BULL PLUME #2 B: *An image of a horse with its ribs showing would mean the starving of horses.*

"…the snows lay so deep that many of our horses perished." [*Brings-Down-The-Sun to McClintock*] [*Old North Trail*] *Ewers correspondence with McClintock shows the date to be 1842. (Ewers; 1943; 605)*

BLOOD

BAD HEAD: Itake-piskiopi akokinu Large number of lodges camped near the Porcupine Hill at the place called "Women Pound".

WHITE BULL: Large number of camps camping near women swimming pound in Montana

LEGAL: *A large number of Bloods gathered at Women's Buffalo Jump near the Porcupine Hills, in south-western Alberta, and killed many buffalo.*

PERCY CREIGHTON: Inside Cutter, a well known woman, was accused of infidelity by her husband and took an oath of her innocence. Had she been guilty, she would have died.

NORTH BLACKFEET

CRANE BEAR: Sixipiskan (Black Buffalo Jump) The Blackfeet make a pound enclosure in newly burned country and there trap many buffaloes.

YELLOW FLY: The year of the Big Denial. This concerned the whole tribe.

RUNNING RABBIT: Black Ration *[Piskan, ed.]*, White Eagle born.

MANY GUNS: Siksipiskan (Black piskan) So named because the enclosure made of burned stuff since a bush fire had burned over the ground.

LITTLE CHIEF: Still at Blackfoot Crossing not much moving around just hunting for Buffalo the late White Eagle was born he was made a head chief treaty No. 7 he died in the year 1908

1843

NORTH PEIGAN

BULL PLUME #1: When the white men shot at "Old Sun"

BULL PLUME #2: When the white men shot at "Old Sun"

BULL PLUME #2 B: *Two rifles would indicate a battle, i.e. shooting at Old Sun.*

BLOOD

BAD HEAD: Sorkoyenamay sixikay iteskimarpi napekwax A white man named "Karkoyomarkan" – Running Wolf – at (Fort) Benton fired the cannon at a party of Blackfeet and killed thirteen of them.

WHITE BULL: American white men attacked South Peigan Indians camps near Fort Benton with Cannon fire by white man called him Running Wolf. Killed thirteen of them.

DEMPSEY: Big mouthed gun/Blackfeet hunted by/ white man.

Some North Blackfoot coming to trade at Fort McKenzie were fired upon with a cannon by A. M. Harvey, who was known in Blackfoot as Running Wolf. This action was supposedly taken in retaliation for the theft of cattle and the killing of a Negro employee during the previous year. E.A.C. Hatch (cited in McDonnell, 1940:268) said the incident occurred on Feb.19, 1844, and that six Indians were killed and several others were wounded.

In the fall of 1843, a group of twenty Blackfoot warriors stopped at Fort McKenzie on their way to raid the Crows. When the felt they were not treated the way they should have been, they left, driving off the cattle which belonged to the fort.

A Negro employee of the company, named Tom Reese, started after them with a dozen men. George Weippert, a witness to the event, tells what happened next, "...in the pursuit (he) made a show of bravado and made many threats. The consequence was he was shot dead when he endeavored to carry his threats into execution." (Wheeler; 1940;248)

Chardon, the head trader, and A.M. Harvey, the chief clerk, both swore they would have revenge. Their chance came that spring. A band of North Blackfeet, under their chief Old Sun, arrived at the fort with robes to trade. The two chiefs were invited into the fort and feasted. They were also securely locked in a room until their people came to trade in the morning. "Harvey had the cannon loaded to the muzzle with all kinds of missiles, and in the morning when the Indians in quite a large body had come up in a line along the fort in front of the gate and asked for their two chiefs...Harvey trained the loaded cannon in the bastion so as to rake through the line when fired...and touched off the cannon himself." (Wheeler; 1940; 248) Four fell dead and seventeen were wounded. The survivors mounted and fled as fast as possible, leaving the robes and other furs where they had unloaded them. The two chiefs had mysteriously escaped. Harvey eventually was dismissed from the company for this action. The fort had to be abandoned for fear of revenge attacks by the Blackfoot.

PERCY CREIGHTON: The Blood built a huge buffalo pen & had a successful killing. They called this Black Buffalo Run (beyond Shell Butte).

NORTH BLACKFEET

CRANE BEAR: A Blackfeet (Napiskonaketaw) (Old Sun ____, ed.) is killed by an American cannon.

YELLOW FLY: Black Pis Kun year, or Black Buffalo Trap year.

RUNNING RABBIT: The White mans shoot Indians [Whiteman and Blackfoot war]; Frost feet (Prairie White Man)

MANY GUNS: Itsa piskunapani yopi. "Time a white man was shooting as in the states." The first chief Low Horns (Ikuskine) was killed by Crees near Drumheller.

Low Horn, North Blackfeet-Blackfoot chief, courtesy Northern Natural Gas Co. Omaha, Nebraska. The shell covered otter hide worn by Low Horn was mentioned by Thompson in the early 1800's. "They have a civil chief and military chief. The first was Sakatow, the orator, and the office appeared hereditary in his family, as his father had been the civil chief, and his eldest son was to take his place at his death and occasionally acted for him...he was always well dressed, and his insignia of office, was the backs of two fine otter skins covered with mother of pearl, which from behind his neck hung down his breast to below the belt; when his son acted for him, he always had this ornament on him" [Tyrrell,1968; 346]

For more details of this event see Dempsey story on Low Horn's death "The Amazing Death of Calf Shirt", U. of Oklahoma Press, *1994 and "Paul Kane's Country", J. Russell Harper, U. of Toronto Press 1971, 147*

LITTLE CHIEF: A Mr. White Man shot and killed Mr. Frost Feet he got killed about Mr. White Man's wife

Scalp-Roller, Blood-Blackfoot, was 85 when he told the following story to R.N. Wilson in 1893.

"We of the Blackfoot Nation never strung up young men [in the torture rite]. In early days, 45 or 50 years ago I guess it was, we were all camped beyond the Sweet Grass Hills, below us were the Gros Ventres in camp. We were all having, our O-Kon; *[Okan, or Sun Dance, ed.]* our people then first saw the string up of men, the Gros Ventres were doing it. I was then a married man, at any rate I know that. The Gros Ventres had learned the practice from some distant south eastern people, whom they had visited some years before. These people they call in Blackfoot nam-istch or uks-i-tupie, [People of the East], we call them also Nu-s-e-po-ya *[Nitsipoyi, "Real Speakers", or Blackfoot speakers, ed.]* because some few of our people [who went there with the Gros Ventres] said that they easily understood them. These people also fought with the Wolf People, Pawnees. Gros Ventres used to tie buffalo heads to the back sticks [skewers] in O-Kon, but we did not do it, our 3 tribes always put [tied] the shield there. Our people never tortured in O-Kon as bad as Gros Ventres and the people they learned it from; we do not cut as big a strip of hide [on the Indian's breasts]. I think that the sacred lodge was called O-Kon because it is so large. We do not consider torture, bravery or [that there is] any connection between the two; boys often do so before they are old enough to go to war, and many brave men never were tortured, it is religious, sacred; fingers were always given to Sun 'to eat' by young men." *[Scalp-Roller to Wilson, March 28, 1893; Godsell, 1959; 232]*

Piercing at the Sun Dance ca. 1892 Blood Reserve, R.N. Wilson photo, Glenbow Archives

1844

NORTH PEIGAN

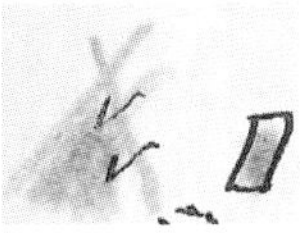 BULL PLUME #1: When they fought at the Belly River. *Blackfeet, Blood, Peigan, Sioux.*

 BULL PLUME #2: When they fought at the Belly Buttes. On the Blood Reserve.

 BULL PLUME #2 B: *A deer or antelope head.*

In many cases the "Sioux" referred to are actually Assiniboines.

BLOOD

BAD HEAD: Hayak-etorpommaop The Bloods separate in to two parties for trading, the one going to (Fort) Benton and the other to Rocky Mountain House.

This would be the result of the trouble some had with the traders at Fort Benton the previous year.

PERCY CREIGHTON: Blackfoot (N.) had a battle with white fur trader. Many were killed on both sides.

NORTH BLACKFEET

CRANE BEAR: A Blackfeet (Kataomarken) (Not Running, ed.) walking alone in the Sand Buttes, on the present Blackfoot Reserve, meets a Cree who kills him. (1845, MANY GUNS & RR, ed.)

YELLOW FLY: When the whites first shot the Indians.

RUNNING RABBIT: Kind Whitemans came; Good Eagle born

MANY GUNS: Axsapiapikueiks = Good White Men. The year the traders came. Akokimam = Many Feathers (was killed by Cree).

LITTLE CHIEF: The Indians first saw the white men I suppose that is the year the white came here the first Indians that saw these white men seen that they had so short a hair the Indians ran away from them afraid of them which the white were trying to stop them and give them some thing to eat they ran to the camps and told the Chief we saw some water man coming out of the water they got no hair so all went to meet the white men the white men give the Indians a lot of grub they were soon friends

James Doty, in 1854, wrote that ten years prior [1844], five Blackfoot followed the eastern slope of the Rocky Mountains until they reached Taos and towns between there and Santa Fe. [This was Far-off-in-Sight, from the Bloods, and James Bird.] [Doty, James to Isaac Stevens, 1854, December 20, Indian Office Records, U.S. National Archives]

1845

NORTH PEIGAN

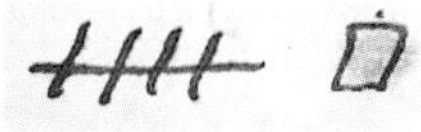 BULL PLUME #1: When the Peigans line of march was broken by the Sioux.

 BULL PLUME #2: When the Peigans line of march was broken by the Sioux.

BULL PLUME #2 B: *No second pictograph.*

There is no doubt a misidentification happened here. Somewhere through time, interpretation, or just mishearing the tribe was identified as Sioux instead of Crow. We have a good record of the event mentioned, since it was so significant to the Blackfoot people. It was the near extermination of the Small Robes Band with one hundred and thirteen killed and one hundred and sixty women and children captured [DeSmet, p524].

"We camped for a time on the Judith River, and then determined to move over on the Musselshell, follow it down by easy stages, and return to the Missouri by way of the east slope of the Snowy Mountains. About noon of the second day we came to the divide separating the two streams. Our column was loosely scattered along four or five miles of the trail that day, and most of the hunters were behind, away to the east and west, skinning buffalo and other game they had killed; ahead of us a mile or so rode our scouts, some thirty or forty men. It was a warm day; the horses felt lazy as well as their riders, and the big camp moved slowly along the trail, widely scattered as I have said. The scouts far ahead, gave no sign that they had seen anything to make them suspicious. The old people dozed in their saddles; young men here and there were singing war, or hunting songs; the mother crooned to the babe at her breast; all were happy. The scouts passed out of view own the south slope of the gap, and the head of our column was nearing the summit, when out from a large pine grove on our right dashed at least two hundred mounted Crows, and fell upon us. Back turned the people, the women and old men madly urging their horses, scattering travois and lodge poles along the way, shrieking for help, calling on the gods to preserve them. Such fighting men as there were along this part of the line did their utmost to check the rush of the Crows, to cover the retreat of the weak and defenseless. Hearing shots and shouts, back came the scouts, and from the rear came charging more men to the front. But in spite of stubborn resistance the Crows swept all before them for a distance of at least two miles, strewing the trail with our dead and dying people – men, women, children, even babies. They took not one captive, but shot and struck, and lanced to kill, scalping many of their victims.

But at last the Peigans bunched up in some sort of order, and the Crows drew off and rode away to the south, singing their songs of victory, taunting us by waving in triumph the scalps they had taken. So badly had our people been stampeded, so stunned were they by the terrible calamity that had betaken them, that they simply stood and stared at the retreating enemy, instead of following them and seeking revenge.

Right there in the gap the lodges were pitched, and search for the dead and missing began. By night all the bodies had been recovered and buried. On every hand, in nearly every lodge, there were mourners cutting their hair, gashing their lower limbs, crying and wailing, calling over and over again by the hour the names of the loved ones they had lost. Yes, it was a camp of mourning. For weeks and months, when evening came, the the wailing of the mourners, sitting out in the darkness just beyond the circle of the lodges, was pitiful to hear. It was a very long time before singing and laughter, and the call of the feast-giver were again heard. I happened to be with the scouts that day, and when we charged back did my best with them to check the Crows. But they so far outnumbered us, had so demoralized the people by their unexpected and fierce assault, that we were well-nigh powerless until our men in the rear came up. More than half of the scouts were killed. I got an arrow in the thigh. In all one hundred and thirteen Peigan were killed, while we shot down but seven of the enemy. *[Hugh Monroe to Schultz, 1973, 194-196]*

The Crow side of this event was related to Edwin Denig, trader to the Crows at Fort Union, by Rotten Belly, chief of the Crow.

When arrived at the sole command he left off heading small parties and carried war into their enemies' country on a large scale. The first grand battle was with about 80 lodges of the Blackfeet on Muscleshell River. Rotten Belly had his spies out watching movements of this camp for months beforehand, and having collected the whole Crow Nation maneuvered them in such a way as not to raise the suspicion of their enemies. He appeared to be marching out of their country when in reality he was encircling them. His wish was to come upon them on some plain, and take them unprepared.

When by his runners he knew that the time and situation were favorable to his views, he, by forced marches, placed his camp near them without being discovered. Under cover of the night about 400 warriors placed themselves still closer. Early in the day when their enemy's camp was on the move, scattered over a level plain of some miles in extent, he gave the word to charge. Terrible was the storm that swept over the Blackfeet. The Crows were well armed, mounted, and prepared, the others embarrassed with their women, children, and baggage. Their long and weak line of march was literally, "rubbed out" by their savage foes. Whoever endeavored to defend was killed, the women and children taken prisoners. Most of the men of the Blackfeet were in front of the traveling van. They soon rallied and returned the charge but were outnumbered. Although they fought bravely for some time they soon were obliged to leave their families and seek safety in flight. Others died defending their children. In the end, after a severe battle of a few hours, 100 and upwards of the Blackfeet lay dead on the field. Two hundred and thirty women and children were taken prisoners and more than 500 head of horses fell to the share of the Crows, besides all the lodges, camp equipment, provisions, etc. The Crows lost 22 men in this battle, besides others badly wounded. *[Rotten Belly, Crow, to Edwin Denig]*

Crow delegation to Washington, D.C. 1873, Henry or Julius Ulke photo, Washington D.C.;Back row left to right; Long Horse; Thin Belly; Bernard Paero, interpreter; Blackfoot's wife; Agent Pease; Iron Bull's wife; Pierce Shane, interpreter; Mo-mukh-pi-tche; middle row; Bear Wolf [Packs the Bear]; White Calf; Blackfoot or Sits in the Middle, principle chief of the Mountain Crow; Iron Bull, chief of the Mountain Crow; One-Who-Leads-the-Old-Dog; Old Crow; Front Row; Stays With The Horses; Bear Wolf's wife; Good Medicine Pipe; Old Crow's wife.

BLOOD

BAD HEAD: Otsitsestarkapipi natosepokomiw A Blood named "Going with the Sun" hides himself from the Crees and escapes.

DEMPSEY: When he crawled under/Going to the Sun

LEGAL: A Blood named Going to the Sun hid in a hole to escape from the Crees.

PERCY CREIGHTON: White man came to the Indians – gave them gifts and food. This happened a year after the battle. These whites were called The Good White Men Came.

NORTH BLACKFEET

CRANE BEAR: At High River a Blackfeet (Akkaekimaniw = Many Feathers) kills a Cree. *[1844, LITTLE CHIEF; 1844, MANY GUNS, ed.]*
YELLOW FLY: When the first generous White Man arrived.

RUNNING RABBIT: Not Running, killed (Mrs. Weasel Calf born)

MANY GUNS: Kotaumaxkan = Not Running. He was a Blackfoot, ambushed and killed by Crees in the Sand Hills.

LITTLE CHIEF: The late Good Eagle was born Mr. Not Running was killed in a battle with the Crees also Mrs. Wolf Calf was born

1846

NORTH PEIGAN

BULL PLUME #1: "The Horse" slipped out of tent and ran away. *"The Horse" was a prisoner.*

BULL PLUME #2: "The Horse" slipped out of tent and ran away.

BULL PLUME #2 B: *No second pictograph.*

The symbols show he had taken refuge in a Medicine Pipe owner's lodge [embracing the Medicine Pipe], and could not be harmed.

Medicine Pipe hanging over door with tripod and "Chief" drum leaning against tipi, in South Peigan-Blackfoot camp. ca. 1906, McClintock photo, Beinecke Archive, Yale University

BLOOD

BAD HEAD: Etsipiksikamotspi Sapow The Crows came right in front of the camp to steal horses.

PERCY CREIGHTON: A well known Indian – No Runner was killed by the Crow.

NORTH BLACKFEET

CRANE BEAR: The Band of chief of the Sayex [Crow Shoe's camp] Blackfeet kill a Whiteman named Kakatosew *[Star, ed.]*

YELLOW FLY: The year "Did Not Run", warrior, was killed.

RUNNING RABBIT: Bull Rations [Piskan, ed.] (Tied Up Many Feathers On His Head) *[See Little Chief, ed.]*

MANY GUNS: Ite stamiksipiskiopi = "Piskan with only bulls," no cows at all caught.

During a part of the Buffalo Calling Ceremony young girls danced in imitation of the buffalo.

"They collected all the little girls to dance. One old man, Maistopan [Crow Arrow] was sitting at the door. The girls were dancing with their robes wrong side out so fur is outside 'so as to imitate buffalo.' The old man was so excited, he jumped up to dance! Men are not supposed to dance. Consequently the next day sure enough the piskin was half full of buffalo bulls and their meat is tough!" *[Crooked Meat Strings to Hanks,* M8458, Box 1, file 9]

LITTLE CHIEF: Bull Ration was missing for a long time he went out hunting did not show up so they all went to look for him they found him in the bushes tied up to a tree with Feathers on his head just like an offering to the sun

1847

NORTH PEIGAN

 BULL PLUME #1: The year of stealing horses while they were busy buying at the store. *At Edmonton.*

 BULL PLUME #2: The year of stealing horses while they were busy buying at the store.

BULL PLUME #2 B: *No pictograph.*

"Assiniboines carried off 24 horses from Edmonton..." *[Kane,1859; 265]*

SOUTH PEIGAN

BIG NOSE WAR RECORD: West butte of Sweetgrass Hills 300 lodges of Peigans attacked at night By 53 Cree. All Crees killed, Peigan lost 13.

BLOOD

BAD HEAD: Katatsinipoka otsitomosok assinay Not Cared for Child killed by the Crees on Teton River.

DEMPSEY: Not a Favorite Child/ when he was defeated/ Assiniboine

LEGAL: *This Blood Indian was killed by Assiniboine on the Milk River*

WHITE BULL: Great medicine man of all Blackfoot nations, his name is Eat Berries, died that year.

PERCY CREIGHTON: The enemy (Cree) came to the lodge of Many Feathers to steal horses. Feathers killed a Cree at night.

NORTH BLACKFEET

CRANE BEAR: A Blackfeet (Makoyimmarsin) (Wolf Facing the Winter – Wolf Good, ? ed.) is scalped while sleeping by the Crow, but did not die from it, ekamotaw. (He survived, ed.) (1847, MANY GUNS & RUNNING RABBIT & LITTLE CHIEF; 1848, YELLOW FLY, ed.)

YELLOW FLY: The year "Many Plumes" killed the man who was going to steal from him.

RUNNING RABBIT: Wolf Good

MANY GUNS: Makuyim axsin (Wolf Facing The Winter?) This Blackfoot was scalped by Cree but lived.

LITTLE CHIEF: Wolf Good was born not much doing that year all living good lots of food

1848

NORTH PEIGAN

BULL PLUME #1: When the Sioux stole many of our horses.

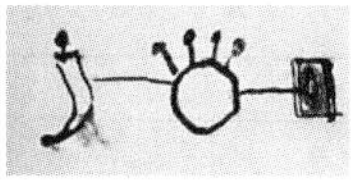

BULL PLUME #2: When the Sioux stole many of our horses.

 BULL PLUME #2 B: *Two rifles indicating a battle.*

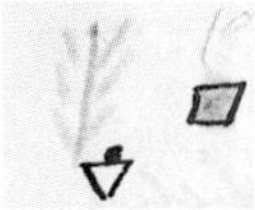 BULL PLUME #1: "Dwarf Black Plume". *Died. [Little Black Plume, ed.]*

 BULL PLUME #2: "Dwarf Black Plume".

 BULL PLUME #2 B: *Grizzly bear claw with a series of lines leading to a crescent with two dots.*

Assiniboines reenacting a raid on a tipi for horses,1898 at Wolf Point, Montana. photo by S.W. Ormsby

BLOOD

BAD HEAD: Nisto-matapistotsi Bad Head, *[I, Bad Head, ed.]* with a large band of Bloods, move camp during the winter to go to (Fort) Benton.

WHITE BULL: Bad Head with large band of Indians moving camps during the winter to Fort Benton, Montana, spend winter there.

PERCY CREIGHTON: West Wolf, a Blood Warrior, was killed and scalped by the Cree in a battle.

Fort Benton after it was rebuilt in 1860 of adobe bricks. Fort Benton Historical Society

NORTH BLACKFEET

CRANE BEAR: Orkonokimmew, grand chief of the Sarcee, is killed by the Blackfeet. (1849, RR & MANY GUNS & LC, ed.)

YELLOW FLY: The year "Wolf's Direction", warrior, was scalped alive.

RUNNING RABBIT: Big Crow Eagle, died quickly.

MANY GUNS: Umaxkaistuipita = Big Crow Eagle. A big Blackfoot chief, killed by Crees.

LITTLE CHIEF: Crow Eagle died suddenly near the Blackfoot Crossing very good year for the four tribes

1849

NORTH PEIGAN

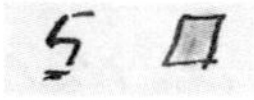

BULL PLUME #1: When the Peigans killed 50 Crees. *Down in bottom near old agency.*

BULL PLUME #2: When the Peigans killed 50 Crees.

BULL PLUME #2 B: *A white man on horseback.*

BLOOD

BAD HEAD: Nisitsippi otsenotsaw assinay Fifty Crees were killed near Milk River on this side of the boundary

WHITE BULL: Blood Indians killed fifty Cree Indians near Milk River on south sides of the Boundary line.

DEMPSEY: Fifty/when they were killed/Assiniboines

"Nitsi-sinawa" Real Crees, was the name for the Assiniboine. In December of 1849 Edwin Denig, a trader, wrote to Alexander Culbertson that fifty-two young Assiniboines Were killed by the Peigans on the Marias River. The Assiniboine stole a number of horses from the camp. The Peigans gave chase and stopped them on the prairie five or ten miles from the camp. The Assiniboine forted as best they could and held out for the best part of the day. The entire Peigan camp turned out and before evening the Assiniboine were wiped out. It was one of the greatest losses the Assiniboine suffered in years.(Ewers; 1952; 145)

Assiniboine war party setting out, [for the Sun Dance pole, ed.]1906, Sumner Matteson photo

PERCY CREIGHTON: Big Crow Eagle – a North Peigan chief, died of illness this year.

NORTH BLACKFEET

CRANE BEAR: Mahestoepitaw *[Crow Eagle, ed.]* chief of the Blackfeet, dies of natural causes, *[1848, LITTLE CHIEF; 1850, MANY GUNS, ed.]*

YELLOW FLY: The year "Big Crow Eagle" fainted.

RUNNING RABBIT: Fight against Sarcees

MANY GUNS: Saxsiwa = Sarsi. Sarsi and Blackfoot had a war – they were usually allies, (so this is unusual)

LITTLE CHIEF: The Blackfeet fight with the Sarcees they did not fight this how it is a Blackfeet had a fight with a Sarcee the Blackfeet went to his tepee took his gun shot the Sarcee the (rel)atives of this Sarcee got mad want to fight the Blackfeet that killed this Sarcee the Blackfeet relatives got mad too wanted to fight the Sarcee so Crowfoot stop this going to be a fight so they made friends again

The confusion in Cree being identified as Assiniboine and vis versa, as well as Plains Ojibwa [Saulteaux] being identified as either group was caused by several factors. First, the Cree and Assiniboine had a longstanding alliance and they often had camps of mixed Assiniboine and Cree. As a result they had many shared cultural traits, as well as inter-marriages. They were both familiar to the Blackfoot since they were the intermediaries in the trade for European goods for years before trading posts were established in Blackfoot territory.

The years following 1820, with the merging of the Hudson's Bay Company and Northwest Company, caused a great shift on the northern plains. The measles and whooping cough epidemic of 1819-20 decimated the eastern groups of the Cree, Assiniboine, and Ojibwa. Small groups of Ojibwa [soon to be called "Saulteaux"] had already made their way to the plains area around 1780 after the smallpox epidemic greatly reduced the populations of the Cree and Assiniboine, and adopting many of their cultural traits.

"About the year1780, smallpox overtook them, and decimated them fearfully. Thereafter…the Saulteaux left the forests… and entered on the plains of Red River…The Saulteaux found the Assiniboines and the Crees encamped at the Pembina Mountain... and after smoking and feasting for two or three days, the children of the forest were formally invited to dwell on the plains – to eat out of the same dish, to warm themselves at the same fire, and to make common cause with them against their enemies the Sioux…"Your presence," they said, "will remove the cloud of sorrow that is in our minds and strengthen us against our enemies" *[Gunn, 1860]*

After 1820 the Cree and Ojibwa [Saulteaux] began leaving the fur trade and moving to the plains in greater numbers. In addition, due to the merger of the trading companies two-thirds of their work force, the majority of whom were Metis, were dismissed. This population kept their hunting life style and formed groups of their own, or joined their Native relatives on the plains. Thus the Blackfoot were confronted by enemies on their eastern border consisting of mixed groups of Cree, Assiniboine, Saulteaux and Metis pushing westward in ever greater numbers. The identification, by writers of the winter counts, could thus vary with each story teller as to which group was involved. Case in point being the battle at Lethbridge in which Cree, Assiniboine and Saulteaux were all involved yet identified as "Cree".

1850

NORTH PEIGAN

BULL PLUME #1: When the Bloods stole many horses. *From states.*

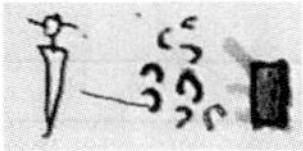

BULL PLUME #2: When the Bloods stole many horses.

Different drawings for BULL PLUME #1 & 2

BULL PLUME #2 B: *A shield with feathers hanging down.*

SOUTH PEIGAN

BIG BRAVE: Fall of year Gambler killed on warpath; Peigan wintered on Marias.

ELK HORN: Camped down at Mouth River; Gambler killed; Sun Dance at Crow Garden.

MRS. BIG NOSE: Gambler killed; in the winter many people died from sickness, some Chiefs. Summer Piegans had a Sun Dance at Crow Gardens; winter camped at Fort Benton.

BLOOD

BAD HEAD: Pitaonistaw otsenitarpi Eagle White Calf killed by a Cree near Sweet Grass Hills

WHITE BULL: Eagle White Calf or By killed by Cree Indians on north side of the Red River

PERCY CREIGHTON: Blackfoot & Sarcee had a big battle with the Sarcee – Many were killed on both sides.

NORTH BLACKFEET

CRANE BEAR: Mahestopapiw, an old Blackfeet dies of old age. "It is at the time that I am born," said old Makoyatosew (Crane Bear). *[1848, RUNNING RABBIT, ed.]*

YELLOW FLY: The year of the Sarcee War.

RUNNING RABBIT: Crow Tribe killed

MANY GUNS: Maistoitapiwa = Crow Person (A Blackfoot) was killed by Crees.

LITTLE CHIEF: The four tribes Blackfeet Bloods and the Peigans Sarcee had a big battle with the Snake tribes the four tribes killed every one of these Snake Indians

1851

NORTH PEIGAN

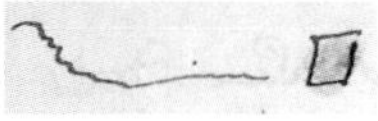
BULL PLUME #1: When the river flooded in winter.

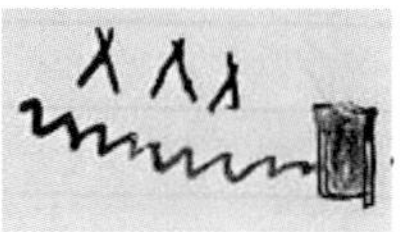
BULL PLUME #2: When the river flooded in winter.

[BULL PLUME # 1& #2 different pictographs]

BULL PLUME #2 B: *This appears to be a hand axe.*

SOUTH PEIGAN

BIG BRAVE: Big Lake, chief of Don't-Laugh *(band, ed.)* dies in fall of year; Peigan wintered on Marias which was high and flooded their camps; Sun Dance at Sweet Grass Hills; Bobtail Horse killed; a woman also killed.

ELK HORN: Camped near Fort Benton; moved to Yellowstone Country; some Crow escape by climbing down rope from rock *(see 1853, ed.)* Yellow River, place of Sun Dance; camped where Bad-Tail killed a Sioux.

MRS.BIG NOSE: Winter camped at Fort Benton. Some Crows escaped by letting themselves down by a rope, this place is named Snake Nose, south of the Missouri River. In winter camped near Yellowstone a place called Where the Foxes Society were transferring their dance to others. (see 1853, ed.) (Labeled as 4th year) In winter some Peigans and Blackfeet went on warpath and fought with Snake Indians and killed many of them. It was very cold had to use mittens while loading guns and fighting. Captured all the tipis and other property of the Snakes. Same winter ice broke up in river of Marias as ice broke up all of a sudden, the people all run out of tipis while the water swept or overflowed the camps. One of the tipis was the Black Buffalo lodge. While the rest of lodges was all carried down by the ice and water, the Buffalo Lodge was not budged and the next day all went and seen that the water made a circle around the lodge and leaving the only dry spot in the lodge. Because the lodge came from the water, the water did not harm it. *[Duvall notes, 1911, 568]*

BLOOD

BAD HEAD: Itsto-tokakoyew Plenty snow and the weather becoming mild, a freshet occurred in the wintertime. The Bloods fought the Snake Indians.

PERCY CREIGHTON: Bloods, Blk *(Blackfeet, ed.)* & North Peigan had a big battle with Cree. Crow Man – a well known Blood, was killed.

NORTH BLACKFEET

CRANE BEAR: The Snakes *(Shoshone, ed.)* (Pixexinnaetapix) are defeated by the Blackfeet. *(1850, LITTLE CHIEF, ed.)*

YELLOW FLY: The year of the war with the Crow, "Gens".

RUNNING RABBIT: Snake Tribe, killed them all

MANY GUNS: Piksiksinetapiwa =Snake People. Blackfoot killed some Snake Indians.

LITTLE CHIEF: The Blackfeet had a big battle with the Crow Indians in this battle they killed all the Crow Indians up south this battle took place after the battle the Blackfeet moved north

1852

NORTH PEIGAN

BULL PLUME #1: When "Wolf Chief" died suddenly.

BULL PLUME #2: When "Wolf Chief" died suddenly.

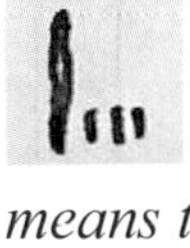
BULL PLUME #2 B: *A man figure with three lines next to him. This usually means three people.*

SOUTH PEIGAN

ELK HORN: Crossed Missouri River to camp; traded at Fort Benton and spent most of winter on Marias; a fight with Snake (Indians, ed.); ice broke up in winter (unusual); Sun Dance near this place; some Peigan killed by enemies. (1851-52)

BIG BRAVE: Leaves-Big-Lodge-Camp-Marks clubbed a Flathead but did not kill him; Peigan kill some Sioux on Marias in summer *(1853, ed.)*

BLOOD

BAD HEAD: Itapatorstoyeniw Manistokos "Father of Many Children" (the same who gave the present account) winter(ed) this side of the boundary line. *(aka, Bad Head)*

WHITE BULL: Many Feather on Head warrior, he life all alone. He sleep at the junction of Belly and St. Mary's River. Some spirit or soul gave him a power.

LEGAL: *Bad Head (or Father of Many Children) wintered in the northern part of the hunting grounds while the rest of the Bloods and the Peigans went to Fort Benton.*

PERCY CREIGHTON: - a battle with the Snake in which many of the latter were killed.

NORTH BLACKFEET

CRANE BEAR: A Blackfeet chief (Ketokeeapiw) *(Prairie Chicken Old Man, ed.)* is killed.

YELLOW FLY: The year of the Victory of the Snake Indians.

RUNNING RABBIT: Old Prairie Chicken Man, killed

MANY GUNS: Two entries:
(1) Kitokiapi = Prairie Chicken Old Man was killed by Cree
(2) Sisawa (is a man who does the contrary) Was killed by Cree. When he was young he always acted contrariwise. [*Query: " Why?"*] " I don't know why – he must have gotten a notion into his head. Maybe he istoxsin" = vow, pledge – i.e. vowed to do this.

LITTLE CHIEF: Mr. Old Prairie Chicken was killed in a battle with the Crows the Blackfeet suffered and lost lot of men in that battle

The Medicine Lodge *[Sun Dance, ed.]* was held at the time when the berries were ripe – about the end of July. Some time previously to that messages were sent out to notify all the bands where and when to meet. <u>The camp circle is formed only when all the bands</u>

are together. The tongues are then gathered for the Medicine Lodge. Scouts locate a suitable spot to erect the Lodge. A number of camp circles are made on the way to this site. The ceremony lasts four days. At the conclusion of the ceremony, camp is broken and each band goes its own way. In the camp circle all the members of a band camp together. *[No Coat to Collier, 1938, 30]*

Societies regulated the pitching of the tipis informing the camp circle. Only the tipis of the chiefs [bad] and of the societies were allowed within the circle. If a man camped too far outside the circle, the societies would tell him to move on. If he refused they would not punish him but take his tipi down and put it where it belonged.

In the camp circle:
The society leaders and the camp chiefs hold a council to settle plans – where to camp, when to hunt, etc. Scouts are sent out to locate camping sites and buffalo herds. Full Bear was the camp crier. He announced the plans to the whole camp, and gave advice on behavior in the camp and on the hunt. While in the camp circles individual hunters could get permission from the societies to hunt if they went to hunt in the opposite direction from that in which the camp was moving; in this way they would not frighten the herds that would be available to the whole camp. *[Green Grass Bull to Collier, 1938, 33]*

When the bands are in the camp circle societies police hunts. Punishment for breaking hunt rules; society members break bow, gun; cut horse's ears and tail; tear off all clothes of offender. The societies had police functions only during the circle camps. *[Calf Tail to Collier, 1938, 33]*

1853

NORTH PEIGAN

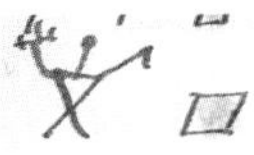
BULL PLUME #1: When "Tatoo" went crazy.

BULL PLUME #2: When "Tatoo" went crazy.

BULL PLUME #2 B:

SOUTH PEIGAN

BIG BRAVE: Black Tattoo became crazy; Goose killed in spring by Sioux; Goose's father killed some Crow; some Crow escape by letting themselves down a cliff with rope. *(1854, ed.)*

ELK HORN: On the Marias; man named Goose killed *(1854, ed.)*; in autumn hunted south of Fort Benton; traded at Fort Benton. (1853-54)

BLOOD

BAD HEAD: Otsitsapapimarpi assinaekivan mammapin The Crees coming after the Bloods make shelters of branches in the (newly abandoned) camp.

WHITE BULL: Cree Indians worries after the Blood Indians and make shelter of branches in the newly abandoned camps.

DEMPSEY: When he made a shelter of branches/Assiniboine/abandoned camp

PERCY CREIGHTON: - a battle with the Cree. Prairie Chicken Old Man, a well known Blood, was killed.

NORTH BLACKFEET

CRANE BEAR: The children *(i.e. people, ed)* of a Blackfeet (Akekakatosapiw) (Many Stars Old Man, ed.) are killed. *(Meaning the band of Many Stars Old Man, a chief, were wiped out., ed.)*

YELLOW FLY: The year "Prairie Chicken Old Man", warrior, was killed.

RUNNING RABBIT: Two camps, killed them all

MANY GUNS: Apsaokikin = Took a Cree Medicine Pipe. *(Meaning they captured a Cree Medicine Pipe. Ed.)*

MANY GUNS 65.68: White Flat Head and Now White Face and Wolf Big.

MANY GUNS 65.69: White Flat Head

LITTLE CHIEF: Two camps small camps got whiped *[wiped, ed.]* out by the Crees one Blackfoot camp and the other mixed Bloods Peigans

1854

NORTH PEIGAN

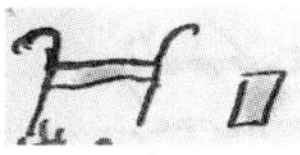

BULL PLUME #1: When they eat dogs.

 BULL PLUME #2: When they eat dogs.

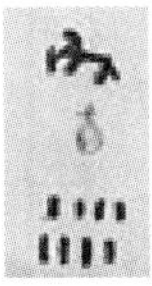 BULL PLUME #2 B: *This may indicate the event in Many Guns .68 when the Americans [Big Knives] feed the people.*

This again, indicates starvation times.

SOUTH PEIGAN

BIG BRAVE: Still Smoking killed; Peigan steal sorrel horse from Flathead. Peigan go on warpath south of Missouri; encounter white settlers, where Last Bull kills a Sioux Indian visitor.

ELK HORN: Wintered on the Teton; spring moved down the Missouri; killed – a man named High Ridge; made two Sun Dances; went to Bear Paw Mts.

BIG NOSE WAR RECORD: In Snake country 124 Peigans found lodge with father, mother, and two Grown sons. The men were killed and the woman spared. Took 36 days to return on foot.

BLOOD

BAD HEAD: Itaomitaohoyop The Indians are starving and eat their dogs.

PERCY CREIGHTON: Blood & Blackfeet were on the warpath. They made a raid on 2 lodges (Crow) & killed them all. This was known as the Raid On Two Lodges.

NORTH BLACKFEET

CRANE BEAR: Old Akekakatosapi *(Many Stars Old Man, ed.)* defeats the Cree by himself, somewhere on the Saskatchewan.

YELLOW FLY: The year two tepees were conquered and taken.

RUNNING RABBIT: We eating our dogs

MANY GUNS: Two entries:
(1) Aawa = Robe. Year the Blood Indian used his robe to get blood.
(2) Itspiotamiso = Coming Over The HN.*[Hill, ed.]* Took a Medicine Pipe from Cree.

MANY GUNS .68: The time we were eating dogs and the Big Knife *[American trader, ed.]* treated us.

MANY GUNS .69: The time we were eating dogs. Big Wolf and Many Stars Old Man.

LITTLE CHIEF: It was a very bad year for the four tribes they could not find the buffalo they got so hunger that they started to eat dogs later they found the buffalo if they did not eat dogs they would be all starve

CHAPTER 7

THE TREATIES BEGIN

The trickle of whites became a flood into Blackfoot country. With it came the treaties. At first asking for small concessions and peace the began to ask for more and more. The Americans began in 1855 with the Lame Bull Treaty to guarantee peace among the northern plains tribes and the use of a small piece of Blackfoot territory. Then the 1865 and 1868 treaties granting land to the new comers, which were never ratified by the United States Congress but took the land anyways. The Canadians followed suit in 1877. Life was changing for the Blackfoot, without their comprehension of the true nature of the treaties.

1855

NORTH PEIGAN

BULL PLUME #1: When treaty was first paid, in Montana

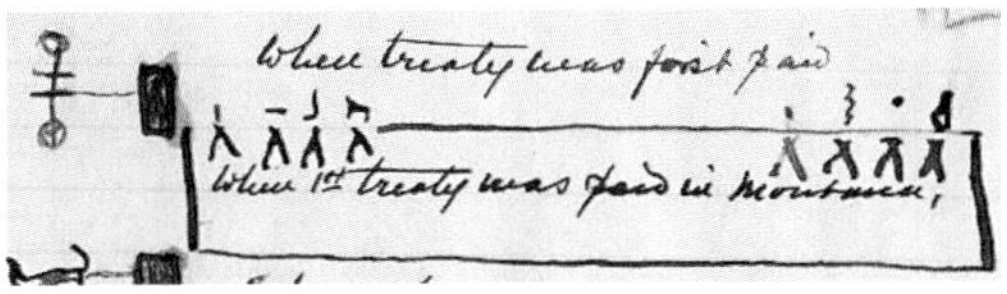

BULL PLUME #2: When 1st treaty was paid in Montana. *In addition to the original symbol there are a series of tipis drawn below the written description. Each tipi has a symbol above it that indicates each different tribe that took part in the signing.*

BULL PLUME #2 B: *The secondary pictograph to the right has the numeral 5 and five lines below it.*

SOUTH PEIGAN

BIG BRAVE: In fall, treaty made with Govt. at mouth of Yellow River – seven tribes there. Mountain Chief winters on Belly River. His daughter's clothes catch fire and she burns to death. During summer Mountain Chief has hiccoughs (sic.).

BIG BRAVE 2: Big Brave is 7 years old.

BIG NOSE WAR RECORD: 60 lodges of Peigans and 10 lodges of Pend d'Oreille camped together. 400 Sioux attacked. Sioux lost 16, Peigans & PD lost 11.

Cypress Hills – 200 lodges of Peigans were camped. Two Sioux stole horses, BN killed one.

Near Cypress Hills – 400 lodges of Peigan & Bloods, 8 Sioux stole horses were overtaken and all but one killed.

ELK HORN: Went toward Crow country; John Monroe came to tell Peigan soldiers were near to issue ammunition and some did not go because they were skeptical; six Flathead came there for ammunition, some Nez Perce, two North Blackfoot, a few Blood, four North Peigan and some Gros Ventre, but no Sarcee; camped on Two Medicine river; Missouri River; deep snow; Sun Dance at Yellow River. (1855-56)

BLOOD

BAD HEAD: Nitsitsitorkotspi Ennaken The Indians of different tribes received a large distribution of goods from the American soldiers whose commanding officer called "Ekkakisiw" or "Short Man" (Stephens) – is very much renowned amongst them.

WHITE BULL: White man named Red Hair make a treaty with Blood Indians and South Peigans in Yellow stone River, Montana and same time 99 years lease was surrendered by Bloods and Peigans to Red Hair.

DEMPSEY: When we were first paid/soldiers

PERCY CREIGHTON:
First treaty with the 7 tribes:

1. Blood
2. Peigan
3. North Blackfeet
4. South Peigan
5. Gros Ventre
6. River Crows
7. Nez Perce

Two Commissioners: A. Cummings & Isaac I. Stevens made the treaty on the Yellowstone River. The Blood chiefs who signed:

1. Onestay-say-nak-que-in [*Calf Out OF Sight, ed.]*
2. Father of All Children
3. Bull's Back Fat
4. Heavy Shield
5. Sun Calf
6. Calf Shirt

NORTH BLACKFEET

CRANE BEAR: There is war between Cree and Blackfeet at Paxatis, a small butte about east of Namaka (between Gleichen and Cluny).

YELLOW FLY: The year we ate dogs.

RUNNING RABBIT: States pay us first Treaty. (Three Sun born)

MANY GUNS: Two entries:
(1) Pitokus (A Blood) Eagle died. Took a lance from Cree (Atsina). *(The name "Atsina" means Gros Ventre. Asinawa means Cree. Which is intended is unknown. ed.)* A war at Hammer Hill – where there is now a monument (Note symbol). *[The symbol referred to is a syllabic writing.]*
(2) Pitospita = High Eagle = was killed by Cree.

MANY GUNS .68: Eagle Child and Tall Eagle and Kinakawa.

MANY GUNS .69: Eagle Child

LITTLE CHIEF: The united states paid the first treaty in the states at the place they call Yellow River

October 18, 1855. 3500 Blackfeet, Nez Perce, Flathead, Kutenai, and Pend d'Oreille attended the council with fifty-nine prominent chiefs from ten separate tribes present. This was an inter-racial "peace" treaty rather than an inter-racial "land" treaty. It was also a treaty of friendship between the plains and western tribes. It took place at the mouth of the Judith (Yellow) River on the Missouri.

For concessions granted at this council, the United States agreed to spend $20,000.00 annually on "useful goods and provisions for the four tribes of the Blackfoot Nation for a period of ten years..

Bloods arriving at the treaty grounds, 1855, Gustav Sohon watercolor, Washington State Historical Society, Tacoma, WA.

FROM BULL PLUME #2:

Signing of the Lame Bull Treaty 1855, Lame Bull and Isaac Stevens

Peigans

Bloods

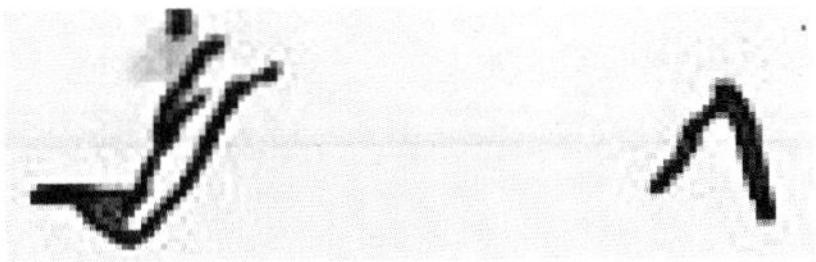

Blackfeet [Siksika]

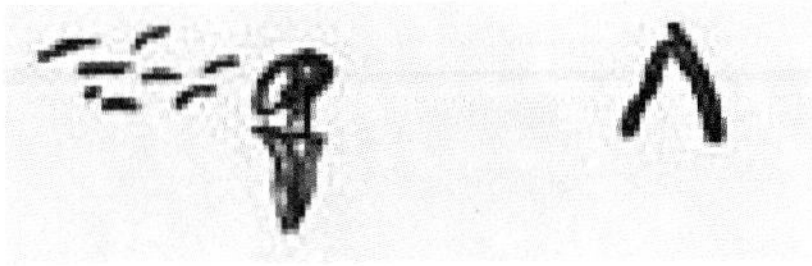

Sarcee

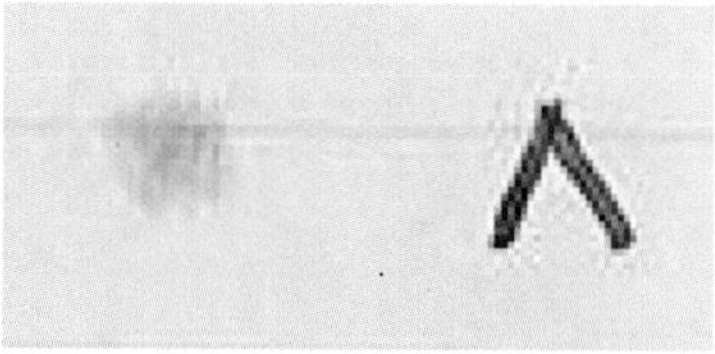

Nez Perce

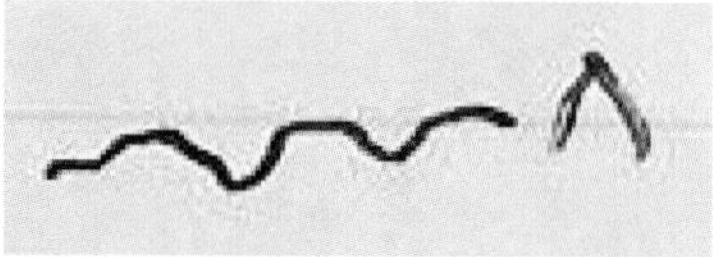

River People [Pend d'Oreilles]

Flathead

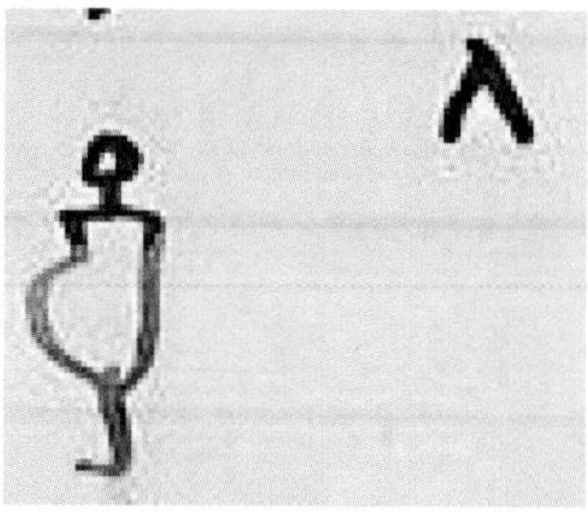

Gros Ventre

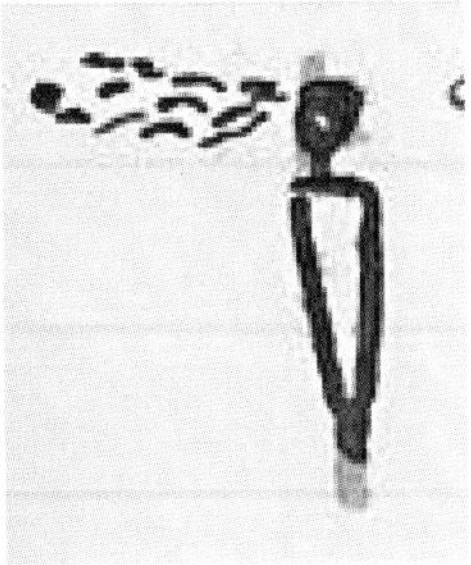

Sarcee

Drawing All Suns to Him

Spotted Eagle [South Peigan Chief]

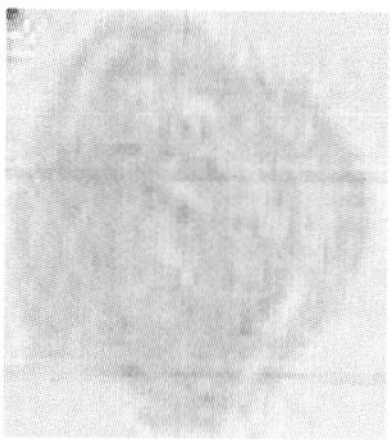

Nez Perce

 Big White Goose

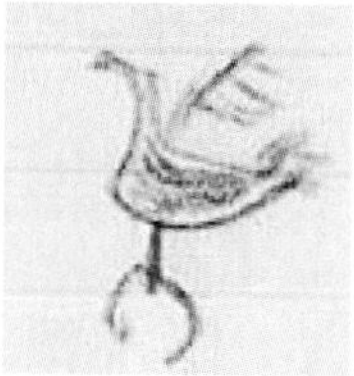 Morning Eagle

 Many White Horses

 Looking Glass

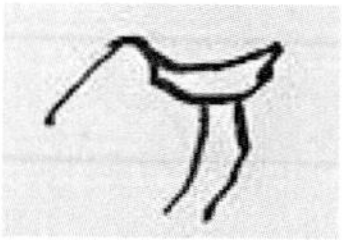 White Crane

Flatheads

Woodpecker

Long Hair

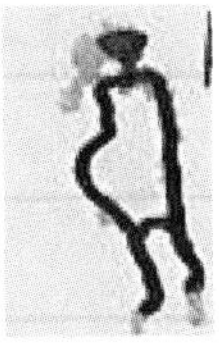
Gros Ventre

Sitting Woman

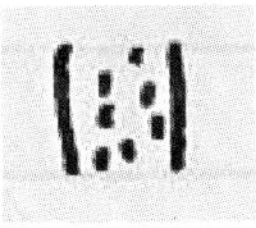
Star Blanket

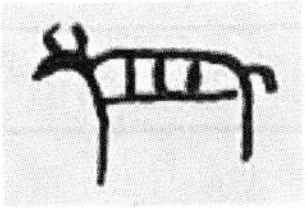
Spotted Calf

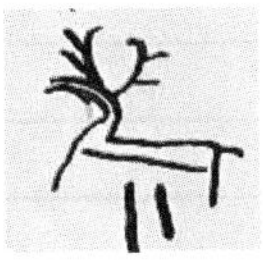
Two Elk

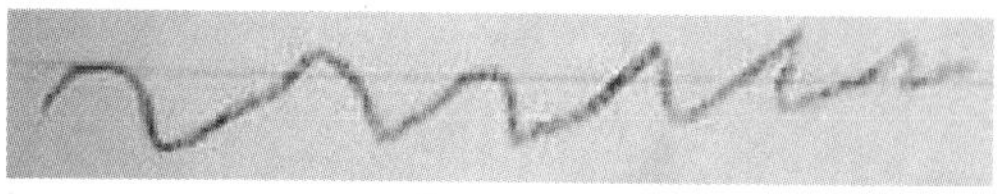
River People

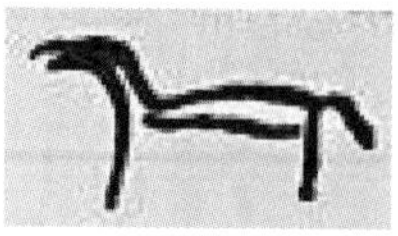
No Good Horses

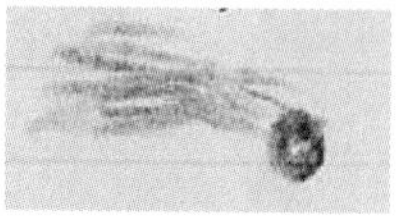
Big Smoke

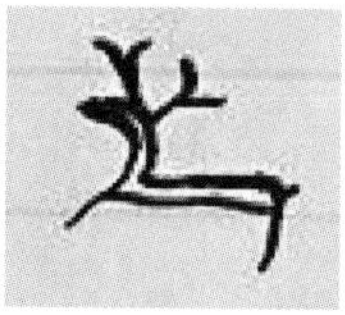
White Deer

Dwarf Coyote

Many Bears

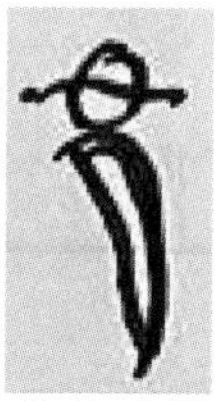
Blood

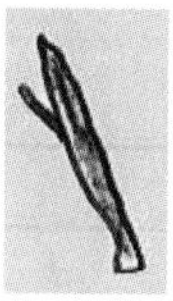
Bull Shoulder *[Buffalo Bull Back Fat]*

Calf Shirt

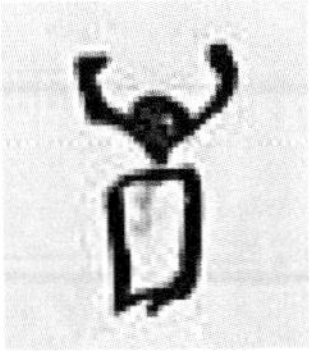 Bull Turning Around

 Sun Calf

 Blackfeet [Siksika]

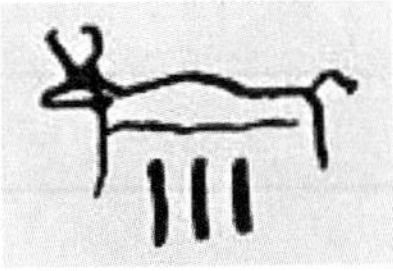 Three Bulls

 Bull Turning Around

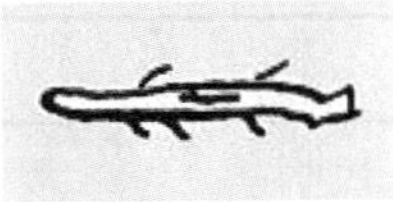 Fish Child

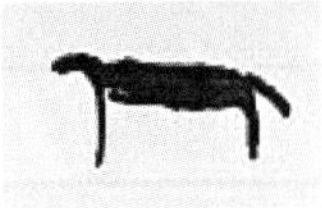 Black Wolf

Peigan

 Lame Bull

 Rattle Snake [Big Snake]

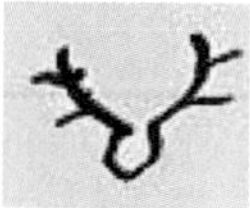
White Elk

Had Horses Before

Many Horses

Running Crane

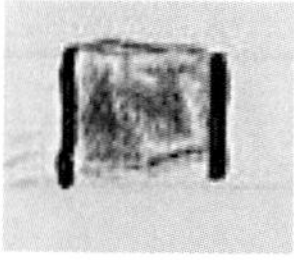
Chief Mountain

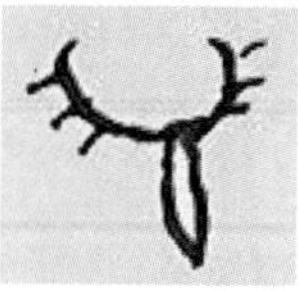
Elk Tongue Chief

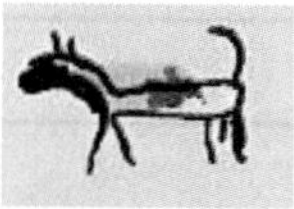
Young Pup

The following drawings of Blackfoot Chiefs present at the 1855 Treaty were done by Gustav Sohon and are in the collections of Washington State Historical Society.

Lame Bull, Peigan, *[Only Chief, ed.]* 1855, Gustav Sohon drawing, Washington State Historical Society, Tacoma, WA.

Chief Talker, Peigan, 1855, Gustav Sohon drawing, Washington State Historical Society, Tacoma, WA.

Big Snake, Peigan, 1855, Gustav Sohon drawing, Washington State Historical Society, Tacoma, WA.

Elk Tongue, *[Elk Tongue Chief, ed.]* Peigan, 1855, Gustav Sohon drawing, Washington State Historical Society, Tacoma, WA.

Mountain Chief, Peigan, 1855, Gustav Sohon drawing, Washington State Historical Society, Tacoma, WA.

White Bull, Peigan, 1855, Gustav Sohon drawing, Washington State Historical Society, Tacoma, WA.

Kutenapi, Blackfeet *[Kutenai Old Man,Siksika, ed.]*, 1855, Gustav Sohon drawing, Washington State Historical Society, Tacoma, WA.

Three Bulls, Blackfeet/Siksika, 1855, Gustav Sohon drawing, Washington State Historical Society, Tacoma, WA.

15th October 1855
Keh-ci-pu-nis-taw
White Buffaloe on the side-hill

White Buffalo on Side Hill, Peigan, 1855, Gustav Sohon drawing, Washington State Historical Society, Tacoma, WA.

Bad Head, *[Blood, ed.[*, 1855, Gustav Sohon drawing, Washington State Historical Society, Tacoma, WA.

Tatuye, Fox, Blood, 1855, Gustav Sohon drawing, Washington State Historical Society, Tacoma, WA.

Ninaonesta *[Chief Calf, ed.]*, Blood, 1855, Gustav Sohon drawing, Washington State Historical Society, Tacoma, WA.

Nis-tas-sa-na kwim
Blood indian Chief
Brother in law of Mr Colberson

Far Off in Sight *[Seen From Afar, ed.]* Blood, 1855, Gustav Sohon drawing, Washington State Historical Society, Tacoma, WA.

Heavy Shield /Middle Sitter, *[Sits-in-the-Middle, ed.]*, Peigan, 1855, Gustav Sohon drawing, Washington State Historical Society, Tacoma, WA.

Mikiapi *[Red Old Man, ed.]*, Peigan, 1855, Gustav Sohon drawing, Washington State Historical Society, Tacoma, WA.

Medicine Calf, Blood, 1855, Gustav Sohon drawing, Washington State Historical Society, Tacoma, WA.

Apyecaye ***[Apikai, Skunk, ed.]*** **Blood, 1855, Gustav Sohon drawing, Washington State Historical Society, Tacoma, WA.**

Low Horn, Blackfeet *[Siksika, ed.]*, 1855, Gustav Sohon drawing, Washington State Historical Society, Tacoma, WA.

1856

NORTH PEIGAN

 BULL PLUME #1: When the whole prairie was covered with ice.

 BULL PLUME #2: When ground was covered with ice.

 BULL PLUME #2 B: *A pictographic symbol for a white man. This may refer to 1857 or 1855.*

SOUTH PEIGAN

BIG BRAVE: Slippery winter – so much ice. In summer Mountain Chief and band went to Canada and killed thirty Sioux.

BIG BRAVE 2: ...place called Big Pile of Rocks.

ELK HORN: Slippery winter; some Peigan killed by Snake *[Indians, ed.]*.

BLOOD

BAD HEAD: Itestsikarkoy The ground is very slippery on account of glazy frost.

WHITE BULL: The slippery winter, ice all over the Prairies

PERCY CREIGHTON: A difficult winter – deep snow – no game. Dogs were killed for food. Winter called Feeding On Dogs.

NORTH BLACKFEET

CRANE BEAR: O. – The autumn snow is terrible, the ground remains slippery, and many buffalo die.

YELLOW FLY: First White Treaty at Yellowstone River in Montana.

RUNNING RABBIT: Icing everywhere.

MANY GUNS: Two entries:

(1) Otsitostsikaku = Slippery winter. Lots of deep snow at 1 degree. Chinook came, thawed, then froze so terribly slippery.

(2) Ksisxuksisiwa = Sharp Pointed Nose, a Blackfoot, killed by Crees.

MANY GUNS .68: The time the ground was slippery.

MANY GUNS .69: The time it was slippery. The time the Big Knives treated us.

LITTLE CHIEF: The four tribes were camping north for the winter they had a fair winter only there was ice all over a lot of water than it frozen up the ice just covered the ground

1857

NORTH PEIGAN

BULL PLUME #1: "Prairie Whiteman" committed murder.

BULL PLUME #2: "Prairie Whiteman" committed murder.

BULL PLUME #2 B: *A difficult image to interpret. A circle with lines around it and dots inside [usually means an Indian camp]. Above it a square shape with an opening at the top and dots inside [this usually means a white man's dwelling of some sort].*

[See Creighton 1858 for details of this event.]

SOUTH PEIGAN

ELK HORN: Camped on Cut Bank; went toward Missouri; Lame Bull killed by fall from horse (chief of tribe); traded at Sun River. (1857-58)

BIG BRAVE: Peigan camp on Marias. Blood kills a Flathead. Lame Bull, chief, killed by fall from horse in summer.

BIG BRAVE 2: camped below Shelby on Marias River.

1857 Camp Circle:
When, in 1857 Big Nose, chief of the Melted Fat band in which lived the Medicine Woman, came to the camp of Lame Bull, chief of the Hard Topknots, and offered him the

pipe in invitation to come to the camp circle, Lame Bull refused the pipe, saying that he had to go over to his wife's grave [somc distancc away] to recover some important papers that were buried with her. Big Nose knocked the tobacco from the pipe, and went on to invite the other bands. Lame Bull took his band to where his wife was buried. While there his horse stumbled in a buffalo chase and he was killed. Big Buffalo Stone succeeded him as chief and took the band back to the camp circle. This is the only case that Green Grass Bull has heard in which a band chief refused the pipe inviting him to the camp circle. It was thought to be bad luck, especially after this incident. *[Some people say it was because he was a major signer of the 1855 Treaty. ed.] [Green Grass Bull, South Peigan-Blackfoot; Collier, 1938, 34]*

A long time ago before the time of Green Grass Bull a chief got angry and left the camp circle with his band. The societies did nothing to stop him. After that he had bad luck. All his horses were stolen by an enemy war party. This year is known as the year "Bear Head disobeyed the orders of the Medicine Woman". This happened when Green Grass Bull's father was a Youngman. *[Green Grass Bull to Collier, 1938, 34]*

BLOOD

BAD HEAD: Sawkiapekwan enitsiw nectarta-tpekwan "Prairie Man" kills a Ped'oreilles [Pen D' Oreilles, ed.].

WHITE BULL: The Blood Indian named Prairie White Man killed south Peigan had a narrow escape. This was happen on south side of now present town of Shelby, Montana, place called Shade.

DEMPSEY: Prairie White Man/killed/Pend d'Oreille Indian

PERCY CREIGHTON: Heavy snow storm came. After that it rained. Then north cold winds forming ice everywhere. The Icy Winter

NORTH BLACKFEET

CRANE BEAR: A white man or Metis, by name of Saekiapekwan *[Prairie Whiteman, ed.]* kills a savage (Indian) of the tribe of Neetartayetapiw (Pend d' Oreilles, ed.), on the other side of the mountains.

YELLOW FLY: The Slippery year. There being ice all over the prairies.

RUNNING RABBIT: First three Rations *[first three pen Piskan, ed.]*

MANY GUNS: Inyokskaipiskan = 3-pen-pisken. This was 1 percent *[first ?,ed.]* of the 3-pen-piskens.

LITTLE CHIEF: The four tribes moved to the south there they had three buffalo traps there was sure a lot of buffalo that year they stayed there nearly all summer after that they moved east near Medicine Hat from there they moved south in the fall they moved back to Blackfoot Crossing for the winter

ORIGIN OF THE INISKIM [Buffalo Stone and Buffalo Medicine]:

"There was a camp and they were starving. A girl, youngest and neglected wife of a husband, four times went for wood and each time she heard singing on a cut bank. Fourth time she looked and saw earth falling. Lo, there was an Iniskim *[buffalo stone]* there all greasy. She heard it singing a song, 'Here woman take me, I'm very holy.' She put it into her dress next to her breast touching the skin. She told her husband at night: 'Taki tato yin.ai.' 'I'm going to be a holy person.' She told husband part of what she saw. She asked for <u>fat</u> so she could get food. Husband sought all over the camp. Finally he scraped a piece of buffalo stomach with his finger nail and got a bit. He brought it to her to grease the Iniskim. Then she asked for buffalo hair, rubbed off when they scratch themselves, 'for the Iniskim to <u>sit</u> on.' The old hair was gotten from an old buffalo skin hat. Then she cleared a place, put dung own. Then white sage, laid the Iniskim on it. A meeting was called. The Iniskim was passed around the room, kissed by each one and prayed over. It was passed around the tipi from door to door. Then she sitting at head took it and told them how she got it. Then she said, 'Tell the others not present, i.e., outside, a buffalo bull will come tonight from the east, others behind him. This bull will rub against every tipi, but no one must look out. Dogs will chase him, but don't seek him.' All went to bed. Before falling asleep they heard the bull go through, but no one looked out. At dawn a man got up, hungry, and looked out. He saw to the east the buffalo 'just like a mist' at the far entrance of a piskin. The men tied up all the dogs. The younger men then rounded the buffalo up and killed them. <u>Hence</u> they got the buffalo into a piskin. They had it built, but couldn't get any buffalo into it until she got the Iniskim.

Then the woman said: 'Bring me these parts:

1. Liver
2. Suet
3. Suet from head
4. Kidney

to feed the Iniskim.'

So these four things were brought in and placed beside the Iniskim, everything in little pieces.

In a piskin, four men chosen to distribute the meat get homologous parts of each buffalo, e.g. one man, on one day, will receive all the o'kin to hand out. Next morning, same four take different parts to distribute. The interior parts are all carefully differentiated and allocated to each quarter.

If a buffalo is divided, these are the named parts:

1. otatsisuim – or oskitsi or sotatsisuoxts – or heart
   statsisum was given first to the women. Every buffalo's otatsisum goes first. Half of every right side is given to the women.
2. o'kin –chest and leg; ataxts, chest and ayistsuist – vertebrae; all the shoulder bones and left front leg.
3. o'koan – stomach and one leg; i.e. all the stomachs and left leg.
4. otsists – guts and one leg; i.e., all the guts and right leg
5. manui – belly and flanks
6. ipaixi – rump and back

Every bit of buffalo eaten – except bones. Blood drunk fresh, especially if starving, so they won't get indigestion on first square meal. Otherwise they get indigestion.

They took all the cow meat [no bulls, which they left in the piskin, except for a few parts]. After all the meat was taken home, a chief called out that all should cook for the woman, so all the roasted ribs and tongue for the woman were put into her tipi, also the upper vertebrae. Of course they cooked meat for themselves too then. They piled up the extra meat in caches. All the bones smashed for marrow, and boiled in store pails set in hot coals.

When the woman died the Iniskim was given to her husband, and he gave it to someone 'he was fond of.'

No one danced when the woman had it, but when the second owner had it there were girls dancing, at a certain time in the proceedings. *[see 1846, ed.]* ...

1. aa'topa.tan – Man [and wife] with whom come in and sing all the old men [collecting men to come in and sit by themselves]
2. awatoyin.skyi - making himself holy to get meat

Piskin Crooked Meat Strings witnessed. The Three Pen Piskin.

1. Omaxkisiskua, - aatopatan -, who had the buffalo medicine [*aatopatan - man and wife who call all the old men in to sing, ed.]*.
2. Kti-saxsi – driver *[driver of the buffalo, ed]*. Both are Paxsinamayin. Aatopatan called Kti-saxsi to come into his tipi to ask him to go out to be the one to do the chasing.

At Red Deer River some Paxsinamayi camps were camping.

Crooked-Meat-Strings was in a Paxsinamayi camp with Omaxkisiskua in the same camp. Natoaioka – Holy-Sleeping – is oldest of the Paxsinamayin chiefs and head of the Paxsinamayi camp in which Crooked-Meat-Strings and Omaxkisiskua lived. Of course Omaxkisiskua was director of ceremonies. Omaxkisiskua used to always be the driver regularly when young, later his brothers went for him, but Omaxkisiskua did it in a pinch. To begin the whole thing, Omaxkisiskua told the chief, 'I think we better put up a piskin so we can have meat and skins to tan for HBC." [Chief did not command Omaxkisiskua's services.] Natoaioka told Omaxkisiskua to go to Saiyeks and tell Ninepiksi and Ixtapaka chiefs of Saiyeks that there was to be a piskin. 'Tell them to come along and bring the people.' Many Blackfoot went therefore with this piskin, i.e. as visitors, but not all the Blackfoot. These piskin are not tribal affairs. [The name of the chiefs means he and his People.] Saiyeks and Paxsinamayi great friends because they camped side by side in camp circle.

Someone called out 'Omaxkisiskua is moving north to put up a piskin where there are lots of woods. Omaxkisiskua is going to move north near Kinaksisaxta [Fort Saskatchewan River, where all the buffalo are].'

When the camp approached the region where they were planning to set up the piskin, people were searching for a good place to build the piskin, men were sent ahead. Men returned, said, 'We're going to move tomorrow.' Ako.totsipiskin – 'Now we are approaching the piskin.' Tipis were pitched in the thicket. Camps had to be far away from the piskin lest the buffalo get scared.

The piskin is built as follows: No rail fence but a mass of sticks and logs propped up strongly – using growing trees as main braces. Props and buttresses embedded in the ground. Thick logs and very strong construction, for the buffalo can break out easily otherwise. The wings of the piskin went out 3-5 miles. Center dividing line is to separate the herd into two or more manageable parts. Hillocks are twenty feet apart. As the buffalo approach the people close in on them, so all have to run fast with the herd. Big boys, not women, are allowed behind hillocks; 'women can't run fast, and little boys might stampede the herd mischievously.'

Crooked Meat Strings was right there as they cut the piskin logs, tied with rawhide ropes.

In this hunt Keteisaksi 'He-couldn't-go-out' went out to drive in the herd – Stamikso'tokan was the scout and stood on a hill. At the right time he announced the herd in sight herded by Keteisaksi and told the boys and men to run to the hillocks. When the buffalo run and fall in, people stand around and shoot at them. Anyone could shoot to kill. No special group designated. Then Stamikso'tokan, when all are killed, enters the piskin. Takes a stick, and points up to sky, says:

1. Omaxkisiskua is to have all the 'hearts' [oskitsi]
2. Keteisaksi is to have the okuan
3. Isapaki is to have the o'tai
4. Sikutamiso manues Black-Coming-Over-the-Hill – the manue
5. Matsimin.ai –Tongue-man [old man] o'paix

6. Stamikso'tokan himself got o'kin

These are the head men of the camp. Natoaioka's name was not mentioned, but he was to help himself to divide among his close followers. Each of these six took homologous parts of each buffalo to hand out to all the people. All men jumped on rail, but women were outside. Men butchered and handed meat over the fence [no windows] to women who have ready the horses and travois. The killers, i.e. shooters, took the hides of the animal they had shot, hence avid shooting. Bull skins are cut into strips to tie up the piskin walls again, bull meat being left. The cold always freezes these strips solid, so the raw hide is very strong. When all are home, women are told to hurry to fix the meat, dry meat and skins, for 'when it is finished we'll have another hunt.' Meat is dried over fire, frozen and stocked up. Some of the strong women scrape the skins, tied onto old tipi poles-frame until frozen, clean the fat and hair off them, for a raw hide.

This was the nyokskaipiskien – three-times-piskin, which was sufficient for the two bands. Some larger piskin hunts on other occasions hunted more days.

A few days later Keteisaksi got ready for the next hunt, for all meat previously taken dried and skins ready. After Natoaioka called out. So Keteisaksi went out, pulled up hay for his horse so it would be in the best condition, for horse was tied up [some horses running wild but not this horse]. Then on a given morning Keteisaksi started off when Morning Star rose, went slowly. Keteisaksi leads the buffalo, riding upper right and left. Buffalo ride towards a leader. First time the piskin was not filled but this time it was so full you could walk on the animals. Crooked Meat Strings was just learning to shoot gophers, but saw everything at the piskin, 'being a curious boy.' Crooked Meat Strings was 15 and so couldn't shoot the big buffalo, not being strong enough. When he was 30 he first used bow for a buffalo; used guns before that time.

Meat skinned and butchered, and taken home to be put away. Every night while the women were busy with meat [two weeks] Omaxkisiskua had a singing-meeting, letting the little girls dance toward the end.

Man said, 'What next? We have all this meat.' Then at night Natoaioka, older and superior to 1-3, went out shouting:

1. Omaxkisiskua!
2. Stamiksotokan!
3. Sapaki !

'Think among yourselves! Make up your minds! After this meat is fixed, we're going to put a piece on the piskin, because it's too small.' Although the chief said 'You think,' they 'took his word' and proffered no opposition. *[It was a case of just being nice – Hanks]* The three said to him, 'That's what we were just thinking. It is too small. You are right. We'll do it.' The 3-some executed his orders, picked out the side to be opened. Chief Natoaioka did not 'of course' do this. They decided to put on 'another room.' All men then started to work again.

Then Omaxkisiskua told Keteisaksi to go for the third run, because he was so good the other two times. 'Get grass for your horse tonight for all women have boiled the bones for fat drippings, meat dried and pounded, i.e. all put away.'

Before dawn Keteisaksi went out to seek the herds when Morning Star came up. Stamiksotokan as scout sent the boys up to the akiosi. Buffalo came in as before – with good luck. Both the 'rooms' were filled, so they had more buffalo than before. Same four-some divided the meat; each man in camp had an absolutely equal share. Unborn <u>calves</u> were given to <u>Omaxkisiskua</u>. Of course some bulls there, but only the insides and skins were taken and tongues, meat left. In spring or fall bulls eaten if hard up, but now none taken.

When meat all home Omaxkisiskua's cooked meat brought to his tipi. Omaxkisiskua called for all the big men to come to an Iniskim-meeting. There Natoaioka then said again: 'Think again. Spring is coming and this is the only place we can get enough skins for trading. In spring we can't get skins like this in the north hunting, for then when we get ten then we are lucky. I think we should make another piece on.' Now spring was almost there, for they had been many weeks at this place. The others, eating, agreed. 'We'll wait for the women to dry meat. Then we'll have our third hunt.' At this time there were dozens of napi *[old men, ed.]* in that tipi. Then later Omaxkisiskua called out, invited the men and Natoaioka to a feast and talk in his tipi again.

At the meeting, Natoaioka again said, 'Let's have a third drive, for spring is near. You know how hard buffalo in spring are to find.' All agreed. So Omaxkisiskua said, 'This time it will be Stamiksotokan 'to lead the buffalo around' [a strong word] because he is very lucky.' So Stamiksotokan got ready the following night, went out at same time. At daybreak Keteisaksi was scout and saw so many 'like dragging a buffalo robe on the snow' i.e. He 'always brought so many it was as if he pulled a buffalo on a string and the others followed him.' Both rooms were filled…

All day they worked, skinned, and cooked for Omaxkisiskua. At the nightly tipi meeting of Omaxkisiskua all the elders and eminent gathered to eat this freshly cooked meat. Having eaten they smoked. Natoaioka then said: 'Now my younger brothers [because very old], how about another piece? For a fourth time. This will be the last one for the spring will soon be here.

So they agreed. This was called the three *[piece –Hanks]* – piskin because of three enlargements. Thicket cleaned out for new rooms. Lots of work. Only time they ever had to enlarge thus. Natoaioka said, 'We are only a few moons from spring. Stamiksotokan will be the driver for he does better than Keteisaksi [no jealousy from Keteisaksi]. So men went to work, cleared the new piskin attachment. Stamiksotokan then brought the buffalo in. 1 was empty [jam full of dead buffalo]. 2 was half full, 3 was jam full, so same thing started again as to fixing – storage. In 3 too full to mill around, but in 2 they could. Killed them all – and one whole day for skinning. Women took all afternoon, just to get meat home. They prepared Omaxkisiskua's meat for him. Not every tipi prepared for Omaxkisiskua – six women, including the chief's wives. Some of the wives of the six recipients cooked. Eight ribs fried, calves, tongues.

1 of Sapaki's wives
1 of Keteisaksi's wives
1 of Stamiksotokan's wives
1 of Natoaioka's wives

These women were all second wives, not real wives, for husband never wants his real wives to cook like this or work hard. 'Ninawa.ki – real wives.' That meeting Natoaioka said they had enough meat – they were loaded with meat and hides. Then Natoaioka said, 'Let's not move but wait till we shoot the geese from here. Then we can go to Edmonton to trade from here when grass comes up.'

A list of piskins remembered:

1. This was the nyokskeipiskeitsi – three piskins put up by Paxsinamayi and Saiyeks. The Paxsinamayi invited the Saiyeks and were the leaders in it. One of the most famous of piskins because it was a three room. It took pace pre-small pox and way north of Red Deer River.

2. Omaxkisis.kun gave one after small pox. Not so full of meat as number 1.

3. Near Okotoks a big rock, one given by I'kuskini - Front Back after Omaxkisiskua died. I'kus.kini took Omaxkisiskua's medicine after Omaxkisiskua's death.

4. Siksipiskin – Black Buffalo trap [or utsipi.piskin – Willow Buffalo Trap] near Sarcee Reserve. Paxsinamayi put up #1- 4.

5. From Buffalo Lake runs a stream – no name. Otxko'tamiso [Yellow-Coming-Over-the-Hill] gave this one.

6. Heard about: The Crees built their own between Red Deer and Omax [Ft. Saskatchewan River] in a thicket. Crooked Meat Strings slept in the tipi of the person who gave it – a two-some piskin, first full of old meat, second empty. Ato'sawato – a Cree chief, gave it, though half Blackfoot.

7. Nak'sin.a – head of Sarsi, gave a piskin. Alias Stamikso'tokan [a Sarsi, not the Blackfoot]. Same year the Cree piskin took place. These were initiated by the Paxsinamayi; Saiyeks always invited in to participate.

Way north he heard Many Swans put one on in the fall. The fall piskin of Many Swans was a small one. The only time a piskin was given not in winter was when Agwmaxkayi *[Many Swans, ed.]* gave one in the fall, but Crooked Meat Strings doesn't know of another piskin given that winter too…

The five piskins not given on successive winters. The other times they were scattered and didn't have piskin. Only when together do they have piskins. These were given alternate years. When buffalo are scarce up north no piskin; when plentiful you give one. When buffalo scarce, you scatter out to seek them.

Omaxkisiskua among the Paxsinamayi put the piskin on for the Paxsinamayi alone. No other band in the tribe could call on Omaxkisiskua to lead them. Other bands though could put on a piskin if they wanted, e.g. Natosapi put on one, and Many Swans did, too. [Natosapi took the role of Omaxkisiskua in his piskin]. *[Crooked Meat Strings, North Blackfeet-Blackfoot, to Hanks 245-257]*

Crooked Meat Strings, North Blackfeet [Siksika], 1938, Lucien and Jane Hanks photo, Glenbow Archives

1858

NORTH PEIGAN

 BULL PLUME #1: When the Peigans broke the Kootenay Indians' gun. *In the foothills.*

 BULL PLUME #2: When the Peigans broke the Kootenay Indians' gun.

 BULL PLUME #2 B: *Shows a man with a single feather in his hair. Death of Big Snake in Big Brave account?*

For eleven days a battle continued between the Kutenai (Kootenay) and the Peigans. It started in the foothills on the east side of the mountains near Pincher Creek, Alberta, and eventually made its way to the Tobacco Plains in Montana near the British Columbia border. (Hamilton; 1900; 77)

According to North Peigan oral history, this was the last time the Kutenai came onto the Plains of Alberta to hunt buffalo. (At Where-we-Fought-the Kutenais River?)

SOUTH PEIGAN

ELK HORN: Sweet Grass Hills; spent spring on Marias; in summer went south; Big Snakes (chief) killed; ammunition issued. (1858-59)

BIG BRAVE: Mountain Chief wintered on Milk River and found extra large buffalo chip (three feet across). Chief Big Snake killed in summer (1859).

Big Snake [Omaxsitsisinakoan – Big-Snake-Man] was chief of the Buffalo Dung band of the South Peigans [100 lodges], and a signer of the Lame Bull treaty of 1855. His war party was said to be responsible for running off the cattle, and shooting an employee, at Fort McKenzie in 1843 leading to the traders shooting at Old Sun and his group the next spring. [See Winter Count for 1843 for further details.]

"Big Snake had power from frog, and bore a live frog inside him He claimed that as long as the frog was unharmed, he would not be hurt in battle. In an engagement with Flatheads *[some say Crees, ed.]* the frog inside Big Snake was struck by a bullet, thus causing his death. *[On Deep Creek west of Choteau, ed.]* Jim said Dusty Bull was brother of his mother's father, Big Snake and took latter's name after his death." *[Jim White Calf to Claude Schaefer,47, 1950]*

"Big Snake wounded in battle and died later. Before taking him to burial place, his stomach was opened to preserve his body. Hence the dead frog was found and cause of death ascertained. Big Snake had a good war record. He had two brothers… Big Snake used to shake his gun and sing, 'My gun wants to eat a person,' and then get up and dance, as a sign he was going on the war path." *[Mrs. John Mountain Chief to Schaefer,150-47, 1950]*

BIG NOSE WAR RECORD: On Milk River near Chinook, MT. camp of 500 Peigan lodges. Twenty miles away nearly the same number of Crows & Assiniboines were camped. Fighting began about midway between camps. Crows & Assiniboines defeated with seven killed – one Peigan killed. Sitting Woman – a Crow chief disgraced himself by hiding in the brush.

Crow delegation to Washington, D.C. 1872, Smithsonian photo. Mo-mukh-pi-tche; Thin Belly; One-That-Leads-The-Old-Dog

BLOOD

BAD HEAD: Itomarkitseskaop The Bloods make a large sweat bath.

WHITE BULL: Gives the killing of Hind Bull and Fish Child for this year

PERCY CREIGHTON: A Blood, Prairie White Man, killed a Kootenay whom he met while crossing a river & who refused to surrender his beautiful bow. He had to flee from his group of Bloods because they were most annoyed at the trouble he had caused. He returned after a few years.

NORTH BLACKFEET

CRANE BEAR: Sotenaw *(Rainy Chief, ed.)* grand chief of the Blood, is shot by the Cree close of Sarkimats (Red Deer River), but was not injured.

YELLOW FLY: The year of three Pis-Kuns in one place. Pis-Kun meaning Buffalo or antelope traps.

RUNNING RABBIT: Dry Wood Rations. *[piskan, ed]*

MANY GUNS: (1) ekniksi iskiupa = All Dried Wood Pisken
(2) Sikstsisuitsiyii = Moose Hills where the pisken was held.

LITTLE CHIEF: That year they camped east of here the wood had to be ration out the dry wood all winter

1859

NORTH PEIGAN

BULL PLUME #1: When "Fish Child" and "Hind Bull", two brothers, were drunk and killed each other. *Blackfeet*

BULL PLUME #2: When "Fish Child" and "Hind Bull", two brothers, were drunk and killed each other.

BULL PLUME #2 B: *Shows a man with a wavy line coming off his head. This wavy line indicates an altered state of consciousness. It can mean "drunk", or also "spiritual power". At the time of its introduction the effects of alcohol were thought to be a spiritual state. It wasn't long before the Blackfoot determined that this was not a positive state, or anything resembling "spiritual". Also, with the red coming out of the body showing bleeding this is no doubt explaining the conditions and effect during the shooting.*

SOUTH PEIGAN

ELK HORN: South of Missouri; Blood fought among themselves; first time steam boats came to Fort Teton. *[Fort Benton ?, ed.]*

BIG BRAVE: Lazy Boy killed. In summer Blood camped at Yellow River and fought among themselves; Calf Shirt killed some of his own people.

BIG BRAVE 2: Bloods camped at Yellow Mountains.

BIG NOSE WAR RECORD: Prickly Pear Valley, near Helena, MT.- BN party of 21 left camp at Badger Creek. Found camp of 60 lodges at Prickly Pear – captured 6 horses – one Peigan killed in the camp.

BLOOD

BAD HEAD: Otsitsipotsenitsiyaw sakoyestanik ke Mamiokossi Two Indians of the Blood Tribe, Hind Bull and Fish Child, kill each other at Rocky Mountain House.

DEMPSEY: *These two brothers were chiefs of the Many Fat Horses band. While drinking near Rocky Mountain House, Hind Bull took his daughter away from her husband and Fish Child objected. In the argument that followed, Hind Bull shot Fish Child but, before dying, the latter stabbed his brother to death (Dempsey mss. 1955).*

WHITE BULL: Sun Old Man died and Pe-kat-ka or Wonderful Foot warrior was killed

PERCY CREIGHTON: Two Blood chiefs who had trouble with one another killed each other. Hind Bull & Fish Child.

NORTH BLACKFEET

CRANE BEAR: Two brothers (Mamiokas and Sakoyestamik) *(Fish Child & Hind Bull, ed.)* are celebrating and kill each other.

YELLOW FLY: The year when the Pis-Kuns were made out of rotten poles.

RUNNING RABBIT: Eagle Leggings, killed.

MANY GUNS: Pikikawan = Bad Foot ?, a Blackfoot, killed by Crees.

MANY GUNS .68: Fancy Foot was killed and the time when Holy White Horse jumped across a deep crevasse. (Holy White Horse is the name of a famous war horse.

MANY GUNS .69: Mysterious Foot was killed. Cranky Inlet Holy.
LITTLE CHIEF: Mr. Eagle Leggings was killed in a battle with the Crees

1860

NORTH PEIGAN

 BULL PLUME #1: When "Four Horns" scalp was taken off by his own people by mistake.

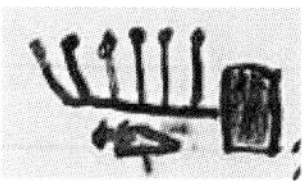 BULL PLUME #2: When "Four Horns" scalp was taken off by his own people by mistake.

 BULL PLUME #2 B: *This is an interesting pictograph, but doesn't seem to have anything to do with the events of the year. It shows a Grizzly bear with short lines coming out of its mouth. This usually means a sickness or disease of some sort. The curved line above it indicates this was in the hills.*

This possibly occurred in the battle with the Assiniboine by the Peigan and Pend d'Oreille. "The Indians are still at Buffalo. Alexander the Pen De O'reille Chief with his camp was attacked on the Eastern Slope of the Rocky Mountains by a large band of Assiniboines. The Pend De O'reilles were Completely Surrounded & No doubt would have been entirely exterminated, had it not been for the providential & timely arrival of assistance from the Peagan Camp. Alexander had Some Seventeen men Killed & a Number wounded. Among the former was a Son.

They lost many horses leaving the Camp barely Sufficient to Carry their Lodges & Children. It rests to be seen how these Indians will receive their Annuities in payment for their lands." [John Owen, Flathead Sub-agent, December 3, 1860; Owen 1927;Vol. 2, p 234-235]

SOUTH PEIGAN

ELK HORN: Camped at Bad Waters; Sioux after Peigan; this camp north of Missouri; killed 7 Cree; a fight with the Crow and lost two chiefs, Good Raven and Mad Plume.

BIG BRAVE: Man named Peacemaker killed. Eagle Child killed in the summer; a Blood wounded by arrow of Sioux.

BIG BRAVE 2:...a Blood was shot with an arrow through the face but did not get killed from Sioux.

BIG NOSE WAR RECORD: Fight with Crows on swift stream that empties into Yellowstone River near Fort Keogh. Killed one Crow.

Judith Basin – Captured horse from 60 lodges of Pend d'Orielle..

BLOOD

BAD HEAD: Neetartaytapi otsit-otas-kak assinay The Crees steal horses from the Pend' Oreille, near sweet Grass Hills.

WHITE BULL: Cree Indians attacked Blackfoot camp near Elk Waters north side of Red Deer River.

DEMPSEY: Pend d'Oreilles/when their horses were taken/Assiniboines

The Pend d'Oreilles, under their chief Alexander, were hunting buffalo along the Milk River when they were attacked by a large war party of Assiniboines and Crees. The Pend d'Oreilles had twenty killed, including the chief's son, twenty-five wounded, and 290 horses taken. Only the timely arrival of some Peigans prevented the complete extermination of the camp. This happened late in November, 1860. (Owen, 1927, vol.2, 234-5, 238-9, 262).

PERCY CREIGHTON: A well known Blood by the name of Bear Robe, fought a battle with the River Crow or Flatheads. The Cree were chased away.

NORTH BLACKFEET

CRANE BEAR: Many Cree are killed in battle at Turnip Hills (Masitomow), on the present Blood Reserve.

YELLOW FLY: The year "Pe Kai Ka" was killed. "Pe Kai Ka" Long Foot, Warrior.

RUNNING RABBIT: Old Sun died.

MANY GUNS: Natosapi = (Big) Old Sun, bigger chief than Crowfoot, died that year.

September, 1860, Old Sun, a leading chief of the North Blackfoot, was killed going to trade at Fort Edmonton. (Ft. Edmonton journal, entry for 25 Sept. 1860 in HBC Journals & Correspondence; HC Arch. B.60/a/31)

LITTLE CHIEF: Mr. Old Sun died just moving around not much going on

1861

NORTH PEIGAN

BULL PLUME #1: Eclipse in summer. *(The closest recorded solar eclipse we could find occurred in July,1860, ed.)*

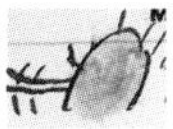 BULL PLUME #1: When "Red Fish" was killed by "Crow Eagle". (The image for this is in BULL PLUME #1 but the description is missing.)

 BULL PLUME #2: When "Red Fish" was killed by "Crow Eagle". Eclipse in summer.

BULL PLUME #2 B: *No pictograph.*

SOUTH PEIGAN

ELK HORN: On the Marias; first fight with the Gros Ventre (1862, ed.); summer camp on the northeast side of Sweet Grass Hills (Canada).

BIG BRAVE: Peigan fought with Gros Ventre and Many Butterflies was killed. Peigan kill five Sioux who had a horn spoon.

BIG NOSE WAR RECORD: Fight with Pend d'Oreille Peigans 11, PD 60, One Peigan wounded, one PD killed.

BLOOD

BAD HEAD: Otsitotorpi Natoyeketokew Visit of Medicine Pheasent *(Medicine Prairie Chicken, ed.)*, great chief of the Crows. He was half-breed Peigan and Crow

WHITE BULL: Old man Cree half Blackfoot Indian was killed by a Cree Indians. *(Old Man, Napi, was a half Blackfoot/Cree, see MANY GUNS 1862, ed.)*

DEMPSEY: When he got there/Medicine Prairie Chicken

PERCY CREIGHTON: There was a Peigan, Achto (a nickname). Everyone killed him. He was a thief – seducer of the women. He was considered an enemy of the tribe.

NORTH BLACKFEET

CRANE BEAR: A Blackfeet (Kitsiponistaw) *(Spotted Calf, ed.)* is hunting, and is surprised and killed by 9 Stoney.

YELLOW FLY: "Old Sun" Senior died. Really pronounced "Sun Old Man".

RUNNING RABBIT: Elk Water (Duck Chief born)

MANY GUNS: Ponokoiyoxki = Reindeer Lake (Elk Lake, ed.), the Blackfoot had a war with Crees there up north. Stamiksisokikin, his son-in-law, and brothers were killed here.

LITTLE CHIEF: The Blackfeet Bloods Peigan and the Sarcee all moved to Elk water they stayed there till fall came back to Blackfoot Crossing

1862

NORTH PEIGAN

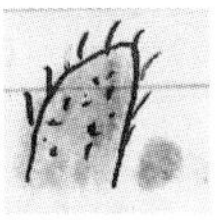

BULL PLUME #1: Smallpox

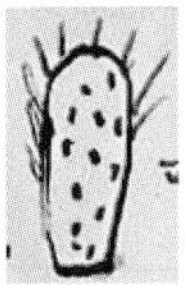

BULL PLUME #2: Smallpox

BULL PLUME #2 B: *A tipi with lines around it indicating a number of people.*

Calf Tail, a South Peigan, was seven years old at the time.
"Winter of Measles. They were camped on Old Man's River, this side of Porcupine Tail River. Iron Breast was chief of the Worms...The camp was large." *[Calf Tail to Collier, 1938; 15]*

SOUTH PEIGAN

ELK HORN: Few cases of smallpox; fight with the Kutenai in which many killed; during summer Mountain Chief attacked by Sioux; a Peigan killed by Gros Ventre. (1862-62)

BIG BRAVE: Chief Coward killed by Crow Indians. In summer Peigan attacked camps of Gros Ventres and killed many of them. Also some Peigan were killed while hunting.

BIG BRAVE 2: ...same time, some Peigans went out to hunt for hide to tie Sun Dance *[Lodge]* with and was killed on way.

BLOOD

BAD HEAD: Tartowa itsenitarpi An Indian named Tartowa (?) gets mad and is firing through the camp. He is killed by his two brothers

WHITE BULL: The Blood Indian named Sleeps on High died with disease

LEGAL: *The name (Tartowa, ed.) has been translated a Prepared Moccasins and as The Fox*

This may well be the Blood chief Tat-tu-ye (The Fox) signer of the Stevens Treaty in 1855, who would be important enough to include in the winter counts of the Bloods and Peigan.

PERCY CREIGHTON: A Blood chief – Striped Calf was killed by the Stoney Indians, another Blood – Puts His Black Leg on Top, was killed at St. Mary's Lake in a battle with the Cree.

A Party of Blackfoot leaving Fort Edmonton were attacked and one killed and another wounded.

NORTH BLACKFEET

CRANE BEAR: The Sayex, Blackfeet, then of the Crow Shoe camp, are met near Nonokaorkiw by the Cree, and many are killed in the 2 enemy camps.

YELLOW FLY: The year when the Crees attacked the Blackfeet at Elk Water.

RUNNING RABBIT: The Old Man, killed. (Little Back Bone gun talk)

MANY GUNS: Napi = a Cree, was killed. (Napi = Old Man). Bill Bear Chief's father = Apaokuyi, Stamiksisokikin is related a brother to Napi, a Cree, and Natosawato, Sun Walker (Cree). Stamiksisokikin was wounded in 1861 (see entry). Then they told him (Stamiksisokikin) his brothers (the Crees) had killed his own son and his son-in-law. So Stamiksisokikin told Apaokuyi, White Wolf, to come along to revenge these 2 deaths. So in 1862 White Wolf killed Napi because Stamiksisokikin didn't want to kill his own relations. White Wolf was "hired" –was told to come and do it. Now Napi is Grandfather of Paul Fox and Mrs. Fox granddaughter of Apaokuyi.

LITTLE CHIEF: Mr. Old Man was killed in a battle with the Crow Indians both tribes had heavey *[sic.]* loses

1863

NORTH PEIGAN

 BULL PLUME #1: When we sold lots of buffalo hides. *To HBC, I.G. Baker.*

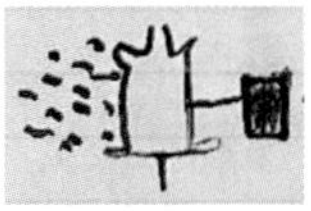 BULL PLUME #2: When we sold lots of buffalo.

 BULL PLUME #2 B: *Ermine Horse [?] See Legal's description.*

SOUTH PEIGAN

ELK HORN: Captured a double barrel shotgun; Sun Dance at High Ridge.

BIG BRAVE: Assiniboine attacked Mountain Chief's camps on Big River in Canada *[North Saskatchewan River, ed.]*, at night, but no one killed. Peigan fought with Gros Ventre in summer and Half-Breed *[name of a man]* killed.

BIG NOSE WAR RECORD: North Cypress Hills on the Elbow River. Large war party of Peigan came upon 4 Sioux in thick timber who had dug a pit. Peigans surrounded them and fought them all day with 4 killed and 17 wounded. BN killed all 4 with double barreled shotgun loaded with bullets. Although they had been shot at many times the large limbs of a tree leaning over them saved them.

BLOOD

BAD HEAD: Nisokimix itomotsarpi Four lodges of Gros Ventres whose chief was "Stone" –Orkotok – were destroyed by the Peigans on the Belly River

WHITE BULL: Indians had disease Black pox. Good many died with it. Yellow Tee-pee died too.

LEGAL: *This winter count refers to four lodges of Gros Ventres under a chief named The Stone, who were killed by Peigans on the Belly River. They had been visiting Blood chief Ermine Horse at the time of the attack.*

PERCY CREIGHTON: Scabby Clan, came home from a long war trail. There were 2 large buffalo pens: one put up by the Fish Eaters, the other by the Scabby Clan. Former called the latter's pen "dog pen" because it was so crowded.

NORTH BLACKFEET

CRANE BEAR: Neoiskaatosew, *(Three Suns, ed.)*, grand chief of the Blackfeet, dies – the chief was also called Natosew *(Sun, ed.)*.

YELLOW FLY: The year "Old Man", a Cree half Blackfoot, was killed.

RUNNING RABBIT: Above Sleeper, died. (R. Rabbit and P.Y. Man; ___ made Sundance) *(R. Rabbit = Running Rabbit & P.Y. Man = Pretty Young Man, ed.)*

MANY GUNS: Koyisaiyoka = Sleeps On Top, Blackfoot killed by Crees.

LITTLE CHIEF: Mr. Above Sleeper was kill by the Cree he went away from the camps and the Crees caught him and killed him also took his scalp gun his horse the next the men went to look for him they found him killed

Winter of 1863 [Winter of Measles] *[perhaps this is the winter of 1864-65?,ed.]* Calf Tail was 7 years old. They were camped on Old Man's River, this side of Porcupine Hills. Iron Breast was chief of the Worms.
[Calf Tail to Collier, 1938, 15]

1864

NORTH PEIGAN

BULL PLUME #1: When there was a great massacre of Crees. *Near Lethbridge.(In pencil, ed.)*

BULL PLUME #2: When there was a great massacre by the Crees.

BULL PLUME #2 B: *A series of lines coming together and leading to the left.*

This could be the battle described by Mountain Chief [Big Brave], or possibly the battle described for 1866.

SOUTH PEIGAN

ELK HORN: Flies-Low killed.

BIG BRAVE: Peigan had red smallpox; in summer they attacked Assiniboine's seventy lodges and captured the lodges.

Early one spring [about 1864] Mountain Chief's father was camped in a river bottom with about fifteen tipis. He received a message to join the rest of the Blood Band, but refused because he was going up to Edmonton to trade. Before the departure the camp was attacked by Crees. The rest of the Blood Band, hearing of the fight, joined Mountain Chief's father. The tipi owners of this small camp were as follows; Young Man Chief, Weasel Curley, Head Carrier [from Skunk Band], Running Fox, Sitting in the Middle, Old Man Mountain Chief, Eagle Flat Head, Painted Wing, Yellow Dust [Black Door Band], Big Sunshine, and three women that had their own tipis; Wolf Woman, Light All the Time, and Medicine Stripe. *[Big Brave, South Peigan-Blackfoot; Collier, 1938, 11-12]*

Winter camps:

1864 Camped on Marias River at Bear Creek
1865 Camped on Marias River at Bear Creek
1866 Camped on Teton River just above the Knees.

Tipi owners: Little Plume, Turn Up Hat, many White Horses, Iron Breast, Yellow Robe Out, and White Buffalo Calf. *[Calf Tail, South Peigan-Blackfoot; Collier, 1938,15]*

BLOOD

BAD HEAD: Sikapinosin Black smallpox

WHITE BULL: The Indians recover from the disease that summer.

DEMPSEY: *An epidemic of scarlet fever ravaged the Blackfoot tribes during the winter of 1864-65. By the spring, Father Albert Lacombe reported to traders at Edmonton House that 1,100 Blackfoot had died. (Edmonton House entry for March 24, 1865).*

PERCY CREIGHTON: Black Small Pox (so called) epidemic resulted in numerous deaths.

NORTH BLACKFEET

CRANE BEAR: Sokapisin, *(Black Small Pox, ed.)* black small pox.

YELLOW FLY: The year "Sleeps on High", warrior, died.

RUNNING RABBIT: Black Pox year

MANY GUNS: Sikapiksin = Black small pox

LITTLE CHIEF: Black Pox that mostly all the four tribes got that Black Pox it was some thing like small pox but it was bigger and Black a lot of them died when they was so many died of it they moved away from the place one family would died of that Black pox then just leave the tepee as it was a (lot) of them were left that way that is way east of Drumheller

1865

NORTH PEIGAN

BULL PLUME #1: When the Sioux came into camp

BULL PLUME #2: When the Sioux came into camp

BULL PLUME #2 B: *A buffalo head connected to a tipi. This could indicate the Buffalo Tipi design, or a name.*

SOUTH PEIGAN

ELK HORN: Many Peigan visited Southern Gros Ventre (?) *(Arapaho, ed.)*; ammunition issued; summer camp above Sweet Grass Hills; a fight with Flathead; also with Gros Ventre; returned to Two Medicine.

BIG BRAVE: Gov't gave Peigan clothes, etc. at Benton; white man who issued them called Black-Horse-Owner. At Benton made peace with Gros Ventres. In summer Little-Dog killed and Peigan fought with Crow, Assiniboine and Gros Ventre, who were allied. Peigan defeated them all. *(1866, this was just the Crow and Gros Ventre, ed.)*

BLOOD

BAD HEAD: Itesam-orkimaop The Indians are kept waiting a long time for the trader.

WHITE BULL: Weasel Horse went for his warriors with bunch of Bloods, Blackfoots killing Cree women and strong force of Crees, attacked and Bloods-Blackfoots retreated. About 50 Bloods-Blackfoots killed by Crees. They were drove to where the deep snow banks are on south side of Red Deer River. Just before the warriors started, Many Feathers on Head he exchanged his power to White Man Smart.

DEMPSEY: *This refers to a long wait for traders who were supposed to come to the Blood camps. In the previous year, hostilities had broken out between Americans and the Blackfoot. After the epidemic, the Blackfoot harassed the British traders at Rocky Mountain House, blaming them for the disease (Edmonton House entry for March 28, 1865). As a result, traders were reluctant to visit the camps and some Indians were afraid to go near the trading houses.*

PERCY CREIGHTON: A Cree chief – Buffalo Head Banner, was killed by arrow by the Blood. The same summer 11 white men were killed as were many Cree women. Big Snake, a Blood warrior, was shot in battle that was fought with the Cree at Three Pens.

NORTH BLACKFEET

CRANE BEAR: A battle between the Cree and Blackfeet at Neskiskapiskan *(Three buffalo jumps = where they had three buffalo jumps, ed.)* where Father Lacombe is shot by Cree without being wounded.

YELLOW FLY: The year of the Black Epidemic.

RUNNING RABBIT: Three Rations. *[three piskans, ed.]* Bear Arm left behind at the big hill)

MANY GUNS:

(1) Otsimin = Foreleg (of a bear). He was shot and wounded they left him on the butte, and he reentered there with three others. Three came back and told the father of Foreleg. Father went over and got Bear Foreleg and brought him home. Father = Nitumo (Hill).

Many Guns won't write down "bear" because he has some kind of anti-bear medicine, so the name is given simply as Foreleg.[Hanks]

(2) Pikuni Atsinawa. Same summer, Peigans chased, and nearly massacred the Atsina (Gros Ventres) at the Dividing Hills (now called Cypress Hills).

(3) Three fold pisken the winter before (no word written in, just the symbol of three piskans.

LITTLE CHIEF: The four tribes moved to the place where they had the three buffalo traps in 1857 they camped there they traped [sic] the buffalo there again while they were there one night towards morning the Crees attacked the camps it was a big battle all day in the evening both stoped [sic] fighting both lost a lot of men

1866

NORTH PEIGAN

BULL PLUME #1: Smallpox (little) *(This would be measles ed.)*

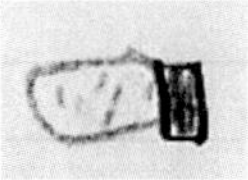

BULL PLUME #2: Smallpox (little)

BULL PLUME #2 B: *Shows a number of people bent over, indicating sickness.*

SOUTH PEIGAN

ELK HORN: Eagle Chief killed; in summer killed, Eagle Horse.

BIG BRAVE: Bear Chief killed south of Missouri and following summer Peigan killed Weasel Horse, a Blood chief.

BLOOD

BAD HEAD: Itayaminotspi A war party falls amongst the Crees, and they fight hand to hand.

WHITE BULL: Still Point Butte, Bloods-Blackfoots *[North Blackfeet, ed.]* attacked Cree camps killed about over hundred Crees. Only one Blood Indian was kill named Insect Wild Ear. The following year double Sun Lodges were held at the Belly River near Standoff.

DEMPSEY: We were captured by hand

In March, 1866, a war party of Bloods and North Blackfoot discovered what they thought was a small Cree camp at the edge of the Red Ochre Hills. They killed two women who had been cutting wood and were following a snow-filled coulee to the top of the hill when they were discovered. The lodges they had seen were part of a larger camp and soon the Crees surrounded the coulee and slaughtered scores of Indians in the snow (Cowie, 1913:314).

PERCY CREIGHTON: Bloods went on the war path & were driven by the Cree into deep snow. Many Blood were killed & wounded. In the summer Buffalo Child & his party were killed by the Cree. There were 2 big Sun Dances on either side of the river at Standoff – one was by the Blood & one by the Blackfeet, A warrior by the name of Handsome Young Man dragged the buffalo head around by a spear in his shoulder. According to Percy Creighton, this was the first time such a vow was made.

NORTH BLACKFEET

CRANE BEAR: The Blackfeet and Blood battle with the Cree below, at the Elbow, and about 50 are killed by the Cree.

YELLOW FLY: The year of the famous three Pis-Kuns, or Buffalo traps.

RUNNING RABBIT: We stuck in the snow. (Double Sundance at Belly *[two Okans, ed.]*) (Crees stuck us in snow)

MANY GUNS: Itayaminotspi = Capturing alive or grabbing you alive. That winter an awful hard snow, deep. Blackfoot and Bloods went to war to Cypress Hills. Killing several women out for wood. Crees and Assiniboines heard of the deaths, chased the Blackfoot and Bloods. Snow so deep, 28 Bloods, 20 Blackfoot killed because they couldn't escape.

Itonamots = getting stuck in deep snow. Driven into deep snow, they were sunk.

(2) In summer, Bloods and Blackfoot had separate Sundances across the Belly River, west of Mokuans (Belly Buttes). Blackfoot had theirs where the old stand-off, (a place where traders were) was. Bloods just across river. Mokuans – natsikapukani – at Belly Butte double Sundance. Thus the Blackfoot were way down in Blood territory. The Bloods and Blackfoot usually have separate Sundances. Once down on the Missouri the Blood and Blackfoot joined in one big circle for Sundance. This happened once. This time there were two circles *(Can't get anything here: I think it is the proximity of the 2 circles, or that visiting possible, that is remarkable. Hanks comments*) Many Guns born 1866? Or the time of 1 circle Sundance.

LITTLE CHIEF: Double Sun Dance the Bloods camped one place not far apart the Blackfeet in one place both camps made Sun Dance in each camp than they all moved to the south near Lethbridge for the winter that winter the snow was very deep the Crees attacked the camps the Crees had home made snow shoes that is the time the Blackfeet suffered lost lot of men women children that was one time we had it bad.

"150 Blackfoot on war path – meet the Crees & fight – they found Cree women gathering wood. Three-Bulls captured one of them & told the Blackfoot not to kill her, but one called him crazy, saying that some Blackfoot had been killed & asked what he would do with the woman. So Three-Bulls killed her and took her scalp. They killed all the women. The Crees heard the shooting and said the women must all be killed. There was 2 feet of snow on the ground – all the Crees had snowshoes. The Blackfoot had none & said, let us turn away, they will kill us all, let us return to the cut bank. But in doing it 50 of the Blackfoot were killed. The Cree were afraid to follow." *[Three-Bulls, Siksika-Blackfoot, to Morris, 1909, 1985;110]*

"Four chiefs each lost at once their minipoka children on a war party. (1) Agawotan

[Many Shields], father of Namaitsis'sapoyistsi alias Axsinamaxka, who was killed. Agawotan had coaxed his son first to go on the war party, saying, 'If you go, I'll be glad to hear you've been killed for I can then pierce myself with four arrows, cut your horse's mane and tail to lead around, and mother can cut her hair and face."

It happened. News came to a circle camp and Agawotan did as he said, pierced calves, etc. with eight arrows. Mother cut her dress to her knees, slashed legs, arms, and sleeves of mother and father; each cut both of their little fingers off. Mother had her hair cut off to ears. Father was 'feeling thankful at being seen thus' and he told his son that he would be glad thus.

(2) Natosapi, also a mourner, was leading his son's horse around the camp, loaded with all his son's things – Ixkeikini, another minipoka, son of Old-Sun. Old-Sun had the most beautiful horse to lead around. All these were marvelous things. Old-Sun did not cut himself as Agawotan.

(3) Saxkumapi *[Young-Man, ed.]* also led a horse, but did not have the beaded stuff that Old-Sun had on his horse. All four chiefs and wives went out of camp, off a ways, and cried. Some of the band members took a smoke and food out to them to try to comfort them. All the people 'are crying with the chiefs.' Every relation was crying, especially if they went out there. The other three chiefs cut one finger off, their wives cut both. Agawotan had the arrows pulled out; being naked except for loin cloth they gave him a buffalo robe to wear. After three days the people pulled the arrows out of Agawotan, doctored all of them. The women retained their oldest dresses though, but were given a blanket.

'In old time we felt very sorry for mourners, not like you today, and all tried to comfort them.' The people after four days begged them to 'put moccasins on' and put away any thought of killing themselves.

Now it was winter when the four sons had gone to war. News came to a first circle camp mixed Blackfeet and Blood. *[This would be the first of four camps made on the way to the Okan, or Sun Dance camp. ed.]* [This happened before the smallpox came. The four were killed among the many who died at the Stuck-in-the-Snow catastrophe.]

Not long after someone organized a revenge party of three hundred. Agwmaxkayi and Nataoxki [Blood chief: Holy Water] were the itamoa, i.e. leaders of the revenge party. There had been Blood and Blackfeet men along on the ill fated party and all had been killed. The Blood chief had lost a son too, but Agwmaxkayi had not.

The two tribal revenge parties joined forces on one party against the Cree. Lots of people went out. All four fathers, although they had long since given up going to war, had to go, i.e. wanted to go in order to pay back for the deaths. All four fathers about the same age – about 70 each. [Old-Sun died at 90 ca. 1898.] Crooked Meat Strings' father was on the party. All the party went out; Agawotan rode his son's horse and went riding among the warriors and as they sat, he began to sing. Agawotani – alias Naistoupiksimaixkini. He was singing seriously, and though people didn't know what it meant, he was actually vowing to avenge his son. All were on horseback. They slept two nights, sent scouts ahead [the best ones and those with best horses]. Scouts zigzagged back, therefore all knew that enemy had been sighted. The messengers said, 'Walk slowly, wait for night.' Two went in advance and strategy was for the two to show themselves so Cree would see them and chase them. Two would then draw them into a trap, where two wings of Blackfoot would fall on. Part divided up. Agawotan was singing [again], 'Tomorrow I'm going to kill a Cree. Even if they run home and into their tipis, I'll pursue them right into their tipis. I don't care anything as long as I kill a Cree.'

The Cree fell into the trap. Cree then fled for home. Agawotan ran into the midst, killed one from the back, ran through the whole bunch of Crees and then came back to Blackfoot! All bullets missed Agawotan! He killed twice a Cree this way. 'This is a tremendously strong thing to do.' [The old man died later of old age.] Agawotan did not have a medicine with him, and Crooked Meat Strings never heard of his ever having one, but he was never wounded.

Blackfoot killed lots of Cree. A Blood saw a Cree chief Ino'takawatan, Buffalo-Head-Flag out in front. The Blood chief decided to go after him. The Cree cried out when shot. So at the victory dance, they sang a song: 'Buffalo-Head-Flag, we made him cry.'...

Apaomaxkan [Weasel-Runner] a half Sarsi married to a Blackfoot, also did a great deed. Crees tried to encircle the Blackfoot, but Apaomaxkan ran out ahead and killed a Cree, grabbed the horse's bridle and got the horse. The horse turned out to be one just stolen from the Blackfoot! So they think it very wonderful to get the horse back home. This one deed would make a man a chief 'of course.' Cree had diarrhea all over the horse before he died so horse was a mess.

Apaomaxkan stole back the horse of Maistosoatsis, original owner, and gave it pronto to his father-in-law who was sitting behind in the battle. Maistosoatsis had been killed when the horse was stolen; but if he had been alive, he would not have gotten the horse back, would have no rights to it. No angry feelings because original owner says, 'It's good that horse is on my side again' and would be glad the other man was such a great warrior. The two [original owner and recoverer] would tease each other much about that horse later, 'You didn't go get that horse, you just let it go!'

When the Cree chief who cried...killed they quit fighting. The old men and non-fighters went ahead, brave ones behind lest Crees chase them. On this war all the young and fast ones were ahead; old ones behind, ready to shoot, but most of them never shot a gun. The young did all the fighting. There were 300 Blackfoot and Blood, over 150 Blackfeet. There were more Cree killed than Blackfoot lost on the ill-fated war party. The 300 came home safe, not a single causality.

Ak'siksim(o)si sa'o – means – we have to try to pay back – revenge party. *[Crooked Meat Strings to Hanks, 1938; 311-315]*

Wolf Carrier, Siksika-Blackfoot, was a member of the revenge war party and recorded the event on a painted robe done for Edmund Morris [now in the Royal Ontario Museum]. He interpreted the drawing as, "Two sons of an old Blackfoot had been killed & to revenge this a large war party of Bloods &Blackfoot numbering over 100. They followed the Bow River down - & on to the camp of the Assiniboine & Crees. They came on the camp & hid in the bushes till morning. It was winter. They attacked but were outnumbered & 50 of the braves were killed, the rest retreated." *[Wolf Carrier, Siksika-Blackfoot, to Edmund Morris, 1907,] [A little confusion with translation occurs here. The two stories (the loss of the 50 and the revenge party) have been mixed as one event. The original story of the defeat in winter begins with, "They came on the camp…".The first part of Wolf Carrier's description deals with the revenge war party.] The painted hide and image of the revenge war party are published in WAR PAINT, by Arni Brownstone published by the Royal Ontario Museum, Toronto.*

1866 Revenge raid:

"A great council was held to decide what steps were to be taken in retaliation. *[For the defeat of a large war party nearly wiped out by the Cree, ed.]* The result of the 'talk' was that the Bloods, Blackfeet, Peigans *[ibid. ed.]*, and Sarcees moved in a single immense camp down the river. A war-camp of the whole nation upon an errand of vengeance. When we had moved a long way down the river, one day 'White Calf' and 'Eagle Head' with a few men went out upon a scouting trip. After they had been gone two or three days, early one morning they appeared in sight riding in circles and as they approached we saw that they were flourishing a scalp. They had discovered a Cree village and at some little distance from it came upon a man and a woman. The former made his escape, but the woman, who was heavy with child, fell into the hands of the scouts who soon dispatched her. The news spread rapidly through the camp, and soon in all directions were to be seen the men catching and saddling their war-horses. A great war-dance was indulged in by the mounted men until all were ready, then off they started, hundreds and hundreds in number, a fine sight." *[Red Crow, Blood-Blackfoot to R.N. Wilson, 1891 in Wilson, 1958, 223]*

Revenge raid pictograph; painting by Night Shoot, South Peigan-Blackfoot, Fort Macleod Museum, Alberta, author's photo

Parade through camp prior to leaving on a revenge raid, South Peigan-Blackfoot Sun Dance camp , 1920, H.F. Robinson photo, author's collection

1867

NORTH PEIGAN

 BULL PLUME #1: When all the tribes first made the corral for the buffaloes. *Or Bull Pen.*

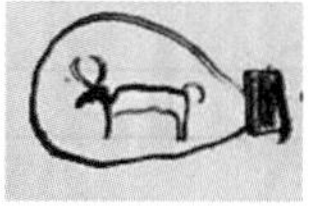 BULL PLUME #2: When all the tribes first made the corral for the buffaloes.

 BULL PLUME #2 B: *This shows the forked Sun Dance center pole and five lines under it. It would most likely mean all five tribes were at the same Sun Dance, or Okan. [North Peigan, South Peigan, Bloods, Blackfeet and Sarsi]*

This should undoubtedly read, "When all the tribes last made the corral for the Buffaloes". Many Guns gives the date of 1871 for this event. Weasel Tail, a Blood Indian, lived with the North Peigan and North Blackfeet in Canada for a number of years. During his lifetime he witnessed two buffalo drives. The last was when he was about fifteen years old and it is entirely possible it is the same one mentioned in this winter count.

Weasel Tail and his daughter Maggie, Thomas Magee photo, H. Scriver collection, author's collection

"I was then among the North Blackfoot near present Gleichen (Alberta). It was in winter. We didn't drive the buffalo over a cliff. We built a corral near the edge of timber toward the bottom of a downhill slope. We made the corral of cottonwood posts set upright in the ground to a height of about 7 feet, and connected by crosspoles of cottonwood or birch tied to the posts with rawhide ropes. All around the corral stakes of cottonwood or birch were laid over the lowest cross poles. Their butt ends were firmly braced in the ground outside the corral. Their other ends projected about three feet or more inside the corral at an angle so that the ends were about the height of a buffalo's body. These ends were sharpened to points, so that if the buffalo tried to break through the corral, after they had been driven into it, they would be impaled on the stakes. From the open side of the corral the fence of poles extended in two wings outward and up the hill. These lines were further extended by piles of cut willows in the shape of little lodges tied together at the tops. These piles were about half as high as a man and were spaced at intervals of several feet. On the hill just above the opening of the corral a number of poles were placed on the ground crosswise of the slope and parallel to each other. The buffalo had to cross these poles to enter the corral. These poles were covered with manure and water which froze and became slippery so that once the buffalo were in the corral they couldn't escape by climbing back up the hill.

Before the drive began a Beaver Bundle owner handled the sacred buffalo stones in his bundle and prayed. He sang a song, 'Give me one head of buffalo or more. *[meaning, '100 head or more', ed.]* Help me to fall the buffalo.'

Then the men of the camp rode out on horseback, got around behind a herd of buffalo and drove it towards the corral...Once inside the corral, the buffalo were killed by men and boys with guns. I have never heard of a buffalo corral made by any of the Blackfoot tribes since the time of this fall in which I participated." *[Weasel Tail to Ewers, 1949, 359-360]*

John Ewers recorded this information in 1947. At that time he estimated the date to be about the year 1872. This was based on the approximate birth date and approximate age of Weasel Tail at the time of the buffalo drive. It is therefore possible that the buffalo corral witnessed by Weasel Tail is the same mentioned in this winter count.

In 1950 Claude Schaeffer also questioned Weasel Tail about this buffalo drive. We attach that story here so the reader may see how a storyteller varies with time and details. Another factor is how well the storyteller and interviewer got along and how, and if, the interviewer questioned the teller for details.

As a youth of 15, Weasel Tail witnessed a bison drive. Saw a mounted man sneak up to the herd unobserved. The herd was facing the drive. He rode alongside and yelled 'Wu...! Wu...! Wu...! The howl started them and they didn't know which way to flee. The hunter then guided the herd towards the drive wings. He continued to howl. They were guided through the wings and over the cliff.

Piles of willows tied together were used instead of rocks for the wings, arranged from three to four feet apart. This was the case in drive which Weasel Tail saw. If any buffalo got too close, the person behind the screen wiggled a finger to turn them towards center of wings. This drive had a log chute leading from edge to corral, instead of a cliff drop. It was covered with manure to make it slippery, so that animals could not retain footing nor turn back. The chute was elevated at far end to conceal brush corral located behind it. The animals ran around inside the corral and were shot with guns.

The willow bundles were supported by piles of rock along both wings. Person concealed behind each one. He remained perfectly still, until bison showed signs of turning, then wiggled a finger to force them back. Weasel Tail's group were short of horses, hence had to make buffalo drive.

Weasel Tail said that at big lakes, wings were constructed in winter to lead out onto the ice. An inclined slope was built at the edge of the lake. Bison were driven out upon the ice, where they were easily killed.

Weasel Tail said that bison move east in spring away from the foothills and by middle of the summer, start to return to the foothills. By fall and winter, they are all back in the foothills again. Long ago, people said, buffalo moved eastward into plains for the new grass and then returned for shelter in foothills in fall and winter. Certain bulls would stay behind in small numbers in foothills, and during spring and summer people depended upon them. If disturbed too much by hunting, bison were thought to leave the country, at least in folktales. *[Weasel Tail, Blood-Blackfoot; Schaeffer, 1950, notes, 3]*

Many bison in country west of Choteau *[Montana, ed.]*, hence many drive sites here. Buffalo were fond of country around Augusta ["Raising Dust" *in Blackfoot*]. Peigan camped in brush along streams around Choteau in winter. Horses fed along creeks here in winter. Peigan camped in bands. *[Green Grass Bull to Schaefer,1950, notes, 29]*

There were buffalo that ranged in the mountains, called Omaxsini, "big buffalo". People prayed to them. They had a song; "I'm sacred standing on the mountain. I walk down in a sacred way."

These animals were said to be larger than the plains bison. People used to find large skulls and great long bones of these animals.

Adam had never heard that any one hunted them. They were considered very wise. The Blackfoot penetrated the mountains for lodge poles but never hunted there much. Elk and deer were hunted in the foothills. Mountain buffalo's song is used by the beaver bundle owner and is sung when the bundle is opened. *[Adam White Man to Schaefer, notes, April 1950]*

SOUTH PEIGAN

ELK HORN: Fought with Crow, Gros Ventre and Flathead.

BIG BRAVE: Mountain Chief camped south of the Missouri and Peigan killed two Flathead near Peigan camps; in summer the Peigan killed thirty Assiniboine, who were picking pine gum.

BIG NOSE WAR RECORD: Near Cypress Hills 6 Sioux attempt to steal horses – 5 killed.

The Worm and Small Robe bands were camped not far apart on the Marias River. Calf Tail, who was with the Worms, was invited by Chief Bull Lodge, the chief of the Small Robes, to camp with him. He went over and staid with the Small Robes all winter. About midwinter Calf Tail went out on a hunting party to get buffalo meat. In this party were: Yellow Wolf [leader], Wolverine, Medicine Weasel, Morning Plume, Bear Paw, Small Robe Old Man, Takes Gun and Calf Tail. They traveled two days until they found the buffalo, made three chases, and got all the meat they could carry back. There were about 25 tipis in the Small Robe band that winter.

Another winter hunting party: The Small Robes were camped near Many Springs [in direction of Sweet Grass Hills]. Yellow Wolf, a famous hunter, lead a hunting party. They traveled one day's journey to find the buffalo. They took along women to do the butchering. They camp in the tipis from the previous year cut small [size of seven skin tipi]. *[Calf Tail, South Peigan-Blackfoot; Collier, 1938,17]*

BLOOD

BAD HEAD: Itaksorpomatiskaopi The Indians have plenty of furs and make a big trade

WHITE BULL: Fort Whoop-up was built by Healy & Hamilton as fur trading post and it was burned down a few years later and rebuilt again. It became know a notorious whiskey trading post. Bear People rushing through the camps killed few.

DEMPSEY: Plenty trade/on trading expedition
The Blackfoot were beginning to obtain repeating rifles and were able to kill larger numbers of buffalo. As a result, more dried meat, robes and leather were taken to the traders (L).

PERCY CREIGHTON: Chief In Sight Far Off, the Blood Indian, took horses & other property away from his sister, Holy (or Sacred) Snake Woman who had married a white man & was not behaving properly. (They were eventually returned to her piece meal.) *(This was Culbertson's wife, ed.)*

NORTH BLACKFEET

CRANE BEAR: A Sarcee, by the name of Assinaetopew *(Sitting Cree, ?, ed.)*, is killed by the Cree.

YELLOW FLY: The year when the Crees trapped the Blackfeet in deep snow and massacred them.

RUNNING RABBIT: Biting Down From Top, killed. Many Shot, died. (Buffalo Child, Three Calf, and Pretty Young Man killed)

MANY GUNS: Akuskunkota = (Many Shot) Blackfoot died. (Not killed)

LITTLE CHIEF: Mr. Biting Down From Top also Mr. Many Shot both died of wounds which they got in a battle

1868

NORTH PEIGAN

BULL PLUME #1: When we met the Sioux in a body and finished them, or ran them down. *[This is obviously the Gros Ventre and Crow referred to on the other counts, ed.]*

BULL PLUME #2: When we met the Sioux in a body and finished them, or ran them down.

BULL PLUME #2 B: *No pictograph.*

[There was obviously some difficulty in the winter count translation for this event.]

The date for this event has been changed from 1866 originally published in 1979. New information concerning events prior to and after, the battle, as well as newly discovered oral history, helped establish the new dating.

Bird Rattle:
"Ever since I can remember, there was the battle of "Retreat Up the Hill", the last great battle fought by the Blackfeet where only Indians took part. It happened a few miles east of here and about this time of year." *[Writing on Stone , Alberta, September, 1924]* I was too young to fight then, and had not taken part in the Sun Dance. But my father fought in that battle, and has often told me of the many strange things that happened. I have also talked it over with Gros Ventre who had relatives killed there...

It was two years before *["after", ed]* the "Small Pox". After being separated for many years, all the tribes of the Sik-si-ka *[Siksikaitsitapix -the Blackfoot Nation, ed]* were together again under one head chief, Ah-kow-tahs, Many Horses. Many Horses was the last great chief under whom all the Sik-si-ka tribes, the Piegan, the Bloods and the Blackfeet, fought as one great tribe. During the summer of this year the Blackfeet had been lucky. The buffalo had been plentiful and many had been killed, until all the lodges were full of pemmican and robes. All the people had horses. That fall the tribes went into winter camp in the Milk River coulees heading in the Sweet Grass Hills instead of going farther south as they usually did. All All the coulees between the Sweet Grass Hills and the Milk River were full of lodges. Wherever there was a spring, there would be a village of lodges. These villages were in all the coulees from the east to the west of the Sweet Grass Hills.

All during the summer A-ki-o-pee, Sits-Like-a-Woman, head chief of the Gros Ventre, had been making preparations for a raid on the Blackfeet, and had made a vow to kill them all. He was very bitter against the Blackfeet. The Gros Ventres were camped on the Big River [Missouri] below Fort Benton, and it is said that some of the white men added to the hatred of Sits-Like-a-Woman by telling him stories of the things the Blackfeet had said about him; that he was too fat to fight, and was only fit to sit around with the women and tell stories. But not all the Gros Ventres wanted to fight the Blackfeet. So there was much talk one way and the other, and Sits-Like-a-Woman was a long time getting his war party together...

Now it was the custom of the old men from the Blackfeet villages to come down to Milk River to read the signs on Writing-on-Stone. Every day they found new signs. Some days there were only a few, and on other days many. Usually the signs told of strangers passing through the country, or where the buffalo could be found. One day some of the old men found pictures of many Gros Ventres and they were making the sign for peace. The old men went to their chief, Many Horses, and told him what the signs on Writing-on-Stone had said, and the Medicine Men advised Many Horses to take a party and go down to the Big River and make a big peace with the Gros Ventres. Many Horses, however, would not listen to his old men. He said, 'No, let us wait. If the Gros Ventres want peace they will send one of their men to us and invite us to come down.'

So they waited, but no one came. You will see how Many Horses might have lived to see his braves win a great victory if he had followed the advise of his Medicine Men, and sent a peace party toward the Gros Ventres camp.

Sits-Like-a-Woman and his big war party of Gros Ventres, Crows and Crees came up the Milk River slowly. He had sent out some of his scouts to the Crows and also to the Crees inviting them to send war parties to join his braves and attack the Blackfeet. So after Sits-Like-a-Woman had left camp a few days he ran across a big party of Crows who made peace and joined his band. A few days later they met a large party of Crees who also made peace and went along. It was late in the fall when the war party reached the Sweet Grass Hills.

Quite early one morning Many Horses and his wife, Lone Coup, went out to gather buffalo brains for tanning hides. Their lodge was pitched in the farthest east village of the Blackfeet, which was just north of the east butte of the Sweet Grass Hills. They knew a coulee about two miles from their village where some buffalo had been killed a few days before, and they went there to get the brains. Hardly had they commenced cracking the buffalo skulls and taking out the brains when they found themselves surrounded by a party of six Gros Ventres. The chief of the party, who was Sits-Like-a-Woman himself, approached Many Horses and told him to prepare to die. Sits-Like-a-Woman went on to boast of the many thousands of warriors he had concealed but a few miles further east, and he announced that he had come up from the Big River to kill all the Blackfeet. He said that he would leave none.

Many Horses then addressed Sits-Like-a-Woman, 'You have me in your power, and you can kill me at any time. There is no hurry. I am not afraid to die. I am old, and it doesn't matter to me whether I go to the Great Spirit now or in a little while. I have one request to make. Let us sit down and smoke. I have some things to say to you. Then, after we have smoked, if you still want to kill me, I have nothing to say.'

So they sat down, with Many Horses and his wife in the center. They lit their pipes, and smoked.

After the pipes had burned a while, Many Horses spoke, 'Word came to me about one moon ago that the Gros Ventres wished to make peace with the Blackfeet. Good, the Blackfeet will make peace. Today the Blackfeet are all one tribe. They are all my children. Their lodges fill the coulees as far west as the eye can see. There are many thousands of lodges. They are well armed. They have plenty of horses. If the Gros Ventres wish peace, I invite you to come, you and all your people, and camp with us. We have much food. We will eat and dance and make peace. You have come a long ways and many of you are on foot. From my many horses I will give each warrior who is with you a horse to ride home. But if the Gros Ventres want war, if they kill me, the head chief, then the Blackfeet will not make peace until the last Gros Ventres is driven out of the country. I have spoken.'

This talk caused a heated argument to break out among the Gros Ventres, a part headed by Sits-Like-a-Woman insisting that they kill Many Horses, and go on with their plans for attacking the Blackfeet, and a part headed by Weasel Horse advising peace. Sits-Like-a-Woman, being the head chief, carried the more weight. It was finally decided that Many Horses must die. Now when Lone Coup, the wife of Many Horses, saw that the Gros Ventres were determined to kill her husband, she seized the ax which she had been using to crack buffalo skulls, and knocked down one of the Gros Ventres warriors, and would have killed him but another saw her, and shot her before she could strike the second blow. In the confusion they also shot Many Horses. When they had killed Many Horses, 'counted coup', and taken his scalp, they returned to their camp.

This party which killed Many Horses and his wife was scouting. They had seen only the small village where Many Horses had his lodge, and they had not believed him when he told them that the coulees to the westward were filled with thousands of Blackfeet lodges. So Sits-Like-a-Woman told his war party what he had done and seen. Then they could capture the village without any fighting. He told a party of warriors to go along the crest of a nearby ridge in pairs, each pair of Indians to carry a blanket over them so that at a distance they would resemble a herd of buffalo going down to the river. The men could see for themselves that the village was small. The Blackfeet would take them for buffalo, come out to take some meat, and be ambushed and killed. Sits-Like-a-Woman's plan was followed. The sun was just coming up, and the Gros Ventres, made up to resemble buffalo, were plainly visible from the Blackfeet camp, although about two miles away. At first, the Blackfeet were fooled, and knowing nothing of the death of their chief Many Horses, they began to get ready to go after what they thought were buffalo.

But one of them, Pinto Bear *[Spotted Bear, ed]* had better eyes than the others. He looked for a long time, then cried, 'Since when are buffalo white, and red, and green? Those are not buffalo, they are enemy spies!' Immediately, all the Braves prepared for battle, and a runner was sent back to arouse the other villages.

The day before Ah-kow-tah – Many Horses – was killed, several old men of the Blackfeet left their lodges and went down to Writing-on-Stone. When they reached the place, they were amazed to find no writings, no signs. There was nothing but the weather-beaten grey surface of the sandstone cliff, without a scratch or mark. A few days before, they themselves had seen and read many writings, where now there was nothing. This was something unheard of. Of course, some days the writings were less than others, but as far as they knew, there had never been known a time when there were no writings on the stones.

They thought about this thing a long time, and talked among themselves, but could make nothing of it. On the way back to their lodges, they agreed they would return very early the next morning to see what might happen. Their story about Writing-on-Stone created quite a stir in their village, so that the next morning there was quite a party of men that went down to the river to see what writings might have been made during the night.

As the party approached from the high land on the other side of the river, and while still a great way off, they could see that there were writings, many high up on the overhanging face of the cliff, far out of reach of any person even on horseback. They hurried up and ran down to the river, crossed, and came up to the cliff, crying all the time, 'Ho! Ho!'

There were writings now, more than they had ever seen before, and the older men, more wise than the others in these matters, began to read the signs. Their high spirits at finding the writings were soon turned to dismay, for there on the cliff was shown the dead lodge, and on it there was plainly seen the mark of their great chief, Many Horses. This could mean but one thing – Many Horses was soon to die. They hurried along the cliff to other writings, talking excitedly to one another as they read. Here they saw a small party of Gros Ventres and before them Many Horses and his wife, Lone Coup, dead. Wildly they looked further. Here was a battle and Gros Ventres running away. They could tell the different kinds of Indians by marks on their shields, so it was easy to identify Crees and

Crows, some dead and some running away. The writings covered all the cliff, and even around the point where it turned back into a coulee and was covered by earth.

Hurrying back to their camp very much excited, they gave the war cry, and caught their horses and raced toward the place where their chief pitched his lodge. Each village they passed through was told that a big battle was on. In this way the news that an enemy of the Blackfeet was in the country spread from the villages at both ends of the camp, many miles apart, at almost the same time. Part were warned by messengers sent back from the camp of Many Horses, and part were told by the men who had seen the signs of Writing-on-Stone. Within a short time after Pinto Bear saw the enemy spies, all the Blackfeet villages were sending warriors on horseback to the chief's village. This caused a curious thing to happen.

The village where Many Horses had his lodge, the one that the Gros Ventres could see, was located on a little flat where two coulees came together. Anybody coming into this village from the west would come down the bottom of the coulee running that way, and could not be seen from where the Gros Ventres were spying. War parties from the other Blackfeet villages came this way. So the Gros Ventres could not see them until they rode through the village where Many Horses had his lodge. The Gros Ventres thought that all these war parties, which they saw, were coming from the same village. A party of Blackfeet would ride out of the village and come up the slope a little way and stop with the first party who had come out. After a little while another party of Blackfeet would come out of the same village and ride up to join the others. They kept coming and kept coming until the Gros Ventres began to get afraid, for they couldn't understand how so many warriors could come from one small village.

They began to whisper to one another, 'What has Sits-Like- a-Woman gotten us into? He told us there was only a small village which we see. But there are too many Blackfeet coming out of it. Are we fighting ghosts?'

The more they talked the more they were afraid. This was one of the strange things about this battle, that the Gros Ventres began to be afraid before they started to fight.

Up until this time no one in the Blackfeet camp knew that Many Horses was dead. The Blackfeet warriors kept coming, party after party, until there were over two thousand of them. They didn't know where the enemy was, nor how many there were. Their head chief was nowhere to be found. All they knew was that some enemy spies had been seen on the ridge nearly two miles away. When the Gros Ventres saw so many Blackfeet on the slope, they thought that their trick had been discovered, and Sits-Like-a-Woman sent back and had all the war party come up. Then they began to show themselves. The Blackfeet were all on horses. Many of the Gros Ventres wee on foot, but the Gros Ventres were higher up than the Blackfeet. So the two war parties began to draw together.

When the two war parties got close together, a loud voice began to speak, so that the men on both sides could hear it. It was loud like thunder, and it seemed to come from the sky.

It spoke plainly so that those who knew the Blackfeet language could understand. It said, 'Blackfeet warriors, your great chief, Many Horses, is dead. He has been killed by the Gros Ventres. Now the Gros Ventres have tried to trick you by imitating buffalo. So, like buffalo, they shall be killed. Ride after them like buffalo, and like buffalo they will run from you. Ride after them until there are no more to ride after.'

The Blackfeet rode at them as though they were hunting buffalo; and everywhere the Gros Ventres ran and tried to get away. Only a few had horses, and these trampled down others in their hurry. They ran back up the hill, which is the reason this battle is called 'Retreat Up The Hill'. *[Bird Rattle, South Piegan to Willcolmb, 1924, Willcolmb, Manuscript, 1968] [Additional versions of the battle are given by Schultz; 1962; 279, Ewers; 1958; 243 and Curtis and Grinnell; 1859; 132]*

The battle is portrayed in petroglyph form at Writing On Stone Park near Milk River, Alberta.

Gros Ventre warriors, 1898-1899, S.W. Ormsby photo

SOUTH PEIGAN

ELK HORN: Straggling (sic) Wolf killed near camp; Peigan killed Crow in revenge.

BIG BRAVE: Strangle-Wolf killed by Gros Ventre while hunting; Chief-Crow killed by Gros Ventre while hunting. Six women with him.

BLOOD

BAD HEAD: Keayetapissiw otsitsetoworpi "Joining the Bear" being drunk, rushed through the camp, and kills many.

WHITE BULL: White Bull adds the following at the end of 1867,"Bear People rushing through the camps kills few."

DEMPSEY: Bear People/shot at people
Some members of the Bear People Band rushed through the camp in a drunken state and killed several people. Legal states they were Peigans.

PERCY CREIGHTON: Short Bull Back Fat, a Blood, killed another Blood, Eagle Tail Feather Chief.

NORTH BLACKFEET

CRANE BEAR: Two old Blackfeet chiefs die.

YELLOW FLY: The year "Many Shots" died.

RUNNING RABBIT: Many Ghosts Place, and Four Bears sell goods. (River Tribe *[Pen d'Oreille, ed.]* killed them all. Crees killed them by mud.)

MANY GUNS: Akainosku = Many-dead. A big battle around Ft. Hooper. *(Ft. Whoop-up ?. ed.)*

Blackfoot, two Peigan tribes, Bloods wintered at Ft. Hooper; Crees, Assiniboines et al. warred. Crees, Assiniboines didn't know there were so many tipis. Blackfoot Confederation tipis were stretched along a river. 1 percent outlying tipis attacked; message went up and all attacked. Many drowned. A tremendous victory for Blackfoot Confederation. Hundreds killed. *[This sounds like the battle at Fort Whoop-up, Lethbridge, Alberta,1870, ed.]*

(2) That summer, Sikutsimi = Chestnut horse, a Crow horse, was stolen and bought to the camps. This a very renowned horse. Blackfoot stole the horse.

LITTLE CHIEF: Mr. Many Ghost also Mr. Four Bear had they first store were selling goods to the Indians

CHAPTER 8

THE AGENCY

It was the United States that first introduced the Blackfoot to the Indian Agent and Agency. At first it was just a specific representative of the government to whom they could address their concerns and who was responsible for issuing their annuities promised in the treaties. In the early days, after the signing of the treaty, these political appointees spent as little time as possible in Blackfoot country, usually distributing the annuities and leaving as quickly as possible. The Agency for the Upper Missouri Indians was created in 1852 and included the Blackfoot Nation after the 1855 treaty. The first agent for this agency was James H. Norwood who was killed later that same year. He was succeeded by Alfred J. Vaughan until 1857 when he was replaced by A.H. Redfield. Vaughan then became agent for the Blackfoot Nation specifically, until 1861. He established the agency at Sun River during this time. [Actually, this was the farm at Sun River, fifteen miles above the mouth of the Sun River. Intended to be an example to the Blackfoot to encourage them to change to farming it didn't last long – ca.1866. (ed.)] This consisted of the North and South Peigans, Bloods and Siksika. [Fort Benton Journals, 1854-1856]

John Ewers states that Edwin Hatch, the first Blackfoot Agent, established the agency at Fort Benton post late 1855. In February he went to Ft. Union for the annuities to arrive and in September 1856 paid the annuities at the Mouth of the Judith River. He was around the Blackfoot for only four months of his nine months in office. [Ewers, 1958]

1869

NORTH PEIGAN

BULL PLUME#1 When "Three Coming Over The Hill" was murdered.

When the 8 Crees were beaten.

BULL PLUME #2: When "Three Coming Over The Hill" was murdered.

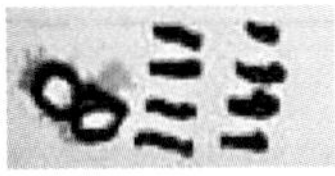

When the 8 Crees were beaten.

BULL PLUME #2 B: *No pictograph.*

SOUTH PEIGAN

ELK HORN: Assiniboine, a Chief, killed.

BIG BRAVE: Peigan had smallpox and soldiers attacked seventy camps, killing many old men, women and children. *(January 23, 1870 Col. E.M. Baker attacked a camp of Peigans killing 173 men, women, and children. ed.)*

BIG BRAVE 2: Summer, Running Raven was wounded by Gros Ventre.

Major Eugene M. Baker of Fort Ellis attacked the camp of Heavy Runner on the morning of January 23,1870. Four companies of the 2nd Cavalry and 55 mounted men of the 13th Infantry attacked the camp, killing 15 fighting men, 90 women, and 50 children under the age of 12. The men were off hunting. As the attack began, Heavy Runner came running out of his lodge towards the attackers. In his hand, he waved a paper written by the Indian Agent, saying he was a good and peaceful man, a friend of the whites. He ran just a short way before being shot down.[Schultz, 298-305, 1962]

Bear Head was a survivor of the massacre and portrayed the event on a pictographic muslin for the Great Northern Railway. He also told the story to James Willard Schultz who recorded it verbatim.

Bear Head, South Peigan-Blackfoot, ca. 1930's, Winold Reiss photo, author's collection

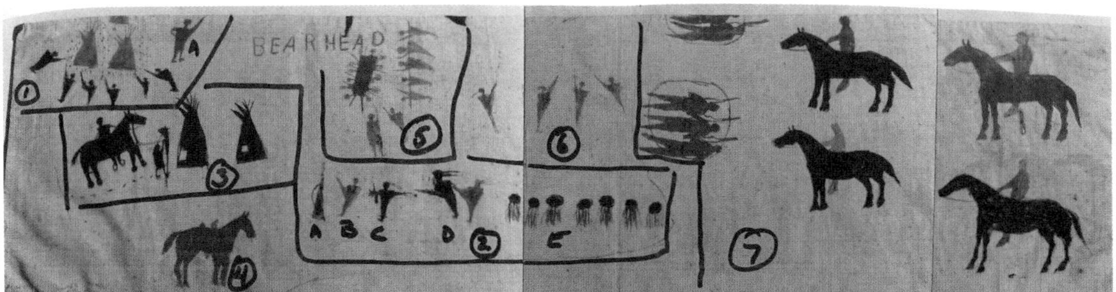

Bear Head's pictograph of the battle, author's photo, Glenbow Museum

Bear Head's Pictographic Story

1. This is the attack of Major Eugene M. Baker of Fort Ellis, on the camp of Heavy Runner of the South Peigans. On the morning of January 23, 1870 four companies of the 2nd Cavalry and 55 mounted men of the 13th Infantry attacked the camp killing 15 fighting men, 90 women and 50 children under the age of 12. The men of the camp were off on a hunting expedition the day before, and were still away. As the attack began, Heavy Runner came running out of his lodge towards the attackers. In his hand he waved a paper written by the Indian Agent, saying he was a good and peaceful man, a friend of the whites. He ran just a short way before being shot down. This is figure "A" in Bear Head's drawing. Bear Head, himself, had been captured prior to the attack when he went out to get his horses and so had a clear view of the attack. He was twelve years old at the time.

"A seizer chief up on the bank shouted something, and at once all of the seizers began shooting into the lodges. Chief Heavy Runner ran from his lodge toward the seizers on the bank. He was shouting to them and waving a paper writing that our agent had given him, a writing saying that he was a good and peaceful man, a friend of the whites. He had run but a few steps when he fell, his body pierced with bullets. Inside the lodges men were yelling; terribly frightened women and children, screaming – screaming from wounds, from pain as they died. I saw a few men and women, escaping from their lodges, shot down as they ran. Most terrible to hear of all was the crying of little babies at their mother's breasts. The seizers all advanced upon the lodges, my seizer still firmly holding my arm. They shot at the tops of the lodges; cut the bindings of the poles so the whole lodge would collapse upon the fire and begin to burn – burn and smother those within. I saw my lodge so go down and burn. Within it my mother, my almost-mothers, almost-sisters. Oh, how pitiful were their screamings as they died, and I there, powerless to help them!

Soon all was silent in the camp, and the seizers advanced, began tearing down the lodges that still stood, shooting those within them who were still alive, and then trying to burn all that they tore down, burn the dead under the heaps of poles, lodge-skins, and furnishings; but they did not burn well.

At last my seizer released my arm and went about with his men looking at the smoking piles, talking, pointing, laughing, all of them. And finally the seizers rounded up all of our horses, drove them up the valley a little way, and made camp…

That night the white seizers did not closely watch the hundreds of horses that they had taken from us. We managed to get back about half of the great herd and drive them down to Mountain Chief's camp. During the day our buffalo hunters returned. With many horses loaded with meat and hides, they came singing, laughing, down the valley, only to find their dear ones dead under their ruined lodges. The white killers had gone, turned back whence they came. As best we could we buried our dead – a terrible, grieving task it was – and counted them: fifteen men, ninety women, fifty children. Forty-four lodges and lodge furnishings destroyed, and hundreds of our horses stolen." *[Bear Head, South Peigan-Blackfoot to Schultz,1962 298-305]*

2. Records Bear Head's first war party at the age of eight. At this time his name was First Rider and his father still held the name Bear Head. Figure "A" shows the gun he took from the dead Gros Ventre; "B" is the Gros Ventre; "C" is little First Rider [Bear Head] holding his powder and ball, five chambered pistol. With his other hand he reaches for the pipe stem his father , "D", is giving him to strike the wounded Gros Ventre with, and count coup on a living enemy. "E" are the seven scalps the war party took, one taken by Bear Head.

"The man was badly wounded, dying. My father handed me the long stem of his pipe, told me to strike the man with it, count coup on him. I stepped to his side; his face, mouth shot and bloody, sickened me; I drew back. 'Hit him! Hit him!' my father yelled at me. 'Hit him, or I will make you to cry.' So at last, I struck the top of his head with the pipe stem, and with that my father and the others shot him again and he died. My father again yelled at me: 'Now, First Rider, out with your knife and scalp him.' And as I hesitated, 'At once scalp him, else you will no longer be son of mine.' Oh, how I hated to do that; but groaning, almost crying, I did it, taking a piece of his head skin from which dropped one of his long hair braids; then my father had me take the dead one's gun and other things, he and the others there with us shouting; 'Young First Rider, little First Rider; he takes an enemy gun; he takes an enemy scalp.' Then how pleased, how proud I was of myself. And I thought, powerful is Sun. Good to me is Sun. I prayed for a gun, and I have it." [Bear Hear, Schultz, 1962, 283-288]

3. Shows Bear Head entering an enemy camp and capturing a horse and Medicine Bundle from outside their tipis.

4. Show another horse he captured on a raid.

5. Shows a battle he was in where the enemy was in a coulee, and the Blackfoot were on a ridge firing down upon them.

6. Shows part of another battle, [The remainder was undoubtedly on a part of the section that was cut off.]

7. Is another story recorded by Schultz of a "sitting on top" [mounted] war party Bear Head went on when he was nine years old. Seventy-seven Peigans attacked a large hunting party of Crees in the Cypress Hills. They caught them out on the plain and killed thirty-three Crees.

"We all lined up in the lower edge of the pines and at a shout from my father raised a shrill war song and charged out upon the plain. Seeing and hearing us, the buffalo went leaping and thundering westward against the wind, and the party of hunters got closely together and with guns and bows and arrows ready, awaited our coming. Well they knew that they could not escape from us by running for their camp. Well they knew that their end was near." *[Bear Head, Schultz, 1962, 290-294*]

Winter – Camped on Marias River in the big bend. This was a mixed camp of which Heavy Runner was leader. *[Meaning there were members of several different bands camped together. ed.]* This was the camp involved in the Baker Massacre. Calf Tail remembers Crow Calf and Holy Man were there. *[Calf Tail, South Peigan-Blackfoot; Collier, 1938,15]*

BLOOD

BAD HEAD: Apinosin Small Pox

WHITE BULL: And again Blood Indians got Small pox. Our head chief, Bull Breast, died with disease. Killed many of his horses beside him near Old Man's River below the Coal Banks.

DEMPSEY: *The disease struck the Blackfoot in the autumn of 1869, again originating with a Missouri River steamboat. By the spring of 1870, the death toll was estimated to be 1,080 Peigans, 630 Bloods and 676 North Blackfoot. (See Winnipeg "Manitoban" for Sept. 16, 1871)*

PERCY CREIGHTON: Blood was traveling in the south along Yellowstone River. Coming north, small pox broke out. Chief-In-Sight-Far-Off died of small pox.

NORTH BLACKFEET

CRANE BEAR: Apikisin, small pox = Apinakoyim *(Pinakuim, Far Off In Sight ?, ed.)*, grand chief of the Blood, dies.

YELLOW FLY: The year "Four Bears", white trader, arrives.

RUNNING RABBIT: Small Pox years. (Three Sun died.)

MANY GUNS: Apiksosin = Small pox (plain, not black) winter of 69-70.

LITTLE CHIEF: The Indians had the small pox it was very bad a lot of them died they moved away from the place they just left the place with all the dead with their tepees a Ghost Camp that was awful.

The first actual agency consisting of staff, stockade and buildings dedicated to the entire Blackfoot Nation was constructed at Choteau, Montana in 1869. Named the Four Persons Agency it was also called the Old Agency for a time. It lasted from 1869 to 1876 before moving to the Badger Creek Agency [soon to be also called "The Old Agency"]. [Three Calf, South Peigan-Blackfoot; Collier, 1938,24] Chiefs Old Mountain Chief, Big Lake, Heavy Shield and Bull Head were buried at the agency site.

Four Persons Agency, Elmer Schock painting, Claire Zion Collection

A knowledge of Peigan history reconstructed from Adam White Man and Tom Spotted Eagle.

A. The Choteau Agency Period, 1869-1876: Buffalo still relatively plentiful and basis of Indian subsistence. Divided into active hunting bands serving as political and residential units, except that old people left near Agency, apparently to be supported by Government largely. Winter camps primary but not entirely on Marias River.

B. Running Crane Agency Period, 1876-1880: Establishment of Agency at Running Crane locality probably dictated more by desire to free area south of Birch Creek to white settlement than to accommodate the Indians. Locality selected because Lone Eaters *[Band, ed.]* had moved there in winter. Buffalo still staff of life but becoming more and more scarce. Rations [weekly] initiated, and beginning of concentration of winter camps on the southernmost tributaries of the Marias [Big Badger and Birch Creek].

C. Old Agency Period, 1880-1895: [Perhaps might be divided into 3 sub-periods -Early, Middle & Late] Early - witnessed extermination of buffalo and greater and greater reliance on rations, hence greater concentration of Indians on Big Badger, ending in starvation winter.

Middle - Complete, or nearly complete reliance on rations for subsistence. The band no longer of importance as economic unit and of little value as political unit - began to break up as residential unit as well. Indians clustered on Big Badger near source of rations.
Late - After sale of Sweetgrass Hills and distribution of cattle and large horses to Peigan, Indians encouraged to spread out over reservation to care for stock. End of horse raiding also had made small, scattered settlements safe. Extension of settlements to Two Medicine, Cut Bank, etc. - further dispersal of bands. *[Adam White Man and Tom Spotted Eagle to Schaefer, notes, 1950, 15]*

1870

NORTH PEIGAN

BULL PLUME #1: When we beat the Crees at Lethbridge.

BULL PLUME #2: When we beat the Crees at Lethbridge.

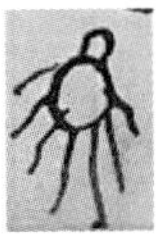

BULL PLUME #2 B: *What appears to be a shield.*

SOUTH PEIGAN

BIG BRAVE: Peigan fought Cree on Belly River (Canada) and killed one hundred. In summer a big battle with Assiniboine and Big-Brave and horse wounded.

ELK HORN: Big Prairie's father killed by own people.

BIG NOSE WAR RECORD: Captured 8 Pend d'Oreille Indians

Winter 1870-71

Calf Tail camped near Porcupine Hills on Old Man River in Canada. There were about ten tipis in this camp. After the Baker Massacre all the bands were scattered.
Tipi owners in this camp: Turn Up Hat [leader], Red Paint, Broad Head, White Buffalo Calf [Calf Tail's father], No Runner, Brings Down the Sun, Chief Coyote and Many White Horses. That spring they went to the Cypress Hills to hunt and returned to the Teton River for the Medicine Lodge. *[Calf Tail, South Peigan-Blackfoot; Collier, 1938,16]*

Green Grass Bull was with the Melted Fat band, camped on the Kutenai River [in Canada]. He was 8 years old and was already riding horseback. This was a very large camp, possibly a hundred lodges. There were some Blood Indians there and some North Peigans. The hunting was good here; hence all the visitors. The tipi owners in this camp were: Big Nose [chief], Big Plume, Generous Woman, Black Bull, Medicine Coyote, Many Horses, Red Plume, Wolf Head, North Chief [North Peigan], Black Bear [North Peigan, son of North Chief], Little Bull, Wolf Coming Up the Hill, Crow Foot, Yellow Robe, Water Bull, and Lone Medicine Pipe. [Green Grass Bull was born in 1862.] *[Green Grass Bull, South Peigan-Blackfoot; Collier, 1938, 19]*

In the winter of 1870, six hundred Cree, Assiniboine and Saulteaux Indians from Saskatchewan set out to eliminate the Blackfoot nation. They felt that the recent small pox epidemic would have claimed most of the fighters and an easy victory would be theirs.

Unfortunately they were wrong on both accounts. The entire Blackfoot nation was camped along the Old Man and St. Mary Rivers. Blood, North and South Peigan, and some North Blackfeet were trading at Fort Whoop-up, for among other things, the new breech loading rifles.

From here the accounts vary with each story teller. The Crees made the mistake of attacking what they thought was a small camp in the middle of the night.

With the first light of dawn, they began to realize their mistake. They had attacked the camp of Red Crow of the Bloods. With the first shots riders were sent to the other camps and re-enforcements were on the way.

The fight began in earnest with the Crees trying to retreat across the prairie to the river. They eventually made it to the coulees where they held off the Blackfoot for a time. The Peigans finally forced them out of the coulees and into the river. The Crees were now fleeing for their lives. They made one last attempt to make a stand on the east side of the river. At this spot they lost an additional fifty men. Those that managed to escape did so by mixing with the Blackfoot and slipping into the river bush. Once there they made their way east through the brush and eventually home, leaving three hundred of the dead behind. (Johnson; 1966)

Mountain Chief [Big Brave], a participant in the battle, gave this account of the battle in 1913.

"The greatest event in my life was in the war of the Blackfeet against the Crees at Hope Up, Canada. *[Fort Whoop Up, Alberta, ed.]* My horse and myself were both covered with blood. Let me tell you about this battle. The war was between the Blackfeet and the Crees. The camp was on Old Man's River. The bands were so many that they were camped on every bend of the river. My father, Mountain Chief, was at the upper end of the camp. I was twenty-two years old at the time. It was in the fall of the year, and the leaves had all fallen. The lower camp was attacked by the Crees at night. The people were just getting up in the morning when the news came that the lower camp had been attacked by the Crees. I got my best horse; it was a gray horse. *[A translation problem here, as the horse is identified as "black" in all the other stories. ed.]* My father led his band in company with Big Lake who that summer had been elected a big chief. We rode up over the ridge while in the plain below the battle was raging. As we rode down the slope, I began to sing my war song. I carried the shield in my hand and this song that I sung belonged to that shield. One of the medicine men dreamed that whoever held this shield would not be hit by the bullets. While singing I put in the words: 'My body will be lying on the plains.' When I reached the line of battle I did not stop, but rode right in among the Crees, and they were shooting at me from behind and in front. When I rode back the same way the men made a break for the coulee. As soon as the men got into the coulee they dug a pit. I was lying about ten yards away on the side of the hill. I was singing while lying there. I could not hear on account of the roar of the guns, and could not see for the smoke. About that time they heard my whistle, and the Crees made a break for the river. Then the Blackfeet made an onrush for the Crees and I ran over two of them before they got to the river. As they were crossing the river I jumped off my horse and took my spear and stabbed one of the Crees between the shoulders. He had a spear and I took that away from him. I jumped off *[on, ed.]* my horse again, and just as I returned there was a Cree who raised his gun to fire at me. I ran over him, and he jumped up and grabbed my horse by the bridle. I swung my horse's head around to protect myself and took the butt of my whip and knocked him down. When I struck him he looked at me and I found that his nose had been cut off. I heard afterward that a bear had bitten his nose off. After I knocked him down, I killed him. I jumped on my horse and just then I met another Cree. We had a fight on our horses; he shot at me and I shot at him. When we got close together I took his arrows away from him, and he grabbed me by the hair of the head. I saw him reach for his dagger, and just then we clinched. My war-bonnet had worked down on my neck, and when he struck at me with his dagger it struck the war-bonnet, and I looked down and saw the handle sticking out, and grabbed it and killed the other Indian. Then we rushed the Crees in the pit again, and my father came up with one of the old muskets and handed it to me. It had seven balls in it, and when I fired it it kicked so hard it almost killed me. I feel that I had a more narrow escape by shooting that gun than I had with the Indians. When we returned I had taken nine different scalps. The Crees who had not been scalped had taken refuge in the scant forest, and my father said to quit and go home. So we took pity on the tribe, and let them go, so they could tell the story. I remember we killed over three hundred, and many more that I cannot remember. When we returned we began to count how many we had killed. We crossed the creek and went to the pit, and they were all in a pile. Then we were all singing around the pit, and I put in the words, 'The guns, they hear me.' And everybody turned and looked at me, and I was a great man after that battle. Then we went home and began to talk about the battle, and the Indians who were dead." *[Mountain Chief/Big Brave, South Peigan-Blackfoot, to Joseph Dixon, 1913;112-115]*

In 1973 the author toured the battle site with Bob Black Plume, Blood-Blackfoot, and Joe Crowshoe, North Peigan-Blackfoot. The details in Johnson's account closely matched those told to the author that day. The following two additional stories came out of that trip.

"Mountain Chief was my relative and he's the one that told me the story. When the Crees attacked, Mountain Chief was at the camp of the Peigans. He jumped on his black horse and went to the aide of the Bloods who were in the first camp attacked. When he got there the Crees retreated into the coulee over there. *[Pointing toward the railroad bridge, ed.]* The Blackfoot were on top shooting at them for a long time. Finally Mountain Chief got angry and decided to break them out of there. He jumped on Sikimi *[his black horse, ed.]* and rode right over the bank and through the Crees. Then he rode back through them again to the Blackfoot lines. That horse just charged right through those Cree. They broke and began to try and swim across the river. There was a big killing that day. Over three hundred Crees whipped out.

'That horse of Mountain Chief's was fierce. It would charge after the enemy and try to bite them. Sometimes he would grab them by the back of the neck and kill the man. Everybody knew that horse. Mountain Chief stole him from the Crows and he was very fast." *[Bob Black Plume, Blood-Blackfoot, 1973, author's field notes]*

Mountain Chief riding through the Sun Dance camp singing his war song and praise song for his horse who is painted with war coups, showing a man figure indicating the horse rode over a man in battle. McClintock photo, Beinecke Archives, Yale University

“It was on the flats on the east side of the river that Minikono, *[Gets-Mad-When-He's-not-Fed, who was the grandfather of his wife, Josephine Crowshoe, ed.]* captured a Medicine Pipe. He was an old man by this time. He charged into the running Cree and saw this Cree woman running away. She was carrying a Medicine Pipe on her back. He just rode right past her and grabbed that pipe off her back. This pipe stayed on the North Peigan Reserve until about 1966.” *[Joe Crowshoe, North Peigan, 1973, author's field notes]*

Minikono [Gets Mad When He's Not Fed], North Peigan-Blackfoot, ca. 1905, Edmund Morris photo, Provincial Archives of Manitoba

Another black horse was made famous during that battle.

"Inokapi [Wonderful-Things] from the North Peigan-Blackfoot, borrowed a black horse from Crow-Flag and rode into battle. Ten times he charged the enemy and each time he captured a gun. *[An outstanding feat for one battle, ed.]* Because of the power of this horse the North Peigans formed the Black Horse Riders Society [Sikimiokitopiks], a Kaispa, or Parted-Hairs Society, to honor that horse and deed" *[Wilford Yellow Wings, North Peigan, 1976, author's field notes]*

From the exploits of both these famous black horses two dance societies were later formed; the Black Horse Kaispa Society of the South Peigans, and the Black Horse Riders Kaispa Society of the North Peigans.

BLOOD

BAD HEAD: Assinay itomatsarpy akaenasky Great battle with the Crees on Belly River near Coal Bank – 200 to 250 Crees are killed.

WHITE BULL: At Fort Whoop-Up Cree Indians attacked the Blood Indians camps along between two rivers, Old Man's River and St, Mary's River, and strong force of Blood Indians on war path. Crees retreated killed about over 250 of them.

DEMPSEY: Assiniboines/when we defeated them/Fort Whoop-Up

PERCY CREIGHTON: Indians had small pox resulting in many deaths. On Jan. 23, Chief Red Horn, Peigan, & Chief Bear were killed by Colonel Baker & army on the Bear River. This was a punitive expedition. The following fall, the Bloods had a big battle with the Cree on St. Mary's River near Lethbridge & killed 250 Crees.

NORTH BLACKFEET

CRANE BEAR: Many Crees are shot and drowned close to Lethbridge, on the present Blood Reserve, at Akainioskoy *(Many Died, ed.)*

YELLOW FLY: Another epidemic year.

RUNNING RABBIT: Pull out to little where to mountains. (In summer time _____ Rough Neck drain *[drowned, ed.]*. Crees killed them all)

MANY GUNS: Itenaksitatotsupi = Moving camp over the hills. They went over to Porcupine Hills.

LITTLE CHIEF: The four tribes moved to the Mountains they stayed there till spring

Scalp Dance, the women wear clothing and headdresses of their relatives and carry guns and scalps captured by the returning warriors. Night Shoot, South Peigan-Blackfoot, pictograph painting, Field Museum collection, Arni Brownstone photo

From here the original journals (BULL PLUME #'s 1&2) read again from bottom to top of page.

1871

NORTH PEIGAN

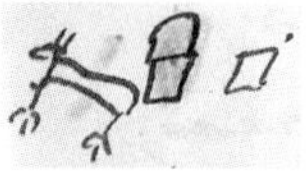

BULL PLUME #1: When "Bear Chief", Blood Indian was murdered.

BULL PLUME #2: When "Bear Chief", Blood Indian was murdered.

BULL PLUME #2 B: *A buffalo torso.*

SOUTH PEIGAN

ELK HORN: Body-Sticking-Out killed by own people.

BIG BRAVE: A Peigan, Red-Old-Man, killed by Gros Ventre near Bear Paw Mountains while he was on a raid. Black Eagle, a Peigan, killed an Assiniboine and wife in summer.

BIG BRAVE 2: Red-Old-Man…while he was trying to steal horses from camps.

Winter 1871-72

The following winter camped with the Worm Band again. Little Plume, Calf Tail's father's brother was chief. Calf Tail was not yet married. His Father was alive. This camp had about thirty tipis, the owners of which were: Under Bull, Calf Bossribs, Little Plume, White Buffalo Calf, No Runner, Brave, Spaniard, Bull Butte, Old Child, Turn Up Hat, Many White Horses, Striped Dog, Chief Coyote, Front Leg, Tall Chief, and two women, Cut Finger and Buffalo Stone.

They stayed on the Marias all that winter. In the spring went toward the Cypress Hills, where there was an abundance of game. The buffalo herds used to go to the Cypress Hills to drop their calves. The Medicine Lodge was held at Elk Water [a lake] near the Cypress Hills. The next winter they spent on the Marias River. At this time each of Calf Tail's father's four wives had four parfleches of dried buffalo meat. *[Calf Tail, South Peigan-Blackfoot; Collier, 1938,16]*

They camped on the Kutenai River again. There were whiskey peddlers about and much drunkenness. Because there was so much fighting over whiskey Green Grass Bull went with Big Plume and White Swan to camp with the Hard Topknot band. They moved down to Cutbank River near Browning. All their horses were stolen by the Cree. Big Buffalo Stone was chief of the Hard Topknots at this time. Then Green Grass Bull went with a cousin to stay with relatives in the Small Robe band because they had plenty of

horses. They stayed with Little Dog all that spring...Late in the spring of 1872 the Small Robe band went up to the Cypress Hills.
When Green Grass Bull went to live in the Small Robes band after his father's death [1871] there were 50-60 tipis in the camp. Some of the tipi owners were: Yellow Wolf, Wolverine, Medicine Weasel, Eagle Head, Chief Lodge Pole [chief of the camp], Five Crows, Small Robe Old Man, Bear Skin, Little Wolf, Little Dog, Morning Plume [North Peigan], Fine Bull, Three Bears, Red Eagle, Iron Pipe [Blood Indian], and Boy Chief. *[Green Grass Bull, South Peigan-Blackfoot; Collier, 1938, 20]*

BLOOD

BAD HEAD: Spitsi napekwax etawpiyaw Some white men settle on High River

WHITE BULL: Seven Cree Indians destroyed by the Blood Indians near place called Whiskers Butte and know white men gave it named Seven Persons River, Alberta. Calf Shirt himself captured another Medicine Axe, like his father in 1827.

PERCY CREIGHTON: At the gathering of the Bloods, a man "Pounder" was shot & killed in a center lodge at a dance because of the jealousy of a husband with whose wife he was dancing.

NORTH BLACKFEET

CRANE BEAR: A Blood man (Ninixinorkeayo) (Chief Bear ?, ed.) is drinking and is killed by the people of the Akaprokax *(Many Children, ed.)* clan. (Of the Blood tribe)

YELLOW FLY: The year the Blackfeet moved over the Rockies.

RUNNING RABBIT: Weasel Child, died of drunk. (Many Swan made fall ration *[piskan, ed.]*)

MANY GUNS: (Itaokui) piskiopi = Fall pisken. i.e. autumn

MANY GUNS .68: The time we built old buffalo jumps.

MANY GUNS .69: The time we went ahead and built a Buffalo jump. Pierced Head and Big Delicious Woman.

LITTLE CHIEF: In the spring the four tribes moved to Blackfoot Crossing they never moved far away again Mr. Weasel Child got killed by Crees

1872

NORTH PEIGAN

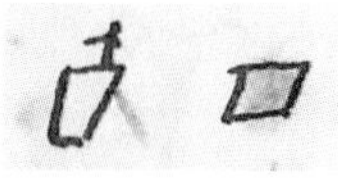
BULL PLUME #1: When “White Child” was murdered.

BULL PLUME #2: When “White Child” was murdered.

BULL PLUME #2 B: *A circle (indicating a tipi) with four people [red lines indicating bleeding] inside and a number of lines around the front.*

[See Many Guns and White Bull this year, and Yellow Fly 1973 for more.]

SOUTH PEIGAN

ELK HORN: Three Eagles killed by own people.

BIG BRAVE: Bull Chief and High Wolf died; while on warpath in summer White-Man’s-Horse and his war party nearly all killed.

BIG BRAVE 2: Codul’s *[Cadot? Pierre Cadot (Cadotte) an employee of Fort Benton who died on the Blackfeet reservation in 1873]* colt died. White-Man’s-Horse war party was killed twenty in all – fifteen killed.

When Old Man Mountain Chief died in the spring of 1872 Mountain Chief *[Big Brave]* was on a war party. Upon the death of the chief the band split. Most of the older men followed Fast Buffalo Horse [Mountain Chief’s father’s brother’s son]; the young married men went with Topknot [Mountain Chief’s father’s brother’s son]. Mountain Chief went with Topknot. At this time Mountain Chief was married and had his own tipi. Topknot was a generous man. Topknot’s camp moved to the mission [on Two Medicine Creek], thence to Lion Slide and up to the Cypress Hills. Visited the Blood Medicine Lodge. The following winter Mountain Chief was with Topknot’s camp. A large number of the young men of this camp were killed on a war party. Mountain Chief felt lonely and went to stay at Shoto [Choteau] where he had two brothers-in-law.

Although the Blood Band was now separated into two camps under different leaders, they were both still known as Bloods, and they camped together at the Medicine Lodge.

The following summer Topknot was killed by his son in a drunkcn brawl. Mountain Chief camped for a time with the Melted Fat Band, and then joined Fast Buffalo Horse as did the rest of Topknot's followers. Wintered on Badger Creek. Across the river was the Melted Fat Band. In the spring Mountain Chief went over to be with his brother-in-law at Shoto [Choteau], in order to visit his sister.

Many Scouts, chief of the Don't Laugh Band, was killed in an encounter with a Cree war party that summer.

Later Mountain Chief moved with the Blood Band to the Milk River and up to the Cypress Hills. There was a fight with the Assiniboines. Later Mountain Chief met in the none too friendly Kutenai camp an old friend of his father, who presented him with a good horse. This man and some other Kutenai returned with him to his camp [Blood Band], were given presents and a peace was made, largely through the good offices of the friend. Then the band proceeded to the Cypress Hills to hold the Medicine Lodge, but were interrupted by a fight with the Assiniboines. The ceremony was held later.

That winter Mountain Chief camped with his band on the Marias River. When that winter camp was made he had eight parfleches of dried buffalo meat. During the winter he went on a war party against the Crow and Gros Ventre. *[Mountain Chief, South Peigan-Blackfoot; Collier, 1938, 13]*

BLOOD

BAD HEAD: Attsitstoyemiyah spitsi napekwax They winter there again.

DEMPSEY: *In the autumn of 1872, Howell Harris and Asa Sample were sent by I.G. Baker & Co. of Fort Benton to build a post on the Highwood River. (Dempsey, 1963:31)*

WHITE BULL: Old Man Chief was stabbed by White Pup up north near Red Deer River.

PERCY CREIGHTON: A well known chief, named Mad Chief Bear was killed by the Assiniboine in a battle with the Blood.

NORTH BLACKFEET

CRANE BEAR: A Blood man (Onistasaenakoyim) (Calf Shirt, Inistaxsisokasim, ed.) is killed by Whitemen.

YELLOW FLY: The year "Weasel Child" died from over-drinking rum.

RUNNING RABBIT: White Man Child, killed. (hit by knife. Thunder, lightning in wintertime)

MANY GUNS: Napiepuka = White Man Child, a Blackfoot Indian died. Stabbed during drinking. *[See Yellow Fly 1873]*

LITTLE CHIEF: Mr. White Man's Child was killed by Crees the four tribes just stayed at Blackfoot Crossing they was a boot legger west of Blackfoot Crossing selling whiskey to the Indians some very bad whiskey the white man used to put tobacco in the whiskey they sold to the Indians the Indians were dying fast account of that bad whiskey

1873

NORTH PEIGAN

BULL PLUME #1: When "Calf Shirt" was drowned.

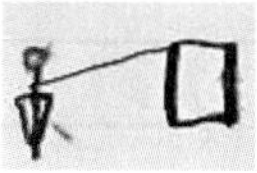
BULL PLUME #2: When "Calf Shirt" was drowned.

BULL PLUME #2 B: *A man figure with a circle containing a few dots above him. This could indicate the ice hole they threw Calf Shirt into.*

Calf Shirt was a Blood Indian who was feared by all the people. He had a terrible temper and was known to have killed at least five of his own people. When at Fort Kipp at the mouth of the Old Man River, he demanded whiskey from Joseph Kipp, the trader. When he was refused he shot at Kipp and missed. Kipp returned the fire and hit Calf Shirt in the left shoulder. Calf Shirt staggered out the door where he was shot sixteen more times by the fort employees, who thought he had killed Kipp. They took the body and dropped it in an air hole in the river ice. The body came up in another air hole down the river, where it was recovered by Calf Shirt's wives. He had given them instructions as to what they should do to bring him back to life when he was killed. When they tried to get help to sing and pray over the body, all refused. No one wanted Calf Shirt alive to kill more of his people.[Schultz; 1962; 66, Ewers; 1958, Dempsey; 1994]

SOUTH PEIGAN

ELK HORN: Many Horses, a chief, died.

BIG BRAVE: Calf Chief killed two Flathead near Peigan camps. Black Eagle killed by North Blackfeet in summer. (1874)

BIG BRAVE 2:...two Flatheads in the camps who was about to steal horses.

Lone Eater camp 21 tipi owners; Running Crane [chief], Bull Shoe, White Man, Painted Wing, Liar, Good Calf, Little Bear, Wolf Eagle [2], Bad Man, Elk Collar, Big Lips,

Rattle, Mad Plume, Bear Skin, Bear Shoe, Big Crow, Last Tail Feathers, Morning Gun, Black Bear, and Small Lance. *[No Coat, South Peigan-Blackfoot; Collier, 1938, 29]*

BLOOD

BAD HEAD: Onistarsesokasin otsenitarpi Calf Shirt is killed

WHITE BULL: The year Blackfoots moved camps over to the Rockies.
The year Calf Shirt was crowned (drowned) by whiskey traders post located at the junction of the Old Man and Belly Rivers.

PERCY CREIGHTON: Chief Calf Out In Sight was killed by the Cree as a result of which thunder howled in midwinter.

NORTH BLACKFEET

CRANE BEAR: A Blood man (Onistars) *(Calf, probably Calf Shirt, ed.)* dies below the Entrails *(Belly, ed.)* Buttes. (Tribe of Bloods)

YELLOW FLY: The year "Old Man Child" was stabbed by White Pup.

White Pup and his wife, North Blackfeet-Blackfoot, ca.1874, author's collection

RUNNING RABBIT: Poor Wolf, killed. _____ Many Cholt tepe (sic.) *(Many Ghost Tipi, RUNNING RABBIT 2, ed.)* Both Calf Shirts killed

MANY GUNS: Inistaxsisokasini = Calf Shirt = a renowned Blood Chief. But very vicious, drowned in the river and killed by Joe Kipp, a White trader in whiskey.

LITTLE CHIEF: Mr. Poor Wolf was killed by Crees still a lot of bad whiskey sold to the Indians one gallon keg the old Indians said that the White Man put it half and half each he put a lot of twist tobacco than fill the kegs with water this way the Indian would get sick when he drink to much get sick and die

In winter:
They used to camp around the agency *[the Blood Melted Fat Band, ed.]* at Choteau, then would go over to the Marias River, then to Riding *[Writing, ed.]* on Stone *[North of the Sweet Grass Hills]*. They camped were not many breaks where the enemy could hide. Then they went over to Belly River. They never staid in one place long. In the spring they would come near one of the trading posts *[e.g. on the Marias River]*, and would tan hides in preparation for trading. They never went on the south side of the Missouri. In summer they would stay close to the Blood or Sarsi, so if the enemy came they could send word for assistance. *[The North Blackfoot went to Edmonton to trade.]* When the Piegan and Blackfoot met the Blackfoot used to give their Piegan relatives Hudson Bay trade goods. The Piegans had the most horses, and they used to give their Blood and Blackfoot relatives horses. *[The Cree, whom the Blood and Blackfoot raided most, had few horses; the Piegan had more opportunity to steal horses – from the Flathead, Shoshone and Crow.]* When the Piegan and Blackfoot [or Blood] camps were near they used to visit back and forth and exchange presents. At this time there were marriages between the Blood, Piegan and Blackfoot *[arranged marriages and elopements, not to mention absconding]*. These marriages brought the Blackfoot people closer together. When a Piegan went to visit the Blood he always had some relatives there *[blood and affiant, or both]*. *[Three Calf to Collier, 1938, 24]*

1874

NORTH PEIGAN

BULL PLUME #1: When "Holy Milk" killed his wife.

BULL PLUME #2: When "Holy Milk" killed his wife.

"Holy Milk" listed as "Pox" or "Woman's Breast" in police records was a Blood Indian who beat his wife to death in the spring of 1875. He fled to the States for a time. When he eventually returned he was arrested by the Northwest Mounted Police. However, at his trial he was acquitted and set free. (Turner 1950; 255)

The following entries for both Bull Plume 1 and 2 are located to the right of the Holy Milk entry.

BULL PLUME #1: When the police came.

BULL PLUME #2: When the police came.

Two pictographs here. The top one is an image of a Mounted Police man with his red coat, pointed hat and carrying a sword. Below him is a person outside a tipi with blood coming out of them while the occupant has his hand out holding a club or gun; possibly the "Holy Milk" incident.

In this year the Northwest Mounted Police, later to become the Royal Canadian Mounted Police, were guided into the Blackfoot country by Jerry Potts. Potts was hired to take them to Fort Whoop-up so that they could stop the whiskey trade among the Blackfoot. (For a more detailed account of the effects of this trade among the Blackfoot see Dempsey; 2001.)

By the time they arrived at Whoop-up the traders had long gone. They then pushed on to the present site of Fort Macleod, Alberta. Bull Head, chief of the North Peigans, allowed them to spend the winter there. After that they were to move on. However, Bull Head died that winter and the Police stayed and Fort Macleod became their permanent headquarters.

Fort Macleod, Northwest Mounted Police fort. Watercolor and pencil on off white paper by D.B. Robinson, 1874. Glenbow Museum Collection, 82.35.1.53/54

"Head Police – Bull Head came over to settle the Indians, to make peace. He gathered the different tribes of Indians in Macleod and made the first laws there. He told them that they should quit stealing and killing one another. It was then also liquor was forbidden among the Indians. Their chief pleasure was to go from one reserve to the other stealing horses so he put an end to it, and peace was among the Indians.

He told them this law is not made by me but by the Government, himself. The Indian that breaks the laws will be punished, and be kind to their wives not to treat them as slaves… After the laws was read out, he told the chiefs if they were satisfied with them, the Head Chief, [Indian] Bull Head stood up and said, 'Yes we will take them.' He gave him his name there, [Bull Head]." *[Bull Plume Journal #2; 35]*

SOUTH PEIGAN

ELK HORN: Many buffalo and many trading posts on Marias, (1874-75)

BIG BRAVE: Hog's heads issued as rations; in summer Big-Nose took four Assiniboine prisoner.

BIG BRAVE 2:…Assiniboine who were in the brush.

BLOOD

BAD HEAD: Ennahen otsitotorpi akapoiyis The (Mounted) Police are at Macleod.

WHITE BULL: Royal North West Mounted Police first arrived here at Fort Macleod and this district.

PERCY CREIGHTON: At the beginning of the year Chief Calf Shirt was killed by traders – 16 shots were fired into his body which was put into a hole in the river; The following summer, red coats (North West Mounted Police), arrived.

NORTH BLACKFEET

CRANE BEAR: A Blackfeet (Kisstsikomiapiw) *(Thunder Old Man, ed.)* is killed. The Police arrive in the country.

YELLOW FLY: The year "Little Coyote" was killed by "Running Rabbit".

RUNNING RABBIT: Mountain police came. *[Mounted Police, ed.]* (11 Crees, killed them all)

MANY GUNS:
(1) Iinakiks = Policemen. First time the red-coats came. There was a killing of 11 Crees just before Mounties came. A certain band of renegade Bloods were killing Blackfoot. Turned around and killed a Blackfoot leader, Stamiksotakaopi (Bull Turning Around). Then Blackfoot killed the leader and others. It was just a family.

"Stomiksotakawpi *[Bull-Turns-Around, ed.]* told one of his three wives to get Buck Running Rabbits' father to come to his tipi. Ninauaksistaumaxkan *[Buck-Running-Rabbit, ed.]* came; Stomiksotakawpi said to go to the store and get booze. Ninauaksistaumaxkan went to get a good horse and ride over. Both got horses tied outside tipi. Sowatsixkinei *[Feather-Necklace, Ninauaksistaumaxkan's father, ed.]* came out of tipi and saw the horses outside. Sowatsixkinei asked where are they going?... Ninauaksistaumaxkan said he was going with Stomiksotakawpi to the store. Sowatsixkinei told Ninauaksistaumaxkan he did not like him to go and took the saddle off of Ninauaksistaumaxkan's horse and turned him loose. Ninauaksistaumaxkan took his father's word to stay home. Then Stomiksotakawpi knew that Ninauaksistaumaxkan would not go. Stomiksotakawpi then sent his wife to Stomiksoskinei [Bull Horn]. Bull Horn went to Stomiksotakawpi and Sowatsixkinei came out and saw that there was another horse there. Sowatsixkinei said, 'I am telling them to stop!' The two started to the store and got there. At the store the Kyaiyetapi *[Bear People, ed.]* were at the store and setting out in a circle. Another came from the camp, Pretty-Young-Man's father Makuiyomaxkan *[Running Wolf, ed.]* They started to drink; Stomiksotakawpi and Bull Horn. Makuiyomaxkan joined them. Stomiksotakawpi started to hit Makuiyomaxkan. The Kyaiyetapi were sitting outside and Makuiyomaxkan told them that Stomiksotakawpi fighting him. One person did not like to hear that; he was called Manikapiatos and took his gun and shot and killed Stomiksotakawpi. All took their knives and cut the face of Stomiksotakawpi.

Then two other persons who came to the store; Motokanipo and Sowatsixkinei came to store after Stomiksotakawpi was dead and did not recognize him immediately. Bull Horn had left too because he was afraid of being killed. The two looked at this man's face and recognized him as Stomiksotakawpi. They could see the camp of the Kyaiyetapi and said they had killed Stomiksotakawpi. When they saw the camp they saw a man on horseback coming toward them. It was Manikapiatos. When he was 100 yards away Motokanipo stopped and asked who killed Stomiksotakawpi. Manikapiatos did not talk; he got off horse and tightened saddle. Then Motokanipo said: 'I am going to kill you; why don't you answer me instead of tightening saddle?' Manikapiatos said, 'They killed themselves.' Both of two ran to Manikapiatos and Manikapiatos ran toward them shooting and both were shooting each other. Manikapiatos made the sound of a bear, 'sh—sh.' They came face to face, shot Manikapiatos right in chest. Sowatsixkinei was running behind and had a gun all loaded. Manikapiatos was not dead; Sowatsixkinei came up to shoot him in face. Manikapiatos said, 'I am badly hurt: I don't want to get dead.' Then Sowatsixkinei said, 'You should not have killed Stomiksotakawpi,' and shot him in the head.
The two went home; Bull Horn who was with the deceased and coming back, cried loudly. All went toward Bull Horn and asked him why he was crying. He said Bear People killed Stomiksotakawpi. Then all got their horses and started toward the camp of the Bear People.

All the men ran toward Bear People and they could see the dust. Bear People beat it into the bush. Then father *[chief, ed.]* of the Bear People got a fast horse and left immediately in rush. _____ ran after him and shot but missed him. Then they went to Bear People's camp. They took all that was in camp: women, tipis, holy things. Before they started out, a man named Three-Eagles took the wife of the man who ran away and said, 'I take this woman for my mother.' Another man asked, 'Why is that woman who is wife of man who ran away alive?' Then he shot the woman and killed her. Two others had been killed while the others were fighting in the camp, called Akasskohnata [two men with same name] Akasskohnata were fighting and killed Akasskohnata of the Kyaiyetapi!

After all was finished, they took everything to camp and wiped all but fire place. All felt bad that Stomiksotakawpi was dead and were quiet.

There was only one Bear Person who got back to the Bloods. This was Stamiksekixsipimi. These Kyaiyetapi were always making trouble for the Bloods and tried to get back and make trouble for the Bloods.

After all was over, one man went to Bloods and said, 'There are no more Bear People.' He said, 'The Akostsikeks did it and now there was no more doubt.'" [*Buck Running Rabbit, Siksika-Blackfoot, to Lucien Hanks, 1941, Field Note Book; 30-34]*

[For more details of this event see Dempsey, 2002; 138-139]

These two events were the last killings before Mounties. This year Crowfoot's boy was killed by Crees. The 11 Crees killed avenging the boy's death.

LITTLE CHIEF:
Our friends the R.N.W.M. police came west and saved the Indians from drinking that bad whiskey ever since then they look after the Indians

1875

NORTH PEIGAN

BULL PLUME #1: When there were many buffaloes.

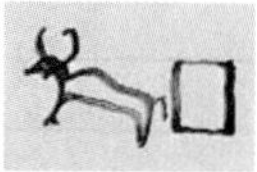

BULL PLUME #2: When there were many buffaloes.

BULL PLUME #2 B: *Three human figures.*

The I.G. Baker Company at Fort Benton, Montana, shipped out 75,000 buffalo hides in the spring of 1876. These were hides taken in trade with the Blackfoot primarily. In addition the people kept a large number for their own use. (Ewers; 1959; 49)

SOUTH PEIGAN

ELK HORN: Man tried to kill wife, she (Sarcee woman) stabbed him, he killed her; in summer Home Chief died. (1875-76)

BIG BRAVE: Plenty of buffalo and many Assiniboine visit Peigan. In summer Agent known as Wood, issued clothing, etc. Peigan made peace with Crow at Sweet Grass Hills.

BIG NOSE WAR RECORD: Cypress Hills Two hundred lodges of Peigan were camped. Four Sioux were discovered in a thicket. Big Nose crawled in among them and convinced them to surrender.

Camp Circle:

At the conclusion of the Medicine Lodge it was announced that large bands of Cree and other enemies had been discovered by the scouts. It had been decided that the camp circle would not break up because of the danger. The bands moved southward, remaining in the circle. The circle was maintained for two months after the Medicine Lodge. The societies continued to meet, keep the peace and control the hunt. There was not difficulty in keeping the bands together because of fear of attack. Then a treaty was made with the Crow, Gros Ventre and Assiniboine. The danger being past, the bands then scattered. *[Green Grass Bull, South Peigan-Blackfoot; Collier, 1938, 32]*

1875-76 Winter
Camped on Marias *[River, ed.]*. Game was scarce in the first part of the winter, and it was necessary to send out hunting parties as far as the Sweet Grass Hills because the buffalo did not come near the Marias. Then a heavy blizzard came and drove the buffalo south. Then there were *plenty. [Night Shoot, South Peigan-Blackfoot; Collier, 1938, 63]*

Dried Meat:
Dried meat was reserved for bad weather when it was impossible to hunt. Except in bad weather it was possible to get fresh meat [buffalo, deer, antelope] all winter. 8 parfleches considered good store of dried meat. One horse carried 3 parfleches. One parfleche weighed 50-60 pounds. One carcass made about 100 pounds of pemmican. Usually there was some dried meat left in the spring. *[Sanderville, South Peigan-Blackfoot; Collier, 1938, 64]*

When Big Skunk was chief of the Skunk band, at the time of making the winter camp Lazy Boy's family had 8 parfleches and 4 hide sacks [hold about twice the amount of a parflech] of dried buffalo meat. By spring they had one or two parfleches left. The family could live ten or twelve days on a parflech unsupplemented by fresh meat. *[Lazy Boy, South Peigan-Blackfoot; Collier, 1938, 64]*

Sharing Kill:

In the concealed approach method, the kill was equally divided among the hunters in the field. One who was willing to accept the last portion, offered his companions their choice of the following arbitrary portions.

1. Boss ribs [and one side of backfat, one side of ribs and one shoulder]
2. Flank meat [and other side of backfat, ribs and other shoulder]
3. Heart [and brisket]
4. Entrails [and one hind quarter]
5. Tripe [and other hind quarter]
6. Flanks [and kidneys and tongue]

The above method of butchering was considered a fair and equal method of dividing the kill. Each hunter further divided his share upon reaching camp. This was practice when a number of persons cooperated in hunting. There was no quarreling over division of meat, each hunter receiving his share.

The bison was butchered by cutting the hide down the spine, dividing the former in two. Each half of hide was given to any hunter that wanted it.

If a hunter killed an animal and a friend came who desired some of it, the former allotted such portions as he wished the other to have.

If two hunters killed a buffalo, one asked the other which portion he wanted. The later might wish the rump. There is a certain way to remove the meat from the hip bones and then remove the flank with the kidneys, so as only to leave the spine with ribs attached behind.

In butchering the flesh and fat were removed so as to leave most of the bones behind. *[Yellow Kidney, South Peigan-Blackfoot; Schaeffer,1950, 99]*

BLOOD

BAD HEAD: Itsenowatorpi napiorki Whiskey trading is stopped.

WHITE BULL: Mounted Police stopped all whiskey traders keep from selling any more whiskey, and Sun Lodge was held at Side River near Medicine Hat, Alta.

PERCY CREIGHTON: The Blood were roaming on the Plains for Buffalo. They can find only old buffalos.

NORTH BLACKFEET

CRANE BEAR: A Blackfeet woman then of the camp of Yellow Horse, searches for a supply of meat on the other side of the river, and on returning with a large amount of meat she breaks through the ice and perishes below it, in springtime. *(1876, MANY GUNS, ed.)*

YELLOW FLY: The year the Royal North West Mounted Police arrived.

RUNNING RABBIT: Gooder Woman, killed. *(Ghost Woman?, ed.)* Police gave out dancing outfits, and Fox died. (Yellow Blanket killed himself) *(Police is the Seizers Society, and they transferred to new members. ed.)*

MANY GUNS: Ponokamiteiksitakoxpumataxpi = Horses – bought many. Time they began to buy White Man's horses. This year, they bought many of them.

MANY GUNS .69: Roaring This Way and Thunder

LITTLE CHIEF: Mr. Good Woman *(Ghost Woman ?, ed.)* counted a coup also a gun this going on war party was not much of it when the police came

1876

NORTH PEIGAN

BULL PLUME #1: Year when all the horses were frozen to death.

BULL PLUME #2: The year when all the horses were frozen to death.

BULL PLUME #2 B: *A single human figure with blood coming out his body.*

This year the Grease Melters Band of the South Peigan were camped near the Sweet Grass Hills. They were much farther north than the rest of the Peigans. They, along with the Bloods, lost nearly all their horses that winter. The animals had become so weak from the storm they could not paw through the snow to the grass. (Ewers; 1934; 606)

"The winter of 1875-76 was a hard one. Deep snow, hardened by violent winds, stayed on the ground for six months. It would only be in January that the buffalo would arrive, in very large numbers." (Doucet; 45)

SOUTH PEIGAN

ELK HORN: Chief Old-Woman-Child dies; an open winter (1876-77).

BIG BRAVE: A Peigan killed his wife who was a Sarcee woman; in summer Calf Chief died.

BLOOD

BAD HEAD: Itakainiskoy Plenty buffaloes.

WHITE BULL: Plenty of Buffaloes. Sun Dance camps keep moving back and forth lake to lake.

PERCY CREIGHTON: The Indians had their Sun Dance gathering at Cow Foot Butte. After the dance was over, the Bloods went in 2 parties – one went north, the other south. At the beginning of winter, a woman named Ghost Old Woman fell into the ice in the river & drowned.

NORTH BLACKFEET

CRANE BEAR: A Blackfeet, Natoyeyew, *(Holy Blanket ?, ed.)* kills some Crees.

YELLOW FLY: "Pe Noo Wa" killed a Cree Indian. The last incident of this nature.

RUNNING RABBIT: Quite horse bought, and Holy Blanket kill Cree.

MANY GUNS:
(1) Stoipitaki = Ghost Woman was drowned.
(2) Itxkutspi = Time when we were given. *[Treaty gifts, ed.]*
(3) Spitapikuan = Tall White Man (David Laird) Meaning we're given first treaty *(actually occurred fall of '77)*

MANY GUNS .69: The horses. The time we started ahead.

LITTLE CHIEF: Quiet Horses was given a holy Robe by one Indian than he went south he met a Cree he killed the Cree he nearly got caught by the police he stayed up south for one year than every thing was forgotten than he came back home

NORTH PEIGAN

 BULL PLUME #1: Treaty Blackfoot crossing.

 BULL PLUME #2: Treaty Blackfoot crossing.

 BULL PLUME #2 B: *Nine tipi figures with a man to their right holding his hand up as if talking to the group.*

"David Laird was at Blackfoot Reserve, the Bloods and Peigan, Sarcee, Stoney were all there, 'I come to make some laws among us and I want you all to listen. I am glad you all come. You all going to make peace now, I am going to buy your land. I'll give you $12.00 a piece. The reason why I am going to buy it, you'll be miserable after a while. They'll be no Buffalos, Deer, Rabbits, Duck, Chickens [Prairie chickens, ed.], Fish. Don't kill the females any more. You'll all have houses to live in, to farm. Your children will be educated. I am glad stop fight and steal. There'll be a time; a bad man, will be jailed and the white man is just same. He'll suffer for what he does. You'll all be allowed to camp any place, same for every thing, wood, water. You'll get this $12.00 is ___ your lives." *[Bull Plume, Journal #2; 34]*

On September 22, 1877 the North Peigan, North Blackfeet, Bloods, Sarsi and Stoney-Assiniboine tribes entered into treaty with the Canadian Government. At Blackfoot Crossing on the banks of the Bow River, Treaty Number Seven was signed, which was to change forever the life of the Blackfoot Nation.

"September. From September 17 to 23 would be held the signing of Treaty Seven at Blackfoot Crossing. This Treaty was concluded between the Canadian Government and the three tribes of the Blackfoot, the Crees from Hobbema, the Assiniboines from Morley and the Sarcees.

Present were about six thousand Indian people…at least. The lieutenant governor of the North West Territories, Mr. Laird, Colonel McLeod, chief of the Mounted Police and the Superintendent of the Indians, all arrive with a large detachment of Police. Father Lacomb had been named judge of the interpreters by the Government, but he fell sick on the way from Winnipeg and had to turn back. Father Scollen attended in his place.

Some difficulties: Old man Bird [James Bird, ed.] was chosen as official interpreter, but he was blind and almost deaf. They therefore had to chose Munro (or Piskan) and our famous Jean L'Heureux in his stead. Their job was to explain to the Indian people the purpose of the Treaty. But they were not very capable; the Indians did not understand.

They had to surrender their lands to the Government, with the provision that they would receive in return a proper compensation agreed upon by the two parties. But Jean L'Heureux was not reliable. Everything started to become very confused and threatened to be prolonged indefinitely, when they asked Fr. Scollen to serve as interpreter.

Fr. Scollen spoke the language of the Blackfoot and enjoyed their confidence. He therefore explained more clearly what it was all about. The people understood, difficulties were smoothed out and the treaty was concluded, signed by the main chiefs: Crowfoot of the Blackfoot, Rainy Chief of the Bloods, Bird Tail of the Peigans, Bear's Paw of the Stoney, Bull's Head of the Sarcee and Bob Tail of the Crees from Hobbema.

Conditions of this Treaty, as signed by the Chiefs.

- *The Blackfoot would receive a certain area of territory in exchange for the lands that they would surrender to the Government.*
- *The Blackfoot proper or Siksika, along with the Bloods and the Sarcees, would receive a common area, quite poorly defined, along the Bow River until it meets with the Deer River. The Peigans immediately received a special reserve near MacLeod that they still occupy today.*
- *They would all receive in money every year $25.00 for each head chief, $15.00 for each minor chief, and $5.00 per head for the others, men, women and children." (Doucet;53)*

SOUTH PEIGAN

ELK HORN: Killed seven Assiniboine.

BIG BRAVE: Open winter, no snow all winter. Big Buffalo Rock died during summer.

BLOOD

BAD HEAD: Itsiparkap otomiop Spring is very late. The Indians lose many of their horses.

WHITE BULL: The Blackfoot treaty on Bow River east of Calgary. Head Chief Crow foot 47 years old at time of treaty. He died 13 years after. Later or at the age of Sixty. Head Chief Red Crow he is 47 years old at the treaty. He died in 1900 age of sixty seven, twenty years in power.

PERCY CREIGHTON: The Indians were called to go to Blackfoot Crossing (also called Crow Foot Butte) to make a treaty with the government under David Laird, the Commissioner. The following winter was so mild that there was no winter to talk about.

NORTH BLACKFEET

CRANE BEAR: The year of the treaty.

YELLOW FLY: The year of the Blackfoot Crossing Treaty.

RUNNING RABBIT: Queen Victoria, paid Treaty and Ghost Old Woman, drain. *(drowned, ed.)*

MANY GUNS: Itsistuyis = No winter

MANY GUNS .68: The Treaty. Tall White Man. *[David Laird, ed.]*

MANY GUNS .69: Ghost Old Woman and the first treaty and Tall White Man.

LITTLE CHIEF: That was the big year that is the year we made peace with Her Majesty Queen Victoria the biggest treaty ever paid to the Indians of North America the five tribes Blackfeets Bloods Peigan and Sarcee also the Stoneys oh that was a big day lot of Indians on horse back riding back and forth singing war songs finely Crowfoot's brother told him you go and sign treaty the buffalo is gone now we have to live the white man way or we starve so do not forget our people and the future generations try and keep as much land as you can the future generation will make use of it

Three Bulls, Sitting on Eagle Tail Feathers, Crowfoot, Red Crow; The four principal Blackfoot chiefs signing Treaty #7. Glenbow Archives

Bull Head, Sarcee chief and Sitting on Eagle Tail Feathers, North Peigan chief, Glenbow Archives

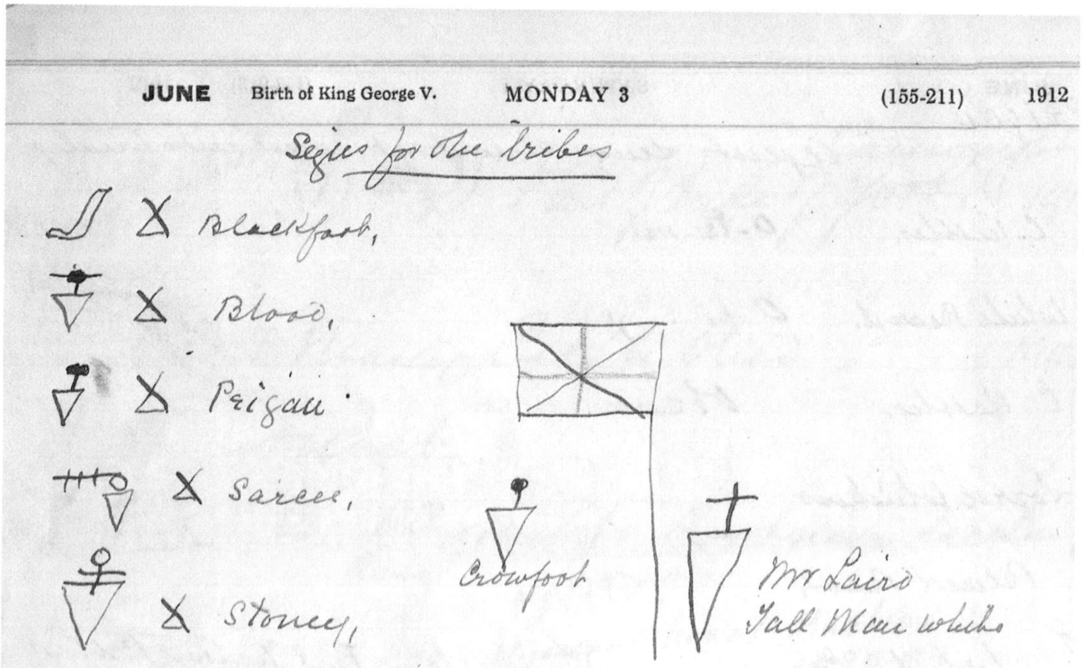

JUNE Birth of King George V. MONDAY 3 (155-211) 1912

Signs for the tribes

X Blackfoot,

X Blood,

X Peigan

X Sarcee,

X Stoney,

Crowfoot

Mr Laird
Tall Man white

Blackfoot Treaty,

Treaty #7, Bull Plume #1

From Bull Plume #2

Sarcee

Bull Head

Carrying Eagle

Drum

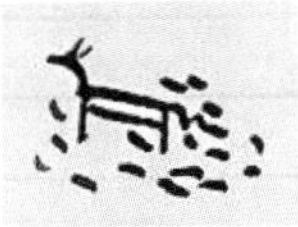
Many Horses

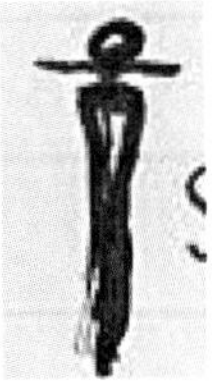
Stoney

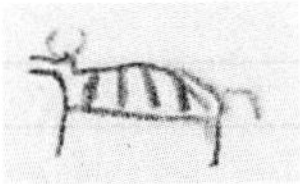
Spotted Calf

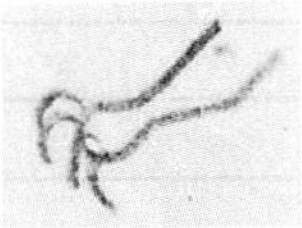
Bear Shoe

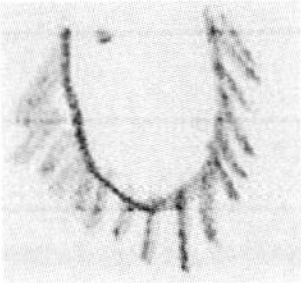
Buffalo Necklace

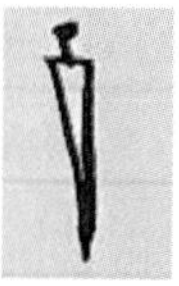 Tall Man

 Riding Three Horses

 Two Young Men

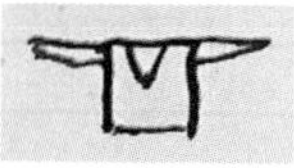 Calf Shirt

 Peigan

 White Tail *Feathers [Sitting on Eagle Tail Feathers]*

 Big Swan

 Morning Plume

 Crow Eagle

 Running Wolf *[Brings Down the Sun]*

Blood

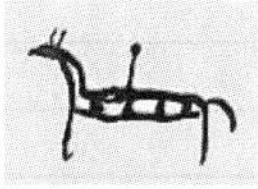
One Spot

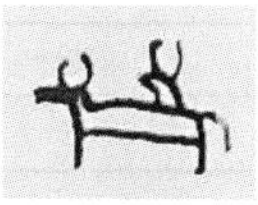
Hind Bull

Eagle Shoe

Eagle Head

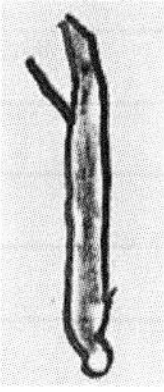
Bull Shoulder

White Deer [or Elk]

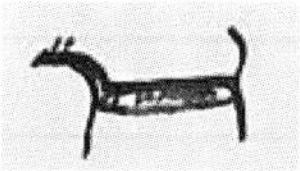
All people Belong to Him *[Father of Many Children]*

Bull Turning Around

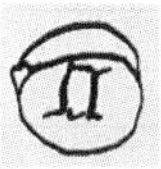
Seen a Long Way Off *[Seen From Afar]*

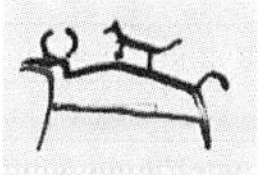
Weasel Bear

 Rainy Chief

 Red Crow

 Dirty Head

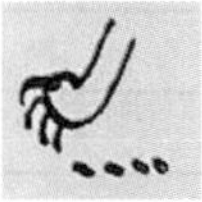 Bear Going

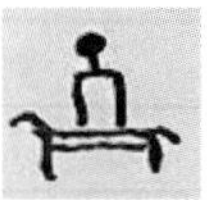 Wolf Collar

 Moon

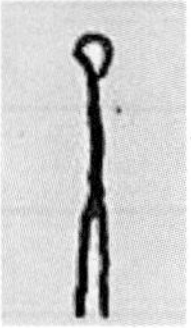 Heavy Whipping

 Many Spotted Horses

 Blackfeet *[Siksika]*

 Only Chief

 Eagle Ribs

White Eagle

Running Rabbit

Weasel Calf

Big Swan

Elk Bull

Crowfoot

Old Sun

Carrying Wolf

Three Bulls

Horses Before

Wolf Collar

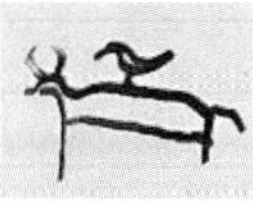

Eagle Calf

 Bear Child

 Big Plume

 Calf Robe

1878

NORTH PEIGAN

 BULL PLUME #1: Mild winter.

 BULL PLUME #2: Mild winter.

BULL PLUME #2 B: *No pictograph.*

SOUTH PEIGAN

ELK HORN: *From here on Elk Horn's count varies with some confusion, as he had trouble remembering. In the original copy the events are just numbered with no dates. It appears years are left out. Some events recorded are known for specific years from other winter counts and historical records. Again, this shows the importance of the winter counts as teaching lessons and not necessarily concerned with actual dates according to non-Native calendars.*

ELK HORN: Crossed the Missouri; Sitting Bull killed many Peigan.
Camped south of the Missouri.

"In 1878 a war party of 13 young men from the Small Robes was wiped out by the Sioux. There was great sorrow in the camp. Big Plume said that his luck was no longer good, and surrendered the leadership to Little Dog. Big Plume returned to the Melted Fat Band." *[Green-Grass-Bull, South Peigan-Blackfoot, to Donald Collier, 1938, Field Notes.]*

[The Sioux refugees under Sitting Bull were camped near the Cypress Hills. Since the Blackfoot were also camped near the Hills, and the Peigans and Bloods were strong enemies of the Sioux, frequent small encounters occurred. ed.]

BIG BRAVE: Weasel Moccasin killed by Assiniboine; had a Sun Dance; cattle tongues first used for Sun Dance. Agency moved to present location(?) (Old Agency).

Badger Creek Agency also called Old Agency, built after moving the first agency from Four Persons Agency at Choteau, Montana. Montana Historical Society

"In 1878 Bear-Chief was with Weasel-Moccasin when he camped with the Peigans on Middle Creek. Then Joe Kipp, a Mandan half-breed, was staying with Bear-Chief in Weasel-Moccasins' lodge, trading with the Indians.

Towards the spring of 1879 they left the camp for a buffalo-hunt, taking many horses and small lodges with them. They were accompanied by the women. During the night the Sioux made a raid on them, and stole horses. Chief Big-Plume [Omaxksapop] led the Peigans to chase the Sioux. They overtook the Sioux on Beaver Creek. There were seven Sioux. Weasel-Moccasin and his followers ran after these Sioux, he himself being on a swift horse before them all. When Weasel-Moccasin was near the Sioux, he dismounted to fight. He soon got shot about the heart, and died on the way to the camp. The Peigans killed six of the seven Sioux. One Sioux escaped. Bear-Chief was not with Weasel-Moccasin when he died. He had stayed at home. They buried Weasel-Moccasin right where he died." *[Bear-Chief to Uhlenbeck,1879, Original Blackfoot Texts][In this story the "Sioux" referred to are actually the Assiniboine.* ed.]

BLOOD

BAD HEAD: Ipsa stoyew Very mild winter

WHITE BULL: Very hard winter, late spring. Indians lose many of their horses. Another treaty was held at Macleod. *[i.e. Paid out treaty payments. ed.]*

PERCY CREIGHTON: This was the year the buffalo went out of sight. The Bloods had their middle treaty payment.

"September. The Bloods then traveled to old Fort Kipp, near the junction of the Old Man and Belly rivers, to receive their annual treaty payment from a Mounted Police captain...

I counted 254 lodges in this Blood camp, lodges which would usually hold at least 10 people, in those days. In Macleod, there were at least 100 Peigan lodges, with about half (or 50) belonging to the South Peigans...

The Blackfoot, on the other hand, were paid at Blackfoot Crossing. A number of Cree lodges were visiting the Blackfoot at the time. (Doucet; 58)

NORTH BLACKFEET

RUNNING RABBIT: Fine winter. (Middle Treaty)

MANY GUNS: Itsimikustuyimiupi = We-had-it-deep. *i.e. deep snow*
Each sign, e.g. 1877. Note: 1875 means the 1875 winter through to the winter of 1876; i.e. winter of 75-76, summer of 1876.

MANY GUNS .68: The winter with a deep snow

MANY GUNS .69: The time we had no winter.

The winter of 1877-78 was a very mild winter while the winter of 1878-1879 was very cold with numerous blizzards. ed.

LITTLE CHIEF: Was very quiet all winter not much of a winter the four tribes had a good winter by this time each tribes went to live on the reserve that were given to them

CHAPTER 9

NO MORE BUFFALO AND GOVERNMENT CHIEFS

Two years after the 1877 Treaty life changed completely for the Blackfoot. They found they were no longer an independent people in control of their own land. The annuities and food they thought were payments for the use of their land now became part of the purchase price for that same land. And the governments that distributed those payments became more demanding, and controlling of their day to day lives. No more hunting the buffalo, roaming or raiding their enemies. Suddenly they were permanently confined to a small area that would become smaller as the governments made more demands and rules.

1879

NORTH PEIGAN

BULL PLUME #1: Deep snow.

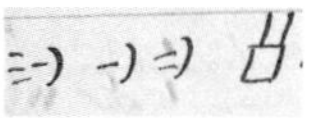

When they move camp.

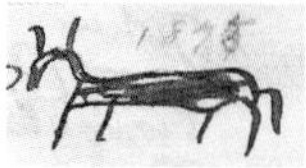

When the buffalo disappeared.

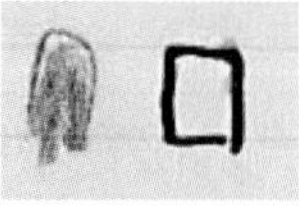

BULL PLUME #2: Deep snow winter.

When they moved camp

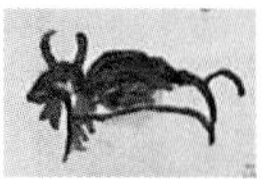

When the buffalo disappeared

For both Bull Plume #1 & # 2 the buffalo entry is to the right of the original entries.

By the summer of 1879 the buffalo disappeared forever from the Canadian Plains. Prairie fires had swept through the grasslands west of the Cypress Hills in 1878 and forced the main herds south. They were never to return to the Canadian Plains.

"By 1879 starvation faced the Blackfoot again. Nearly three thousand North Peigan and Bloods gathered at Fort Macleod calling upon the Government for help. The government was not prepared to feed so many. (Just the year before the Blackfoot had been totally self-sufficient.) Indian Commissioner Edgar B. Dewdney managed to give them some

provisions and told them to follow the herds south across the line. North Peigans, South Peigan, North Blackfeet, and Bloods all went south across the Missouri to the Judith Basin for the last great buffalo hunt of the Blackfoot Nation". (Ewers; 1958; 279)

St. Peter's Catholic Mission built on the North Peigan Reserve 1879

SOUTH PEIGAN

ELK HORN: Camped south of the Missouri

BIG BRAVE: Peigan moved and camped south of Missouri; in summer Peigan brought back to reservation by soldiers.

BLOOD

BAD HEAD: Itsistsitsisawwenimiopi The buffalo are no more.

WHITE BULL: Very mild winter, hardly any snow on ground. All buffaloes are disappear. Sun Lodge was held place called Like Belly Buttes in Montana.

DEMPSEY: When first/no more buffalo

PERCY CREIGHTON: The Indians had their Sun Dance gathering at Cypress Hills, put up by a woman named Koomai (Round). The following fall the Bloods received treaty payment at Fort Macleod.

NORTH BLACKFEET

RUNNING RABBIT: Deep snow, and first time, hard up. (for food)

MANY GUNS: Amskapots = South whole Blackfoot wintered in the states.

MANY GUNS .68: They packed home lots of meat.

MANY GUNS .69: The big time we went and envied. White Fat died.

LITTLE CHIEF: That winter was a very hard winter for the Blackfeet at Blackfoot Crossing they were hard up for food but the got along alright they pull through the winter they got meat from deer and a very few buffalo

"February. The buffalo disappear.
The buffalo are moving out towards Montana (U.S.) and the Indian people are forced to spread out hunting for them. This is the beginning of the great famine. Three Bulls and his people head north as far as Battleford. Others head south. But everywhere, the game is missing. Many are saved by the Mounted Police at Fort Walsh (Cypress Mountain). There is trouble and disorder everywhere." (Doucet; 61)

"October. After receiving their pay (treaty payments, ed.), the Blackfoot leave for Montana where they have heard are still some buffalo. A large number of Bloods and Peigans would also go down there...

Our Indian people stayed two winters and one summer in Montana, especially in Judith Basin, where the buffalo were still abundant. Many Indian people, both Canadian and American, were gathered there for the hunt. A large number of Metis also, white people, adventurers, whiskey traders, etc. There were quarrels between the different tribes, horse thefts, disorders of all kinds...By the spring of 1881, the American authorities forced the Canadian Government to call back its Indian people." (Doucet; 65, 66)

1880

NORTH PEIGAN

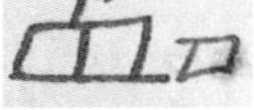

BULL PLUME #1: When they built the first houses.

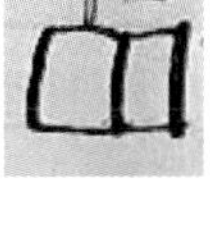

BULL PLUME #2: When they built the first houses.

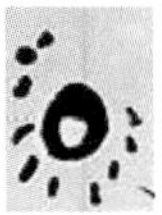 BULL PLUME #2 B: *Black circle with white center and a series of lines around it.*

For the North Peigans this would be when they went to have their Sun Dance with the Bloods and saw the Bloods build their first houses at Belly Buttes.

 OLD AGENCY: *When they built the first houses.*

 *Horse Sun Dance*

SOUTH PEIGAN

ELK HORN: Camped on Two Medicine River; White Dog, chief of Assiniboine, killed by Piegans; after this Piegans confined to reservation.

BIG BRAVE: Peigan wintered south of Missouri; Black Cheek killed by Flathead. In summer Peigan moved back to reservation and Indian accidentally shot by Agency doctor during Sun Dance.

BIG BRAVE 2:...Summer, Wide Ribs was killed by half breed.

BLOOD

BAD HEAD: Itorkoneopatotsop All the Indians of the Blackfoot tribe leave the territories of all the States and come to this side of the boundary.

WHITE BULL: Sun Lodge put by Pretty Owl Woman and Holy Feather on Head. Blood Indians went after and return horses. Killed bad Cree Indian. Chief One Spot captured Cree medicine pipe.

DEMPSEY: When we all moved camp *The starving Indians began drifting back at the end of the winter of 1880-81 and by May the entire tribe was camped along the Belly River. (Blood Agency letter book, entry for May 7, 1881).*

PERCY CREIGHTON: Bloods had their Sun Dance with the North Peigans after Chief Red Crow & a big party of the Bloods went to Belly Buttes & there built the first house. Others went south. Little Shield stole numerous horses from the Crow.

NORTH BLACKFEET

RUNNING RABBIT: Pull out to South, and stoled horses one to another with Crees.

MANY GUNS: Itsokuyisopi = flooded out. They also wintered south in states. They had a flood there. That same summer we drifted north and ever since have been here up to 1938. That was the last time they ate wild buffalo 1880-81 winter.
Note: All circle signs mean the woman who put up the Sundances. Before the circle signs started, up to 8 women put up Sundances.

MANY GUNS .69: The time the little children were massacred and when the Peigans were sent home by the police.

LITTLE CHIEF: The Blackfeet moved south to the Bloods from there they stole horses from the Crees

LITTLE CHIEF 2: The Blackfeet moved south and raiding the different tribes stealing their horses as the Blackfeets were short of horses. Also Rev. Father Lacombe by the assistance of the Dominion Government started to build the first industrial school in Alberta east of Okotoks where the High Wood River empties into the Bow River. Lumber was rafted down the Bow River from Calgary to the High Wood from there was hauled by team to the site. Bricks were hauled by team from Calgary. It was opened in the year 1884 it also stood on six sections enough stock to make it self sufficient.

1881

NORTH PEIGAN

BULL PLUME #1: Mange among the horses.

BULL PLUME #2: Mange among the horses.

BULL PLUME #2 B: *A double line with a number of lines on both sides of it, and two tipi forms at the top. This could indicate the when the tribes were sent back across the international line.*

OLD AGENCY: *Mange among the horses*

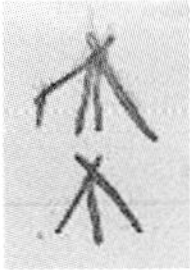 *Two tipis, a four pole and a three pole base [meeting of two different peoples?]*

Peigans and Bloods lost horses in this epidemic." ...about half of the horses these Indians owned died." [Young, South Peigan agent; Reports of the Commissioner of Indian Affairs, 1882; 100]

SOUTH PEIGAN

ELK HORN: Wolf Eagle shot in the arm by Cree

BIG BRAVE: White Dog, an Assiniboine, killed by Piegan. Big Brave and many others lived on Birch Creek seven winters and summers.

BIG BRAVE 2: …no more traveling around.

BIG NOSE WAR RECORD: Judith Basin, MT. 40 lodges of Peigans were camped – three Sioux Attempted to steal horses. They were discovered and all three killed by Under Bull & Young Bear Chief.

BLOOD

BAD HEAD: Inna-askew ossa otsitotoyu Visit of Marquis of Lorne – son-in-law of the Queen

WHITE BULL: Sage brush Sun Lodge was put by Gambler's mother; Swindle Cross Capture Woman.

DEMPSEY: Queen Victoria/her son-in-law/ when he came *The Marquis of Lorne, Governor-General of Canada and son-in-law of Queen Victoria, visited the Bloods at Fort Macleod in September 1881, during a tour of the west. (MacGregor, 1964,1).*

PERCY CREIGHTON: Sun Lodge was put by Pretty Owl Woman & Sarcee Feathers On Head. The Bloods went after their horses that were stolen by the Cree – one of whom was killed.

NORTH BLACKFEET

RUNNING RABBIT: We came to stop at Reserve, and Looks Like Woman, killed. *[From this time on they lived on their Reserve, ed.]*

MANY GUNS: Akieto = Brush on slope of hill. This was the place where Sundance was given. On top of east end of Sand Hills.

MANY GUNS .68: Hillside bush. Shedding Face

MANY GUNS .69: He has mule design on his tipi. *[Many Guns bought the Mule Tipi design, ed.]*

LITTLE CHIEF: The Blackfeets settle down on the Blackfoot reserve Mr. Looking Like A Woman was killed by Crees

LITTLE CHIEF 2: These Blackfeets that moved in the year of 1880 south raid some tribes south came back to Blackfoot Crossing and stayed for good and that was the end of they stealing horses from different tribes.

1882

NORTH PEIGAN

BULL PLUME #1: When the ration house was burned.

BULL PLUME #2: When the ration house was burned.

BULL PLUME #2 B: *Three tipi forms with a double line of dashes leading away from them. This could represent the horses being stolen from the Bloods.*

OLD AGENCY: *When the ration house burned.*

Eagle Sun Dance or Eagle put up Sun Dance.

SOUTH PEIGAN

ELK HORN: Many Indians died of sore throat; Chief Birch Bark die.

BIG BRAVE: In summer Big Brave moved to Blacktail Creek and wintered there.

BIG BRAVE2: Spring Raven Feather was shot and killed by Wolf Moccasin.

BLOOD

BAD HEAD: Miskhestow itsikamapi The Crees steal the horses of Red Crow.

WHITE BULL: Sun Lodge was held the same flats. Horn Societys exchange to Bull Shields took over the White Cane. *(Leader's staff, ed.)*

DEMPSEY: In August 1883, Red Crow, head chief of the Bloods had eighty horses stolen by a war party of Crees. Although the Bloods pursued them towards Cypress Hills, the raiders were not caught. (Blood Agency letter book, entry for Aug. 25,1883).

PERCY CREIGHTON: A Sun Lodge was put up by Gambler's mother, Elk Woman.

NORTH BLACKFEET

RUNNING RABBIT: We very poor for horses and things, we made tents with an sacks. (Mrs. R. Rabbit, Mrs. Iron Head made Sundance)

MANY GUNS: Akieto = Brush on slope of hill. Second Sundance held here. Therefore two years in succession. First C.P.R. train in summer of '83.

MANY GUNS .68: Hill side bush. Fake Gun Woman

MANY GUNS .69: Sun Dance was put up by Sheding Face by the bushes on the hillside.

LITTLE CHIEF: That year the Blackfeet had hardly any horses also they had to use gunner sacks to make tents Sun Dance was made just north west of Dick Bad Boy's across the Bow River

LITTLE CHIEF 2: Was a hard winter the Blackfeet just made it till spring each Chief and his band had garden had potatoes and some vegetables just lasted till spring. In the spring some was lucky to get some game all their tepees were all old and had no money to buy new canvas to make a tepee so they had to make their tepee or tents with guner *[gunny, ed.]* sacks that how poor the Blackfeet were but by the help of the Agent stock man they got canvas to make their tents.

"A few of the Blackfoot had gone to war and came back with some horses they had taken from their enemies in Montana, U,S, Sowatisikin [Feather Necklace, ed.] who was one of the group drove his share of the herd to Crowfoot's camp. They were immediately seized by the Mounted Police and later returned to their owners. Because of Crowfoot's interventiion, however, Sowatisikin turned himself in and was then released without any Punishment." (Doucet; 82)

1883

NORTH PEIGAN

 BULL PLUME #1: Year of disease.

 BULL PLUME #2: Year of disease.

 BULL PLUME #2 B: *The Sun Dance center pole with a man attached to the top by a rope. This would indicate a piercing at the ceremony.*

 OLD AGENCY: *Chiefs went to Winnipeg?*

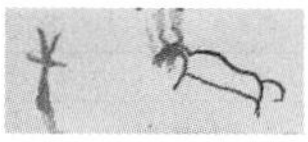 *Buffalo Sun Dance*

SOUTH PEIGAN

ELK HORN: Crow Big Foot visited Piegan; Crow came to steal horses.

BIG BRAVE: Mares issued to Piegan and Little Dog received two buckskin mares. The government began issuing larger horses to cross breed with the smaller, tougher, buffalo horses in order to get a larger horse to be used for farming.

BIG BRAVE 2: …others got horses. *[Meaning they got studs and geldings, ed.]*

BLOOD

BAD HEAD: Istsienakas otsitotorpi The railroad is built across the country.

WHITE BULL: Sun Lodge was much closer to the River. Same flats. Another treaty was made in 2nd day of July 1883. Indians called Middle Treaty.

DEMPSEY: Fire wagon/when it arrived

PERCY CREIGHTON: Sun Lodge was put up by Turn Up Foot, which is known as The Bushy Lodge. Great Chief was made head chief & died soon thereafter. The Bloods left the Gleichen territory & came to their present territory necessitating another treaty.

NORTH BLACKFEET

RUNNING RABBIT: C.P.R Co. came. *(Canadian Pacific Railway, ed.)* (Mrs. Eleven, Mrs. Calf Sitting, Mrs. Little Old Man made Sundance) (Bear Shirt born)

MANY GUNS: Itamisiksisapukaopi = West below river bottom Sundance. Place where Sundance was held. i.e. west of where it had been held two years before. (This year,1938, it was held in the same spot).

MANY GUNS .68: That time we had a Sun Dance in West Valley. Pretty Woman

MANY GUNS .69: Bushes on the Hillside. Killed at Close Range and Ambush Woman and False Gun Woman

LITTLE CHIEF: The C.P.R. went through on the Blackfoot Reserve when the Indians saw it first they did not know what it was

LITTLE CHIEF 2: The C.P.R. came through on the Blackfoot reserve the C.P.R. had some trouble with the Blackfeet but Crowfoot stop those troubles also Rev father Lacombe was a great help to the C.P.R. and helped Crowfoot to stop those troubles so the C.P.R. went right on.

"The construction crews for the CPR had already reached Crowfoot Creek when they were spotted by the Blackfoot. Very angry that these strangers had overstepped their boundaries and crossed into their lands, the Blackfoot wanted to stop them at all costs, with force if need be. Tempers were beginning to flare when someone notified Father Lacombe of the situation and he hurried to their side. He held an impromptu meeting with Crowfoot and the leaders of the tribe. He began by passing out 20 lb. bags of sugar, bags of flour and some tea. He then told them: 'These workers are given orders by their chiefs, and they only obey. I have telegraphed the Lieutenant Governor, and asked him to come here as soon as possible to settle this difficulty. At that time, if his offer doesn't please you, it will still be time to expel these workers'...

Father Lacombe was thus able to reason with them, and helped them to surrender a strip of land to the CPR as a right-of-way for the railroad, with the agreement that extra land south of the river would be given them in compensation. The Lieutenant Governor Dewdney promised it immediately; it was then formally ratified on February 7, 1884, during a meeting held at the Mission at Blackfoot Crossing, attended by Honourable Dewdney, Colonel Macleod, and several CPR officials." (Doucet; 87)

1884

NORTH PEIGAN

BULL PLUME #1: When the Chiefs went to Winnipeg.

BULL PLUME #2: When the Chiefs went to Winnipeg.

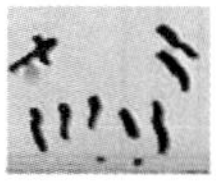

BULL PLUME #2 B: *A cross with a number of lines next to it. This would be a white man leading a group (to Winnipeg).*

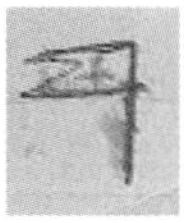

OLD AGENCY: T*he government taking the chiefs to Winnipeg?*

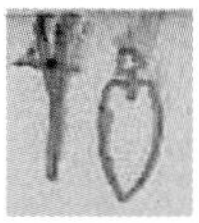

Tall Man Sun Dance

Cree and Metis had been trying to get the Blackfoot to join in their rebellion against the Canadian Government. Governor Dewdney, of the Northwest Territory, decided to impress the Blackfoot chiefs with the power and numbers of the whites. He invited Sitting-On-An-Eagles-Tail-Feathers of the North Peigan, Red Crow of the Bloods and Three Bulls and Crowfoot of the North Blackfeet to visit Winnipeg and Regina. There the chiefs saw the full power of the whites, which influenced their decision not to join the rebellion. (Dempsey; 1972; 160)

Sitting on Eagle Tail Feathers, Three Bulls, Crowfoot and Red Crow on the way to Winnipeg, Hall & Lowe photo, Winnipeg, Glenbow Archive

SOUTII PEIGAN

ELK HORN: Eagle Child died.

BIG BRAVE: Big Brave moved to Whitetail Creek and lived there two winters and two summers.

"Each year, after 1880, Agent John W. Young, from his Agency then on Badger Creek, a few miles south of the present Browning [Montana, ed.] drew attention to the situation, with urgency, in his annual reports...

Congress had tragically underestimated the necessary appropriations, and freighting in emergency rations in the winter when the coulees were snow-filled was nearly impossible. Agent Young spent a heartbreaking winter watching his Indians daily grow weaker, sending out frequent and urgent requests for aid, which in this remote and inaccessible country, was discouragingly slow in coming and insufficient in quantity when it arrived. He resigned and when his successor, Reuben Allen, arrived in April, 1884, he reported that he saw, in a tour of inspection of twenty-eight lodges, only a rabbit cooking in one, and a steer's hoof boiling in a pot in another. During those months 600 died and the Army carpenter was kept busy building crude wooden coffins which were placed on a slight rise to the south of Old Agency. The Indians came to refer to this dreary elevation as 'Ghost Ridge'." [The Starvation Winter of the Piegan Indians, 1883-84; Helen B. West; n.d. U.S. Department of the Interior; Museum of the Plains Indian, Browning, Montana, Information Leaflet No. 7]

BLOOD

BAD HEAD: Ekorpipastsimasin Epidemic of Erysipelas.

WHITE BULL: Side Belly Butte, Sun Lodge was put up by Mrs. Red Crow or Before Singing Woman and Holy Feather on Head. Eagle Calf was make sacrifical brave. *[meaning he pierced at the Sun Dance, ed.]* Chiefs visit to Ottawa. Railroad was built through the Reserve.

PERCY CREIGHTON: Side Butte Lodge put up by Mrs. Red Crow (Holy Feather on Head) (Pretty Owl Woman) (Mrs. Hind Bull). Eagle Calf hung up twice on the Lodge Pole.

NORTH BLACKFEET

RUNNING RABBIT: Crow Foot and Red Crow, went east, and Crow Collar didn't paid a Medicine Pipe. *[He got a Medicine Pipe without paying for it, ed.]* (Mrs. Spot Calf, Mrs. Eagle Ribs made Sundance) (Mrs. Spotted Calf, ed.)

MANY GUNS: Itakxkoxkapi = Sundance on side of the hill, at Eagle Ribs point or bend, or graveyard (a recent name for the bend).

MANY GUNS .68: We had the Hillside Sun Dance. Two Cutter Woman
MANY GUNS .69: The only Sun Dance in the valley put up by Pretty Woman

At this point in our stories we should bring in some facts that caused entries in the winter counts to change, and also had tremendous impact on the Blackfoot People.

In 1876 the Canadian Government enacted the "The Indian Act, 1876" to consolidate it's control over the Indians of Western Canada as well as those in effect in the east. Before 1884 the Indian Act dealt with property, Indian government, and education. But after that year the government passed a series of amendments that allowed it to directly interfere with the ceremonies of the Northwest Coast and Prairies Indians in an attempt to "civilize" them. At this point it was not illegal to hold the Sun Dance, but allowing it was up to the digression of the agent.

The act dealt with stopping the potlatches among the Northwest Coast Native peoples by outlawing them. "Every Indian or other person who engages in or assists in celebrating the Indian festival known as the 'Tamanawas' is guilty of a misdemeanor, and shall be liable to imprisonment for the term of not more than six nor less than two months in any goal or other place of confinement; and any Indian or other person who encourages, either directly or indirectly an Indian or Indians to get up such a festival or dance, or celebrate the same, or who shall assist in the celebration of same is guilty of a like offense, and shall be liable to the same punishment."

The government's opinion was that the huge giveaways did not foster thrift, or economic acquisition necessary for acculturation into Canadian society. This so-called "Potlatch Law" was initially directed solely towards the people of the Northwest Coast tribes, but became the basis for stopping cultural events on the Plains as well.

This giving away of material goods became the justifiable reason to prohibit Sun Dances, Medicine Pipe transfers, Society transfers and any other cultural activity that incorporates exchange of material goods. In effect, every part of Blackfoot traditional culture was affected since exchange of property was a part of Medicine Bundle transfers and Society membership.

The Blackfoot, of course, resisted in every possible way; which is why we start to see the noting of "Lodges" and Sun Dances, or just the names of the women sponsoring them, in the winter counts from here on. To put up a Sun Dance or transfer a Medicine Pipe, or Society membership, became, in effect a brave deed in the face of imprisonment or fines, or both.

NORTH BLACKFEET

LITTLE CHIEF: Crowfoot also Red Crow of the head Chief of thc Bloods wcnt cast for Conference same year Mr. Crow Collar was given the Medicine Pipe

LITTLE CHIEF 2: Crowfoot and Red Crow head Chief of the Blood band were called east on some government business matter when Crowfoot got back he told his people Now my children in the future you will live like white man if you try hard to keep the laws of the white man he R.C.M. Police are our friend they will watch and protect you and help you the future generation will have a horse this horse will have a bad smell he fore seen the cars of to-day and the smell of the gas for the cars they will live like white man but my children do not act like a white man even if you look like a white man because you will never be a white man I don't care how white or fair an Indian is there is something that will give him away of being an Indian so never try to be a white man you will never be one be proud of being an Indian stay an Indian as the Great Spirit made you an Indian and he was right.

1885

NORTH PEIGAN

BULL PLUME #1: When the Sioux came to look for their horses.

BULL PLUME #2: When the Sioux came to look for their horses.

BULL PLUME #2 B: *Two horsemen facing each other would show the white man (in hat) coming to ask for the stolen horses to be gathered for return to the Sioux.*

OLD AGENCY: *When the Sioux came to look for their horses.*

Three pole tipi with lines – Sioux came?

Horse raiding was still going on despite attempts by the Indian Agents to stop it. The agents were often in contact with each other and one of the methods they used was to send some of the people who lost horses to the reserve of the suspected tribe. In this way the horses would be returned to their original owners and hopefully, discourage future raids.

SOUTH PEIGAN

ELK HORN: Many cattle died.

BIG BRAVE: Moved to Blacktail and has been living there ever since, nineteen winters and summers he has lived there.

BLOOD

BAD HEAD: Itakaenigapotskinay Plenty cattle died.

WHITE BULL: Sun Lodge was put up by Tiny Woman and Otto *[Otter, ed.]* Woman, cross the river from Weasel Moccasin's flats. Weasel Running killed his wife.

PERCY CREIGHTON: Yellow Sun Lodge. Northwest Rebellion; police & Cree. (Chief Standing in Middle hung up on Lodge Pole.)

NORTH BLACKFEET

RUNNING RABBIT: ___________ (River side brush made third Sundance) Mrs. R. Wolf, Mrs. Y. Horse made Sundance. *(Running Wolf & Yellow Horse, ed.)*

MANY GUNS:

(1) Akieto = another Sundance at this place. (cf. 1882)

(2) Matsitokaopi = we had another Sundance. Meaning a 3rd Sundance at this same place.

MANY GUNS .68: Hillside bush. Roaring The Opposite Way and Nice Snake

MANY GUNS .69: The time we were going to have a Sun Dance. Two Cutter Woman. The Crees were exchanging gifts.

This could be when the Crees sent gifts and tobacco to the Blackfeet to get them to join the rebellion.

LITTLE CHIEF: That was the year that the Crees had a war with the white men police lot of Crees came here to the Blackfoot Reserve later the police put all the Crees chiefs in jail some got hang

LITTLE CHIEF 2: The rebellion was on Reil meet Crowfoot in Montana Crowfoot Reil what do you get out of war so when he came back at Blackfoot Crossing he told his band not to join that rebellion stay out of it Crowfoot adopted a boy at the time of the rebellion he was a young man his name was Wolf Small Leg (Mo-ko-ye-ko-ke-na-ke-ma) *[This may well be Poundmaker who was adopted by Crowfoot and was a leader in the rebellion., ed.]* it happen that this adopted son of Crowfoot was among the Crees that fought in that rebellion he also joined in that battle when it was over the police arrested all the Cree Chiefs also Mo-ko-ye-ko-ke-na-ke-ma was arrested all was sentence to be hang included among that was going to be hang was Mo-ko-ye-ko-ke-na-ke-ma just before the time they were going to be hang Wolf Small Legs told the head police please let my father know that I am among the ones that are to be hang the police told him who is your father say Wolf Small Legs my father is Chief Crowfoot tell him that your son is going to be hang alright the police wired east of Cluny about one mile and a half Old Croutney's place it was a store to tell Crowfoot that his son was about to be hang when Crowfoot go the news he went right up he told the store keeper wire the police that is my son that they are going to hang also tell them to let him out and see that he is send home to me which the police did and that is how Ma-ko-ye-ko-ke-na-ke-ma did not get hang all the rest got hang

1886

NORTH PEIGAN

BULL PLUME #1: When many cattle died.

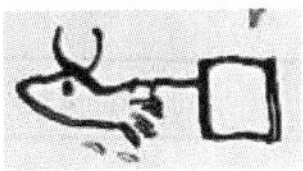

BULL PLUME #2: When many cattle died.

BULL PLUME #2 B: *Three pairs of parallel lines with red coming from them would indicate the six Bloods killed by the Gros Ventre in Creighton's winter count.*

OLD AGENCY: *Stockman with pipe in mouth and coughing cow [facing right]. When many cattle died.*

That simple statement could not show the severe winter that wiped out many of the northern plains ranchers. It started, November 17, 1886, "It has been blowing a blizzard since early this morning and every railroad is more or less blocked...". February 2, 1887, "The temperature at 2 o'clock to day was 42 below zero, with a gale blowing from the north...". March 9, 1887, "Our losses in cattle are simply immense...we cannot tell how severe." It also was the inspiration for Charles M. Russell's watercolor, "Last of the 500", which was the answer to a rancher's question regarding the condition of the herd Russell was caring for. (The Charles M. Russell Book; Harold McCracken; Doubleday, 1957; 102-104)

"This winter of 1886-87 is a very rigorous one: intense cold, deep snows... Because of this long and hard winter, thousands of cattle and horses have died." (Doucet; Peigan Reserve; 109)

SOUTH PEIGAN

ELK HORN: Stallions issued. *This was part of the program to improve the size of the Blackfoot horses. When it was discovered that one of the studs was a famous race horse Many Guns, of the North Peigans, smuggled one of his race horse mares down to Montana. He had her bred by the stud without he government officials finding out, and took the mare back to Alberta. Her foal was the first in a long line of great race horses among the North Peigan, and the blood line is still owned by the Many Guns family. [Joe Crowshoe, personal interview, 1979]*

BIG BRAVE: White-Dog, an Assiniboine, killed by Peigan. Big Brave and many others lived on Birch Creek seven winters and summers.

BIG BRAVE 2:... no more traveling around.)In summer Big Brave moved to Blacktail Creek and wintered there.

On February 11, 1887 the Blackfeet [South Peigans] ceded all lands except those within the boundary from the mouth of Cutbank Creek north to the Canadian border and along the south on Birch Creek to the mountains, which are the boundaries of the present Blackfeet reservation. From this time on the Blackfoot were confined to the reservation only being allowed to travel with a pass from the agent. For all this land they received $150,000 per year for ten years. In Blackfeet oral history it is referred to as "when we sold the Sweetgrass Hills".

BLOOD

BAD HEAD: Otsntsennapi-krisahoy ninnan The Chiefs of the Blackfeet are taken down on a visit to Ottawa.

WHITE BULL: Sun Lodge was put up by Elk Woman and Otto *[Otter, ed.]* Woman. Long Time Bird was shot by mistake. Six Blood Indians killed by Gros-Ventres Indians near Sweet Grass Butte.

PERCY CREIGHTON: Six Bloods were killed by Gros Ventre at Sweet Grass Butte. Sun Lodge put up by Tiny Woman & Otter Woman. Running Weasel killed his wife in the fall.

NORTH BLACKFEET

RUNNING RABBIT: Eagle Ribs place, made Sundance, and Calf Chief and Three Sun went war. (Mrs. Sitting Eagle, born.)

RUNNING RABBIT 2: Mrs. Many Guns born

MANY GUNS: Many Guns was at the Bloods so nothing was recorded.

MANY GUNS .68: Ambush Woman and Coming Singer. The time when the tongues were carried around the camps. *[This occurred on the Blood Reserve, ed.]*

MANY GUNS .69: No Sun Dance at Bushes on the hillside. Opposite Roaring died.

LITTLE CHIEF: Mr. Calf Chief the late Three Sun went on a war party they got away with it only the Chief Crowfoot took the horses they stole back to the Crow Indians Sun Dance was at Eagle Rib's flat north of the Bow River Mrs. Sitting Eagle was born

LITTLE CHIEF 2: The Blackfeets had their Sundance at Eagle Rib's flat also the late Mrs. Sitting Eagle was born also Calf Chief (O-ne-sta-na) and Three Sun (Ne-o-k-to-se-wa) went on war party without Crowfoot knowing it.

1887

NORTH PEIGAN

BULL PLUME #1: When "North Axe" was made Chief. *Head Chief of the Peigans.*

BULL PLUME #2: When "North Axe" was made Chief?

BULL PLUME #2 B: *A Sun Dance center pole with a man lying at its base would indicate someone died at the Sun Dance.*

A second drawing, between 1886 & 1887, shows a white man,

 OLD AGENCY: *When the Bloods made peace with the Gros Ventre and Assiniboine?*

 *When North Axe was made chief?*

He succeeded his father, Sitting-On-Eagle-Tailfeathers, signer of Treaty Number Seven.

North Axe, chief of the North Peigan-Blackfoot, ca. 1886, F.A. Russell photo, Lethbridge, Alberta, Glenbow Archives

SOUTH PEIGAN

ELK HORN: Mares issued

BIG BRAVE 2: Wintered on Blacktail. Spring, Raven Feather was shot and killed by Wolf Moccasin in summer.)

BLOOD

BAD HEAD: Sapomanika otsitawayyok atsenaw Crow Foot goes to visit the Gros Ventres, and is knocked down by a drunken Indian.

WHITE BULL: Sun Lodge was put up by Lizard Head or Girl, south side Kootenay Bridge. Red Crow exchanged his medicine pipe to Weasel Horse and Joe Healy and Grost-Good [sic] Looking were struck by lightning. *[Healy and The Ghost (Mitchell Hughs, an Agency employee) were struck in 1888. [Dempsey, 1994]*

PERCY CREIGHTON: Shaggy Hair Woman (Weasel Tail Woman) put up Sun Lodge at Stand Off Flat. Long Time Bird was shot by error.

NORTH BLACKFEET

RUNNING RABBIT: _______ Big Plume, made Sundance. (Mrs. Benedict Iron Head born)

MANY GUNS: Many Guns was at the Bloods so nothing was recorded.

LITTLE CHIEF: Mr. Big Plume made the Sun Dance

North Peigan Sun Dance. 1886 Unknown photographer. Back row; Sgt. Gaigen [N.W.M.P.], 3 unknown, Runs Among Buffalo, Mr. Springett [Indian Affairs Official], Kidney, 1 unknown, Jerry Paisley, Crow Shoe, Constable George Manfield [N.W.M.P.], Running Wolf, N.W.M.P. constable, Jerry Potts, 3 unknown, Corporal M. Hayne [N.W.M.P.],1 unknown. Front Row; Good Young Man, Little Plume, Running Eagle, Shining Double, Bull Plume, Green Grass Bull and Black Chief.

1888

NORTH PEIGAN

 BULL PLUME #1: When the moon died. (Eclipse)

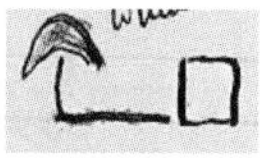 BULL PLUME #2: When the moon died. (Eclipse)

 BULL PLUME #2 B: *A Sun Dance center pole with five lines around it may indicate the trouble at the Blood Sun Dance.*

 OLD AGENCY: *When the moon died.*

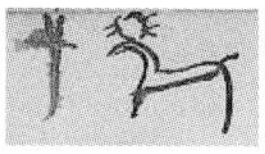 *Big Elk [?] Sun Dance*

SOUTH PEIGAN

ELK HORN: Two Indians arrested and died in prison; in summer cattle were issued.

BIG BRAVE: Mares issued to Peigan and Little-Dog received two buckskin mares

BLOOD

BAD HEAD: Itsaskinapastsimesop Epidemic of Influenza
(BAD HEAD/WILSON winter count ends here.)

WHITE BULL: Sun Lodge was put up by Crook Foot of Black Snake and First Striker, and Blood Indians had trouble with Mounted Police north side of Kootenay River, sun dance was held there.

This simple statement of "Blood Indians had trouble with Mounted Police" has enough of a story and drama, that is well worth reading. Details are given in two books; the first is told by White Calf, a participant in the war party that initiated the trouble. [PIEGAN, Lancaster, 1966; 300-345].The second book is "The Last War Party", THE AMAZING DEATH OF CALF SHIRT; Dempsey, 1994; 119-137.

A war party to the Crows returned and several members were arrested by the Mounted Police. Calf Robe and Prairie-Chicken-Old-Man had not been arrested and eventually all charges had been dropped against the party. A group of three Mounties and an interpreter were at the Sun Dance of the Bloods when they saw the two men. Unknown to the Mounties the charges had been dropped but as far as they were concerned the men were still wanted. The fact that the Mounties didn't have a warrant, didn't prevent them from trying to arrest the men in the middle of the Okan holy lodge. This was the Holiest of Blackfoot ceremonies. As Staff Sergeant Hilliard drew his pistol and pulled the rifle from Calf Robe's hands, the other Mounties grabbed Prairie-Chicken-Old-Man, and both headed to the entrance to the lodge. The lack of respect for their Holy ceremony and rough handling of the war heroes caused a violent reaction among the warriors. They quickly freed the two men and took the Mounties weapons away. In the process the famous scarlet uniforms were torn and disheveled, and the Mounties very lives were at risk. It was only the intervention of three Blood chiefs and the Black Catchers Society that saved their lives. They were led to safety at the edge of the camp and told in no uncertain terms to keep away from their holy ceremonies.

PERCY CREIGHTON: (Girls) Sun Lodge at Rocky Bridge. Looking Safed *[Saved, ed.]* was struck by lightning.

NORTH BLACKFEET

RUNNING RABBIT: ______ Big Road, made Sundance. (Mrs. Jack Wolf Leg born.)

MANY GUNS: Many Guns was at the Bloods so nothing was recorded.

LITTLE CHIEF: Mr. Big Road made Sun Dance

1889

NORTH PEIGAN

BULL PLUME #1: When the Thunder Pipe was sold.

BULL PLUME #2: When the Thunder Pipe was sold.

BULL PLUME #2 B: *No pictograph.*

Two possible interpretations can be read in this count. The first, which is the most probable since it is an act of courage, is defiance of the "Potlach Law" that stated payments could not be made for any ceremony. The transfer of a Medicine Pipe Bundle would entail payments of horses, blankets, and other goods to compensate the past owner for the loss of his bundle. All the Blackfoot tribes were defying government attempts to eliminate their culture and religion by holding Sun Dances, transferring the Holy societies, and various Medicine Bundles. At times these were held far from the agent's eyes. Some agents aggressively tried to stop these, while others turned a blind eye to the happenings.

Another interpretation would be the transfer of one of the Medicine Pipes off the North Peigan Reserve to one of the other tribes of the Blackfoot Confederacy.

North Peigan Sun Dance Camp 1889, in defiance of the government laws. Unknown photographer, Steele & Company, Winnipeg, Manitoba, Glenbow Archives.

SOUTH PEIGAN

ELK HORN: Wolf Coming Over Hill died

BIG BRAVE: Big Brave moved to Whitetail Creek and lived there two winters and summers.

BIG BRAVE 2: Then has lived on the Blacktail Creek 19 winters now, ranch.

BLOOD

WHITE BULL: Sun Lodge was put up

PERCY CREIGHTON: Bloods had a ___*(blank, ed.)*

NORTH BLACKFEET

RUNNING RABBIT: Dick Bad Boy, born

MANY GUNS: Isapomaxsika = Crow Big Foot. Crowfoot died (Spring 1890)

MANY GUNS .68: Crow Big Foot and Looking Together

LITTLE CHIEF: Mr. Dick Bad Boy was born
LITTLE CHIEF 2: No Sundance Dick Bad Boy was born

1890

NORTH PEIGAN

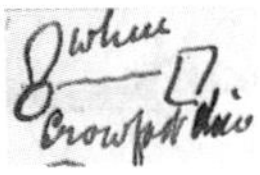

BULL PLUME #1: When "Crowfoot" died.

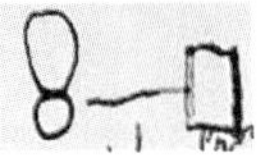

BULL PLUME #2: When "Crowfoot" died.

BULL PLUME #2 B: *No pictograph.*

OLD AGENCY: *The Old Agency pictographs seem to skip 1889 for the next entry is the death of Crowfoot.*

Bear Moccasin[?] in the timber.

The next two pages of the agency book don't seem to match up with any nearby year events so are presented here separately.

 *Fight in the timber?*

 *Tall Woman[?] Sun Dance .*

Crowfoot was a North Blackfeet chief who had considerable influence during the signing of Treaty Number Seven with the Canadian Government. He died April 25, 1890.

SOUTH PEIGAN

BIG BRAVE: Big Brave moved to Blacktail and has been living there ever since, nineteen winters and summers.

ELK HORN: Chief Walking Through the Beach dies.

BLOOD

WHITE BULL: Sun Lodge was put up by Mrs. Holy Walking Down or Noisey [sic] Under Ground. Bull Black, Gros Ventre Indians flashing light to our Sun dance camps from the top of the Belly Butte. Chief Crow foot died that year.

PERCY CREIGHTON: No Lodge. Peigans here to sell their dance outfit. *(Kaispa Society?, ed.)* Sheep Old Man died. Crowfoot died at Crowfoot Butte.

NORTH BLACKFEET

RUNNING RABBIT: Crow Foot died, 25th of April, aged 60 years

MANY GUNS .68: Double Chaser

MANY GUNS .69: Crow Big Foot

LITTLE CHIEF: It was a sad year for the Blackfeet they lost their great chief Chief Crowfoot died April 25th 1890 at the ages of 69 years

LITTLE CHIEF 2: Our Chief Crowfoot died in April 25th all those in the tepee heard Crowfoot tell them in a little while I will go I will leave you my children be good to each other as I was good to you all mind the Red Coats because they are our friends they look after us also be kind and mind our missionaries the long coat that is what they call the

Catholic priests also the short coats that is the Anglican Ministers which are also our friends I am not sorry that I am going to die I know I will go to a good place try and come to were I will go from who where we coming from and nowhere we go be good to each other and a few minutes Chief Crowfoot left the world to God's place.

1891

NORTH PEIGAN

BULL PLUME #1: When many cattle died.

BULL PLUME #2: When many cattle died.

BULL PLUME #2 B: *No pictograph.*

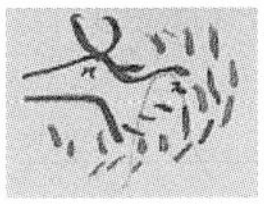

OLD AGENCY: *Many cattle died.*

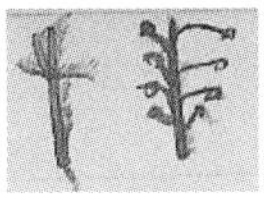

Many Berries Sun Dance

SOUTH PEIGAN

ELK HORN: Crow Big Foot dies.

BLOOD

WHITE BULL: Sun Lodge was put up by Shaggery Hair Woman or Mrs. No Chief. Late in fall Mr. Steel was shot by Mounted Police.

PERCY CREIGHTON: Sun Lodge put up by Mrs. Shaggy Head Woman. Pigeon Society killed dogs around the camps. In the fall Steele was shot by the police between

Kootenay & Belly River straight across from Morning Owl's place. *[October 19, 1891. See Dempsey, 1994, p 150-60 for the complete story.]*

NORTH BLACKFEET

MANY GUNS: Nyokskaistauuk = Three Bulls. Became Chief in fall of 1892 after Crowfoot died.

MANY GUNS .68: Three Bulls and Sun Old Woman

LITTLE CHIEF: The Blackfeet were without a head Chief like Crowfoot they was sorrow still on the Blackfoot reserve

LITTLE CHIEF 2: No Sundance it was a hard winter but the Blackfeet got through the winter

1892

NORTH PEIGAN

BULL PLUME #1: When the deer were easily caught in deep snow.

BULL PLUME #2: When the deer were easily caught in deep snow.

BULL PLUME #2 B: *No pictograph.*

OLD AGENCY: *When the deer were easily caught in deep snow.*

Five people

SOUTH PEIGAN

ELK HORN: Yellow Medicine dies.

South Peigan Sun Dance. Left to right; The first Holy Woman, wearing her Natoas headdress is at the far left with her group. Gives to The Sun, another of the sponsors of the Okan [wearing the Natoas headdress just behind pole], Mad Wolf [her husband who put it up with her], White Calf [in white shirt], Running Crane, Little Dog, Little Petrified Rock, Black Snake. Their husbands, painted black and wearing black robes, sit to their left. And the third is behind the middle support pole. Boss Ribs leads Iron Breast carrying his Beaver Pipe for the Holy Party to smoke. This was a "triple" Sun Dance, meaning three women made vows and sponsored it that year. Thomas Magee photo, McClintock photo collection, Beinecke Archives, Yale University

BLOOD

WHITE BULL: Sun Lodge was put up by two women, Mrs. Holy Walking Down and Wolverine Woman. She make a vow for Mr. Steel to get well soon.

PERCY CREIGHTON: Sun Lodge put up by Mrs. Walking Around, Under Wolverine Woman. She made a vow for Steele when he was shot by the police.

In 1892 seven women fulfilled their vows [to put up a Sun Dance, on the Blood Reserve ed.]. that was an extraordinary number. In '92 the seven women and the husbands used four lodges only in which to reside during the rites, three were in one [Big Wolf's]. Four sweat lodges were made for them, one for the inmates of each lodge, and by four different societies; all the work and ceremony was performed at the four lodges simultaneously...The initiation rite was performed in '92 in all four of the lodges. I witnessed that in which three women were initiated at once in Running Wolf's lodge.

[In the procession to the shelter from the Holy Lodge;] No Chief [a priest] walked first, leading the path over some cotton print laid to the doorway. Next the three black men [the women's male partners, ed.], then the women, each a novice, following the one whose regalia she had just received. Very slowly they walked to the south side of the half-built medicine lodge, stopping at intervals to pray, but not loudly. They circled the Medicine Lodge once, taking the course of the Sun, and then sat down in a shelter which had been constructed for them to the west of the Medicine lodge.

This shelter was made up of travois lodge poles and canvas. Those using it sat facing the sacred edifice. The shelter was about 60 feet long and sitting in a row, extending from one end to the other, was seven parties of people each composed of the woman who had sold her O-kon [Natoas, ed.], her husband, the new O-kon, and her husband. Thus there were seven vendors and their seven husbands also seven novices and their husbands, the later painted black.... [R.N.Wilson, 1892, 266-7, 272]

The Shooting of Steel
Steel, a Blood-Blackfoot, was driving his lost horses back to the Reserve off the Cochrane ranch when he stumbled on a group of young Bloods butchering. They had killed one of the Cochrane ranch's cows and were loading their pack horses. He visited with them for a bit as it started to become dusk. At the same time two Mounties, out looking for bootleggers smuggling whiskey from across the border, stumbled on the group. In the dim light they took the group for the smugglers and charged them with drawn weapons. As Steel rode toward the Mounties with his hand raised in greeting, one of the Mounties fired two shots that went sailing past his head. Steel shot the one officer, nipping off his ear lobe and grazing his neck. Spinning his horse to head into cover Steel was shot in the back. As he lay on the ground the Mounties realized their mistake. They tried to get him on his horse but he was too weak to move. They left him on the ground and rode off to the detachment for help.

The boys that had been butchering, meanwhile, had escaped and went to Steel's camp. There they told his wife what had happened and then took off to the States to hide out. Medicine Pipe Woman took one of the horses the boys brought back and hitched her travois to it. She then found her husband and brought him back to the reserve. All expected him to die from the wound. As the Indian doctors worked to save his life, his sister Under Wolverine Woman vowed to sponsor a Sun Dance for him if he recovered.

The Mounties, meanwhile, were claiming Steel shot first and insisted he had been shot in the chest. After Steel had recovered he was arrested for shooting with intent to kill and sentenced to two months hard labor in the Fort Macleod guardhouse. He served his time and lived until 1940. [Man of Steel, THE AMAZING DEATH OF CALF SHIRT; Dempsey; 1994; 150-160]

NORTH BLACKFEET

RUNNING RABBIT: Three Bull, died. (Prairie Chicken born and Antham Wolf Child)

MANY GUNS: Many Guns was at the Bloods so nothing was recorded.

MANY GUNS .69: Alert Old Man

LITTLE CHIEF: Three Bull died head Chief of Blackfeet Crowfoot's brother Mr. Pat Prairie Chicken also Anthim Wolf Child were born

LITTLE CHIEF 2: The Chief Three Bulls died Crowfoot's brother he also spoke to his people Now I am going to leave you my children I will go to where my brother went be good to each other and mind the ones that are looking after you I have been good to you all and help you as much as I could if you are good we will see each other some day in the happy hunting grounds Good by

1893

NORTH PEIGAN

BULL PLUME #1: When children died with measles.

BULL PLUME #2: When children died with measles.

BULL PLUME #2 B: *A square building with church steeple and lines inside and out would indicate the mission school where the children died.*

 OLD AGENCY: *Children died with measles.*

 *Tall Whiteman Sun Dance*

This was an epidemic of small pox and "grippe". The North Peigan population dropped from 932 in 1888 to 471 in 1909. A Siksika elder had a dream instructing him to tell the people to have their children painted with the holy red paint. It is said that those who were painted survived this epidemic.

SOUTH PEIGAN

ELK HORN: Three Bulls dies.

BLOOD

WHITE BULL: No Sun Lodge. Some of our Indian children were sent to schools. Some went to Dunbow school, some went to St. Paul mission school. Heavy snow storm that winter. Head Chief Crow Foot died.

PERCY CREIGHTON: This fall is remembered as the year the children were sent to different schools; some to Dunbar – others to the Elkhorn School; some to the St. Paul's mission. Heavy snowstorms in the winter of '93 as the Blood returned from Browning, many deer were caught alive in the snow.

NORTH BLACKFEET

RUNNING RABBIT: (Mrs. May Field *[Mayfield, ed.]*, killed by train.) (Jim Black and Big Tobacco born)

MANY GUNS: Many Guns was at the Bloods so nothing was recorded.

LITTLE CHIEF: Mrs. May Field was killed by train

LITTLE CHIEF 2: Some of the Blackfeet went to the timber west of Banff to cut logs for their Huts while they were still up there they where almost through cutting logs One woman her treaty name May Field we call her in Indian (E-pa-mo-mo-wa) She went across she got kill by the train the Blackfeets that was up there moved right away for home they were afraid of her they said she is a Ghost now she will tease us to-night

1894

NORTH PEIGAN

 BULL PLUME #1: When "Scraping High" killed "No Skunk", Blackfoot Reserve.

 BULL PLUME #2: When "Scraping High" killed "No Skunk" the _____ on Blackfoot Reserve.

 BULL PLUME #2 B: *Symbol for white man would indicate the murdered stockman at Gleichen.*

 OLD AGENCY: *Scraping High killed No Skunk.*

 *Many Horses Sun Dance [In 1973 John Yellowhorn, former chief of the North Peigans, told the story of this Sun Dance. Many horses were given away in defiance of government laws forbidding any sort of giveaway. [John Yellowhorn, North Peigan, author's field notes]*

Scraping High threw his life away [iskohtai-im-ohksiow] when his son died from being at the residential school. He went in search of Rev. Tims, who was in charge of the school, to kill him. Tims was in Calgary, so he sought another high official to kill before he was killed. He found No Skunk (also known as Owl Eyes, Mr. F. Skyner), stock man for the agency, and killed him. (For the complete story see Scraping High and Mr. Tims, Dempsey; 1994; 186)

Scraping High's son contracted a form of tuberculosis at Tims' residential school. When he wanted to take his son home Tims refused, finally allowing him to take the boy when the boy was about to die. White-Headed-Chief was the nephew of Scraping High and tells the story;

"One night Atsaowan's *[Scraping High, ed]* boy very sick and they were fixing him up [i.e. had the medicine man in]. Atsaowan went over to Tsipistapini [Eyes-of-the-Owl], *[aka No Skunk, ed.]* the white, ration man- to ask for food for his boy. The ration man began instead to swear at Atsaowan. Atsaowan went home. He found the boy almost ready to die. Atsaowan, 'What do you think of me, son? You are about to die.' Boy; 'I love you much father. I want you to come with me.' Atsaowan, 'All right, we'll both go in the same way.' When boy had died, Atsaowan's brother [Pitonista] took Atsaowan away to his camp. Atsaowan told people to bury boy on a hill. Atsaowan then told his brother, 'I'm going to <u>fix</u> that white man, for he refused me food. White man think we Indians are like children.'...Pitonista, blind, tried to talk to Atsaowan to stop him from killing. So finally Atsaowan said: 'I'll take your word, I won't hurt him. But I'm leaving the reserve, going south.'

Shortly after that Atsaowan was playing cards with five men. One of them, Duck-Chief, said to Atsaowan; "Friend, everyone is making fun of your name for saying you were going to kill a white man, and now you are not doing anything.' Atsaowan; 'Do you mean that?' Duck-Chief; 'Yes, they're taking your name for fun.' So Atsaowan got up from the table, got gun and went down to a bunch of white men and families who lived near the mines and worked there. He was going to kill any one of them, he didn't really care which, though they had nothing to do with this fight, but then he had pity on them. 'I can't kill them, but I'll go to Tsipistapini, the man who disappointed me.' So he went up to Tsipistapini's barn, saddled Tsipistapini's horse with Tsipistapini's saddle. Then went over to the house. Atsaowan knocked. Tsipistapini opened door and at that moment Atsaowan fired, killing him instantly. The brains were found in the kitchen. Then Atsaowan mounted and rode the horse over to Running Rabbit, head chief at the time. Atsaowan told him; 'I've killed the ration man.' Atsaowan rode then to his brother Pitonista and said; 'I've done it. If they send you up to get me, don't come. If you do, I'll kill you and you'll be the first dead.'

Then Atsaowan went over and told White Eagle, Pitoxpikis, and told both the story. 'They'll find me on the hill where my boy is buried.' This was all done the same night he killed the ration man. After telling all the Cluny people he went back to the ration house, put the horse back in stable and killed it. Then he walked up to his son's grave. It was dawn.

In the morning, Running Rabbit came up to Gleichen, mentioned it to the Mountie. They phoned to Calgary for a whole lot of police. They all gathered at the foot of the hill where Atsaowan was in a coulee by Duck Chief's house and near Pitoxpikis'. There were piles of Indians and whites, and the police were there too. The police came up to Running Rabbit; 'What are we to do with this man?' Running rabbit; 'Try to catch him.' Police sent for Pitonista *[Atsaowan's blind brother, ed.]* to go up to get Atsaowan. At that White-Headed-Chief said to Pitonista; 'Don't you go! You are my stepfather and I want to save your life. I've heard Atsaowan will kill Pitonista.' But Pitonista jumped on his horse and in a flash made for Atsaowan. White-Headed-Chief and Inagaowotan chased Pitonista on a horse too, to head him off. Now Atsaowan had marked a line over which no one was to pass. The three horses crossed this line. Atsaowan said; 'Look out, my friends,' and fired. Bullets missed the three, but whizzed over the manes of the horses, making the hair rise. Pitonista was brought back safely however…

Then the Mounties began to shoot Atsaowan who fired back. Atsaowan almost got a policeman, for the bullet ricocheted off a rock behind which the policeman was shooting. At last Atsaowan's firing ceased, for a bullet had stuck. Atsaowan ran down the back of the hill to the bushes in a long coulee. White-Headed-Chief quietly jumped on his horse, ran down too and tied his horse by a house near where he knew Atsaowan was. White-Headed-Chief then went into the bushes to find Atsaowan. When White-Headed-Chief saw Atsaowan, Atsaowan said, 'Give me your coat' – yet was afraid lest the coat be noticed and he be shot in the coat. Blanket then taken instead but also given back. The blanket and coat were each asked for because it was cold. Atsaowan; 'My gun has jammed. What shall I do? I'm going to disappear for four days. They'll see me at the same place after I fix up my gun.' White-Headed-Chief; 'Go to the coulee by ration house. All the Indians are at Pitoxpikis' place and you'll be safe.' But Atsaowan didn't do as White-Headed-Chief said. Went into the open place down by the river.

They searched everywhere for Atsaowan all day. Near the old ration house was a lake, and a road thick with brush on each side. At sunset Atsaowan came down the road. A mountie saw him, fired, caught a vein in arm with the shot. They didn't catch him though, for he fled, though bleeding. Then all police set after him, but he eluded them. There was the house there nearby of John Drunk Chief's. Atsaowan was tracked there. People, Indians and Mounties were all standing around the house, not daring to enter. Maku-yokos came up with his son Turned-Up-Nose. Maku-yokos; 'What are you doing here?' 'Your brother-in-law is in the house.' They were afraid he'd shoot. Maku-yokos was armed, went straight up to door and roughly pulled Mounties aside. Maku-yokos entered and saw Atsaowan was dead. He said to dead man; 'Friend, you should have waited for me. You died too soon [gave up so soon].' Then Mounties came in. Maku-yokos was so mad at the Mounties. He tried to shoot a Mountie but Blackfeet held him. So it was over." *[White-Headed-Chief to Hanks, Box 1 file 4, 1938;129-133]*

White Headed Chief and his wife Aisomyaki [Ambush Woman], North Blackfeet-Blackfoot, Lucien and Jane Hanks photo, 1938

BLOOD

WHITE BULL: Sun Lodge was put up by Yellow Buffalo Stone Woman or Mrs. Eagle Child. The Blackfoot Indian named Blood Juice killed white man call him Owl Eyes.

PERCY CREIGHTON: Sun Lodge put up by Mrs. Eagle Child (Yellow Buffalo Stone Woman). Red Crow purchased cattle. Ah-tsa-wa (a Blackfeet) killed Owl Eyes.

NORTH BLACKFEET

MANY GUNS: Many Guns was at the Bloods so nothing was recorded.

MANY GUNS .68: Emiamomowa (See LC2, 1893, ed.)

MANY GUNS .69 Scalp Old Man

LITTLE CHIEF: Paul Weasel Head also Joseph Little Chief were born the same day

1895

NORTH PEIGAN

 BULL PLUME #1: Visit of Lord Aberdeen.

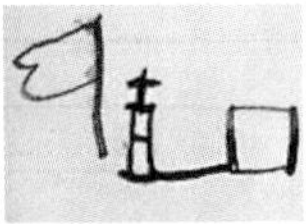 BULL PLUME #2: The year Lord Aberdeen came.
[Governor General of Canada, 1893-1898, ed.]

 BULL PLUME #2 B: *Many Horses Sun Dance*

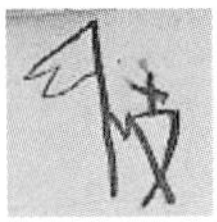 OLD AGENCY: *Lord Aberdeen visit.*

 *Agency Sun Dance.*

SOUTH PEIGAN

ELK HORN: Big Nose dies. *(1896, Also known as Three Suns, ed.)*

BLOOD

WHITE BULL: No Sun Lodge. Wolverine Running died with nose bleeding. The sports were held at Bull Shields flats. Late in fall Charcoal killed Medicine Pipe Crane. The Indian Agent James Wilson stopped the Sun Lodges any more. Ee-tak-poo-cheop or Packs Load of Meat killed his wife.

PERCY CREIGHTON: No Sun Lodge. Running Fisher died of nose bleeding. Ca-tah-poh-chop killed his wifc.

Agent James Wilson, at the Blood Reserve, ordered that all the ration beef tongues would be cut in half. Since the tongues were an important part of the Sun Dance, and needed to be cut by the Holy Woman during a part of the ceremony, this effectively stopped the Sun Dance for that year.

In 1895 the government amended the Indian Act which dealt with stopping the potlatches among the Northwest Coast Native peoples by outlawing them.

"Every Indian or other person who engages in, or assists in celebrating or encourages either directly or indirectly another to celebrate, any Indian festival, dance or other ceremony of which the giving away or paying or giving back of money, goods, or articles of any sort forms a part, or is a feature, whether such gift of money, goods or articles takes place before, at, or after the celebration of the same, and every Indian or other person who engages or assists in any celebration or dance of which the wounding or mutilation of the dead or living body of any human being or animal forms a part or is a feature, is guilty of an indictable offense." [Section 114(c. 35, 58-59 Vict.) of the Indian Act]

The agents took this as their authority not only to actively stop the Sun Dances, but all other traditional ceremonies as well.

NORTH BLACKFEET

RUNNING RABBIT: Scratching Hide *[Scrapping Hide, ed.]*, killed. (Owl Eyes killed) *[Agency ration man, ed.]*

MANY GUNS: Many Guns still on Blood Reserve heard that Atsaowan = (Scrapings from hides made into soup) killed the ration-man.

MANY GUNS .68: Head Old Man and Hide Scrappings
MANY GUNS .69: Hide Scrappings killed Owl Eyes

LITTLE CHIEF: Scratching Hide killed the stock man Owl Eyes

LITTLE CHIEF 2: Henry Scratching Hide (A-ja-wa-na) killed the stockman Owl Eyes (Se-pe-e-sta-pe-ne) he also got killed

1896

NORTH PEIGAN

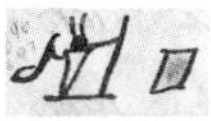

BULL PLUME #1: When "Charcoal" was hung.

 BULL PLUME #2: When "Charcoal" was hung.

 BULL PLUME #2 B: *A human figure next to a line with five lines projecting from it at right angles. This could indicate Charcoal who was owner of a Seizers Medicine Pipe. The Seizers Medicine Pipes have a series of hair locks, or feathers, spaced along the length of the pipe stem as opposed to the Thunder Medicine Pipes which have a fan of eagle feathers at their base. Or, it could be the name glyph of Medicine Pipe Man Returning with a Crane's War Whoop,[aka Medicine Pipe Stem] who was killed by Charcoal.*

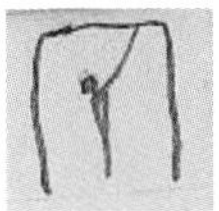 OLD AGENCY: *Charcoal hung*

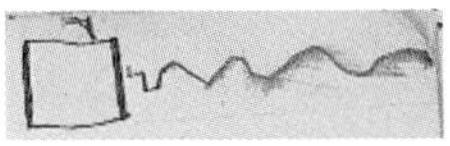 *Flooding[?]*

Charcoal, a Blood Indian, was actually hung in 1897 but started his career as a fugitive in 1896. It all began when he shot his wife's lover. He then went on a rampage, stealing horses and food. Whenever the police caught up with him he would begin firing and eventually escape. After a time he went up into the Porcupine Hills north of the North Peigan Reserve. There he, and his wives, managed to hide out evading the police and stealing horses and supplies from the Peigans. His wives finally managed to escape and make their way back to the Blood Reserve.

It was shortly after this that some Peigan scouts (for the N.W.M. Police) tracked him to the area of Pincher Creek, Alberta. The horses they were riding were tired out so they sent one of their men to the police horse farm in Pincher Creek, It was Sergeant Wilde who came out on a fresh horse to give chase.

Ekistanopataki was a young girl when she visited her brother in the Fort Macleod jail. In the next cell was Charcoal, and he told them the course of events.

"When they were chasing me I was not trying to get away very hard. I was feeling very sad since my wives left me and was thinking of giving up. So I just kept riding along at a regular pace. Pretty soon that mountie *[Wilde, ed.]* caught up to me and began yelling at me; but I just kept riding. Then he began to whip me across my back with his quirt. I got mad right away and leaned over my horse away from his and shot him with my rifle I had stuck in my belt. I was so mad I stopped and shot him again through the head after he fell off his horse. Then I took his guns and rode away." *(Ekistanopataki, North Peigan-Blackfoot to the author, field notes; 1977.)*

Charcoal was eventually captured by his brother and hung at Fort Macleod, Alberta 1897.

Charcoal, Blood Indian who killed Sgt. Wilde, on the way to the gallows. A hat covers his handcuffs, and his face is painted with the Medicine Pipe design [more than likely one of the Medicine Pipe owners came and painted him for a final blessing]. 1896, unknown photographer, Glenbow Archives

SOUTH PEIGAN

ELK HORN: Four Bears dies.

BLOOD

WHITE BULL: No Sun Lodge. In March 16th Charcoal was hung at Macleod. Indians held their sports outside the Sun dance camps.

PERCY CREIGHTON: No Sun Lodge. Sports took place at Bull Shield Flat. There was a bucking contest. Swimming contest won by Tough Bread. Squaw race won by Mrs. Okeefe. Charcoal killed Medicine Pipe Stem & Sergeant Wilde, a policeman.

NORTH BLACKFEET

RUNNING RABBIT: (Charcoal killed Blood Indian and policeman)

MANY GUNS:
(1) A'atsistauyietsiwa = Rabbit Carrier – (chief) died
(2) Summer: Natsikapo matskimawa = Driving a Double Herd. Now Mrs. Weasel Calf put up Sundance.

"A meeting has been called at the Agency (Blackfeet, ed.) for the Chiefs with Mr. Rogers (Agent, ed.). He tries to stop the Sun Dance, 'by order of the Government.' Bitter speeches by the Chiefs. They definitely refuse. The Okan will proceed." (Doucet; Siksika; 39)

MANY GUNS .68: Double Chasing and Home Ward Gun Woman

MANY GUNS .69: Double Chasing and Many Big Swans and Charcoal

LITTLE CHIEF: Rev father Riou in Aug. came from france here on the Blackfoot Reserve

1897

NORTH PEIGAN

 BULL PLUME #1: When Treaty was paid in winter.

 BULL PLUME #2: When Treaty was paid in winter.

 BULL PLUME #2 B: *While next to the winter treaty payment entry this may be an image of a student running away from the school building (which occurred in 1898).*

 OLD AGENCY: *Treaty paid in winter*

Treaty payments, which are five dollars per year, are usually paid in the summer or fall.

SOUTH PEIGAN

ELK HORN: Gets Paint dies.

BLOOD

WHITE BULL: No Sun Lodge. Buffalo Woman Society exchange to Mrs. Red Crow or Singing Before Woman. She took over the pole. *[This is the Women's Buffalo Society, or Motokiks, and she took the leaders position. ed.]* The R.C. School was start to build at near Standoff at Belly river side. *[This is the roman catholic School started by Father Level. ed.]*

PERCY CREIGHTON: No Lodge. On March 16th, Charcoal was hanged at Macleod. During the summer there were sports in the camps.

NORTH BLACKFEET

RUNNING RABBIT: (Mrs. Peter White Pup born. Charcoal hung)

RUNNING RABBIT 2: Charcoal hung 16th of March

MANY GUNS: Nataio = Lynx
Mrs. Pitonista – put up Sundance

MANY GUNS .69: Lynx. The first time the Sun Dance was held up on the hill. Calf Robe. *[Calf Robe was one of the original signers of Treaty Seven for the Siksika-Blackfoot and an accomplished warrior of the old days. This is probably when Calf Robe died according to Many Guns.]*

LITTLE CHIEF: Rev father Riow was sent the Bloods to in charge of the Residential school

1898

NORTH PEIGAN

BULL PLUME #1: The year children were killed Victoria House.

BULL PLUME #2: When children were killed in the snow slide at Victoria House.

Victoria House was a boarding school, built in 1897, at the edge of the North Peigan Reserve. Reverend Haynes was the administrator. Both symbols show a snow slide.

Victoria House, boarding school on the North Peigan Reserve. 1892, R.N. Wilson photo, Glenbow Archives

BULL PLUME #2 B: *A bird with "v" shapes under it over a tipi would indicate the transfer of a painted bird tipi design. Possibly the transfer of the Crow Lodge.*

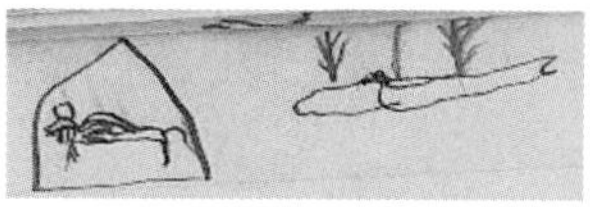

OLD AGENCY: *These two images, on the same page, could well show the opening of ceded land [Act of 1896] to White prospectors searching for gold in the area of now Glacier Park.*

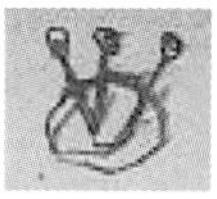 

On two separate pages we have an image of people in a circle [the children dying ?] and a buffalo Sun Dance, or Buffalo put up a Sun Dance.

SOUTH PEIGAN

ELK HORN: Black Living Over Tail dies.

BLOOD

WHITE BULL: No Sun Lodge. The Horn Society exchange. Low Horn was killed by an upset wagon in sun dance coulee. Late in fall Three Persons died.

PERCY CREIGHTON: No Sun Lodge. Mrs. Red Crow (Singing Before Woman) bought the pole of the Moh-toh-kes; R. C. (Roman Catholic) mission built on the reserve near Stand Off.

NORTH BLACKFEET

MANY GUNS: Paiosepiyi = Charging Towards.
Mrs. Maitsoitsikui (Crowshoe) put up Sundance

MANY GUNS .68: Attacking Back

MANY GUNS .69: Spying Back

LITTLE CHIEF: Residential school was finished it was build at Standoff Alberta

1899

NORTH PEIGAN

 BULL PLUME #1: Queen Victoria died.

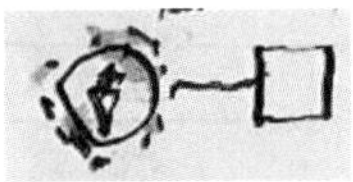 BULL PLUME #2: Queen Victoria died.

 BULL PLUME #2 B: *Shows a funeral wagon with a dead person next to it, which would stand for the Queen's death.*

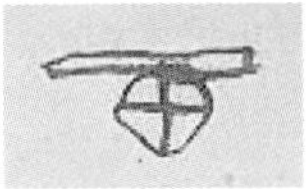 OLD AGENCY: *Cannon [?] Queen Victoria died [?]*

[This actually occurred January 21, 1901, ed.]

 *The next image is a bit of a puzzle. An eagle with a chief's medal around its neck would seem to indicate a chief. But the only reference to a chief anywhere close in dates would be the death of Crow Eagle in 1902 and that would put the image out of sequence.*

SOUTH PEIGAN

ELK HORN: Old Kicking Woman dies.

BLOOD

WHITE BULL: Mrs. Eagle Child or Yellow Buffalo Stone Woman put up Sun Lodge by force.

"As the summer of 1900 approached, it was obvious that there would be another major confrontation. The Bloods had not held a real Sun Dance for six years, but during the winter, Yellow Buffalo Stone Woman, wife of Eagle Child, had promised to sponsor one. Her husband had been ill for several weeks and the vow to the sun had been made in the

hopes he would be restored to health." When the police agreed to Red Crow, the head chief, they would not stop it, the Bloods were elated, and Agent Wilson frantically tried to intervene. "He called for the sergeant of the local Mounted Police detachment to force the Indians to abandon the big camp and to go home, but the ploy was unsuccessful. Instead the Mounted Police scout scoured the reserve, rousing Indians from their beds and hauling them in from their fields, ordering them to gather at the camp. It was a banner year which went down in the winter counts as the time when "Yellow Buffalo Stone woman put up the Sun Dance by force".[Dempsey, 1980 , 212 & 213]

PERCY CREIGHTON: No Sun Lodge. Horn Society exchanged. Low Horn killed in an upset wagon in the cooly [*coulee, ed.]*. Three people died in the fall at the Hay Camp. *[Low Horn died in June 1899. Dempsey, 1994]*

NORTH BLACKFEET

RUNNING RABBIT: Hauled lumber for school. Francis Black born.

MANY GUNS:

(1) Kamosaki = Stealing Woman. Mrs. Nose-cutter Aka kanitoki put up Sundance along with.

(2) Pitaki = Eagle Woman, alias Mrs. Red Leggings Mikutsisuyika (not the Red Leggings who died in 1937)

Crowfoot school worked on.

MANY GUNS .68: Stealing Woman and Eagle Woman and Bee Bumpy Hill.

MANY GUNS .69: Stealing Woman and Eagle Woman and Spring Woman and Lynx Shields

LITTLE CHIEF: father Riou came back to Blackfoot Crossing to take charge of the building of the Crowfoot school it was build a mile west of Blackfoot Crossing

CHAPTER 10

SMALL VICTORIES

At the mercy of the governments for their very subsistence the government agents and resident missionaries now started a campaign to eliminate Blackfoot culture. The Blackfoot resisted, and continued to resist until these unjust rules were changed. As they became more knowledgeable about Euro-laws and process they began to hire non-Native lawyers to plead their cases. Elders tell of having their ceremonies out on the far reaches of the reserves, away from the eyes of the agents. Others, including many of the traditional chiefs, simply openly defied the government rules. In other cases some agents simply chose to ignore what was occurring.

1900

NORTH PEIGAN

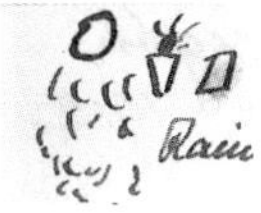

BULL PLUME #1: Rained in winter.

BULL PLUME #2: Rained in winter.

BULL PLUME #2 B: *No pictograph.*

OLD AGENCY: *Rained in winter.*

SOUTH PEIGAN

ELK HORN: Lance Chief dies.

BLOOD

WHITE BULL:Sun dance camps, the Horns Societies took the medicine tongue round inside the camps. Many Killer, she took over the tongue. She make the Sun Lodge and late in fall Chief Red Crow died in age of seventy on Blood Reserve.

Agent Wilson had been successful in preventing the Sun Dance for the last five years with his order to cut the tongues issued to the Bloods. However, the Blood Mounted Police scouts received their rations directly from the Mounted Police and made arrangements to take their rations in whole tongues, which were then used in the Sun Dance ceremony. (Dempsey; "Red Crow";213-214)

NORTH BLACKFEET

MANY GUNS:
(1) Omaxkaki = Big Woman. (Mrs. Big Old Gran-omaxkiapi) (Put up Sundance, ed.)
(2) Ksisikini = Sharp Feet (Mrs. Keg –Aswyin) (Put up Sundance, ed.)
(3) Napinawa = Old Man Chief, i.e. Mr. Markle, arrived as Agent.

MANY GUNS .68: Big Woman and Eagle Woman and White Man Chief and Buffalo Head and Stem Calf.

MANY GUNS .69: Big Woman and Sharp Teeth

LITTLE CHIEF: The Crowfoot school was finished in the fall it was open I Joe Little Chief and my sister was the first ones to go there to school

1901

NORTH PEIGAN

BULL PLUME #1: Visit of Duke of York. Later to become King George V.

BULL PLUME #2: When the Duke of York visited Calgary.

BULL PLUME #2 B: *Fence around cattle with pictograph of eagle above it would be the fencing of the reserve. Crow Eagle and the land surrender.*

OLD AGENCY: *The next three pages also have images that are unrelated to the following dates…*

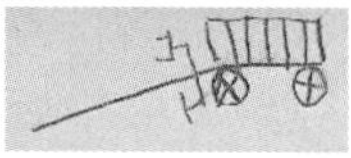
1. Horse drawn wagon.

2. Flag on top of a government building [signified by the cross at the top left corner] of the building.

3. Flag with many short lines running through it. [This would signify the government and deaths. It may well represent the Boer War which Bull Plume recorded in separate pages in his other winter counts.]

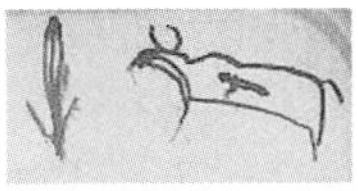

4. Bull Plume's name glyph.

SOUTH PEIGAN

ELK HORN: Fat Buffalo Horse dies. *[Fast Buffalo Horse?]*

BLOOD

WHITE BULL: Sun Lodge was put up by Stealing at the Door Woman or Mrs. Crane Bear. King George visit Calgary. Chiefs went meet him, also Rock Me to Sleep.

NORTH BLACKFEET

RUNNING RABBIT: King George V visited Calgary

MANY GUNS:
(1) Matominiskim = First Buffalo Storie (First Buffalo Stone, ed.), alias Mrs. Apastokis – ermine-skin or Sisimos = Cutter. (two names is bad). (Put up Sundance, ed.)
(2) Spistsomoki = Tall Hat = King George, then Duke of York, arrived with a bear-skin shakes hat in Calgary.

MANY GUNS .68: First Buffalo Stone and High Hat and the people that all burned to death.

LITTLE CHIEF 2: King George V visited Canada he came to Calgary in the fall a big Prairie fire around little Bow a lot of cattle was burn mostly the Blackfeet went and butchered the cattle

During the world tour of the Their Royal Highnesses The Duke and Duchess of Cornwall and York [later to become their Majesties King George V and Queen Mary] undertaken

after the accession of King Edward VII, Canada was visited in 1901. September 28,1901 at Calgary, Alberta nearly two thousand Blackfeet, Peigan, Blood, Stoney, Sarcee, and Cree gathered at Shaganappi Point two miles west of the city.

"The time this picture was taken was the last time we nearly had a war. It was in 1901, and I was a student at the Calgary Industrial School. They told the People, 'Your chief mother [the Queen of England] is sending someone over to meet with you, the Duke of Cornwell is coming.' All the tribes moved camp to Calgary – there were the Blackfoot, Sarcee, and Stoney.

Dressed for war. 1901, unknown photographer, Glenbow Archives

The place where they held the meeting was west of Calgary. There's a big hill there, and the camps were put up right at the bottom, next to the CPR [Canadian Pacific Railroad] tracks. I saw the Duke – we called him Spitz-Omachakan [High Hat]. He didn't go around the camps. He just sat at a special table in the center – a table with fancy coverings. He didn't even sleep out at the camps. I guess he stayed in the Mounted Police barracks, in town. At that time Calgary was quite a town – a lot of shops, though not very many houses. The Mounted Police had big, long houses for their barracks. And they had jails – one for men and one for women. The people in town treated the Indians pretty good in those days.

The first day of the meeting all the chiefs sat with the Prince and the other government officials. The chiefs wanted to know about the Treaty – they said, 'We gave up our lands and we quit fighting, but we never got all the things and the help you promised.' One Blackfoot chief, White-Pup, he stood right in front of the Duke and pointed at him and shouted loud; 'You! When will your promises come true?' The Duke just said, 'It's all coming, wait.' Then White-Pup sat down, but pretty soon he jumped up again, and he said, 'We're safe!' That's his last word, and I don't know what he meant by that. But the meeting broke up.

The second day everyone was really worked up. There was pretty near a big excitement. Lots of people talking about a fight – war. I saw the younger men all wearing paint, carrying Medicines and weapons, riding war horses – all dressed up for a fight, just like this fellow in the picture. You see he's got his rifle, and a Medicine bandoleer over his shoulder, hanging way down. His face is painted and he's got his hair tied up, ready to go. His horse has a war mask – that's Medicine too. And his tail is tied short, for battle. See all the riders on the hillside.

All the students from schools were staying by the train tracks, but when it looked like trouble, our relatives came and got us. My brother, Meki-Api, took me back to his own tipi with his wife. My mother was a widow, by then, and she was staying with them. There was lots of excitement – the men were all nearly naked, and they were shooting off their rifles and pistols.

Finally the Mounted Police came with a lot of meat and flour and other grub, and the people settled down. Pretty soon they started dancing – all kinds of dances and games. They did the Grass Dance and the Horse Dance. The Societies worked hard to keep control. After that day they came and took us students back to school." *[Ben Calf Robe, Siksika-Blackfoot, Calf Robe & Hungry Wolf, SIKSIKA, 80, 1979]*

Blackfeet women dressed for the Kaispa Society dance [Grass Dance] at Shaganappi Point, Calgary, Alberta 1901. Unknown photographer, Glenbow Archives.

1902

NORTH PEIGAN

 BULL PLUME #1: When "Crow Eagle" was frozen to death.

 BULL PLUME #2: When "Crow Eagle" was frozen to death.

BULL PLUME #2 B: *No pictograph.*

"Crow Eagle, son of the first chief Crow Eagle, was chief at the time. He was considered a 'easily influenced' man by some of the people; this plus the circumstances in his appointment as chief led to hard feelings toward him. He was made chief by the agent in charge at the time through a bit of trickery. The agent realized that the majority of old people still considered writing something of a supernatural occurrence. When it came time to appoint a new chief the natural successor (Crow Eagle) was not to the people's liking. But the agent preferred Crow Eagle since he felt he could be controlled. He then called the leaders together and said he would pick a slip of paper from a hat and the name of the new chief would be written on it. After blindfolding himself, he picked a blank slip of paper from the hat and wrote Crow Eagle's name on it. The people accepted the demonstration as an indication as to who should be chief." *[Tom Yellowhorn, author's field notes, 1975]*

Crow Eagle was also a main force behind one of the major land surrenders involving the reserve. He believed they needed the money to improve the situation on the reserve. It was this event that led to his death. Crow Eagle, Big Face Chief, and Big Swan were returning from Fort Macleod and were drinking along the way. An argument started over the land surrender and Crow Eagle was beaten up by Big Face Chief and Big Swan and left by the side of the road where he froze to death. Big Swan and Big Face Chief spent time in the Federal Penitentiary at Regina as a result.

Tom Yellowhorn gave another version of Crow Eagle and the land surrender north of the reserve.

Crow Eagle, North Peigan Chief, 1895, unknown photographer, Glenbow Archives

Big Face Chief, North Peigan, ca. 1920's , Associated Service News Material, Glenbow Archives

"One day our Indian Agent told Chief Crow Eagle to put his signature on a piece of paper as his consent was needed to commence with a fence around the reserve. The chief would not sign, stating that the people knew their country and did not need a fence to know its situation. 'The government says you have to fence it.' Crow eagle said, 'No, I know the area of my land, I do not need to fence it.' At the time the chief was about to leave for Montana. He said he was taking his son along on the journey. The boy was of school age. The agent said, No, you will not take your son. He will stay and you will go alone.' The chief was foolish and insisted on taking his son. The agent said, 'Sign these papers, then you can go with your son.' So the chief then foolishly signed the papers consenting to the fencing of the reserve in exchange for the privilege of having his son accompany him,

"The people were all surprised to know for the first time how little the reserve really was according to the fence. Immediately after the fence was up, white settlers began moving in right next to the fence around the reserve. The area that the Indian people had always known to be theirs was just suddenly not theirs any more." *[Tom Yellowhorn, Interview, 1973]*

SOUTH PEIGAN

ELK HORN: Bites, killed in a runaway.

BLOOD

WHITE BULL: Sun Lodge was put up by Mrs. Black Plume or Long Time Rifle Woman. There were two floods that spring, one in May and the other one in June.

NORTH BLACKFEET

RUNNING RABBIT: Never Use Belt, killed by Thunder, and Crow Shoes made Sundance.

MANY GUNS: Not a extra symbol *(?, ed.)* Paiyosepi = Mrs. Crowshoe put up another Sundance (mother of A Young Man)
(2) Koteiyipsi = Never Having a Belt. This man was struck by lightning and killed. Husband of Mrs. Duck Chief. The tipi was struck. It was a painted tipi, but not one of the lightning ones.

MANY GUNS .68: Looking Together and Wearing No Belt

MANY GUNS .69: Spying Back and (Lacing Woman) and Wearing No Belt

LITTLE CHIEF 2: Never Use A Belt got hit by lightning Crow Shoe's wife made the Sun Dance

1903

NORTH PEIGAN

BULL PLUME #1: Turtle Mountain slide.

BULL PLUME #2: Turtle Mountain fell.

BULL PLUME #2 B: *No pictograph.*

At 4:40 in the morning on April 29, 1903, 90 million tons of rock wiped out the town of Frank, Alberta. The slide swept over one mile of the valley killing 70 people and burying a mine and railway. It occurred in ten seconds.

Ekistanopataki added the following, "We were at the old agency then. *(Northeast of the present Brocket, Alberta, across the Old Man River. Approximately 30 miles from Turtle Mountain, ed.)* We had started to fix breakfast when everything started shaking. We thought it was an earthquake. Later on several people looked over to the mountains and saw the bare rock face. Then we knew what happened." *[Ekistanopataki, North Peigan-Blackfoot, author's field notes, 1977]*

Ekistanopataki [Mrs. Buffalo], North Peigan-Blackfoot, 1976, Richard Naskali photo, from Mrs. Buffalo, author's collection

SOUTH PEIGAN

ELK HORN: Running Rabbit dies. *[This is the Blood/Peigan chief and not the one from Siksika, North Blackfeet. Ed.]*

BLOOD

WHITE BULL: Sun Lodge was put up by Mrs. Eagle Plume or Holy Howling.

NORTH BLACKFEET

RUNNING RABBIT: Three White Mans drain. *(drowned, ed.)*

MANY GUNS:
(1) Kukao put up Sundance. This is a pet name meaning ___. Aistomotstakiwa = real name = Short Victory Woman. She was Mrs. Pitakatsis = Eagle-? (Skunk now has this name on the books.) Atsis = is an old word, meaning unknown.
(2) Namitapikuan = East Man *[Possibly the shortened version of "Namiotsinaikuan" Arapaho Man, ed.]*, alias White Pup. Apsuisksi died – head chief of North camp.

MANY GUNS .68 & .69: The Corner and Eastern Person

LITTLE CHIEF 2: One police man and two white man got drown west of Eagle Rib's flat

1904

NORTH PEIGAN

BULL PLUME #1: When Agent Wilson left.

BULL PLUME #2: When Agent Wilson left.

BULL PLUME #2 B: *No pictograph.*

Agent Robert Wilson [Long Nosed Crow] was replaced by J. H. Gooderham [1904].

"Mr. Gooderham, frustrated at not being able to stop the dances, wrote to the Department asking them to stop at least the Sun Dance which was the occasion for so many disorders. His letter achieved nothing. The Agent was not supported in his efforts; other agents across the country were turning a blind eye to the problem, and the Department did not want to interfere...

The Peigans are preparing for their Sun Dance. One of our recent converts, Bad Eagle's wife, is the one who is supposed to preside over the Okan. She is the one who made the vow to celebrate it this year. Bishop Legal tried to talk her out of it, but she remained

firm in her project. She believed that she was held to her vow. This is not the first time that some of our Catholics have presided over this Sun feast, which is somewhat the center of all Blackfoot beliefs." (Doucet; Peigan; 87)

North Peigan-Blackfoot Sun Dance lodge in 1904, in defiance of government laws, Agent Gooderham and Father Doucet. Clark Wissler photo, Glenbow Archives

South Peigan warrior societies getting ready to dance inside the Sun Dance lodge. McClintock photo, Beinecke Archives, Yale University.

Bull Plume, far right, officiating at the South Peigan-Blackfoot Okan [Sun Dance] next to Red Plume and his wife who vowed the ceremony, McClintock photo, Beinecke Archives

A recorded court case[December 1903] relating to giveaways occurred following the arrest of two North Peigan men, Commodore [Tail Feathers Chief, ed.] and Joe Smith. Smith was accused of giving away twelve horses, a blanket, and other articles during a ceremony...The prisoners were found guilty but released with a suspended sentence with a warning not to have any giveaway dances in the future. [Pettipas, 1994; 121]

SOUTH PEIGAN

ELK HORN: White Calf dies. *(1903, ed.)*

White Calf was the recognized chief of South Peigans in Montana. He died in Washington, D.C. fighting for the rights of his people.

BLOOD

WHITE BULL: Sun Lodge was put up by Capture Rifle Woman near river. Mexican longhorn cattle were lease on Blood Reserve for ten years. Mr. Just Left, head of Horn Societies, he exchange to Weasel Fat. Call them young Horn Societies.

PERCY CREIGHTON: Sun Lodge put up by Mrs. Wolf Child - thrice cul ____ Gordon Ironside. In fall Bloods were in for horse stealing High Crown Hat

NORTH BLACKFEET

RUNNING RABBIT: Womans hand game up north.

MANY GUNS:

(1) Matsiomotsta = Nice Victory. Put up Sundance. She was Mrs. Sepistuisisksi = (Owl With a Lot of Wool Hair) alias Little Raw-Eater; They were the Father and Mother of Charlie Raw-Eater. Her husband was son of Fat Horse = (Old Raw Eater)

(2) Itaiokyotsp = We were closed i.e. quarantined because of rash disease. And old school at Cluny also was quarantined.

(3) Mikiu = Red Body, Duck Chief's brother died. (i.e. son of old Running Rabbit).

1905

NORTH PEIGAN

BULL PLUME #1: Many Rainbows.

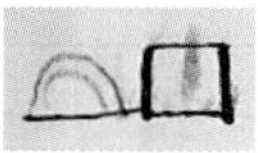

BULL PLUME #2: Many Rainbows.

BULL PLUME 2 B: *A person hangs themselves.*

BLOOD

WHITE BULL: Sun Lodge was put by Mrs. Big Air Top or Cutting Woman.

PERCY CREIGHTON: Sun Lodge put up by Mrs. Heavy Shield (Many Kills) Holy tongue was carried around the camps by Weasel Fat, Eagle Ribs, Running Crane & Little Shields.

NORTH BLACKFEET

RUNNING RABBIT: Henry Calf Robe died up north and Slow Coming Over The Hill made Sundance. All Braves gave out dancing outfits and Prairie Chicken too. *(These are the All-Brave Dogs and Prairie Chicken Societies. They transferred to new members this year. ed.)*

MANY GUNS: Natokiniki = Killing Two put the Sundance up. She was Mrs. Itspiotamiso, Coming Over The Hill, the same one mentioned in 1854! She (or maybe he) died a hundred years of age!)

Story of Itspio and the Believers. He claimed he saved Jesus on a war party, who was crying for help.

MANY GUNS .69 Two Killer and Owl Child and we did a transferal.

1906

NORTH PEIGAN

BULL PLUME #1: Many horses died.

BULL PLUME #2: Many horses died.

BULL PLUME #2 B: *A flag with five lines under would signify treaty payment by the government.*

"The winter of 1906-1907 has so far been a very rigorous one. Storms. Frequent blizzards. Deep snow. Ranchers on every side are reporting huge losses of cattle. I. E. Mandell & Co. The Peigans also are reporting terrible losses. They previously had over 3000 head of cattle on the reserve. A little more than 900 survived." [Doucet; Peigan; 91]

BLOOD

WHITE BULL: Sun Lodge was put by Capture Rifle Woman near the River, or Mrs. Crow Ventral.

(End White Bull winter count)

PERCY CREIGHTON: Sun Lodge put up by Mrs. First Charger (Yellow Snake Woman). Balloon at Macleod. Sports. Old Sitting Bull died.

NORTH BLACKFEET

RUNNING RABBIT: Red Caps visited Blackfoot, deep snow, lots of cattle died, Rose Cutter *(Nose Cutter ?, ed.)* made Sundance and Prairie Chicken too. Braves gave out their dancing outfits. [*This is the transfer of the Braves Society. ed.]*

MANY GUNS:

(1) Kamosaki = Stealing Woman again put up Sundance (cf. 1899)
(2) Mutsiks = Brave Dogs *[Mutsiks = Braves Society, ed.]* got their society, i.e. bought in (including Many Guns).
(3) Imaxsisksomokiwa = Red Cap. He came to visit the Reserve. He was Prince Arthur, son of Duke of Connaught.
(4) Sispistokus = Owl Child, husband of old Mrs. Spotted Eagle, brother of Koteiyipsi who was killed 1902. alias Matsikstonima (Scalp Lock), *(died?...J.H.)*

MANY GUNS .68: Stealing Woman and Wearing A Big Hat.

MANY GUNS .69: Stealing Woman and Spear Chief and Pinto Woman

LITTLE CHIEF 2: Red Cap came to Gleichen deep snow lot of cattle died that almost ended the Indians ways of living

1907

NORTH PEIGAN

BULL PLUME #1: Fire at Macleod.

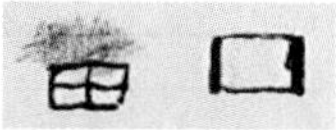

BULL PLUME #2: Fire at Macleod.
[This occurred in 1906, ed.]

BULL PLUME #2 B: *A flag with five lines under would signify treaty payment by the government.*

BLOOD

PERCY CREIGHTON: No Lodge. Crow Flying Against The Wind died. Tail Feathers shot himself. Thunder Chief died. Many Bloods went to the Gros Ventre. Bad September. Storm. New Robe murder case. Blood become farmers.

NORTH BLACKFEET

RUNNING RABBIT: Short Woman died.

MANY GUNS: Three women put up Sundance.

(1) Aistenixki = Coming Singing. (Mrs. Little Old Man – Puksapi)
(2) Matominiskim (see before 1901) *[First Buffalo Stone, ed.]*
(3) Misomiksiskstaki = Long Time Beaver Woman. Mrs. Tsinakuan A Gros Ventre, (daughter of Paiosepi who put up two Sundances).
(4) Many Guns sister died.

MANY GUNS .68: Coming Singer and Long Time Beaver and First Buffalo Stone.

MANY GUNS .69: Coming Singer and First Buffalo Robe and Running Eagle

While the U.S. and Canadian governments tried their best to put a stop to traditional ceremonies, dances and gatherings local non-Native communities began to change things in the other direction. Local agricultural societies, rodeos and western exhibitions began to encourage Indian cultural exhibitions and parades which attracted visitors and monies to their events. Indian agents threatened to cut off rations to those Natives attending. The agricultural societies, in turn, offered not only to pay for transportation expenses, and provide food rations, but also to award money for each traditional dressed rider and tipi set up. The following postcards from Fort Macleod show the participants.

"Blackfoot Indian Braves", 1907, A.Y. & Co. Lethbridge, Alberta, author's collection

"Blood Squaws in War Dress", 1907, A.Y. & Co. Lethbridge, Alberta, author's collection

"Old Time Piegan Squaw with Travois and Papoose"1907, A.Y. & Co. Lethbridge, Alberta, author's collection,

"Chief Running Wolf and Party of Blackfoot Braves", 1907, A.Y. & Co. Lethbridge, Alberta, author's collection

"Blackfoot Indians Returning to Camp After the Parade, Valier, Mont.", Unknown photographer

1908

NORTH PEIGAN

 BULL PLUME #1: Wreck on C.P.R. Brocket

 BULL PLUME #2: Wreck on C.P.R. near Brocket.

 BULL PLUME #2 B: *A flag with five lines under would signify treaty payment by the government.*

A Canadian Pacific Railway train derailed just west of the reserve town site. All the perishable goods were given out to the reserve residents. (John Yellowhorn gives the date as 1908. ed. interview 1975)

BLOOD

PERCY CREIGHTON: Sun Lodge put up by Mrs. Eagle Child (Yellow Stone Woman) (Yellow Buffalo Stone Woman, ed.) Big flood during camp gathering. Many Blackfeet here. New farms at Farm 3.

NORTH BLACKFEET

RUNNING RABBIT: Began Crow dancing, *[this was the Kaispa Society social dancing, ed.]* and took Medicine Pipe, Red Legging, Bear Robe, Turn Up Nose, Crow Collar and made Sundance.

MANY GUNS:

(1) Kukao again (see 1903) (Short Victory Woman put up Sundance, ed.)
(2) Pitakatsis = her husband, (i.e. vower's ? _____ jr.) died after Sundance.
(3) Pitomaxkan = Running Eagle died

MANY GUNS .68: The Corner and Eagle Curve Walk and Running Eagle

1909

NORTH PEIGAN

BULL PLUME #1: All went to the Kootenay Indian Reserve on their first visit.

BULL PLUME #2: All went to Kootenay Reserve to visit.

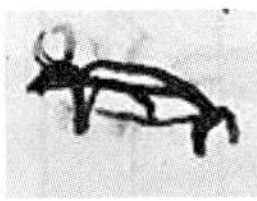

BULL PLUME #2 B: *A cow with red lines symbolizes cattle dying.*

As part of the agreement to allow the railroad to pass through Reserve lands tribal members were given passes to ride the trains free of charge. A few took advantage of this to visit other tribes.

"Around Christmas time people from here *[Peigan Reserve, ed.]* would travel to the Kootenay Reserve over at Cranbrook *[British Columbia, ed.]* to visit them. A lot of Peigans went over there. Some even married there. They would have five houses set up for their ceremonies. Each one of their different reserves had a house to themselves; the ones from Bonners Ferry, Tobacco Plains, Elmo *[Montana, ed.]* and their own group. Then they'd have one for just the visitors from Piikuni *[Peigan Reserve, ed.]*. They just turned over the whole house to us. Each night we were there they'd have a big feed at one of the houses and we'd go there. I don't know much about their ways, but we'd go, and before we ate they'd stand around the table and sort of dance in place singing their songs. Then everybody would sit down and eat. They'd give out lots of gifts to the visitors. We all had a good time. When they came over for Indian Days we'd treat them good too." *[Alphonse Little Moustache, author's notes, 2010]*

BLOOD

PERCY CREIGHTON: No Lodge. Horn Society sold out. Dancing hall built. Big Fair at Lethbridge. Little Shield killed.

NORTH BLACKFEET

RUNNING RABBIT: Wolf Shoe *[Wolf Moccasin, ed.]*, died. Carry Kettle, came and no Sundance *[This could possibly refer to the Carry The Kettle Assiniboine coming to the Blackfoot Reserve. They are the ones who transferred the Kaispa Society dancing to the Blackfoot.]*

MANY GUNS:

(1) Matokao = no Sundance at all; because no vower. No one picked up the tongues of the Horns Society.
(2) $4.00 Irrigation ditch built therefore everyone got $4.25.
(3) Makuyisikiu = Wolf Shoe died. (a minor chief)

MANY GUNS .68: Nothing happened. Calf Flat Head

MANY GUNS .69: No Sun Dance Lodge. (Tom) Flat Headed Calf

LITTLE CHIEF 2: White Head Chief (A-po-pe-na) went to Sask. To visit a Sioux Indian and when he got there he saw mostly all the Indians were farming so when he came back he went to see the Agent told him what he saw all those Indians farming down there why should not the Blackfeet be farming. Well he also told the Chief Yellow Horse (O-ta-ko-me-ta-se) so the Agent told Yellow Horse how can the Blackfeet go into farming so they talk about it finely it was decided to sell some of the Blackfeet land south of the Bow River about three miles wide and 36 miles long

1910

NORTH PEIGAN

BULL PLUME #1: Comet

BULL PLUME #2: Comet

BULL PLUME #2 B: *Circle camp of tipis with flag. Possibly the death of Brings Down the Sun.*

July, Running Wolf (Brings-Down-the-Sun) dies suddenly, "stricken by the heat". [Doucet letters to Morris]

BLOOD

PERCY CREIGHTON: Sun Lodge put up by Mrs. Coming Singer. Crop Ear Wolf fainted in his lodge. Star with tail in the west. Many Bloods went to Harlem. Chief Chasing Back, an Assiniboine, killed himself.

NORTH BLACKFEET

RUNNING RABBIT: (Running Rabbit made Sundance and people gave things one to another.) *[Under the Indian Act it was illegal to give gifts at any gathering at this time.]*

MANY GUNS:

(1) Epoxkski = Mrs. Running Rabbit (wife of the old chief) gave Sundance.

(2) Itxkutsiyopi = a lot of giving among each other. That same winter following, Running Rabbit died, husband of the vower.

MANY GUNS .68: The time we exchanged gifts and Shedding Face and Ambush Woman and Eagle Ribs.

MANY GUNS .69: Shedding Face and the time we exchanged gifts. And Ambush Woman.

LITTLE CHIEF 2: Mr. Markley talk it over with the Chiefs well Yellow Horse and Spring Chief also Sitting Eagle Calf Bull. Wolf Collar seemed to like to sell some land to go for farming. Oh there was a big fuss over all the rest of the Chiefs were against not selling any land you could hear some Indians talking bad to the ones that wanted to sell the land some almost fight over it but the ones that wanted to sell the land for the benefit of their tribes so when it was known that it might go into a fight so Mr. Markle put it off for next year so it was decided a vote would be on.

1911

NORTH PEIGAN

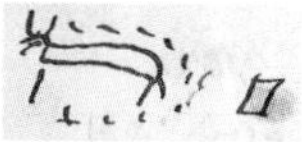 BULL PLUME #1: Many cattle died.

 BULL PLUME #2: Many cattle died.

 BULL PLUME #2 B: *Animal with tracks could be the coyotes that came to feast on the dead cattle.*

In 1973 Tom Yellowhorn, a son of the old chief Yellowhorn, was interviewed concerning cattle on the North Peigan Reserve. He was 70 years old at the time, and going from memory, he gave the date for this as "around 1906".

"In the fall of 1906, the cattle were dipped in hot water *[to kill insects, ed.]*, then it turned cold. As they started to head for the river bottom, they got stranded at the C.P.R. *[Canadian Pacific Railroad, ed.]* fence and could not get to the river bottom. As a result many perished. A man by the name of Emery La Grandeur was stockman then. He was hired to haul away the dead cattle that had died from exposure. The Indian Agent wanted no part of it. The Indians suffered the complete loss." *[Tom Yellowhorn interview, 1973]*

BLOOD

PERCY CREIGHTON: Sun Lodge; Mrs. No Chief & Mrs. Big Wolf. Known as the whiskey camp gathering. (Elbow Woman) died of poison rum. Much grain was threshed in the fall.

NORTH BLACKFEET

RUNNING RABBIT: Running Rabbit died 22nd of January. Morning Coming Over The Hill died no Sundance.

MANY GUNS:

(1) Motokopi = no Sundance. Many Guns took over the calendar.
(2) Apinakotamiso *(Tomorrow Coming Over The Hill, ed.)* one of the calendar owners died this very year.

MANY GUNS .69: Calf Sitting Down and that time there was no Sun Dance Lodge, and New House Woman. Coming Up The Hill At Dawn.

LITTLE CHIEF 2: At the old agency every Indian was up there to vote I just left school I Joe Little Chief I seen what was going on I thought there was going to be a big fight some Indians that did not want to sell the land were on horse back were riding among the Crowd singing war songs and with their whips in the air one old man his name is Bear Hat (A-ke-tis-na) he was on horse back with his whip high up on the air right in front of the table where they were voting was he told these Chiefs yes you want to sell our land just because you want to try get some where you are all very poor we will not sell the land after the votes were counted it was known that the votes were in favor of selling the land. So the same year the government sold the land for the Blackfeet it was decided the government would sell the land for the Blackfeet and that their would get a farm about 40 acres of plowed land and one team harness wagon these were to be pad for in five years time they also got a house a barn and also a ration 7 # (pounds) meat 3# (pounds) flour 1# (pound) tea once a month.

"The Band has surrendered part of the reserve. 120,000 acres. 65,000 of them sold for $1,250,000. The vote was 68 in favor, and 64 against... but half of the people didn't vote." (Doucet; 102)

1912

NORTH PEIGAN

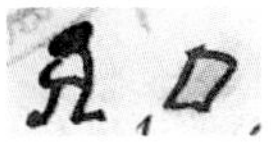

BULL PLUME #1: One person frozen to death.

BULL PLUME #2: One person frozen to death.

BULL PLUME #1: Visit of Duke Cannaught

BULL PLUME #2: Visit of Duke of York.
BULL PLUME #2 B: *End of second pictographs.*

The Duke of Cannaught [named Bear Hat by the Blackfoot] was the Governor-General of Canada at that time. He was also on hand to open the first Calgary Stampede in September, 1912.

The government had still been trying to stop dancing, as well as the Sun Dance with little success. As far back as 1896 there was concern their policy was failing due to an unexpected development – non-native sponsored stampedes, rodeos, fairs and agricultural exhibitions. "I might draw attention to one of the most serious [impediments] encountered in our efforts to secure the final abandonment of heathen rites and ceremonies by the Indians. I refer to the encouragement given to the Indians on reserves adjacent to towns and settlements by that element of the white population which is ever ready to assist in the creation or maintenance of anything which panders to an appetite for the sensational and novel and to whom the resultant effect on the actors therein is a matter of perfect indifference. So long as such 'shows' are patronized and supported by the gate-money of this class of whites, so long will the difficulty of securing a total abandonment of such continue." [Indian Commissioner Amedee E. Forget, Annual Report, 1896]

The visit of the Duke to the Calgary Stampede, complete with Blackfoot people in traditional dress during the parade, setting up traditional tipi camps and demonstrating their traditional dances was a perfect example of such "shows". "For reserve communities, such occasions continued to offer evidence that there was some degree of support for their indigenous practices – a form of support that was also an important source of capital. In addition to the material rewards, the opportunities to socialize and 'act as Indians' provided on these occasions encouraged many Indians to incorporate the fair and stampede circuit into their economic and ceremonial cycle." [Pettipas, 1994;141]

Governor-General of Canada,The Duke of Cannaught opening the first Calgary Stampede. 1912, Glenbow Archives
BLOOD

PERCY CREIGHTON: Sun Lodge; Mrs. Yellow Bull – Night Killer. At Calgary Stampede Tom Three Persons won the championship. There was spring threshing.

At the Calgary Stampede Tom Three Persons, of the Blood-Blackfoot, rode a notorious bucking horse named Cyclone, whose claim to fame was never having been ridden, throwing 129 men before Three Persons rode him to win. In those days the ride was not a timed event but the rider rode the horse to a standstill.

"The fact that Tom Three Persons, a Blood Indian won the belt and championship at the Calgary Stampede in 1912, has been responsible for the condition, that every boy on the Blood reserve between the ages of 17 and 23 wished to be a second Tom Three

Persons, and all they think about is saddles, chapps [sic], silver spurs, Race and bucking horses, etc., a full equipment of the above accoutrements makes him a hero in his own eyes, and in the eyes of the admiring young women on the reserve." (Agent W. Dilworth; To Assistant Deputy and Secretary, February, 1917)

This was not the role model of a hard working Christian farmer and rancher the Government was trying to instill in the Native population.

Tom Three Persons and admirer, 1912, W.J. Oliver photo, Calgary, Alberta, Glenbow Archives

Tom Three Persons riding "Slippery Bill"1919, W.J. Oliver photo, Calgary, Alberta, Glenbow Archives

NORTH BLACKFEET

RUNNING RABBIT: Jim Ham killed police man, start farm and build Indian houses.

MANY GUNS:
(1) Kukao again (cf. 1903, 1908)(Short Victory Woman put up Sundance, ed.)
(2) Maika = Mike Running Wolf, killed the Mountie.
(3) Apiman died. Put Up a Rough Shelter alias Red Squirrel. A bundle owner and always wore robes. Not a chief – ordinary man, but respectable.
(4) Crowfoot school moved to Cluny.

[Mike Running Wolf aka Jim Ham shot and killed a Mountie June1,1912. Dempsey, 2003]

MANY GUNS .69: The Corner and Wolf Shoe and Shorty and the time Shelter killed.

LITTLE CHIEF 2: The farms were plowed all 40 acres four room houses and two rooms build

1913

NORTH PEIGAN

BULL PLUME #1: New agent arrived

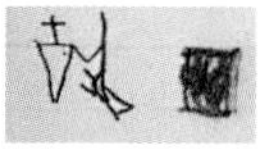

BULL PLUME #2: When Mr. Gunn was agent on the Reserve

From here on the journal for Bull Plume #1 is written in pencil. We know Haynes obtained the previous account from Bull Plume in 1912 so we can only assume that he continued the winter count on his own (or with Bull Plume's assistance until Bull Plume's death in 1920) from this date on. The drawings continue until the year of Bull Plume's death, so it may be possible he continued the drawings.

BLOOD

PERCY CREIGHTON: Sun Lodge put up by Mrs. Wolf Child with Chief Running Wolf on Feb. 24. Single Rider & his wife died of poison rum.

NORTH BLACKFEET

RUNNING RABBIT: Heavy Shield, Cutter, made Sundance, built new school at Cluny. (First Sundance made up Old Agency)
MANY GUNS:

(1) Niteniki = Only Killing. Mrs. Heavy Shield put up Sundance. She is his (Heavy Shield's first wife), i.e. he Heavy Shield now living. She is the sister of Joe Whitefat.
(2) Matominiskuii also put Sundance up
(3) Itauwaxkaopi = to enjoy oneself. (They (some) went to Winnipeg to a stampede).

A GROUP OF INDIANS AT THE "STAMPEDE" WINNIPEG 1913.

1913 Winnipeg Stampede, North Peigan Chief Yellowhorn on white horse. Unknown photographer

(4) Maistawastan (Crow Flag) died.
(5) Maisto opuka (Crow Child) was drowned in Bassano dam. Was on horseback and drunk, fell over cut bank.

MANY GUNS .68: Black Face Chief and First Buffalo Stone and Only Killer and Crow Flag. The time we went to play.

MANY GUNS .69: Only Killer and First Buffalo Stone and the time we went and compete at a fair. *[Winnipeg, ed.]*

LITTLE CHIEF 2: In the spring the farm were given out also the teams harness wagons and the government got Band Machinery the land was seeded by the ones that got the farms

Ever since the Blackfeet been farming and making progress ever since around after the 1940 some of them bought tractors some farm as much as over five hundred acres today 1956 some have all kinds of machinery even some have combines one fellow has to combines and that is P. Yellow Fly. So that is how the Blackfeet from 1913 and the big progress they made on farming to 1956.

1914

NORTH PEIGAN

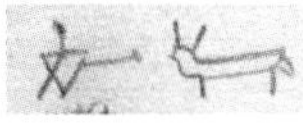

BULL PLUME #1: When 60 or more horses were stolen from the Peigan.

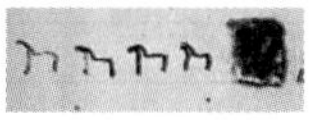

BULL PLUME #2: When 22 head of my horses were stolen from *[by]* Whiteman

BLOOD

PERCY CREIGHTON: Sun Lodge put up by Holy Feathers On Head. Hay contract at Belly River Camp & Ghost Home.(?, ed)

NORTH BLACKFEET

RUNNING RABBIT: Little Old Man, Yellow Horse, made Sundance. (The Crow Indians came to visit to Blackfoot Indians.)

MANY GUNS: Two women put up Sundance:
- (1) Aistomxkin = Coming Singing.
- (2) Natoki sisuyaki = Sharing Twice Woman. Mrs. Yellow Horse (the head chief there). Yellow Horse swam across the Bow River.
- (3) Sikaokas = Black Antelope died.

1915

NORTH PEIGAN

BULL PLUME #1: When Parliament Buildings at Ottawa were burned and big fire at Gleichen.

BULL PLUME #2: When bridge was Brocket down from a river. *[sic.]*

The Ottawa fire occurred in 1916.

BLOOD

PERCY CREIGHTON: Sun Lodge put up by Night Killer (Otter Woman). High Hats bought the Pigeon Society.

NORTH BLACKFEET

RUNNING RABBIT: Mrs. Big Snake, Spring Chief, made Sundance, took Braves, All Brave Dogs and Prairie Chicken. *(These Societies transferred again. ed.)*

MANY GUNS:

(1) Aisomyoki = (my mother) (Ambush Woman) present vower for 1938 *(Okan, ed.)*
(2) Matsiks = "Braves" including Many Guns gave away their society to the ones we have now (1938, ed.)
(3) Piksapi = Old Man Bird died; his wife now Mrs. One Gun *(1938, ed.)*

The government continued its efforts to suppress traditional dances and ceremonies among Indian people. Big Face Chief of the North Peigan-Blackfoot was charged and convicted by the Supreme Court of Alberta for making a presentation of two mares at a Blackfoot ceremony. ["The King versus Big Face Chief" December 1915; NAC, RG10, vol. 3,826, file 60,511-4, part 1]

1916

NORTH PEIGAN

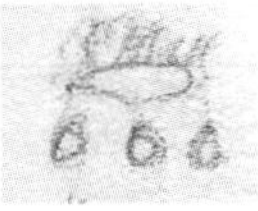

BULL PLUME #1: When Indians went to Omaha and Kootenays.

BULL PLUME #2: When Johnny E. *[English? ed.]* when for long trip to across the line.

This is the last entry for Bull Plume 2.

BLOOD

PERCY CREIGHTON: Sun Lodge; Mrs. First Charger. High Hats bought Crazy Dogs (Society, ed.). Tornado storm on July 1st. Many cases of measles.

NORTH BLACKFEET

RUNNING RABBIT: Wolf Leg made Sundance. (Sold outfit Crow Carrier.) *(The Crow Carrier Society transferred to new members. ed.)*

MANY GUNS:

(1) Iinimaki = Catching Woman Mrs. Wolf Leg, Makuiyokut, of Chicago (the village), (not Mrs. Jack Wolf Leg)

(2) Maistaxpa takiks= Crow Carriers bought in. This is Many Guns bunch. (see 1906, 1915)

1917

NORTH PEIGAN

BULL PLUME #1: When crops were a failure.

BLOOD

PERCY CREIGHTON: Sun Lodge by Mrs. Panther Bone. Sports & Fair at the Lower Agency Camp Gathering.

NORTH BLACKFEET

RUNNING RABBIT: Calf Collar, Rainy Chief made Sundance and took the Horns. *(They took over membership of the Horn Society. ed.)*

MANY GUNS:

(1) Aisomyaki and

(2) Kukao, put up Sundance again.

(3) Omaxksistsiksinekuan = Big Snake died (husband of the vower Aisomyaki) that fall.

1918

NORTH PEIGAN

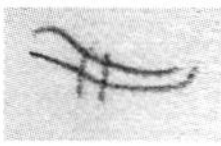

BULL PLUME #1: When Indian Agent Guin left, and new Agent I.H. Graham came. "Itu" and young "Mansae" drowned at old agency. *Pictograph of Agent Guin's Indian name [Na Ma]*

"Agent Gun has been accused of improper dealings at the Peigan Agency; he wanted to defend himself, but friends advised him to resign...which he did...Tom Graham, farm instructor for the Bloods, becomes the new Agent at Peigans." (Doucet;123)

BLOOD

PERCY CREIGHTON: Sun Lodge Mrs. Bull Plume. Two Indians by name of Bull Plume died at the same time. One was a Peigan. *[North Peigan Bull Plume died in 1920, ed.]* Flu epidemic. Great prod____, at least $6.00 per head.

NORTH BLACKFEET

RUNNING RABBIT: Yellow Horse made Sundance, and lease across the river ($6.00) and we registration.

MANY GUNS:
(1) Natokisisoyaki Again. Mrs. Yellow Horse (made Sundance, ed.)
(2) Namistoyi = Just Eating Two died that year
(3) Otsitoksikokupi = eclipse of sun. (June)

MANY GUNS .69: Two Cutter Woman and Only Two Eater and The Sun and Chief Moon and the eclipse of the sun.

1919

NORTH PEIGAN

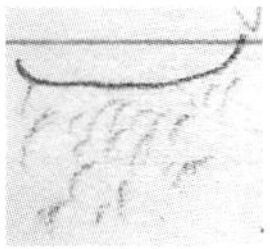

BULL PLUME #1: When it rained in winter January 24th and many rainbows. Mild winter

BLOOD

PERCY CREIGHTON: Sun Lodge; Mrs. Coming Singer. Hay was cut until Feb. 15th; hay dried up the following summer. A snow storm on Sept. 21st killed many stock. Snow & storms lasted 7 months.

NORTH BLACKFEET

RUNNING RABBIT: Weasel Calf made Sundance near Gleichen.

MANY GUNS:
(1) Natsikapomatspina = (Double Chaser, ed.) Mrs. Weasel Calf had it on prairie at
(2) saokyokan (in the open).

(4) Mikutsistamik = Red Bull alias Little Old Man, died.

1920

NORTH PEIGAN

BULL PLUME #1: "Bull Plume" died and "Big Swan", two minor treaty chiefs.

Big Swan. 1907, Edmund Morris photo, Provincial Archives of Manitoba, Winnipeg

BLOOD

PERCY CREIGHTON: Sun Lodge; Mrs. Hairy Bull. Chief Weasel Fat, Maxwell W.T., Young Pine & Goose Chief Gambler died. Farm 4 farmers bought horses (?, ed.). R.N.

Wilson went to Ottawa to represent the Bloods. Long Time pipe bought by Sorrel Horse *[Long Time Medicine Pipe, ed.]* Robbers held up train. Tom Basoff hanged Dec. 22.

NORTH BLACKFEET

RUNNING RABBIT: Calf Collar made Sundance, Stampede, Gleichen, was little Sundance.

MANY GUNS:
(1) Aisomyaki = put it up (Sundance, ed.)
(2) Iksimiawotan (Iron Shield) died
(3) Mr. Gooderham Sr. died
(4) Ispuxtsitaupi = Sitting High, a Catholic bishop died
(5) Ixkuksankin (Little Axe, a wealthy man) died

MANY GUNS .68: Ambush Woman and Crow Big Foot and Only Chief, and Owns Axe

MANY GUNS .69: Got Ahead and Stabbed and the place of many ghosts and Crow Big Foot and Only Chief. Last Flying Woman.

1921

NORTH PEIGAN

BULL PLUME #1: When Indians got their cattle to look after and they were taken away again.

From here on there are no drawings in BULL PLUME #1. Yearly notations in pencil from here to the end of Bull Plume #1 are believed to have been done by Reverend Canon Haynes.

BLOOD

PERCY CREIGHTON: No Lodge. Red Shirt bought the Horn Society. (Red Shirt Society, ed.) Vow by Mrs. Hairy Bull. Running Wolf died in a dispute at a dance by Heavy Shield & others.

NORTH BLACKFEET

RUNNING RABBIT: Yellow Horse died, Nose Cutter made Sundance, stampede at Sarcee, all hail out, and Hind Bull died.

MANY GUNS:

(1) Kamosaki = again put up Sundance

(2) Utxkuimyotasi, Yellow Horse, died

(3) Akoinikaisumi = Many Names alias Sakuistanaik, Hind Bull, died.

MANY GUNS .68 & .69: Stealing Woman and Buffalo Child and Many Names

CANADA

DEPARTMENT OF INDIAN AFFAIRS

CIRCULAR

OTTAWA, 15th December, 1921.

Sir,-

It is observed with alarm that the holding of dances by the Indians on their reserves is on the increase, and that these practices tend to disorganize the efforts which the Department is putting forth to make them self-supporting.

I have, therefore, to direct you to use your utmost endeavours to dissuade the Indians from excessive indulgence in the practice of dancing. You should suppress any dances which cause waste of time, interfere with the occupations of the Indians, unsettle them for serious work, injure their health or encourage them in sloth and idleness. You should also dissuade, and, if possible, prevent them from leaving their reserves for the purpose of attending fairs, exhibitions, etc., when their absence would result in their own farming and other interests being neglected. It is realized that reasonable amusement and recreation should be enjoyed by Indians, but they should not be allowed to dissipate their energies and abandon themselves to demoralizing amusements. By the use of tact and firmness you can obtain control and keep it, and this obstacle to continued progress will then disappear.

The rooms, halls or other places in which Indians congregate should be under constant inspection. They should be scrubbed, fumigated, cleansed or disinfected to prevent the dissemination of disease. The Indians should be instructed in regard to the matter of proper ventilation and the avoidance of over-crowding rooms where public assemblies are being held, and proper arrangement should be made for the shelter of their horses and ponies. The Agent will avail himself of the services of the medical attendant of his agency in this connection.

Except where further information is desired, there will be no necessity to acknowledge the receipt of this circular.

Yours very truly,

Duncan C Scott

Deputy Superintendent General.

Thos. Graham, Esq.,
Indian Agent,

Copy of circular from Department of Indian Affairs, Canada. Notice of continuing efforts by the government to stop traditional practices. Courtesy of Dave Sager, Mississauga, Ontario

1922

NORTH PEIGAN

BULL PLUME #1: When Agent Graham died in Calgary January, 1922 . Running Eagle the new Agent came February 1922. *(Chester A. Arthur)*

This may be when Arthur obtained his copy of Bull Plume Winter Count #2. Since Bull Plume's will was contained in the journal it may have been kept for the probate.

BLOOD

PERCY CREIGHTON: Sun Lodge; Mrs. Bear Shin Bone & Mrs. Hairy Bull. Pigeons & Crazy Dogs sold & bought the Cree Society. Treaty 12. July 13 & 14 First annual sports & stampede put up by a Indian Committee Deputy & Member of the (tribe ?, ed.). R.N. Wilson went back to Calgary.

NORTH BLACKFEET

RUNNING RABBIT: Calf Collar made Sundance and Heavy Shield was going put up Sundance and his wife died, Prairie Chickens dancers are sold their outfits. ($10.00). *[Transferred, ed.]* Indian Government came here from Ottawa. D.C. Scott and government *[Governor, ed.]* General visit Calgary.

MANY GUNS:

(1) Aisomyoki put up Sundance

(2) Niteniki = (Mrs. Heavy Shield), ill, had vowed for her husband. He turned worse and died right before Sundance. Isomyaki volunteered to pinch hit, therefore, Joe Whitefat took Aisomyoki for a sister, because Niteniki was <u>his</u> sister.

(3) Inakaowotan = Little Shield died. Husband of the present Mrs. Heavy Shield.

MANY GUNS .68: Ambush Woman and Only Killer and Fox Medicine Hat and Little Shield

MANY GUNS .69: Ambush Woman and the time Only Killer died and Little Shield

1923

NORTH PEIGAN

BULL PLUME #1: *New Agent arrived Mr. Arthur, in the meantime the clerk looked after things. Peigans had their first stampede.*

BLOOD

PERCY CREIGHTON: Sun Lodge; Mrs. Coming Singer. Beaver Woman had a fit. Commissioner Graham here on May 25. Big ____ ____ on May 30. Sites made for agency & school. Blk. ____ died at Lethbridge.

NORTH BLACKFEET

RUNNING RABBIT: Round Face Woman died, Mrs. Wolf Collar, North The Axe, and Nose Cutter, and Eating The Middle. We ration the Buffalo meat. Mr. Jones quit working for Government. Mrs. Wolf Legging (fifth) made Sundance with White Headed Chief, (they didn't let hot bath) *["get the sweat bath", ed.]*

All Braves Dogs sold their outfits; Crow Collar died.
(winter time)
Dancing hall was constructed, fine winter.

MANY GUNS:

(1) Iinimak = again put up Sundance.
(2) Pitopi, Sitting Eagle, died.

1924

NORTH PEIGAN

BULL PLUME #1: *Big Stampede at Macleod. All Blood and Peigans present in big parade.*

[Last entry for Bull Plume #1.]

Parade through downtown Fort Macleod, Alberta. 1924, Yellow Horn, chief of the North Peigan, leads the riders. Unknown photographer, Glenbow Archives

BLOOD

PERCY CREIGHTON: Sun Lodge; Mrs. First Charger. Big crops. Measels [sic] epidemic. Com. Graham here re. leasing of North end of reserve.

NORTH BLACKFEET

RUNNING RABBIT: Dancing hall was burned.
(Summer time) Yellow Horse wife made Sundance with Rex Back Fat. Braves they are sold dancing outfit. *[Mutsix, Braves Society, transferred, ed.]* These are took Medicine Pipes Calf Child, Black Face, and Butter. *[They became Medicine Pipe owners, ed.]* (We made stampede at Gleichen.)

MANY GUNS: Natokisisuyaki = Mrs. Yellow Horse again. *(put up Sundance, ed.)*

MANY GUNS .68: Two Cutter Woman and The Medicine Pipe

MANY GUNS .69: Two Cutter Woman and Sitting Eagle

1925

BLOOD

PERCY CREIGHTON: Sun Lodge; Mrs. Eagle Plume. Dry summer. No winter until the end of March. Big Earrings to the Horn Society.

NORTH BLACKFEET

RUNNING RABBIT: No dance hall, Crees made a lot of dancing. Crow foot sent away. Mrs. Calf Collar, with Many Fire made Sundance, all hauled out. *[hailed, ed.]* _____ died. Mr. Clark and sister both left Cluny, New ration house, My son, Joe Running Rabbit born 7th of July.

MANY GUNS:

(1) Isomyoki = again. *(put up Sundance, ed.)*
(2) Iinimaki (Mrs. Wolf Leg) died.

MANY GUNS .68: Ambush Woman. Laughing Woman was born and Only Announcer and Night Coming Up The Hill

MANY GUNS .69: Ambush Woman and Night Coming Up The Hill and Holding Woman

1926

BLOOD

PERCY CREIGHTON: Sun Lodge; Mrs. Wolf Child & son Mack

NORTH BLACKFEET

RUNNING RABBIT: Water Chief, Sleigh, Mr. Yellow Horse made Sundance (Mrs. Yellow Horse ?, ed.), Mr. Clark work here; Calf Bull died; fine winter; Spance Owl Child his wife and The Calf's wife and Raw Eater's wife died.

MANY GUNS:

(1) Nitsiniku = Killing Person, Mrs. Waterchief *(put up Sundance, ed.)*
(2) Mrs. Yellow Horse again (put up Sundance, ed.)

MANY GUNS .68: Real Killer and Two Cutter Woman and Fish Child

1927

BLOOD

PERCY CREIGHTON: Sun Lodge; Mrs. Coming Singer. High Crown Hats took up Horn Society. P.C. *(Percy Creighton, ed.)* at Baltamore *[Baltimore, ed.]*. Some Bloods went to Banff with R.N. Wilson.

NORTH BLACKFEET

RUNNING RABBIT: Joe Bull Shoes, Under Bear and Red Horn came visit here; *(these are South Peigans, ed.)* Frank Foot On Blanket died; my daughter born 31 of Jan. Spring Chief died March, Weasel Calf died 23rd of June, we received $25.00 a head for lease money, Mrs. Running Rabbit made Sundance. Half of farm not thrashed. Wolf Collar died 29th of Dec.

MANY GUNS:

(1) Epuxkski again.
(2) itsinakokopi = little Sundance. (Just had lodge up. Made a little shelter really, no center pole.)
(3) Crowfoot monument. Crowfoot's remaining camp or lodge fixed

MANY GUNS .68: Shedding Face and the little Sun Dance and Many Back Fat and The Foot Robe

MANY GUNS .69: Shedding Face. The time we had the little Sun Dance. Holy Chasing Back Woman.

1928

BLOOD

PERCY CREIGHTON: Sun Lodge; Mrs. White Man. P.C. went to St. Paul by airplane.

For several years Percy Creighton had been working in Glacier National Park as an interpreter for Winold Reiss, an artist painting the Blackfoot. When Reiss had his big showing of portraits in St. Paul, Minnesota Louis Hill, owner of the Great Northern Railway and hotels in the park, brought several Blackfoot back there as part of a promotional tour. After this initial tour he began to take groups of Blackfoot across the country promoting the park and train travel to the park.

Percy Creighton, center in cowboy hat, interpreting for Winold Reiss' art class at St. Mary Studio, Glacier Park. Winold Reiss on left wearing buckskin jacket. Winold Reiss photo, author's collection.

New York City publicity tour, Hotel McAlpine, 1928, Right to left; Lazy Boy; White Calf and wife; Medicine Owl; Big Top and wife; Fish; Three Bears; unknown; Cecil Ground [8 years old], photo, Great Northern Railway

NORTH BLACKFEET

RUNNING RABBIT: Washed out the bridge. Spring thrashing. Mrs. Water Chief made Sundance. Old Sun school was fire; Sun Walk died, I went to Blood Reserve.

MANY GUNS:

(1) Nitsinikim (put up Sundance, ed.)
(2) Agumaxkay = Many Swans died. Alias Wolf Collar. (Many Guns took over this name.)

MANY GUNS .68: Real Killer and Many Big Swan

1929

BLOOD

PERCY CREIGHTON: Sun Lodge; Mrs. Bear Shin Bone. Chief Talkers took part in Horn Society.

NORTH BLACKFEET

RUNNING RABBIT: Outside Attack died 3rd of Feb. Little Wolk *[Walker, ed.]* and White Headed Chief make vote for Chief Duck to quit. Chiefs make vote of Jack McHugh to left here. Mrs. One Gun and Mrs. Yellow Horse make Sundance. All poor crop and hail out. One Gun open coal mine.

MANY GUNS:

(1) Natokisisuyan = Mrs. Yellow Horse (put up Sundance, ed.)
(2) Insima = Grower Mrs. One Gun. (put up Sundance, ed.)
(3) Manikapine = died, Youngman Chief alias Black Face.

MANY GUNS .68: Two Cutter Woman and Planter Woman and Weasel Flat Head and Bachelor Chief and Stealing From Both Sides Woman.

1930

BLOOD

PERCY CREIGHTON: Sun lodge Mrs. Hairy Bull. High Crowns Horn Society sold out to Good Riders *(Society, ed.)*. Long Time Pipe stolen by Calling First. South Pipe stolen by Plume. New chiefs elected. Running Coyote & 3 Guns died. Mastalon *(?, ed.)* Chief killed in coal pit. Chief Mountain died.

NORTH BLACKFEET

MANY GUNS: Mrs. Water Chief *(put up Sundance, ed.)*

MANY GUNS .69: Real Killer and Sarcee Woman

1931

BLOOD

PERCY CREIGHTON: Sun Lodge; Mrs. First Charger. 5 pipes sold. *(Medicine Pipes, ed.)*

NORTH BLACKFEET

RUNNING RABBIT: Running Rabbit's wife make Sundance. Indian Agent run coal mines.

MANY GUNS: Epuxkski = Mrs. Running Rabbit (stepmother of Duck Chief) *(put up Sundance, ed.)*

MANY GUNS .68 & .69: Shedding Face and Weasel Tail

1932

BLOOD

PERCY CREIGHTON: Sun Lodge; Mrs. Hairy Bull.

NORTH BLACKFEET

RUNNING RABBIT: Arthur White Elk killed.

MANY GUNS: Isomyaki (put up Sundance, ed.)

MANY GUNS .68: Ambush Woman and Crow Game Dwelling Place. The time we had the big snow storm in ice. Horn Medicine Hat.

1933

BLOOD

PERCY CREIGHTON: No Sun Lodge.

NORTH BLACKFEET

RUNNING RABBIT: Mrs. One Gun made Sundance, Little Bear Child died, Rabbit Tail died, Dance hall was constructed.

MANY GUNS:
> (1) Insima again *(put up Sundance, ed.)*
> (2) Piksinotasi (bachelors, i.e. skinny horses) These toughs made an imitation Sundance and paid treaty there.
> (3) Pukokan = we had Sundance together.

MANY GUNS .68: Planter Woman and Turned Up and the Skinny Horse Owners.

1934

BLOOD

PERCY CREIGHTON: Bad winter, Sun Lodge; Mrs. Crow Spreading. P.C. & Tailfeather took part in Sun Lodge.

NORTH BLACKFEET

RUNNING RABBIT: Jim Skunk Tallow died, Feb. Board *[Broad, ed.]* Lock died April. The Sarcee died April, High Eagle died on Wednesday night 11th of April, Good Woman son died on June, Mrs. Little Bear Child made Sundance, Mrs. Yellow Horse died on Sept. Jim Big Eyes died on June. Frank Red Old Man killed himself 19th of Nov. Monday. The Black freeze to death on 23rd Sunday.

MANY GUNS: Isomyaki

MANY GUNS .69: Ambush Woman and Shorty and Fancy Foot

1935

BLOOD

PERCY CREIGHTON: Sorrel Horse killed Black Fox March 6. Geo. Blue Wings killed Black Fox March 6. Sun Lodge; Rhubarb Woman; center pole left overnight. *(This means they did not set up the center pole until the next morning. ed.)*

NORTH BLACKFEET

RUNNING RABBIT: Calf Bull died, Mrs. Peter White Pup died on 28th of May. Mrs. Crow Eagle died Oct. Mrs. Water Chief made Sundance.

MANY GUNS:
(1) Mrs. Water Chief (put up Sundance, ed.)
(2) Frank Raw Eater, died right at Sundance
(3) Alex Stevens, died right at Sundance
(4) King George died, Jan. 20, buried on Jan. 28.
Manstoyi = New winter

MANY GUNS .68: Real Killer and One Spot and Black and Chickadee Shoe and Far Seen.

1936

BLOOD

PERCY CREIGHTON: Bad winter. Weasels trapped for aid. Horn Society exchanged. Only 10 taken in. *[This means only 10 new members joined. ed.]*

NORTH BLACKFEET

RUNNING RABBIT: Crow Eagle died on 10th of Feb. Hard winter, deep snow. Spencer Owl Child out on 8th of Feb. no Sundance.

MANY GUNS:
(1) No Sundance matokopi
(2) Utskuimopitopi = Riding a Blue Roan *(died, ed.)*

MANY GUNS .68: No Sun Dance lodge. Blue Horse Rider

MANY GUNS .69: Nothing happened. Nice Otter Woman and Blue Horse Rider

1937

BLOOD

PERCY CREIGHTON: Very cold winter. Mrs. Hairy Bull made a vow to build Sun Lodge for recovery of Sam Hairy Bull.

NORTH BLACKFEET

RUNNING RABBIT: Joe Bear Robe plow the snow. George Crane Bear died on January. Fat Horse died on 6th of March and Sugar.

MANY GUNS:

(1) Isomyaki
(2) Diamond Jubilee for the treaty.
Itawaxkan (join together)
(3) Maika (Mike Running Wolf died.)
(4) Kamosaki died
(5) Awapxsotas = Fat Horse Son died – chief priest
(6) Francis Wolf Shoe died
(7) Agakitaki = (Winter after New Years 1938) Pilot Fox. Many sticks cut down by beavers
(8) Red Leggings died = Ikitsimyotasi = Owner Of a White Horses.

MANY GUNS .68: Ambush Woman and Shorty and Fancy Foot and Stealing Woman

MANY GUNS .69: Ambush Woman and the King died and Stealing Woman and Owns a Fat Horse.

1938

BLOOD

PERCY CREIGHTON: Sun Lodge; Mrs. Hairy Bull. Crows visited. *(Crow Tribe, ed.)* *[Last Percy Creighton entry, ed.]*

NORTH BLACKFEET

MANY GUNS:

(1) Mrs. Water Chief (*put up Sundance, ed.)*

(2) He will put down Catface's death

(This is the date when Hanks copied down MANY GUNS' winter count, ed.)

MANY GUNS .68: Real Killer and Eagle Head and Owns a Gray Horse and Fake Gun Woman

MANY GUNS .69: Real Killer and Eagle Head and the Old Women and Owns a Gray Horse and Many Piler.

1939

NORTH BLACKFEET

MANY GUNS .68: Magpie and Stripped Eagle and Red Face

MANY GUNS .69: Magpie and Spotted Eagle and Holy Woman and Eagle Moon and Fair Face and the Bishop died and Makikowana. Owns a Mysterious Gun, Heavenly Old Man and the time the King Came.

Visit of King George, 1939, Lethbridge Herald, Lethbridge, Alberta, Glenbow Archives

1940

NORTH BLACKFEET

MANY GUNS .68: Makiikowana, Fair Face

MANY GUNS .69: Real Killer and New Old Man

Okan, or Sun Dance, of the North Peigan main ceremonialists. Left to right; Unknown; Mrs. Crow Flag [instructor to the Holy Woman]; Mrs. Many Guns sponsor of the Okan; Many Guns, partner of the Holy Woman [his wife]; Four Horns, instructor for Many Guns during the ceremony. ca. 1940, unknown photographer, Glenbow Archives

1941

NORTH BLACKFEET

MANY GUNS .69: Planter Woman and Pretty Woman and Heavy Runner

1942

NORTH BLACKFEET

MANY GUNS .69: Real Killer and Only Chief and Only One Getting Up and Eagle Round Face

1943

NORTH BLACKFEET

MANY GUNS .69: Buffalo Stabb and Stripped Killer and Small Woman and Nice Gun Woman

1944

NORTH BLACKFEET

MANY GUNS .69; Real Killer and when Bird Old Man was killed. Running Crane

1945

NORTH BLACKFEET

MANY GUNS .69; Prairie Chicken Crazy and the time we won. *[World War 2, ed.]* Sailer and Water Calf.

Victory Dance at end of World War Two - Europe. Women wearing their male relatives' headdresses and carrying gun cases and scalps on sticks Unknown photographer, Glenbow Archives.

1946

NORTH BLACKFEET

MANY GUNS .69; Ambush and Holy Eagle Woman

Many Guns dies of a heart attack at the Sun Dance July 1. His son took over the winter count after this.

1947

NORTH BLACKFEET

MANY GUNS .69; Home Coming Gun Woman and the snow was deep

1948

NORTH BLACKFEET

MANY GUNS .69; Wolf West and Old Sun and Running Rabbit and Real Killer. No Sun Dance

1949

NORTH BLACKFEET

MANY GUNS .69: Stretched Leg died

1950

NORTH BLACKFEET

MANY GUNS .69; The time Shoe put up a Sun Dance

1951

NORTH BLACKFEET

MANY GUNS .69; Making a Sound Like An Owl. And Ambush Woman

1952

NORTH BLACKFEET

MANY GUNS .69; No Sun Dance lodge was put up

1953

NORTH BLACKFEET

MANY GUNS .69; Blind Woman and Pine Cone and Calling Many Names and Real Killer

1954

NORTH BLACKFEET

MANY GUNS .69; Home Coming Gun

1957

NORTH BLACKFEET

MANY GUNS .69; The time Home Coming Gun called a Sun Dance

1958

NORTH BLACKFEET

MANY GUNS .69; No Sun Dance lodge was put up

1959

NORTH BLACKFEET

MANY GUNS .69; Real Killer

1960

NORTH BLACKFEET

GUNS .69; No Sun Dance lodge was put up

1962

NORTH BLACKFEET

MANY GUNS .69; Home Coming Woman. September 3, we broke camp

1963

NORTH BLACKFEET

MANY GUNS .69; Cree Sun Dance. August 13 we broke camp

APPENDIX 1

TRIBAL NAMES & DATE OF COLLECTION

White Calf: [1962]

Crees	Asinawa
Northern Cree	Ah-paht-o-sey-sinawa
Brush Cree	Ist-tsis-sinawa
Bear Hill Brush Cree	Kyai-yai-toh-mai-ist-tsis-sinawa [Edmonton & Hobbema]\
Rocky Boy Crees	Och-koh-tok-ees-sinawa
Gros Ventre	Aht-tsi- sinawa
Assiniboine	Ni-tsi-sinawa
Yankton Sioux	O-mach-si-kai-sinawa
Assiniboine Sioux	Ai-yak-kyok-sey

Holterman: [1932]

Assiniboine	Asinawa
Blackfeet Indians	Sikxikaizitapi
Blackfeet tribe	Sixikaw
Blackfoot of all tribes	Sokitapi *[Saokitapi – Prairie People]*
Blood tribe	Kaina
Pend 'd Oreille	Nietahtaitapi-w
Frenchman	Nizapikoan [real white man]
Chinese	Apatamiszinimakoan [braid behind person]
Cheyenne	Kihzipimitapi [spotted, dappled]
Osage	Kaximizitapi [sage people]
Cree	Saiyi-w
Metis Cree	Saiyapikoan
Sarcee	Sa-ahsi-w
Crow	Isapowa
Omaha	Iistoiikoan [grow plants]
Sioux [Dakota]	Pinapisina-w [downstream]
Englishman	Suyapikoan [water]
Indian [fullblood]	nizitapikoan
Gros Ventre	Azina-w
Japanese	Zapanikoan
Navajo, Pueblo	Awaipiszimiska-w [blanket makers]
Nez Perce	Kumonuitapi [Blue/green people]
Kutenai	Kuten ai
Ojibwa	Matuyisaiyi-wa [grass Cree]
Peigan	Pikani

North Peigan	Apatosi Pikani
Shoshoni	Pixixinaitapi
Mexican	Spaiyikoan
Flatheads	Kotokspitapi
Sioux	Kaiispa

Lanning: [1882]

People	Ma ta pe oo
Blackfoot Nation	Sow ke ta pe
Blackfeet	Six ik ai ta pe
Blood	Ki no
Peigan	Pa kon a
Crow	Sa po
Gros Ventre	Ats e no
Assiniboine	As sin na
Sioux	Pe nap as sin na
Kootanies	Koo tin a oo
Sarcees	Sa se
Flatheads	Ko tokes pet a pe
Pen Doreille	Ne eti ta pe
Nez Perce	Ko mun i ta pe
Chinese	A pot se pis tax
Whiteman	Nap pe kooin
French	Neat sap pe kooin
German	Kis tap pe ap pe kooin
Mexican	Spi o kooin
Negro	Six app e kooin
Metis	Sia ap pe kooin

Tims: [1883]

American	Omux Istoapiekuun
Blood	Kai nau
Blackfeet	Sixikaua
Cree	Saiekuun
Crow	Is sap po e kuun
Metis [Cree]	Saiapiekuun
Metis [Blackfoot]	Anaukitappiekuun
Indian	Nit si tap pe kuun

Curtis: [ca. 1909]

Crow	Issapo
Arapaho	Ikiotsisaka [red tattoo]
	Ampska atsina [southern Gros Ventre]
Assiniboine	Nitsi sinna [real Assiniboine]
Stoneys	Sahsis sokitaki
Gros Ventre	Atsina
Blackfeet	Sisika
Blood	Kainow
Cheyenne	Kihtsipimitapi [Spotted people]
Chippewa *[Ojibwa]*	Matuyi sayiw [Grass Cree]
Cree	Sayiw
Flatheads	Kutukspitapi [flat headed people]
Kutenai	Kutunai
Nez Perce	Kumunitapi [blue/green people]
Pend d'Oreilles	Niituhtatapi [River people]
Piegan	Pikunni
Sarcee	Sahsi
Shoshone	Pitsiksinatapi
Sioux	Pinapi sinna [downstream Assiniboine]
Red River Half Breeds	Sayapitapi

Buck Running Rabbit: [1934]

"Natosistsi was in the Omaxkietsimani-Sayeks fight [not Sleigh's Big Snake fight] and went down east with the Omaxkietsi. He got there the North Door tipi up east. Old Weasel Calf, Fil *[father-in-law, ed.]* of Mrs. Weasel Calf, was 10 -12 yr old boy when they went down east. There were four tribes down east and the last *[first?]* one spoke same "our" language.

1. Ni'tsi poyi---speakers of real words
2. Aksi tapi---scarlet marked people *[Cheyenne ?]*
3. Tsipist tapi---Owl people
4. Aki tapisaksi---scarlet marked on hip people

#1 talked only a little differently from us, but all are friends, so warred together.

Arapaho Nahm –otsinai [East Gros Ventre]

Scalp Roller, Blood [1893]
"These people they call in Blackfoot nam-istch or uks-i-tupie, [people of the east], we call them also Nu-s-e-po-ya because some few of our people [who went there with the Gros Ventres] said they easily understood them. These people also fought with the Wolf People, Pawnees." *[Scalp Roller to R.N. Wilson, 1893, p.342]*

Two possible identities for this Blackfoot speaking group are given below.

The Arapaho were divided into five divisions; 1. Gros Ventre,[Begging People] 2. Besawunena, [Big Lodge People] 3. Hinanaeina 4. Ha-anahawunena 5.Nawathinehena [South People], and each had its own dialect. The Ha-anahawunena dialect was said to resemble Blackfoot, but they were the first to lose their separate identity. The four divisions south of the Gros Ventre consolidated into the Arapaho and adopted the language of the Hinanaeina. [Fowler,2001; 840]

These "real speakers" could well be the twenty young Blackfeet men that moved down in 1825, and married into the Arapaho and Cheyenne. They would have stayed together as a group, camping and hunting together. George Bent stated he knew several of these old Blackfeet and stated they never learned the Cheyenne language, but always talked to them in sign language. They often went to war as a group, with some Arapaho and Cheyenne joining. [Hyde, 1967, p 33-4]

Old Swan Tribal names 1801-02 [from map]

1. Mandans *[ed.]* -	Mud House Indians [Cho que]
2. Crow -	Is sap poo *[Mountain Crow, ed.]*
3. Kiowa -	Ams cope sox sue Sessews Indians *[South imitation Sarcee, ed.]*
4. Wrinkled Indians -	Sip pe ta ke
5. Beaver Indians -	Kix ta ka tappee
6. Arikara *[ed.]*	Cho que - go to war against No. 1
7. Arapaho	Nee koo chis ak ka - Tattooed Indians *[Arapaho proper, ed.]*
8. Kit Fox [ed.]	Sin ne po tuppe - Grey Fox Indians *[a division of Arapaho, ed.]*
9. Garter Root Indians	Ke ta kap sum - Garter Indians *[another Arapaho division]*
10. Beard Indians	So hoo is tooye - *[another Arapaho division]*?
11. Ak ken nix sa tuppee	*[Many Rosehips People, another division of the Arapaho]*

The last five tribes are located together on the map and more than likely are all today's Arapaho People. The divisions all spoke a very different dialect [one close to Blackfoot and another to Cheyenne] at this period in time.

12. Rib Indians	Pik et a tuppe
13. Thigh Indians	Oo aps six sa tuppe
14. Scabby Indians	Oc sa tup pee
15. Pawnee	Mak que a tuppee - Wolf Indians
16. Grass tent Indians	Mut ta yo que Snake, Northern Paiute

17. Fish Eating Indians	Mem me ow you
18. Root Indians	Ne chik a pa soy
19. Wood Indians	Nis che tappe
20.Sussew Snake Indians	Sox sue chicks sin na tappee *[Imitation Snake Indians, ed.]*
21. Pearl Shell Indians	Poo can nam a tappee
22. Black Indians	Six too k tappee *[Utes, ed.]*
23. Flathead Indians	Cut tux pe too pin
24. Nez Perce Indians	Cum mun na tappee - Blue Mud Indians *[Blue Paint people, ed.]*
25. Ermine or White Indians	Ap pa tupee
26. Kalispell Indians	To kee pee tuppee - Those that collect Shells
27. Pend d'Oreille Indians	Ac cook sa tappee - Paddling Indians
28. Snair Indians	Atcha tappee [became extinct in the early 19th century]
29. Lower Kootenay	Cut tux in na mi - Weak Bow Indians
30. ?	Patch now
31. Kootenay	Cotton na
32. Long Hair Indians	Pun nus pee tup pin [Interior Salish ?]

Melting Tallow [1966]

Si kchi ka wa	Blackfoot
Ams kaup si kchi ka wa	South Blackfeet
Ah ka na Many Chiefs, or	
Au au paitsi ta pi	Blood Indians
Ah pa toh si pi ka ni	North Peigans
Ams ka pi pi ka ni	South Peigans
Ki tsi sah si	Higher Sarcee
A pa tohs sah si wa	Northern Sarcee or Chipeweyans
Sah sas so ki ta ki	Stoney Indians [Morley]
Ni tsi sah sas so ki ta ki	Stoney Indians [Eden Valley]
Ist tsi si na wa	Wood Crees [Hobbema]
Pi na i si na wa	Swampy Crees
Ki ea eo tsi si na wa	Bear's Paw Crees [Plains Cree or Rocky Boy]
Koo to nai wa	Kootenay Indians
Is twi ta pi kch	Eskimos
Tsin a wa	Gros Ventre
No moo tsi na wa	Eastern Gros Ventre
Is sa po wa	Crow Indians
Kha kchi mo s tsi ta pi	Osage Indians
Pa kchs toh kih ni ni tsi ta pi	Flat Head Indians
Pi tsi kchi na ta pi	Snake Indians [Shoshone]

Kcha ko yi	Navajo Indians
Kih tsi pi mi ta pi	Pinto Indians [Cheyennc, cd.]
Ko mo ni ta pi	Idaho Indians [Nez Perce, ed.]
Ah yah kioh si	Rowers Indians

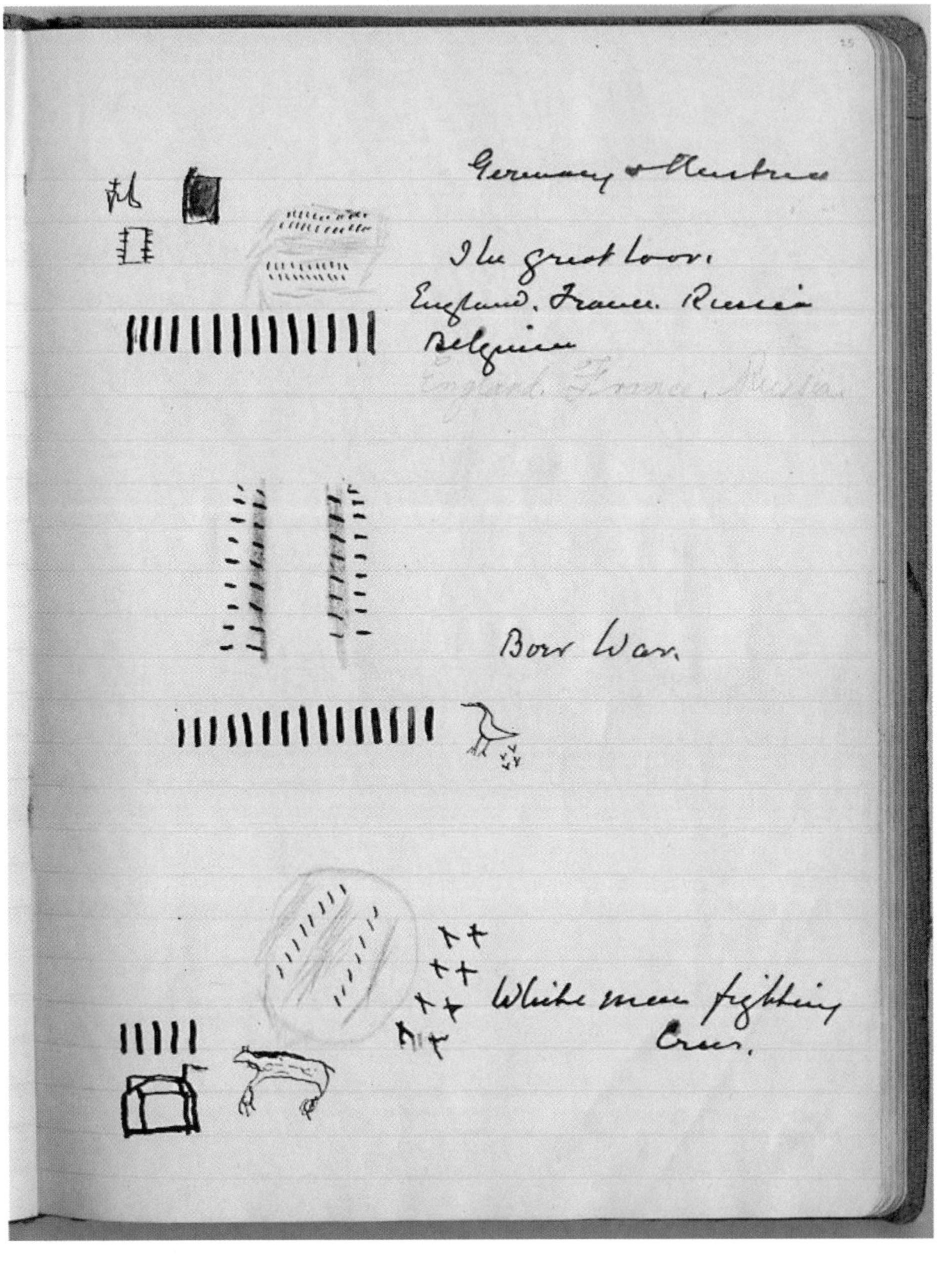

The Great Wars: Bull Plume's record of the Riel rebellion [at bottom] with a name glyph for Northwest Mounted Police Colonel A.G. Irvine [Black Bear], who was an officer in that war. Above that is the Boer War in South Africa and the name glyph for R.N. Wilson [Long Nosed Crow] who served during that war. And at the very top is "The Great War" [World War I] with Germany and Austria against England, France, Belgium and Russia.

WINTER COUNT BIBLIOGRAPHY

Bradley, James H.
1900 AFFAIRS AT FORT BENTON FROM 1831 to 1869, FROM LIEUT. BRADLEY'S JOURNAL, Historical Society of Montana, vol.8, Helena, Montana,

Brennan, L.
1959 NO STONE UNTURNED. AN ALMANAC OF AMERICAN PREHISTORY, Random House, New York

Brownstone, Arni
1903 WAR PAINT BLACKFOOT AND SARCEE PAINTED BUFFALO ROBES IN THE ROYAL ONTARIO MUSEUM, Royal Ontario Museum, Toronto

Calder, James M.
1977 THE MAJORVILLE CAIRN AND MEDICINE WHEEL SITE, ALBERTA, National Museum of Man Mercury Series, Archaeological Survey of Canada Paper No. 62

Calf Robe, Ben, with Adolf Hungry Wolf
1979 SIKSIKA, A BLACKFOOT LEGACY, Good Medicine Books, Invermere, British Columbia

Chittenden and Richardson
1905 FATHER DESMET'S LIFE AND TRAVELS AMONG THE NORTH AMERICAN INDIANS, Harper, New York

Crane Bear
1909 Jules Le Chevallier Papers, Acc. 71.220 Box 165, File 6738, Provincial Archives of Alberta, Archives of the Oblates

Collier, Donald
1938 Piegan Field Notes, unpublished

Cocking, Mathew
1908 AN ADVENTURER FROM HUDSON BAY, JOURNAL OF MATHEW COCKING FROM YORK FACTORY TO THE BLACKFEET COUNTRY, Transactions of the Royal Society of Canada, Series 3, Vol. II

Coues, Elliott
1965 THE MANUSCRIPT JOURNALS OF ALEXANDER HENRY AND DAVID THOMPSON; 1799-1814, Vols. I & II
Ross & Haines, Minneapolis, Minnesota,

Curtis, Edward & Grinnell, George Bird
1898 Manuscript, Seaver Center for Western History Research, Los Angeles, CA.

Dempsey, Hugh
1962 FINAL TREATY OF PEACE, Alberta Historical Review, Winter 1962
1965 A BLACKFOOT WINTER COUNT, Glenbow-Alberta Institute, Occasional Paper No. 1, Calgary,

1972 CROWFOOT CHIEF OF THE BLACKFEET, University of Oklahoma Press, Norman, Oklahoma

1980 RED CROW, WARRIOR CHIEF, University of Nebraska Press, Lincoln

1994 THE AMAZING DEATH OF CALF SHIRT, University of Oklahoma Press, Norman, Oklahoma

2002 FIREWATER, Fitzhenry & Whiteside, Allston, Maine

2003 THE VENGEFUL WIFE, University of Oklahoma Press, Norman, Oklahoma

Denig, Edwin Thompson, ed. Ewers, John
1961 FIVE INDIAN TRIBES OF THE UPPER MISSOURI, University of Oklahoma Press, Norman, Oklahoma

Dixon, Joseph
1913 THE VANISHING RACE; THE LAST GREAT INDIAN COUNCIL, Popular Library Eagle Books Edition, New York

Dodge, Col. Henry
1836 JOURNAL OF A MARCH OF A DETACHMENT OF DRAGOONS UNDER THE COMMAND OF COLONEL DODGE, IN THE SUMMER OF 1835, 24 Congress, 1 Sess. House Document 181, Washington

Doucet, Leon Fr.
1909 Letters, Edmound Morris Papers, MG14 C30 Box3 Provincial Archives of Manitoba, Winnipeg

Duvall, David
1904-1911 DAVID C. DUVALL PAPERS, Glenbow Museum Archives

Ewers, John
1943 WERE THE BLACKFOOT RICH IN HORSES?, American Anthropologist, N.S.45

1945 THE CASE FOR BLACKFOOT POTTERY, American Anthropologist, n.s.,47

1949 THE LAST BISON DRIVES OF THE BLACKFOOT INDIANS, Journal of the Washington Academy of Sciences, Vol. 39

1952 ed.
OF THE ASSINIBOINES, Edwin T. Denig, Bulletin, Missouri Historical Society, St. Louis

1955 THE HORSE IN BLACKFOOT INDIAN CULTURE, Smithsonian Institution, Bureau of American Ethnology, Bulletin 159

1958 THE BLACKFEET, RAIDERS ON THE NORTHWESTERN PLAINS, University of Oklahoma Press, Norman.

Fiddler, Peter
1769-1882 JOURNAL OF A JOURNEY OVER LAND FROM BUCKINGHAM HOUSE TO THE ROCKY MOUNTAINS IN 1792 & 3, Limited edition 1991, Historical Research Centre, Lethbridge, Alberta

Fitz-Gibbon, Mary
1985 THE DIARIES OF EDMUND MANTAGUE MORRIS; Royal Ontario Museum

Forbis, Richard G.
1960 THE OLD WOMAN'S BUFFALO JUMP, ALBERTA
National Museum of Canada, Bulletin No, 180 Contributions to Anthropology, 1960, Part 1

Fowler, Loretta
2001 ARAPAHO; HANDBOOK OF NORTH AMERICAN INDIANS; Vol. 13 part 2. Smithsonian Institution, Washington

Gidley, Mick
1982 A.C. HADDON JOINS EDWARD S. CURTIS; AN ENGLISH ANTHROPOLOGIST AMONG THE BLACKFEET, 1909, Montana, The Magazine of Western History, Autumn 1982, Helena, Montana

Godsell, Phillip H.
1958 The R.N. WILSON PAPERS, Glenbow Foundation, Calgary, Alberta
Bad Head WC
Scalp Roller, p. 342

Goldfrank, Ester
BLACKFOOT PAPERS, Harry Biele Folder, Box 13, National Anthropological Archives, Washington, D.C.

Gregg, Josiah
1967 THE COMMERCE OF THE PRAIRIES, University of Nebraska Press, Lincoln

Grinnell, George Bird
1892 EARLY BLACKFOOT HISTORY, The American Anthropologist, Vol. V, Washington, D.C.

1962 BLACKFOOT LODGE TALES, University of Nebraska Press, Lincoln, Nebraska

1973 TWO GREAT SCOUTS AND THEIR PAWNEE BATTALION, University of Nebraska Press, Lincoln

Hackett, Charles Wilson, ed.
Historical Documents Vol. 3; Carnegie Institute of Washington

Hale, Horatio
1885 REPORT ON THE BLACKFOOT TRIBE, REPORT OF THE BRITISH ASSOCIATION FOR THE ADVANCEMENT OF SCIENCE, London

Hanks, Lucien and Jane
1938 JANE & LUCIEN HANKS FONS, Glenbow Alberta Archives, Calgary, Alberta

Holterman, Jack
1932.1996 A BLACKFOOT LANGUAGE STUDY, Peigan Institute, Browning, Montana

Hewitt, J.N.B. ed.
1970 JOURNAL OF RUDOLPH FRIEDERICH KURZ, University of Nebraska Press, Lincoln, Nebraska

Hyde, George E.
1968 LIFE OF GEORGE BENT; WRITTEN FROM HIS LETTERS; University of Oklahoma Press, Norman

Kane, Paul
1859 WANDERINGS OF AN ARTIST, Longman, Brown, Green, Longmans and Roberts, London

Lanning, C.M.
1882 A GRAMMAR AND VOCABULARY OF THE BLACKFOOT, Fort Benton Montana Territory

Lancaster, Richard
1966 PEIGAN, Doubleday & Company, New York

Legal, Emile
BAD HEAD WINTER COUNT, Mss.
Provincial Archive, Edmonton, Alberta

1909 CRANE BEAR WINTER COUNT, Mss. Royal Alberta Archives, Edmonton, Alberta, Jules Le Chevalier Papers, A.71.220, Box 165, File 6738

Lewis, Oscar
1939 OSCAR AND RUTH LEWIS fonds, Glenbow Museum Archives, M8462

Little Chief, Joe
n.d. LITTLE CHIEF WINTER COUNT, Glenbow Museum Archives, M4394, Files 22 & 27

Macleod, Norman T.
1944 STOKOS OF THE BLOODS; Lethbridge Herald, Jan. 19

Maximilian, Alexander, Prince of Wied-Neuwied
1976 PEOPLE OF THE FIRST MAN, ed. Davis Thomas and Karin Ronnefeldt, E.P. Dutton & Co. Inc. New York

McClintock, Walter
1968 THE OLD NORTH TRAIL; University of Nebraska Press,

McCracken, Harold
1957 THE CHARLES M. RUSSELL BOOK, Doubleday, New York

McGillivray, Duncan
1929 THE JOURNAL OF DUNCAN MCGILLIVRAY, 1794-1795, ed. A.S. Morton, Toronto

Middelton, S. H.
1952 INDIAN CHIEFS ANCIENT AND MODERN
Lethbridge

Milloy, John S.
1988 THE PLAINS CREE, The University of Manitoba, Winnipeg, Manitoba

Morris, Alexander M.
1880 THE TREATIES OF CANADA WITH THE INDIANS OFMANITOBA, THE NORTH-WEST TERRITORIES, AND KEE-WA-TIN,. Willing & Williamson, Toronto

Moulton, Gary E. ed.
1983 THE JOURNALS OF THE LEWIS & CLARK EXPEDITION, University of Nebraska Press

Owen, John
1860 JOURNAL & LETTERS OF JOHN OWEN, INDIAN SUB AGENT IN CHARGE FLATHEAD NATION, Owen 1927;Vol. 2

Peers, Laura
1994 THE OJIBWA OF WESTERN CANADA, The University of Manitoba Press, Winnipeg, Manitoba

Pettipas, Katherine
1994 SEVERING THE TIES THAT BIND; GOVERNMENT REPRESSION OF INDIGENOUS RELIGIOUS CEREMONIES ON THE PRAIRIES, University of Manitoba Press.

Reeves, Brian
1974 CROWSNEST PASS ARCHAEOLOGICAL PROJECT 1973 SALVAGE EXCAVATION AND SURVEY PAPER NO. 2 PRELIMINARY REPORT, National Museum of Man, Archaeological Survey of Canada Mercury Series No. 24 [1974]

Running Rabbit, Houghton
n.d. RUNNING RABBIT WINTER COUNT, Glenbow Museum Archives, D920.3, R943

Schultz, James Willard
1962 BLACKFEET AND BUFFALO, THREE SUN'S WAR RECORD, University of Oklahoma Press

Smyth, David
2001 THE NIITSITAPI TRADE: EUROAMERICANS AND THE BLACKFOOT-SPEAKING PEOPLES TO THE MID 1830'S, PhD. Thesis, Carlton Univ. Nov

Sohon, Gustav
1855 DRAWINGS OF THE CHIEFS, 1855 LAME BULL TREATY, collection of Washington State Historical Society

Swanton, John R.
1952 BUUREAU OF AMERICAN ETHNOLOGY, Bulletin #145, Washington, D.C.

Tims, Rev. J.W.
1889 GRAMMAR AND DICTIONARY OF THE BLACKFOOT LANGUAGE IN THE DOMINION OF CANADA

Turner, John Peter
1950 THE NORTHWEST MOUNTED POLICE, Ottawa, King's Printer and Controller of Stationary

Tyrrell, J. B. ed.
1916 DAVID THOMPSON'S NARRATIVE OF HIS EXLORATIONS IN WESTERN AMERICA , The Champlain Society, Toronto,

Uhlenbeck, C.C.
1911 ORIGINAL BLACKFOOT TEXTS, Michelson, T. (1911), *Original.* American Anthropologist, 13:

West, Helen B.
n.d. THE STARVATION WINTER OF THE PEIGAN INDIANS, 1883-84 Information leaflet No. 7, U.S. Department of the Interior, Museum of the Plains Indian, Browning, Montana

Wheeler, William F.
1940 PERSONAL HISTORY OF MR. GEORGE WEIPPERT, CHOTEAU COUNTY, MONTANA, Notes and References, Contributions, Historical Society of Montana; Vol. X

White Bull, Jim
1969 1806 TO 1960, Kainai News 1969, Standoff, Alberta

Williams, Glyndwr
1971 PETER SKENE OGDEN'S SNAKE COUNTRY JOURNALS, 1827-28. Vol.28, Publications of the Hudson's Bay Record Society

Willcolmb, Roland
1968 Manuscript, File 941-250 to 289, 4/4, Montana Historical Society, Missoula

Wissler, Clark
1910 MATERIAL CULTURE OF THE BLACKFOOT INDIANS, Anthropological Papers of the American Museum of Natural History, Vol. V, Part I, New York

Yellow Fly, Teddy
n.d. YELLOW FLY WINTER COUNT, Glenbow Museum Archives, M4423

Yellowhorn, Tom
1973 Interview, Peigan Reserve, Tape number IH-245, Transcript 3; Office of Specific Claims & Research of the Indian Association of Alberta, Winterburn, Alberta

Index

Titles by the author

"Art of the Blackfoot Indians", Audiovisual production, Department of Native American Studies, University of Lethbridge, Alberta; 1977
"Canadian Indian Dancers", THE BEAVER, Winnipeg, Manitoba; Summer 1978
"Minipoka, Children of Plenty", AMERICAN INDIAN ART, Arizona, Vol. 4, #3, 1979
"Canadian Raiders in the Southwest", Stagecoach Publishing, Langley, BC; 1979
"Blackfoot Artists; Rights and Power", AMERICAN INDIAN ART, Arizona; Vol. 5, #2, 1980
"Bearhead; Drawings, Stories and Deeds of a 'Real Fighter'", THE PEIGAN STORYTELLER, New Bern, NC; Vol. XII, #2, April, 1988
"Sacred Robes of the Blackfoot and Other Northern Plains Tribes", AMERICAN INDIAN ART, Arizona; Vol. 17, #3, Summer, 1992
"Spotted Tail's Warbonnet", RUSSELL'S WEST, Vol. 1, #1, 1993
"Portraits of Change", (Winold Reiss and the Blackfoot) RUSSELL'S WEST, C.M. Russell Museum, Great Falls, MT; Vol.2, #2, 1995
BOOKS:
"Traditions of Northern Plains Raiders in New Mexico", Chap. 3, THE CHANGING WAYS OF SOUTHWESTERN INDIANS, Rio Grande Press, Glorieta, NM 1973
WINTERCOUNT, A HISTORY OF THE BLACKFOOT PEOPLE, Oldman River Cultural Centre, Brocket, Alberta; 1979
WINOLD REISS, PORTRAITS OF THE RACES, C.M. Russell Museum, Great Falls, MT; 1986
CULTURAL IMPACT SURVEY OF THE PEIGAN INDIAN RESERVE, Peigan Tribe, Brocket, Alberta; 1986
KEEP OUR CIRCLE STRONG, Cultural Centre and renewal programming study. Peigan Tribe, Brocket, Alberta; 1989
"Ohkiniksi: War Medicines of the Northwest Plains", Section IV, Chapter 3.PEOPLE OF THE BUFFALO, Vol. 1 THE PLAINS INDIANS OF NORTH AMERICA; MILITARY ART, WARFARE AND CHANGE; ESSAYS IN HONOR OF JOHN C. EWERS; Tatanka Press, Wyk, Germany; 2003
"Trade Goods or Art Supplies?" Chapter 10, NATIONAL FUR TRADE SYMPOSIUM PROCEEDINGS; THE FUR AND ROBE TRADE IN BLACKFOOT COUNTRY 1831-1880, River and Plains Society, Fort Benton, MT; 2003
"Traveling with Spiritual Power; the Weasel in Blackfoot Culture", Chapter 3, GENEROUS MAN; ESSAYS IN MEMORY OF COLIN TAYLOR, PLAINS INDIAN ETHNOLOGIST; Tataka Press, Wyk, Germany, 2008
"Posted: No Trespassing; The Blackfoot and the American Fur Trappers", PROCEEDINGS OF THE NATIONAL FUR TRADE SYMPOSIUM, Three Forks Historical Society, Three Forks, Montana; December, 2010
"Ponokamita Saam – Horse Medicine of the Blackfoot People", Chapter, BRIDLES OF THE AMERICAS Vol. 2; Hawk Hill Press, Nicasio, CA; December 2010

About the Author

“Everything is connected” was what the traditionalist elders said in talking about almost anything in Blackfoot culture. That was almost 50 years ago, and since then Paul Raczka has worked to show those connections between the art, language, music, history and oral traditions. *Niitsitapiiysin*, the “Blackfoot way of life”, is how it is all called, and explained to others. It is a holistic, rather than a segmented look at people, be they Blackfoot or otherwise.

It had its roots in 1969 with his founding of “The Singing Wire” at KUNM.FM, the University of New Mexico's radio station. What began as a half hour show of traditional Native American music expanded all these years later into a four hour show. Still going strong, every Sunday it provides a platform for both traditional and contemporary Native American musicians. A couple of years later, and a move to Alberta, started his long association with the Blackfoot people. As director of the Napi Friendship Centre, his function was to create a bridge of understanding between two very different cultures. Exposing non-Natives to Blackfoot culture through elders on the Piikani and Blood Reserves, it was the first time many longtime area residents saw the richness of traditional Blackfoot culture.

In 1976 he was hired as a Native American Studies Sessional Lecturer, at the University of Lethbridge to develop and implement a course approach to Canadian Native Art History, one of the first of its kind in Canada.

Through the years his numerous articles, book sections, conference, and symposium papers as well as lectures dealing with Native art and history from the perspective of Native traditionalists brought a fresh, holistic, viewpoint. In 2004 those viewpoints were incorporated by the Canadian Government in its new Intellectual Property Policy Directorate validating tribal intellectual traditions.

His work with, and for, the Blackfoot people continued with the Cultural Impact Survey of the Peigan Indian Reserve, consulting on the feasibility study for the Cultural Renewal Facility on the Piikani Reserve, and the Blackfeet Traditional Land Use Survey, Blackfeet Reservation, Montana.

This Winter Count, as well as the first publication of a part of it, has been more of an on going conversation rather than a simple statement. Bull Plume's ledger brought out the stories from those elders still living, and their encouragement as to the importance of the work. Through the years the stories continued to come, almost as if they had been waiting, and the book grew. As Raczka says, “These are not my stories, but stories of the Blackfoot people. Stories that have been waiting for a long time to be heard. Stories of *Niitsitapiiysin*, the Blackfoot way of life.”